# Think Christianly

📖 Ezra Press

# Think Christianly

DEVELOPING AN UNDIVIDED MIND

JOSEPH BOOT

Copyright © 2025 Joseph Boot

The moral right of the author under the Copyright, Designs and Patents Act 1988 has been asserted.

All rights reserved. No part of this publication may be reproduced, stored in a retrieval system, or transmitted in any form or by any means—electronic, mechanical, photocopying, recording, or otherwise—without the prior written permission of the publisher.

Unless otherwise noted, all Scripture quotations are taken from the *Holman Christian Standard Bible*®, Copyright © 1999, 2000, 2002, 2003 by Holman Bible Publishers. Used by permission. Holman Christian Standard Bible®, Holman CSB®, and HCSB® are federally registered trademarks of Holman Bible Publishers.

Scripture quotations marked ESV® are from *The Holy Bible, English Standard Version*®, Copyright © 2001 by Crossway, a publishing ministry of Good News Publishers. Used by permission. All rights reserved.

Scripture quotations marked Knox are from *The Holy Bible: A Translation by Monsignor Ronald Knox*, © Burns & Oates, 1945, 1949. Used by permission.

Scripture quotations marked NRSV are from the *New Revised Standard Version Bible*, © 1989, Division of Christian Education of the National Council of the Churches of Christ in the United States of America. Used by permission. All rights reserved.

Scripture quotations marked KJV are from the *Holy Bible, King James Version*. Public domain.

Scripture quotations marked NKJV are from the *New King James Version*®, Copyright © 1982 by Thomas Nelson. Used by permission. All rights reserved.

Book design: Robert J. Hewitt III, Livingstones Studio

The author gratefully acknowledges the writers whose works are quoted in this book. Where practicable, quotations have been referenced in the footnotes with details of the writer, the title of the book, the publisher, and the date of publication. If any requirement for permission has been overlooked, the publishers would be glad to hear from the copyright holders.

ISBN: 979-8-9916932-3-3

IN GRATEFUL MEMORY OF
HERMAN DOOYEWEERD; PHILOSOPHER,
SCHOLAR, PROPHET AND MAN OF GOD
(1894-1977).

# Contents

Foreword by P. Andrew Sandlin — IX

## Think Christianly

| | | |
|---|---|---|
| 1 | About Everything | 1 |
| 2 | About Christ | 43 |
| 3 | About Church and Kingdom | 67 |
| 4 | About Law (Part 1) | 101 |
| | The Meaning of Law, Natural Law, & Politics | |
| 5 | About Law (Part 2) | 135 |
| | Theonomy, History, and Messiah | |
| 6 | About Apologetics | 183 |
| 7 | About Science and Evolutionism | 221 |
| 8 | About History | 251 |
| 9 | About Marxism | 307 |
| 10 | About Race and Racism | 349 |
| 11 | About Identity and Sexuality | 385 |
| 12 | About Life | 407 |

Bibliography — 433

# *Foreword*

**M**ARK NOLL'S SOBERING CONCLUSION TO his well-publicized thirty-year-old jeremiad, The Scandal of the Evangelical Mind, was that there wasn't much of an evangelical mind. For the previous century, evangelicals had, by and large, retreated from cultivating the intellect as a distinctly Christian virtue, and the cultural decline over that same period was by no means unrelated to this omission. That conservative Protestants (and all conservatives, really) have long been afflicted with a deep anti-intellectual streak was a chief contributing factor to the rapid loss of cultural hegemony that had stamped previous centuries.

Dr. Joseph Boot's cure for this degenerative ailment is not simply to call for a recovery of the intellect but, more radically, of thinking Christianly about all of life. This drastic proposal is not identical to the worthwhile pastoral concern of helping lead Christians to think more and better Christian thoughts. Every sound biblical sermon should do that. In addition, Boot argues, Christians must learn to think in distinctively Christian ways about everything, not just about "Christian things." For too long, the dualism of many varieties has stamped the Christian faith, and intellectual dualism has relegated ordinary matters of life to the realm of the secular mind. Science, music, architecture, history, technology, education, law, politics, vocation, athletics, and entertainment — these and other ordinary areas of life were deemed unworthy of distinctively Christian thought, and we should focus instead on Bible reading, prayer, heaven, hell, and systematic theology. Boot argues, to the contrary, that, unless we are thinking Christianly about all of life, we are not faithful Christians.

Over the last decade, I have listened carefully to and profited from Dr. Boot's extensive, robust, Christianly lectures on thinking Christianly, and I know of few living thinkers who have addressed this problem as biblically, intelligently, and persuasively as he. We can thank God that significant sectors of the church today have awakened from their previous pietistic slumbers and have begun to engage with the culture, particularly in politics. This is a creditable development, but unless it is marinated in the Christian mind, it will be short-lived and, in the end, futile. I enthusiastically commend this latest work by Dr. Boot and suggest that, rivalling The Mission of God, it might be his most important work to date.

**P. Andrew Sandlin**
*Founder & President, Center for Cultural Leadership*

# *Think Christianly*

CHAPTER 1

# Think Christianly About Everything

*Teach me Your way, Yahweh,*
*and I will live by Your truth.*
*Give me an undivided mind to fear Your name.*
— Psalm 86:11 (HCSB)

## A Grateful Mind

**I**F YOU SEE A TURTLE perched on top of a fencepost, you know immediately it didn't get there on its own. Similarly, this human terrapin certainly did not reach his conclusions about Christian thinking by unaided mental acrobatics, so the message of this volume is not a veiled conceit. True, I have thought a lot about thinking over the years and the implications of that thought for human life, which is why I am writing this book—though too much of a good thing is liable to be bad for your health according to the wisest (Eccl. 12:12), so no one should think too much!

Admittedly there is more of others in my thought than there is of me; at least of last month's me as I suppose, once incorporated, their thoughts become part of me as I continue to wend my way through the cloud of witnesses. All of which suggests that we can become our true selves only with the help of others who have submitted their minds to Christ—from apostles, parents, pastors, teachers, friends and colleagues, not to mention the pages we leaf through. I am grateful to the many living and dead believers who have helped me think—the dead through their books as opposed to the illegitimate ingenuity of Saul in Endor (1 Sam. 28:7–20).

## The Life of the Mind

In reference to that cloud of witnesses, it has been observed by thinkers far more penetrating than I, that the ignorance of our own deceived and disillusioned time is currently killing it. Knowledge of Christ has faded from view—we no longer think of Him and so we languish in the stifling embrace of our own presumptuous errors. This neglect of remembrance is not for a lack of seers claiming to be oracles of wisdom for the moment. A long tradition stretching back to the sixth century BC, when an intellectual movement arose in Miletus with a man later called Thales, has given the West what it came to call philosophy (lit. *love of wisdom*). The story of Western philosophy—a discipline looking to search out the boundaries of human experience—is a fascinating one, with many heroes and villains, plots and subplots, but without Christ it is a tragic story. Godless philosophy, for all its purported love of wisdom, has neglected the beginning of wisdom—the fear of the Lord (cf. Prov. 9:10; Ps. 111:10). This faulty start has led to one dead end after another, producing intellectual and spiritual exhaustion. St. Paul understood very well the pitfalls of an autonomous search for wisdom and so placed Christ at the source of all true wisdom and knowledge:

> For the message of the cross is foolishness to those who are perishing, but it is God's power to us who are being saved. For it is written: I will destroy the wisdom of the wise, and I will set aside the understanding of the experts. Where is the

philosopher? Where is the scholar? Where is the debater of this age? Hasn't God made the world's wisdom foolish? For since, in God's wisdom, the world did not know God through wisdom, God was pleased to save those who believe through the foolishness of the message preached. For the Jews ask for signs and the Greeks seek wisdom, but we preach Christ crucified, a stumbling block to the Jews and foolishness to the Gentiles. Yet to those who are called, both Jews and Greeks, Christ is God's power and God's wisdom, because God's foolishness is wiser than human wisdom, and God's weakness is stronger than human strength. (1 Cor. 1:18–25)

The apostle did not intend to say here that intellectual labour is worthless—no doubt Paul's own inspired discourses and letters involved real mental exertion—only that without the proper grafting into the Living Tree, it will fail and fall like a dead leaf because of our sins, and the wind will carry it away. Human understanding and our wisdom traditions outside of Christ can lead only to despair and error, so the apostle warns, *"Be careful that no one takes you captive through philosophy and empty deceit based on human tradition, based on the elemental forces of the world, and not based on Christ"* (Col. 2:8).

Such a basic trust in human reasoning as *sufficient to itself,* a kind of captivity to the immanent, is a humanistic religious dogma and transparently so. All our arguments proceed from obvious or hidden assumptions drawn from elsewhere; it is an impossible demand that all those assumptions should themselves be based on arguments. There is no such thing as an assumption-free, neutral standpoint—what has been called a view from nowhere. Our most fundamental convictions about reality are not the result of "pure thought" via a set of rational procedures. We must already *believe* something in order to justify something else; we can work only with the given, just as we cannot demand of the chef that he bring out a cake without taking for granted he has the ingredients for baking.

In any case, how would one possibly go about establishing that human reasoning is the *highest principle* so that truth must come to rest on logical arguments rather than on aesthetic beauty, as with a piece of music? How can logical reasoning demonstrate that logical reasoning is the highest principle without entering a vicious circle; that is, how might reasoning validate itself without already assuming the very thing to be proved? This would require a transcendent God's-eye view, a higher position from which to judge that it is indeed "logical to be logical, dear Watson." Even if it were possible to ascend to the heights of Icarus without falling into a sea of contradiction, the new god's-eye view would be *beyond logic*, which would belie the original claim, because what is beyond logic cannot itself be reduced to the logical. This is a rather inelegant way of saying that no one can escape the necessity of faith and belief by hoisting themselves up by their own shoelaces to a position of transcendence.

Supra-rational starting points (i.e., those beyond logic) rooted in a religious choice in life cannot be eluded; the boasts of self-sufficient reason are empty—the emperor has no clothes. To be sure, we are able to consider all things through the lens of the logical dimension of reality, but it does not follow that because created things function in a logical aspect—being subject to a law for rationality—that logical analysis is the *ground* of all truth, or that it represents the highest or purest reality. Our experience shows that the universe is subject to all manner of law structures besides the logical. Things in this world also take up space (a spatial dimension); they grow and reproduce (a biotic dimension); they experience sensations (a sensitive dimension); they can be counted (a numerical dimension); they manifest a beautiful harmony (an aesthetic dimension); they have a history (a historical/cultural dimension); in fact, all things function in numerous other dimensions or aspects of reality that could be discussed at great length. So, despite the ambitions of some thinkers and philosophers, there can be no complete *logical* system to give a full and totalizing account of reality any more than the world can be understood through solely physical, spatial or biotic accounts of our experience—reality can be a logical system only for God.

Notwithstanding naïve claims to the contrary, according to God's revelation, all human experience exists in *relationship* to God and the inner-self—the depth dimension of the heart with its beliefs and commitments—governing the *direction* of our life and thought. The Christian philosopher Dirk Vollenhoven explains the unity of the Christian position effectively:

> Christians ground their belief... in the acknowledgment of the true Word-revelation, which, having been put into writing in Holy Scripture, rejects all other

"revelation" as having arisen out of the human heart and which brands every belief in such an alleged revelation as unbelief. Nevertheless, this completely justified sharp opposition within sacred belief does not abolish the similarity that exists between Christian and non-Christian belief. A consequence of this is that the sacred belief of non-Christians continues to be sacred belief....

The Christian revelation belief always inherently includes knowing.... A Christian philosophic conception must, therefore, not only contain thoughts concerning the nature and the task of Scripture belief but must also completely agree with this believing and with the knowledge that is correlated to it, that is, be scriptural or, if you prefer, in line with Scripture. And the deepest motive for our making this demand is not the desire to avoid the sorrow that any division of life brings with it, but respect for God, who forbids fragmenting life in any way.[1]

Nurturing genuine self-consciousness about the underlying heart-motives and beliefs that shape all human thinking is vital for truly Christian engagement with our unbelieving neighbour and wider culture, as well as the development of our own Christian mind. This is because human beings are an enigma to themselves, endlessly distracted by a bedlam of desires, hopes, lusts, fears and dreads dominating the horizon of daily life. Because of sin, nobody is entirely transparent to themselves. It is easy to rationalize our motivations and actions; this is like a man under hypnosis, having been told to open a window, who proceeds to do so when he opens his eyes and when asked why, confidently declares it was because the room was too warm. He doesn't *really* know why he opened the window, but he says something to justify his action and make it seem reasonable. Our culture is awash with endless rationalizations for self-destructive belief and action, covering up the ruling motives of an unexamined life.

Ancient or modern, Athenian or New Yorker, the thinker, artist or scientist is no different—ordinary human beings easily carried along by the

---

1. Dirk H. Vollenhoven, *Introduction to Philosophy*, trans. John H. Kok (Sioux Center, IA: Dordt College, 2005), 13–14.

zeitgeist of the age, rationalizing various motives and moral preferences in the form of high-sounding ideas, theories and totalizing systems. A good illustration is found in the insightful comment of the philosopher of science, Karl Popper, who once tellingly remarked he had come to the conclusion that the evolutionary perspective ubiquitous in our culture was not a scientific theory, testable in the real world, but a "metaphysical research programme—a possible framework for testable scientific theories."[2] There are few better illustrations of a system of intellectual conceit, liberally applied to conceal ethical rebellion, leading to previously unimagined and inhuman cruelties, than the one popularized by the reclusive, emotionally disturbed and spiritually tormented Charles Darwin.[3]

In the cradle of our civilization, with the ancient polis unable to penetrate to the root of the human condition, the intellectual pride and prominence of the Grecian world with its academies and schools of philosophy steadily declined. Cynicism and skepticism set in as people became increasingly exhausted and disillusioned with an endless proliferation of empty rhetoric in an obviously decaying culture. It is easy to see parallels to our waning Western world in the vice-like grip of unbelief and spiritual amnesia. As Soren Kierkegaard poignantly observed:

> Our age reminds one very much of the disintegration of the Greek state. Everything continues, and yet there is no one who believes in it. The invisible spiritual bond that gives it validity has vanished, and thus the whole age is simultaneously comic and tragic: tragic because it is perishing, comic because it continues.[4]

---

2. Karl Popper, *Philosophy after Darwin* (Princeton, NJ: Princeton University, 2010), 167.
3. See the fascinating book by Jerry Bergman, *The Dark Side of Charles Darwin*.
4. Søren Kierkegaard, *The Humor of Kierkegaard: An Anthology*, ed. Thomas C. Oden (Princeton, NJ: Princeton University Press, 2004), 220.

## Idolatry, Folly, and the Natural Mind

Given the nature of the human heart, an idol factory that never goes offline, people are not to be blamed for their suspicion of professional "thinkers" in a tragicomic era of decline. Commonly, instead of people thinking for themselves, the influential "thinker" presumes to think on behalf of all humanity, even identifying their thought with the inner spirit of the heaving masses. Yet their "wisest" thoughts are usually to be applied to everyone but themselves, like that generous and compassionate system of philosophy, still enormously popular, that longs to redistribute your broth and bread whilst living a bourgeois existence on caviar, fine wine, and rare cheeses.

Meanwhile, from another boudoir, the living God is pronounced dead to us all through the bushy moustache of a new kind of prophet, only for a vicious demi-god to emerge in his place, beyond good and evil, resembling a kind of amalgamation of Apollo, Ares, and Narcissus. Far from an emergent Super-man, the thinker's end is insanity.[5] And yet, inspired by God's apparent abdication of His throne, amidst the smoke of Parisian cafés when a little leisure might be taken from the labour of seducing philosophy students with his mistress, we learn from Jean-Paul Sartre that we all stand on the edge of an infinite abyss—for existence precedes essence. Life confronts us with a lonely and naked choice; and note that we are already trapped in hell with "No Exit," for hell is *other people*.

Similar illustrations could be multiplied *ad nauseum* from the chronicles of Western thought. None of these notorious 'insights' foster widespread confidence in "thinkers" or the labour of thinking—so why bother with thinking at all? Why not just be pragmatic and act intuitively? Perhaps because, on the other hand, unthinking enthusiasts are people of whom we do well to be equally wary. These "influencers," agitators and activists, both inside and outside the church, loud and sweeping in opinion—alleged victims of past generations and ready to act instinctively as judge, jury, and

---

5. The particular thinker in mind here is the nineteenth-century German philosopher, Friedrich Nietzsche.

executioner—like revolutionaries with metaphorical guillotines, go about trying to liberate the triangle from its three sides. Invariably making haste to dispense with careful thought and get on with "changing the world," they head off to get a selfie of themselves conquering Mount Everest without knowing where it is on the map. They are ready to sternly excoriate the pastor for his privilege, alleged phobias, and participation in the patriarchy before listening to his sermons or being able to find Zephaniah in the Bible, never mind quote from the minor mouthpiece of divine revelation. Consequently, it is not an easy task to persuade readers to adopt a particular sort of careful thinking in disillusioned and thoughtless times and harder still to make appealing the kind of Christian thought which is unconcerned with the self-justifying abstractions so popular in our woke culture for what is radically transformational—which is to say, cutting to the root of human selfhood, and by extension moving out like ripples on a lake, to touch all of life.

The self-justifying ideology that dominates society today, with its shameless moral posturing—the jiggery wokery of the West—is especially difficult to deal with because it is a form of stupidity which is less self-aware than rank evil and is no respecter of persons. It seems immune to reasoning and inconvenient facts. "When the mouth blathers pure drivel, it is futile to try to deliver a coherent discourse;...."[6] Intellectuals, scholars, political elites, and journalists are frequently afflicted with this brand of stupidity—indeed more so than ordinary people forced to consume their vacuous messaging in every form of media. Stupidity is a peculiarly human condition that arises, not because of a lack of intellectual capacity, but because of a herd mentality formed around powerful propaganda—a collective stupidity. It is the abstraction Kierkegaard railed against—public opinion:

> the public is a kind of colossal something, an abstract void and vacuum that is all and nothing.... [This public is] the most dangerous of all powers and the most

---

6. Søren Kierkegaard, *Kierkegaard's Writings*, vol. 14: *Two Ages: The Age of Revolution and the Present Age. A Literary Review*, ed. and trans. Howard V. Hong and Edna H. Hong (Princeton, NJ: Princeton University Press, 2009), 106.

meaningless.... Now everyone can have an opinion, but there must be a lumping together numerically in order to have it. Twenty-five signatures to the silliest notion is an opinion.[7]

The collective folly that emerges is a kind of sociological phenomenon which evidently undermines rudimentary human capabilities, depriving people of their inner independence—their ability to think and assess individually and decide for themselves as an image-bearer before God. This they are prepared to renounce, with varying degrees of self-consciousness, in order to adapt their behavior to the prevailing ideological situation. In the early 1940s the noted Christian martyr in Nazi Germany, Dietrich Bonhoeffer, had time to reflect whilst languishing in prison, on how and why the highly educated German people had become afflicted with collective ideological stupidity. His comments are startlingly reflective of our own cultural moment:

> The fact that the stupid person is often stubborn must not blind us to the fact that he is not independent. In conversation with him, one virtually feels that one is dealing not at all with him as a person, but with slogans, catchwords, and the like that have taken possession of him. He is under a spell, blinded, misused, and abused in his very being. Having thus become a mindless tool, the stupid person will also be capable of any evil and at the same time incapable of seeing that it is evil.... Yet at this very point it becomes quite clear that only an act of liberation, not instruction, can overcome stupidity.... The word of the Bible that the fear of God is the beginning of wisdom!! declares that the internal liberation of human beings to live the responsible life before God is the only genuine way to overcome stupidity.[8]

---

7. Kierkegaard, *Two Ages*, 93, 106.
8. Dietrich Bonhoeffer, "On Stupidity," in *Dietrich Bonhoeffer Works*, vol. 8: *Letters and Papers from Prison*, ed. Christian Gremmels et al., English ed. John W. de Gruchy, trans. Barbara and Martin Rumscheidt (Minneapolis, MN: Fortress, 2009), 43–44, 44.

## Transforming the Mind

The need of the hour in the West is the liberating reality of Jesus Christ and the recovery of the Christian mind—the mind of Christ (1 Cor. 2:16). Merely political and sociological arguments will not suffice because collective folly is an abstraction, a slogan and one cannot simply reason people out of it. Liberation must come from the outside, which involves the recovery of an inner independence in confrontation with the truth.

So, what is the Christian mind? Where do we begin? From the standpoint of scriptural revelation, truly Christian thinking must be concerned first and foremost with Jesus Christ, following Him and having His Word dwell and abide in us by His Spirit. But submitting oneself to being a humble follower doesn't come easily to anyone—especially professional thinkers. The human inclination is always toward autonomy, preferring to live the illusion that we can legislate for ourselves as kings without a country. Being a professing Christian in the church does not entirely remove the temptation or inclination to strike out alone and follow our own desires, living by our own priorities and setting to one side the awesome and all-consuming call to be a disciple of Christ; to come and die in order to truly live. Yet this is precisely what Christ calls us to. Being a "*living sacrifice*" (Rom. 12:1–2) sounds excruciating and involves a transformation of the mind which implies the pain and suffering of rejection by a world conformed, in the final analysis, to a very different spirit. But the divine midwife insists this is the only way. We must be reborn, transformed and given a new heart, a new mind.

As Christians we may claim to follow Christ, but the lifelong challenge in developing a truly Christian mindset requires regularly asking ourselves if we have followed Him far enough? Have we been to Jordan and seen the dove descending, but hung back from the mountain to avoid His exposition of the law and radical insistence that only those who teach and obey that law can be great in the Kingdom? Have we fallen asleep in pious satisfaction at the gates of Gethsemane, or lingered from a safe distance at Golgotha, never making it to the slopes of Olivet or to the Upper Room in Jerusalem with the dancing flames of fire? Is it possible that we are not yet Christian enough? It is all too easy to follow Christ only as far as is convenient, till the tarrying is just too tiring. If we are unwilling to stand under Christ's Lordship in all of life, then we are uninvolved in key aspects of the drama of redemption and miss the significance of God's full act in history.

The entire work of Christ in all His offices must become contemporaneous with us if we would truly be transformed by the renewing of our minds. It is not sufficient to appreciate Christ washing Simon Peter's feet at the last supper as a model of service if we refuse to see Him, let alone join Him, where the bloodied Stephen saw Him—exalted in heavenly places, standing up from His seat of total authority at God's right hand (Acts 7:55; Eph. 2:6). Unambiguously, we must surely see Him as priest on the road to Calvary, but we must also recognize Him on the footpath to Emmaus as resurrected Lord, the gardener of creation among Arimathea's roses, if we are to truly follow Christ and know the renewal of our minds (Lk. 24:13-25; John 20:11-16).

In a hostile context, the temptation is to follow Him just as far as culture permits. When the storm rises and dread grips us is precisely the time we are called to step out of the boat and walk upon the Word—despite the wind and waves of the world's antagonism. We must not suddenly become hard of hearing. And if we will not *hear* that Word over the inimical clamour of idolatry, we certainly cannot then *speak* it. If our cultural moment is allowed to determine how far we follow Christ, then we cannot follow Him at all. We may perhaps hear Hosanna's from a distance, but we will not be found stammering with the doubter, "*My Lord and my God*" (John 20:28)! We may even be permitted by our age to stand near the wooden cross of a brave martyr, a moral teacher, but not upon the mountain of ascension with the ruler of the kings of the earth (Rev. 1:5).

The sad end of hearing and heeding only the word our culture will permit is first an unwillingness, then a tragic inability to speak the whole counsel of God as faithful prophets. As priest and prophet Christ was hated, knew the world's enmity, and warned that the spirit at work in the children of disobedience would naturally hate His followers also. But we cannot follow our prophet nor share in His sufferings if we refuse to prophesy. Many contemporary priests would rather predict with Balaam to preserve their living than stand with Elijah against Baal. It is certain an ass has spoken with more wisdom in the annals of prophetic utterance than many English bishops in the Church of England in recent years—hirelings who would flog the meekest of God's prophets if they could for hindering their progress in vexing the church. Always loquacious but lacking true substance, they deceive and flatter themselves that their goal is unity when, in reality, it is revolt. Like powdered-wigged courtiers fighting over who will fetch the kings chamber pot, much of the Western church's leadership, even amongst evangelicals, simply courts the culture—ingratiating themselves with the influential, the powerful, the professors, even senior clergy who have whored themselves to the spirit of the world. Largely in the name of scholarliness they are avidly committed to half-measures, truth to a "certain degree."

The moment that God's people call a truce and reach a settlement with the spirit of the world, the mindset of the age, is the moment they set aside the Christian mind and overturn true Christianity. The kingdom of God is indeed in this world, but not of it; it is surely *present* here, but it is not *from* here—its power, authority and mandate derive from a transcendent source. In history, the church is always the church militant not triumphant. The struggle will continue over our graves till the king comes who will open all graves. We are called to victory but not to peaceful collaboration. It is only where the battle is fiercest that the fealty of Christ's soldiers is proved. To desert the frontline but deny cowardice and disloyalty because you once served up beans in the officer's mess is to lie to oneself.

When God's people say *"peace, peace,"* when there is no peace (Jer. 6:14), and sign a treaty with a rebel world, it *pretends* to be the church triumphant, that the struggle against lawlessness and spiritual darkness is complete—but before the consummation of Christ. Declaring an armistice with sin or striking a deal with an idolatrous state is not a victory nor faithfulness to God's kingdom. For example, if the church acquiesces to accepting or blessing homosexual relationships to make peace with the culture, like the Church of England's Synod, or meekly surrenders Christ's authority over public worship, preaching, healing, and sacraments to the State, like many Christian leaders during the Covid-19 debacle, defeats are being dressed up like conquests. It is a tragic irony that those who preach truth, righteousness and hope for history through following Christ to the uttermost, bringing them into direct conflict with the spirit of the world on the frontlines of battle, are charged with "triumphalism," whilst popular collaborators who claim neutrality with the world, making a compact of surrender or privatizing of the faith to the applause of culture, are thought pious and realistic. In reality *they* are triumphalist—seeking to immanentize a false eschaton by denaturing the Word of God, abstracting it from the affairs of daily life and coating what remains in honey so as to avoid any bitter taste in society's mouth—for a church no longer at war is a church triumphant.

This compromised situation is one we Christians should feel ashamed and embarrassed about, for today's unthinking Christianity, so in harmony with the world, humiliates itself; like an old man dressed up in the latest youth fashion, strutting about and believing he appears cool and trendy makes himself an object of ridicule. The accommodation of the Christian mind to the ever-changing whims of society takes the bread whose flour is eternal and reduces it to play dough for children, devoid of nutriment and molded to the petty preferences of a superficial and malnourished generation. But Christ will not be reduced to a part-time waiter satisfied with bringing out whatever the customer demands. Neither is the baker answerable to the dough; the bread of life is indeed available without money, but not without cost and only on His terms.

## Reformational Thought

An unadulterated Word can therefore be the *only* foundation for thinking Christianly and thinking Christianly is the prerequisite for Christian work, for action—they are bound together and involved in each other. Superficiality, which marks our culture and deeply infiltrates the contemporary church, always adulterates the Word because it breaks down the distinction between hiddenness and revelation; it is a revelation of emptiness. It puts on a good show as over-compensation for the reality that the depth and substance of the essential Word-revelation has never been allowed to truly settle and take root. There is often much noise, talk and activity, but it is banal, hollow, glib, and frequently incoherent. Its effect is passing and insignificant. It may bring laughter, yet not lasting gladness. We can be sure superficiality and frivolity do not mark the heart and mind *transformed* by the Word and Spirit of God. The counterpoint is depth, weight, profundity, and true humor, all leading to joy unspeakable. The expression I frequently borrow to describe this faithful way of thinking—a mind in self-conscious surrender to Christ by the Spirit—is *reformational* due to the conviction that Christian thought must always be reformed in terms of God's *Word* and geared toward both personal and cultural reformation within God's *world*. It involves a *living* faith in Jesus, an abiding trust and confidence in His Word, which leads by the Spirit to having *"the mind of Christ"* (1 Cor. 2:16). Because such a mind is alive, it is growing and unfolding, manifesting itself in faithfulness in all of life.

The religious root of life thus means obligation to follow Christ and live for Him in all things, times and places—in all human activity and cultural spheres. The word "culture" shares a common root with everyday and earthy words like "cultivate," showing up in agrarian terms like "agriculture," "horticulture," and so on. They all point to growth, development and a fruitful unfolding of potential. Its origin and significance are hidden in the term "cultus" which is tied to worship. Every person will worship and has been placed in this world as in a garden, to tend, develop and care for it. As such, the question is not *whether* human thought will lead to developing and shaping life and culture but simply what *kind* of civilization our lives will cultivate. This will be determined, in the last analysis, by whether we have been transformed by the renewing of our minds. It only remains to be seen, in each generation, whether we will, as an offering of praise to the living God, imitate the original gardener who planted Eden and tended the resurrection garden, or impersonate idols in the despair of defiance.

## Reformational Thought is More Than Thinking About Thinking

The reformational perspective is not simply concerned with analytical thinking as such, for its own sake, but with what *living life to the full* is all about—for that is why Christ was made manifest (John 10:10). Happily, reformational thinking is not interested in a narrow, intellectualized faith or the misguided hubris of a rationalistic apologetic for Christianity—as though the faith depended on the fragile character of our petty demonstrations. Though Christians must joyfully obey Christ's command to love God with all their *mind* (Mark 12:30), it would be a mistake to regard intensive and focused reflection on the full implications of God's Word-revelation in Christ as a merely abstract, speculative intellectual exercise bearing little relationship to our everyday life in the world and the everlasting matters of Christ's kingdom. Where Christianity is explained speculatively and in terms of a so-called "natural theology" the result is invariably paganism and elitism.

Christian thinking worth the name does not terminate with tweed jackets, dusty libraries, pipes, and slippers (pleasant as those things are), nor high-brow essays crafted for bohemian scholars living in academic echo chambers. On the contrary, the Christian life-view is very much concerned with *every aspect* of real life as God has created and is redeeming it through His Son. Rigorous, philosophically oriented thinking in the grip of Scripture must be an act of faith and obedience directed toward the reconciliation of all things to God, beginning with our own hearts and with a passion passed down to those coming after us (2 Cor. 5:19). A merely propositional faith not renewed through Christ in each generation at its religious root, the subjective heart of the believer, becomes like a page whose copy is in turn recopied, so that the hundredth genealogical copy is faded and illegible.

## Reformational Thought Shuns Intellectual Idolatry

As I have already suggested, making clear the true purpose of Christian thinking is vital because much of our Western thought heritage stems from the pagan Greeks. I have also observed that many believers are understandably wary of anything that smacks of philosophy—considering it indicative of people's effort to trust *ultimately* in human reason as an alternative source of certitude to faith in Christ and His Word. This is in part because philosophy has been falsely viewed as the pagan or secular *alternative* to theology; philosophy as the "non-Christian" discipline and theology the truly

"Christian" science. This presumed antagonism between the two disciplines is problematic for several reasons. First, it overlooks the fact that philosophical assumptions, categories, and concepts are always operative in the work of every theologian, whether he or she is conscious of them or not. And second, it assumes without any justification that there can be no such thing as scriptural thinking (or philosophy) truly built upon Christ and His Word.

There is a certain irony in the hostility to philosophy because two of the great theologians of the church, St. Augustine of Hippo and Thomas Aquinas, were deeply influenced by the works of Plato and Aristotle respectively. As D. J. O'Connor had the audacity to point out, "the philosophy of Aristotle could hardly have had its massive influence had not St. Thomas tried to show that it could be tamed to serve theology."[9] I am not suggesting that this Thomistic effort was ultimately a good thing; in many respects what we call Western philosophy was transformed during the medieval period by attempting a synthesis between biblical Christianity and the Greek philosophers. Vollenhoven makes many uncomfortable when he explains:

> In the same way that Augustine had used Plato in the explanation and defense of church doctrine, Thomas did with the philosophy of Aristotle. To be sure, he met with vehement opposition from his contemporaries but finally Thomas did prevail, to such an extent that Aristotelian philosophy became the basis of all medieval scholasticism.[10]

A certain suspicion of *pagan* philosophy among many Christians is certainly well justified. The intellectualism of the classical Greeks (and modern secularists) which regarded human reasoning and indeed thought itself in almost *divine terms,* went as far as to suggest that intellectual contemplation was the highest kind of life, manual work was contemptible, and the abstract ideas of the philosophers qualified them (in their own minds) to be

---

9. D. J. O'Connor, *Aquinas and Natural Law*, New Studies in Ethics (London: Macmillan, 1967), 5.
10. Cited in Bernie Van Der Walt, *Thomas Aquinas and the Neo-Thomist Tradition: A Christian Philosophical Assessment* (Jordan Station, ON: Paideia Press, 2021), 20.

philosopher-kings governing the unsophisticated masses. In my judgment, as Asalo of St. Victor once stated, "the spirit of Christ cannot rule where the spirit of Aristotle prevails."[11] The same is true of Plato or any other philosopher. Human theoretical reasoning must be kept in its provisional place, fully submitted and subordinated to Christ and His Word.

In contrast to the poisoned chalice of humanistic thought, a reformational perspective holds that the most fundamental and foundational questions of life *cannot* be answered by man's theoretical reasoning. Confronted with the great boundary questions of life—the origin of all things, the nature of the cosmos, the ground of truth and meaning, the basis of the relationship of unity and multiplicity, constancy and change—our analytical capacities alone are helpless, human systems fail. Finality and system imply each other, but our human existence is anything but the finality of God's perspective. We cannot transcend ourselves. At what point are we outside ourselves? Truth cannot be attained by the mind alone as final and complete. It is like the difference between being a talented high-jumper and being able to fly. Creaturely existence always exhibits this kind of restraining influence. So, we stand in need of *revelation* and the kind of certainty that is rooted in faith in Christ.

The Word of Christ Jesus concerns *all of life* in all its aspects, diverse relationships, and structures which come to focus in the *heart* of the human person—the religious root of our being, bringing together the temporality of our life with eternity in the heart. As such, truly Christian thought is oriented toward the *totality* of life and is not restricted to any one *function* of it (such as analytical thinking), while recognizing the limitations of human understanding in grasping that totality. One of the wisest men who ever lived, king Solomon, well understood the profound limitations of all human theoretical inquiry:

> Who is like the wise person, and who knows the interpretation of a matter...? When I applied my mind to know wisdom and to observe the activity that is done on

---

11. Cited in Van Der Walt, *Thomas Aquinas and the Neo-Thomist Tradition*, 19.

the earth (even though one's eyes do not close in sleep day or night), I observed all the work of God and concluded that man is unable to discover the work that is done under the sun. Even though a man labors hard to explore it, he cannot find it; even if the wise man claims to know it, he is unable to discover it (Eccl. 8:1, 16–17).

What the inspired Hebrew philosopher seems to be describing here is the human inability to fully *comprehend* or grasp in a manageable *concept*, the unity and totality of God's work in history: which is to say, we cannot intellectually tie neatly together the meaning-*fullness* of all God's work in creation and culture by mere logical inquiry—by philosophical systems. I can form an easy *concept* of a chair, bringing various elements together, as an object used for human comfort with four legs and a seat—it is a part of my everyday human experience. But whilst I can have an *idea* of God's sovereign work in all creation and history, I cannot form a simple *concept* of it because it transcends my ability and experience to unify all its infinitely diverse elements. I must rely on God to tell me the truth about it—to give me a true idea of His sovereign work without being able to fully comprehend it. As Solomon writes again, *"I resolved, 'I will be wise,' but it was beyond me. What exists is beyond reach and very deep. Who can discover it?"* (Eccl. 7:23–24)? We simply cannot independently uncover the work God has done from beginning to end (Eccl. 3:11). Why? Because we are creatures. And more, because we are dust—fully embedded in the creation we are investigating—and to dust we shall return (Gen. 3:19). There is for us all a time to be born and a time to die (Eccl. 3:2). A moment comes when those that look through the windows grow dim, the embers burn low, the light fades:

> I have seen the moment of my greatness flicker,
> And I have seen the eternal Footman hold my coat, and snicker,
> And in short, I was afraid.[12]

---

12. T. S. Eliot, "The Love Song of J. Alfred Prufrock," in *T. S. Eliot: Selected Poems and A Critical Reading of the Selected Poems of T. S. Eliot* (Croydon, UK: Faber and Faber, 1954), 6.

The Christian mind bows low in the face of its creatureliness, acknowledging the root and transcendent unity of meaning lies *beyond* creation in Christ who contains all things. The idolatrous demand of our humanistic age to be the measure of all things—a desire to be deceived by life rather than learn from it—is a ten-thousand-tongued rumour calling forth confusion and despair. We know the rumour to be false but lack the integrity to admit we've enjoyed the gossip. We love the lie and so darkness descends. Thus, light must shine into the heart from the living God if there is to be real hope. Christian thought is, of necessity, rooted in the soil of submission to Jesus Christ and the light of His self-revelation.

## Reformational Thought Recognises a Primary Religious Knowledge

This posture of humble submission does not mean we cannot have a view of life that is all-encompassing. The grand narrative of the Christian faith revealed in Scripture is indeed a cosmic story rooted in the creation of all things by the living God that captures all of life. But this comprehensive view is not humanly *constructed* from our own thought in any rationalistic sense. Rather, it is grounded in the *givenness* of primary faith knowledge which contains true, inescapable ideas that we cannot manage without because they form the indefinable and irreducible categories of all human thinking—life, love, beauty, energy, motion, logical distinguishing and more.

This intuitive "idea" knowledge is like a skylight shedding light upon life from above even when we cannot fully comprehend that revelatory knowledge in comprehensive concepts (cf. Psalm 139:6). This certitude of faith extends to biblical teachings like the status of the human heart as the invisible centre of our person; God's eternal relationship as trinity; the apparent paradox of the two natures of Christ; God's creation of all things from nothing "in the beginning"; His sovereign government and sustaining of all things by His law-word at every moment; His covenantal love and redemptive plan for His people in history; His everlasting truth and justice; the realm of heaven, angels and demons. We cannot *fully* comprehend these truths and they are not *inferred* from other beliefs but are part of the givenness of God's revelation to us and in us.

This real knowledge goes *beyond* our ability to fully grasp in simple concepts, yet as primary, practical, religious knowledge given in creation and in Scripture it is the real *foundation* for every other kind of knowledge. So reformational thinking, truly Christian thinking, is not a form of "rational theology" for a Christian intelligentsia, constructing an independent knowledge of God and the world from theoretical inquiry. It is founded in *acknowledgement* of God's revelation of Himself.

## Reformational Thought is Confessional

This recognition means that reformational thought is also *confessional*, because its foundation is the Christian *confession of faith*, contained in Scripture and summarized in the ecumenical creeds, as it seeks to explore and develop faithful answers to the great questions of life. Stated simply as a *world-and-life view*, our basic confession can be summarized as a firm belief in the *creation* (in Christ), *fall into ruin* (in Adam), and *redemption* of all things in Christ (the last Adam), by the regenerating and consummating power of the Holy Spirit. In the language of Scripture, we *confess* the all-pervasive reality of the *kingdom of God* under the sovereignty of Christ the King. This knowledge is not a development or "system" worked out by professional theologians but constitutes the first principles of Christian life and thought revealed to the heart by the Holy Spirit in the encounter with His Word. It is the *basis* of all true theology and philosophy.

In approaching the broader questions of philosophy, reformational thought affirms that the majestic beauty and rich *diversity* of creation which we experience is given to us in the divine *order of creation* (Gen. 1:20–31; Ps. 19), whilst the *unity* of that coherent diversity in creation cannot be found in anything created, but only in the transcendent fullness of all things *created in Christ Jesus* (Col. 1:15–17; John 1:1–3). The apostle Paul teaches that Christ is the *origin* who contains all things (Eph. 1:23; 1 Cor. 3:19–23; Eph. 2:10) so that the rootedness of the cosmos in Christ is the most important feature of the creation in its essence. This same Lord Jesus Christ is also the *destination* of all creation, for He is reconciling all things to Himself (Col. 1:19–23) and will one day liberate the totality of creation, which holds together and consists *in Him* (Col. 1:17), from its subjection to futility (Rom. 8:19–23). To abstract our thinking from this *faith foundation* in any area of life is the essence of *secularization*, the spiritual uprooting of reality, and the eventual destruction of all meaning.

So, truly Christian thought is confessional, but confessionalism is not unique to Christian thought. Reformational thinking recognizes that *every other worldview* is equally characterized by a *religious* confession because all answers to questions of origin, meaning, unity and destination within creation are answered by a conscious or unconscious non-Christian or Christian *faith* perspective. All worldviews involve an articulation of an attitude to life or "ethos" at the spiritual root of human existence. This means that in Christian apologetics, the contest is not between science and Scripture, or between reason and faith (as though the sciences and our reasoning are neutral instruments operating without basic presuppositions)—Christians struggling on the backfoot to show that despite their views, despite being rooted in faith, are nonetheless rational. Rather, faithful apologetics recognizes a confrontation between *religious worldviews*, between opposing *philosophies of life* that put human understanding (reason) and the various tools of the sciences to different uses, cutting in different directions. Biblically founded Christian apologetics will lay bare this antithesis, whilst graciously pointing people to Christ *alone* as the one in whom all things find their origin, meaning and resolution. Vindication of the Christian standpoint consists in helping people to see that it is only biblical faith that does not collapse under its own weight.[13]

The humanistic perspective has no category for anything other than the *immanent frame*, which is to say, everything must be accounted for, find its meaning and origin, from *within* creation—perhaps reason, or number, or matter and energy, or historical eventuation, or pure will etc., can "stand in"

---

13. See Boot, *Why I Still Believe*, for a detailed explanation of the transcendental direction for cultural apologetics.

as the origin and source of unity and diversity in creation. By contrast the Christian perspective finds its root in Christ as transcendent over all things—their source, origin and meaning. It is a mistake to try and use the confessional tools of immanent thinking to validate Christianity. Undertaking to counter the thought and progress of an era from *within* its own assumptions and norms is like trying to halt the progress of a train by tugging on the seat in front of you. A drowning man in a river cannot be helped by another non-swimmer caught in the same undercurrents and a hiker sinking down in quicksand cannot be rescued by another flailing inside the bog. Christ must reach in by His Word and Spirit and if we would cooperate with Him in the task, we must work from scriptural presuppositions.

## Reformational Thought is Not About Making Everyone a Theologian

This openly confessional basis does not mean that reformational thought tries to privilege the science of theology over other disciplines as "queen," nor over other vocations. Theology is an important subject and is a professional vocation for some, but it is only one among many equally important fields in which to study, work and serve God in terms of a Christian world-and-life view grounded in a scriptural confession. Theology as a science is the human *theoretical* interpretation of biblical revelation, doctrine and confessions, it is not revelation *itself*. Revelation is not a systematic theology text, it is God revealing Himself *in creatures*—in creation, in the Bible, in man himself (Rom. 1:19) and supremely in Christ who is the firstborn (i.e., inheritor) of creation, both God and man. His revelation is the norm and normative content of our faith. So, theology, like philosophy, both of which when faithful can *deepen* our understanding, must be kept in their provisional place.

Scripture does not offer us a *theoretical* account of human knowing, a detailed philosophy of history, a theoretical description of the precise relationship of the inner and outer person (of the relation of spirit and our bodies), nor a theological systematics or church dogmatics—it does not intend to. The Bible does not offer "theories" of any kind because it is the Word of God:

> God's Word is itself not a science, but it stands above all science, and is the norm for every science which seeks truth. The Bible is the divine guide that ought to lead our scientific thought. The guide, however, does not do away with scientific activity, but requires and calls it into existence. The Word of God does not relieve us of the responsibility of examining the great works of God scientifically....
>
> [T]o solve a philosophic problem serious intellectual struggle and study are required. God calls his children to engage in science and philosophy and He is glorified through that philosophy which permits itself to be led by his Word.[14]

This is important because many Christians are confused about the relationship between the Bible, philosophical thinking, and theology—as though theology is Christian and philosophy is pagan, so that a "theology" of everything must be developed. However, all theology has its philosophical prolegomena (lit., to say before). The theologian brings all kinds of philosophical assumptions to his or her work. This prolegomena will either be scripturally rooted and derived or not, and will determine the shape of a given theology. It is for this reason that there are numerous theological schools that don't agree on a variety of doctrinal questions. The philosophical prolegomena also accounts for why there are many bad theologians, some of whom are not even Christians at all.

A faithful biblical theology requires an equally scriptural philosophy as its prolegomena so that both disciplines share the same foundation. Only a truly Christian philosophy can provide an adequate introduction to theology and even then, its conclusions cannot be given the authority of Scripture itself. Whilst we should value the results of faithful theological labour, we do not put our faith in theology, nor in theologians, but in Christ. After

---

14. J. M. Spier, *An Introduction to Christian Philosophy*, trans. D. H. Freeman (Philadelphia, PA: Presbyterian and Reformed, 1966), 10.

all, if theology is directly equated with the Word of God, who or what can stand in judgement over the systems of the theologians? Every true Christian with access to Scripture and subject to the Holy Spirit must test the theologies of men. Theological knowledge is not a measure of faith or fidelity to Christ any more than philosophical sophistication gauges the depth of a Christian life. There were no professional theologians present at the cross or resurrection, and the apostles were not academic theologians. Their ministry provides the material for theologians to work with, but far too many people today are taken up with pontificating about "theological schools" rather than with speaking about Christ, His Word, and a life of obedience. Rather than heading for Jerusalem to be endued with power for witness, many of today's theological scholars would have set up a new seminary at Olivet to develop various views of the ascension. Amongst some Christians, pastors, and scholars today, theology must be dethroned and must become a servant, and not pretend to be "queen" by claiming that only theology and the theologian can speak Christianly to the various areas of life. Ultimately, faith comes and grows by hearing the Word of God, not by having a pristine theological system.

Biblically, to have true faith is to believe, trust, and serve God with the *whole of our being* (Heb. 11:4–12; Luke 10:27; John 14:15). Without revelation, there is no possibility of faith because faith, the function of believing (Heb. 11:1), is always in *response* to divine revelation. As such, faith is actually a *constitutive aspect of being human.* Those who reject God's *norm* for faith have not stopped putting their faith somewhere, nor have they lost their human faith function; they have simply reacted to revelation by placing their faith elsewhere. Faith remains the guiding function in all our lives—including that of the theologian. It gives form and shape to all we are and do because it refers us to the religious root of life, concentrated in our hearts.

Whilst reformational thought is not seeking to turn everyone into theologians, it *is* concerned with authentically understanding and expressing our faith in *all disciplines* and *areas of life.* True faith is worked out and developed by *practicing faith* (not just hearing lectures or sermons), because believing matures by doing, by applying, by testing, trial and error (Jas. 1:22; 2:18–26). This means that whether we are bankers, butchers, homemakers, heart surgeons, midwives, theologians, truck drivers, carpenters, investors, apologists, or philosophers, our life and work are shaped and directed by our faith as we *respond* to God's revelation in obedience or disobedience. We have a response-*ability* by virtue of our humanity, and all of us, not just the theologian, have access to God's revelation to guide our believing, thinking, acting and speaking.

## Reformational Thought Sees Man as God's Image-Bearer with a Cultural Task

The scriptural distinctives of *genuine faith* make it abundantly clear that human beings have a real-world task as God's image-bearers, called to reflect His will and purpose back to the rest of creation (Gen. 1:26–27). In the biblical world-and-life view, a certain *dynamic* has been written into creation because all things are created *from, through* and *unto* God (Rom. 11:36; Acts 17:28). Everything is oriented toward the maker of all things in total dependency—the one in whom all things consist and are brought to their destination (Rev. 22:13). This includes human beings who occupy a unique and royal station within creation; a privileged position rooted in Jesus Christ.

Scripture reveals that man (both male and female) is an image-bearer of God and of Christ in whom he is created (Gen 1; Col.1). The first man, Adam, was created as head of the race and in himself represented and comprehended the unity of all human beings who would come from him. The Bible teaches that as human beings we were all *in Adam* who was "son of God" (Luke 3:38; Rom. 5:12). In an important sense, then, we are royal representatives of God the Son, and we too were in paradise and fell into sin *in Adam*. It was here we fell from our *original unity* in Christ. As believers, it was and is our creaturely bond with the *human nature* of Christ (the last Adam) in the depth dimension of the heart which, stupendously, brings us into his central position in creation (Ps. 8)! Redeemed humanity's kingly role is consequently bound to Christ's identity for we are *joint heirs* with the king of kings (Rom. 8:16–17; 1 Pet. 2:9; 1 Cor. 15:22). If we fail to recognise this, we entirely miss the religious root of cosmic reality and our place as Christians in it (Heb.

2:10–12). We may then end up living much of life as though Christ did not exist, as though we are not *in Him*, and as if He is not of central relevance to the entirety of our life in the world.

Reformational thought further recognises that the task given to us in Christ is to participate in His ministry of reconciliation (John 20:21–23)—the restoration of all things to God. If we truly are *in Him*, not just by virtue of creation but also of redemption, by rebirth and faith, this ministry is inescapably bound to us (John 14:12; 2 Cor. 5:17–18; Eph. 2:6–7). Christ is the true vine, the Father is the gardener, and we are the branches called to remain in Him and bear fruit by the Spirit (John 15:1–8). In a broader sense the whole world is God's Garden (Matt. 13:38), and He is restoring paradise and glorifying His creation through the renewing work of Christ (2 Cor. 5:17; Rev. 21:5).

The cultural task is therefore beautifully illustrated for us in Scripture employing this metaphor of creation as God's Garden. The Son was there from the beginning (Prov. 8:22–31), walking by evening in the world's first garden with the man He had formed—a garden which the Lord Himself had planted (Gen. 2:7–8). Adam and Eve's task was to tend and keep that garden and to have dominion in the earth (Gen. 1:28; 2:15; 2:18, 21–24). This meant working in and watching over what God had made, turning *creation* into a God-honoring and Christ-glorifying *culture*. We know from Genesis that because of sin and rebellion our first parents were forced to leave the garden to struggle in a creation now subjected to futility and producing thorns and thistles. Yet at the same time God made a promise to send the *Son of man*, the seed of the woman (Gen. 3:15), both the *root* and *offspring* of Jesse, the true vine and last Adam, to restore the garden and fellowship with the divine Gardener. To that glorious end (Gal. 3:16), He called a royal-priestly people in Abraham (Exod. 19:6) and promised them a taste of paradise restored in Canaan, a land flowing with milk and honey (Exod. 33:3), if they were obedient. Due to their repeated idolatry and apostasy that fertile garden-land was also forfeit.

Finally, the first Gardener, the Lord of the vineyard, enters His garden again to walk with His image-bearers—this time as a Son of Adam, born of a virgin (Mark 12:1–12). He entered the garden of Gethsemane and yet His disciples slept, once again leaving the divine Gardener alone in His garden as he knelt and offered up prayers and supplications with strong cries and tears (Matt. 26:36-46; Heb. 5:7). There He confronted the death which He had pronounced on His loved ones in the first garden and then went out to taste the bitterness of death for everyone by hanging on a tree (Gen. 3:19; Heb. 2:9).

At the cross a remarkable exchange occurs concerning God's creation-garden—the restoration of paradise. One of the criminals crucified next to the Lord, now under the inspiration of the Holy Spirit, asks, "Jesus, remember me when you come into your kingdom." Jesus replies, *"I assure you: Today you will be with me in paradise"* (Luke 23:42-43). Here, the kingdom of God and paradise are synonymous. Christ explicitly reveals that *on this very day* the paradise, lost in the garden of Eden by the first Adam, is being reinstated by the last Adam. Soon after, Jesus cries out, *"It is fulfilled"* (John 19:30). It is at this very moment all the Father's requirements for redemption and the restoration of creation are fully met and Jesus' specific promise to the converted criminal is realized. At that marvelous and awe-inspiring instant, *in Christ,* all God's people in history had their passports stamped for resurrection life in *paradise restored*—a renewed earth and heaven liberated from its bondage to corruption (Rom. 8:21). Scripture records for us that as Jesus declares these words, the curtain of the temple which separated people from the holiest place (the temple itself being an image of the garden of Eden) was torn in two from top to bottom, ensuring the believer's direct access to God, even as our first parents had enjoyed immediate access to Him (Matt. 27:51). Paradise is again accessible to the people of God, the children of faith, in and through the Lord Jesus Christ. As a result, we are given the assurance, *"I will give the victor the right to eat from the tree of life, which is in God's paradise"* (Rev. 2:7).

Near the place our Lord was crucified was another garden with a new sepulchre in which no-one had ever been entombed. There the crucified Lord was buried alone, His grave sealed with a great stone. On the glorious morning of death's defeat, Mary Magdalene wandered distraught in the garden tomb and mistook the Lord for the gardener as He walked there in resurrection power and glory (John 20:15). To mistake Him for the gardener suggests He may well have been doing some gardening at the time!

Now, the great Gardener of creation has been exalted and is seated at the right hand of God, pruning His vines and bringing all things into subjection (Ps. 8; Heb. 2:5–12). Truly reformational thinking must recognize that *in Christ*, we are raised up and seated in the heavens, *participating* in Christ's ministry, rule, and authority as He subordinates everything to Himself (Eph. 2: 6, 10). As such, the same Lord walks with us again as His people by the Holy Spirit. God is in Christ reconciling the world to Himself (2 Cor. 5:19) and we are *in Him* restored to our calling to cultivate creation into the garden city of God. The Lord Jesus called this cosmic garden the *Kingdom of God* and we are entrusted with spreading and advancing the good news of this kingdom.

In view of this wondrous and profound story of Scripture, reformational thinking is necessarily enthralled with the joy, mystery, and privilege of our royal-priestly calling to represent the covenant love, will, and purpose of God to all creation, in every sphere of life and thought, delighting in the Lordship of the constant Gardener.

## Scholasticism or Reformational Thinking

So far, we have seen that a Christian mindset is unashamed of Christ and His claims and openly attaches to the true vine, speaking prophetically as circumstance demands. I have described this mentality as a heart-motive, a spiritual ethos, discussing its implications in a reformational approach to Christian thought that keeps both philosophy and theology in their provisional place, accepts the limitations of human understanding, and seeks to apply the Word of God to all of life by cultivating obedience in all spheres, beautifying God's good creation. In so doing I have stressed the unity of the Christian mind—a mind productive of an undivided life which subjects all things to Christ Jesus by seeking to follow Him to the uttermost.

This perspective is not without opposition and is the minority view in much of the Christian community. In fact, the Christian church in the West remains strongly influenced by many of the thought-forms which marked the pagan world of ancient Greece and Rome—ideas which contributed to their decline and collapse. It is my conviction that we need ongoing reformation in the Christian community in the West (and throughout the globe) so that we are enabled, by grace, to move away from an intellectual schizophrenia which divides our life and thought, undermines passionate commitment, weakens resolve, hinders self-sacrifice and subdues us under apostate religious motives. We can either be subject to Christ or steadily subjugated by the grand levelling of pagan religious commitment.

## The Root of Creation

We have already seen that the New Testament reveals explicitly the role of Christ Jesus as the one *in whom* all things are created and hold together and *for whom* all things exist (cf. Col. 1:15–20). The apostle Paul deepens our understanding of creation and redemption profoundly by showing that the triune God is the root and end of all things: *for from Him and through Him and to Him are all things*" (Rom. 11:36). This truth is supressed by unbelievers in unrighteousness because they have exchanged the truth about God for a lie and worship and serve something created rather than the creator (cf. Rom. 1:25–32).

The twentieth-century Dutch philosopher Herman Dooyeweerd drew out some important implications from these scriptural truths when he taught that it is not only the Christian world-and-life view, but all human thought which is embedded in a religious ethos oriented toward an idea of origin and law-order. That is to say, every person, believer and unbeliever, inescapably has a world-and-life view that, self-consciously grasped or not, contains ideas concerning the origins and laws of the universe. In his work, *A New Critique of Theoretical Thought,* Dooyeweerd expressed this biblical reality in philosophical terms:

> All meaning is *from, through* and *to* an origin, which cannot itself be related to a higher ἀρχή [origin]....

All genuine philosophical thought has therefore started as thought that was directed toward the origin of our cosmos.[15]

This is part of what makes the Christian perspective utterly unique in its understanding of reality. In the Greco-Roman cradle of Western civilisation, there was no room in philosophical thought for a free *creation* by an infinite-personal God as revealed in the Bible. This is because the Greek understanding of *nature* (as it comes to full flower in Aristotle) was ruled by a dualistic "form-matter" framework that regarded reality as consisting of an *uncreated,* amorphous *chaotic matter,* which by a forming activity of an impersonal divine principle achieves a coherence of "form and matter." This duality had the effect of *dividing reality* into two realms—the sensory and supra-sensory—the former being the realm we can experience with our senses and the latter being the realm which we cannot. This latter realm was nonetheless thought to be knowable by the intellectual contemplation of "rational souls"—an idea which influenced the thought of Augustine, for whom the soul was conceived as an immortal substance.

In our understanding of what it means to be human, the eventual result of these ideas was that human beings came to be seen as assembled from two components, distinct in principle: a mortal, material body, and an immortal, rational soul. Plato considered the soul-substance of the human being primary, whilst regarding the body as merely its "tool," akin to the way a person drives a car. For Aristotle, form was the divine, higher principle that is embedded in non-divine, chaotic matter providing its essential unity. Together they make up a substantial unity in which the rational soul is considered the "essential form."[16]

---

15. Herman Dooyeweerd, *A New Critique of Theoretical Thought*, in *The Collected Works of Herman Dooyeweerd*, Series A, vol. 1: *The Necessary Presuppositions of Philosophy*, trans. David H. Freeman and William S. Young (Jordan Station, ON: Paideia Press, 1984), 9.
16. D. F. M. Strauss, "Scholasticism and Reformed Scholasticism at Odds with Genuine Reformational-Christian Thinking," *Nederduitse Gereformeerde Teologiese Tydskrif* 5, no. 2 (March 1969): 97–114.

This view is a radical departure from biblical revelation, in which there are no independent substances that exist apart from the all-conditioning Word of God, the Lord Jesus Christ. In Scripture creation is from nothing by the Word of God. It is *distinct* from Christ but not *separated* from Him. The apostle Paul therefore shocks the Greek philosophers in Athens with his application of this truth: "for *in Him* we live and move and exist" (Acts 17:28). As Andree Troost puts it, "[Christ] is with God the Father, the creator and bearer of the entire cosmos which was created *in* Him."[17] We will see the vital importance of this radical difference in religious commitment concerning origins and how compromise with pagan thought impacted Christian thinking.

## Scholasticism

Scholasticism was a medieval movement within Christian centres of learning and is much more than a set of neutral procedural tools for doing theology; it was an effort to blend Christian theology and the ancient Greek dualism just described. As Dooyeweerd notes, "Scholasticism seeks a *synthesis* between Greek thought and the Christian religion. It was thought that such a synthesis could be successfully achieved if philosophy, with its Greek basis, were to be made subservient to Christian theology."[18] In the thirteenth century, Thomas Aquinas brought Roman Catholic scholastic thought to its apogee by officially interpreting Aristotle's views for the church. In 1263, Pope Urban IV reminded Christian scholars that a decree of Pope Gregory IX, which forbade the teaching of Aristotle as mediated by the Arabs, at the same time called on them to interpret Aristotle for the Christian faith:

---

17. Andree Troost, *What is Reformational Philosophy: An Introduction to the Cosmonomic Philosophy of Herman Dooyeweerd*, trans. Anthony Runia (Jordan Station, ON: Paideia Press, 2012), 166.
18. Herman Dooyeweerd, *Roots of Western Culture: Pagan, Secular and Christian Options*, in *The Collected Works of Herman Dooyeweerd*, Series B, vol. 15, ed. D. F. M. Strauss, trans. John Kraay (Jordan Station, ON: Paideia Press, 2012), 115.

William of Moerbeke and Thomas Aquinas were summoned to the papal court to assume the task of assimilating Aristotle into the Christian world of thought. Aquinas' purpose reflected a supreme confidence, a confidence shared by many, that an establishment of Christian truth upon the foundation of the reason of autonomous man was possible.[19]

Aquinas' project was to try to accommodate the form-matter dualism of the Greeks to the Christian faith. In this unfortunate marriage, "matter" was the principle of imperfection, and the "rational form" was the "thinking soul" which participated in the divine.[20] As a result, Aquinas divides the creation order into *natural* and *supernatural* realms. That legacy has remained with us in various permutations ever since.

The religious superstructure built up around this philosophical dualism steadily and inexorably divides *all of life* into two domains, the natural and the supernatural (spiritual)—a worldview expressed in the polarities of *nature and grace*. Here nature is conceived as form and matter, and grace (supernatural faith) as an additional gift to bring the immortal soul to perfection. This Scholastic perspective is antithetical to the scriptural reality of the creation of human beings as a *unity*, along with a *life-comprehending* apostasy in sin and rebellion at the Fall so that humanity is in need of an equally *life-comprehending* redemption at the root of our being. Instead, though our "rational soul" is thought wounded by sin and deprived of the gift of faith, it is not seen as radically perverted and depraved by the Fall. Scholastic thought teaches the Fall really robbed us only of a supernatural gift of grace (i.e., true faith) which is restored through Christ and the church—the church being the one *supernatural institution* of grace.

---

19. R. J. Rushdoony, *The One and the Many: Studies in the Philosophy of Order and Ultimacy* (Vallecito, CA: Ross House Books, 2007), 198.
20. Dooyeweerd, *Roots of Western Culture*, 119.

## Reformed Scholasticism

Though the Reformation broke with much of this mischaracterisation of life and sought a renewal of the biblical understanding of a life-comprehending Creation, Fall, Redemption and Consummation by the power of the Holy Spirit, it did not completely destroy Scholasticism's artificial bridge from Aristotle to Christianity. Consequently, a "Protestant Scholasticism" soon became entrenched and has strongly persisted into modern evangelicalism. As Dooyeweerd explained, "Protestant scholastics thought they could strip Greek philosophy of its pagan features by depriving it of all independence and turning it into a 'handmaiden.' Thus, it was put to so-called formal use in systematic theology and theological ethics."[21] This kind of mistake is easily made when we assume the king of Sodom can make Abraham rich. I am reminded of more recent assertions that Critical Theory can be a "useful analytical tool" for Christians.

The origins of a Protestant Scholasticism are found in the thinking of the early reformers who did so much to bless and recover the church in other ways. The great reformer, Martin Luther, openly claimed to be of William of Ockham's school—a perspective in which he was immersed whilst at Erfurt monastery. Ockham was a fourteenth-century Franciscan monk who denied that there was a real point of contact between the realms of nature and grace. Aquinas had tried to tie the Greek concept of nature to the faith of the church, but Ockham denied that these could be held together. He held to the idea of a divine arbitrariness; human reason could neither discover nor prove God. Belief in God was simply a matter of faith, not of knowledge. And so, cutting the link between nature and grace, between knowledge and faith, and between creation and redemption, he rejected the idea of Christianized society, holding to the complete sovereignty of *secular* government. In many respects Ockham anticipates the modern period of history, shunting off the *super*natural Christian life, the realm of faith and revelation, to another world

---

21. Herman Dooyeweerd, *Reformation and Scholasticism in Philosophy*, Collected Works of Herman Dooyeweerd, vol. 5, part 2, trans. D.H. Freeman (Jordan Station, ON: Paideia Press, 1984), 5-2:46.

and privatizing Christianity to the church and individual believer. Herman Dooyeweerd observes that Ockham's criticism of the nature-grace link left two options for Christians:

> one could either return to the Scriptural ground-motive of the Christian religion or, in line with the new motive of nature severed from the faith of the church, establish a modern view of life concentrated in the religion of the human personality. The first path led to the Reformation; the second path led to modern humanism.[22]

Luther was profoundly influenced by Ockham's complete separation of "natural life" from the "supernatural" Christian life of grace—thereby driving a radical wedge between creation and redemption. So-called "nature" (the natural order and whole of the cultural life of human beings) was viewed almost exclusively in the light of sin, and reason was regarded as the only guide in this natural domain—clearly entailing the ubiquitous, secularizing notion of a radical separation of reason and revelation. Consequently, "[I]n matters of secular government, justice, and social order, a person possessed only the light of reason."[23]

This fundamental error was expressed also in Luther's attempt to set law (nature) and gospel (grace) in opposition to each other. The law was an order for sinful *nature* which Luther began to regard as antithetical to *supernatural* grace. Gospel love must inevitably overcome the "rigidity" of law. Consequently, the link between creation-law and God's restorative grace was effectively severed. On this view, redemption came to imply the *death* of "nature" rather than its liberation and *renewal*. Though Luther vigorously attacked pagan philosophy, often with great wit and sagacity, due to his lack of insight into the full implications of a biblical world-and-life view, he was unable to direct people to a comprehensive inner reformation of thought itself. As Dooyeweerd explains, "…[H]e did not see that human thinking arises

---

22. Dooyeweerd, *Roots of Western Culture*, 139.
23. Dooyeweerd, *Roots of Western Culture*, 141.

from the religious root of life and that it is therefore always controlled by a religious ground-motive."[24]

Calvin, though clearly and explicitly grasping the sovereignty of God over all creation and its life-comprehending character, was also unable to extricate himself entirely from a persistent and inherited Greek dualism because he lacked a developed, scripturally grounded ontology. Calvin followed Augustine (who unsuccessfully sought to escape the grasp of Neo-Platonism), and this is apparent in Calvin's view of the human person where he conceives of the soul as the noblest "part" of man—an immortal (though created) "being." The flesh is a kind of prison, so that soul and body stand over against each other in uncomfortable tension, never fully encompassing the biblical unity of the human person.

Calvin's reformational emphasis on Christ's rule over all of life is gradually pushed aside by the development of a protestantized Scholasticism, beginning with men like Theodore Beza. Whilst wanting to honor biblical revelation, the period produced no true inner reformation of all thought, and so Christ's kingship and scriptural authority are gradually sequestered in the ecclesiastical sphere—a narrow domain of religious faith and church dogma. The result being, as the church's influence declined, biblical truth is pushed further upward into a spiritual upper story. Inevitably, theology is then honoured as queen of the sciences (i.e., the only truly Christian science), whilst philosophy and other disciplines must simply be adapted, where possible, to the church's theological principles. The thought that philosophy, history, politics, jurisprudence, and the natural sciences, etc., must be inwardly reformed from a scriptural world-and-life view just does not occur. These disciplines supposedly belong to the lower story of nature, natural reason, and natural law, whereas theology is concerned with the higher supernatural realm of faith, grace, and the church.

It is then entirely unsurprising to find the eventual emergence of dialectical theology in Protestantism which "sharply opposes the religious antithesis in the area of worldly life, rejecting the idea of Christian politics,

---

24. Dooyeweerd, *Roots of Western Culture*, 141.

of a Christian political party..., and of Christian scholarship."[25] For example, though reacting against a radical liberal Protestantism, Karl Barth continues the identification of nature with sin, separating nature from the Word of God which he and his followers regarded as "wholly other." Barth rejects a point of contact between the Christian faith, the kingdom of heaven, and natural life so that he completely repudiates the idea of distinctly Christian culture—including Christian art, political life, scholarship, and even social action.[26] In this neo-orthodoxy, the creation law and ordinances recede so far from view that Christian thought effectively begins with the idea of a Fall and then redemption—for Barth there could be no knowledge of creation law and norms.

With this continuation of Greek philosophical dualism in various branches of Protestantism, we can easily see the many ways in which a *division of life* into separate domains has stubbornly manifested itself, producing a mindset accepting of various artificial rifts. Consider some of these familiar oppositions and polarities still emphasized to varying degrees by many evangelical Christians and Protestants of all stripes:

**Body/Soul:** We *are* a "soul"; we *have* a "body." Human beings are made up of two separate substances, one higher the other lower, easily distinguishable and separable. The soul (a complex of higher functions including reasoning and feeling) is the real person; the body is merely a shell. The soul's destiny is Heaven or Hell, the body and the earth are relatively less important.

**Material/Spiritual:** The Christian life is a "spiritual" life consisting of "spiritual" disciplines. It is an inner battle against the desires of the lower part of us—stemming from the body. The material world is an incumbrance, lesser, or evil, and we will eventually escape it when we go to Heaven. In the meantime, we must suppress the desires of our material nature.

---

25. Dooyeweerd, *Roots of Western Culture*, 143.
26. John R. Franke, *Barth for Armchair Theologians* (Louisville, KY: Westminster John Knox, 2006, 50 –55.

**Natural/Supernatural:** Most life activities are just natural and about this world, but Christianity is about a supernatural world beyond this one, and therefore this natural life and creation are not as important as the supernatural world. The natural is mundane, generally humdrum, and carries on largely in terms of its own impersonal laws. However, sometimes God breaks into this natural world do supernatural things like miracles, which are much more significant than everyday events.

**Public/Private:** Our spiritual life of faith with its principles of discipleship are an essentially private matter of personal conviction. We are not to openly argue for Christianity as superior to other ways of life and should not impose our views on anyone else. Our private faith is not for the public space as it does not involve publicly accessible knowledge that everyone can approve based on reason; and in any case, God's kingdom is not of this world.

**Secular/Sacred:** Most of life functions well in terms of neutral, non-religious, secular principles that everyone can agree on. Politics, education, law, science, etc., are secular areas of life which man's common natural reason is sufficient to govern. The church, however, is a sacred institution of grace which, unlike these other areas, is ruled by biblical revelation. This revelation is not to be applied to culture and society, for to Christianize culture is to mix the upper and lower stories of existence, the secular and sacred, the natural and supernatural.

**Law/Gospel:** Law is concerned with the earth, with nature, the material world and sinful natural desires, whereas gospel freedom is spiritual and concerns grace for the soul. The church is the institution of grace not law—which is a matter for the state as a natural institution ruled by reason. Grace throws law aside because grace has no more need for the law than heaven needs earth, or the saved soul has real need for the body.

**Common/Special Revelation:** The natural creation is the realm of common principles, natural theology, and natural law. By contrast, Christ is the source of special grace and special revelation. The one is the proper ladder to the other, but we need the addition of faith and grace in special revelation to bring us to completion, salvation, and perfection.

**Reason/Revelation:** Human reason is sufficient for understanding most of our experience in the natural world and should guide human cultural life including politics, education, etc., in terms of neutral, rational principles. Human reasoning, though prone to errors, is essentially good as far as it goes and can offer high-probability proofs for God's existence acceptable to logical and right-thinking people. However, supernatural revelation in the Bible and to the soul is admittedly necessary for eternal salvation and to disclose certain spiritual doctrines.

**Science/Faith:** The sciences operate only in terms of objective natural reason, and concern religiously neutral "facts" and knowledge of the natural world. The sciences answer factual questions about how things happen in the world. Faith is unrelated to reason and is concerned only with the higher value judgments of why things happen. The only truly Christian academic discipline is theology, because it is concerned with studying religion and faith. There can be no distinctly Christian view of philosophy or science.

**Culture/Kingdom:** The kingdom of God is a spiritual and invisible reality that does not manifest itself outside the heart and supernatural institution of grace—the church. The kingdom of God fundamentally concerns a future heavenly reality, not the present earth and human culture. The earth is destined for total destruction, so nothing in human culture has any abiding value. Getting souls to heaven and preserving them in the institutional church through this veil of tears is our calling.

The reformational tradition has shown that this artificial separation of various domains in life—which are necessarily ruled by different standards and principles—follow entirely logically from the dualistic conception of the human person derived from the *form-matter and substance concepts* in Greek philosophy once synthesized with the Christian view of creation and redemption.

## The Reformational Response

As with all influential errors, Scholasticism's persuasiveness lies in its close imitation of the truth, together with its use of familiar biblical language. It is true for example that scripturally, we may conceptually distinguish an *inner* and *outer* man (2 Cor. 4:11, 16), fully dependent in every way and at every moment upon the sustaining Word of Christ (Acts 17:28; Rom. 11:36). But there is no independent "essence" of human life, no higher and lower substances, or "parts"—the human person is an integrated unity created in the image of God and made a living being from the dust with the breath of God. The "I" or human ego cannot be identified simply with reasoning, feeling, willing, or any other aspect of our existence, because these *functions* all presuppose a deeper unity that transcends them. The "I," our full human selfhood, the *depths of the heart*, is God's mystery transcending the temporal functions of our existence and is grasped only in relation to God who has placed in us a sense of the eternal (Eccl. 3:11). Critically, Christians shall one day follow Christ bodily out of the grave (Col. 1:18; 1 Cor. 15:20). It is the full person that is raised to life (inner and outer man), just as it is the totality of creation which will be released from its subjection to futility when we receive the fullness of our adoption as sons, the redemption of our bodies (Rom. 8:19–23).

Reformational thought therefore resists every inclination to divide up created reality in terms of philosophical distinctions that are entirely foreign to the Bible. Our faith rests on the scriptural truth "that the mediating Word is the religious lifeline which links God and man together in a life-long, *all-embracing* covenant relationship of revelation and response."[27] All of creation in every part is governed by the *mediating Word* of Christ and in no domain of life do we escape the all-embracing relationship we have with Christ and His Kingdom. *All of life* is a religious response to that Word.

---

27. Gordon J. Spykman, *Reformational Theology: A New Paradigm for Doing Dogmatics* (Grand Rapids, MI: Eerdmans, 1992), 94; italics added.

Reformational thinking translates this all-embracing, mediating, and sustaining power of the Word of Christ in terms of what we can call "ontic normativity." This is simply the recognition of a law-Word *for* creation that provides a normative structure for all spheres of life and every entity within creation—it governs the law-conformity of all created reality. As such, Christ cannot be decoupled from a so-called "natural" realm of factual neutrality, an area of creation that can be withdrawn from the sovereign Lordship and authority of Jesus and His written Word-revelation. Christ Jesus, who holds all things together by the Word of His power, from whom, through whom and to whom all things exist, cannot be banished to a supposed upper story of reality, a spiritual world of grace, shunted out of history to a future age, nor imprisoned in the walls of the institutional church so that the Kingdom of God (*Basileia*) is limited to the institutional expression of the *ekklesia*.

The central direction of scriptural revelation is the *unity* and *continuity* of God's creation and redemption within the rubric of the kingdom of God—an all-encompassing Creation, Fall, and Redemption of the whole of life. This inescapable revelation must be the *starting point* for all our activity as Christians, including philosophical and theological activity; it is not a theological *product* of human interpretation but is rather the motive-force of the biblical message. The radical character of this religious motive, argues Dooyeweerd:

> can only be revealed by the Holy Spirit, because he opens our hearts so that our faith will no longer be a mere acceptance of formal articles of our Christian confession, but a *living* faith, serviceable to the central working of God's Word in the heart—the religious centre of our life.... [I]n their radical meaning—as the ground motif of the Word-revelation and the key to true knowledge—creation, fall and redemption are no simple articles of faith; they are rather the Word of God itself in its central spiritual power, directed to the heart, the religious centre of our existence. Confronted by the Word of God in his heart, man can offer nothing, but only listen and receive.... The Word of God... must penetrate to the root of our being and become the central motive-force of our whole Christian life.[28]

---

28. Dooyeweerd, cited in Strauss, "Scholasticism and Reformed Scholasticism," 9–10.

This profound statement means, among other things, that Christ's restorative kingdom life cannot be restricted to a "part" of the human person nor any isolated terrain of human existence or experience such as the institutional church or our personal devotional lives. Rather, taking root in the unity of our heart, it bursts forth in marriage and family, education and entertainment, science and arts, politics and law, business and economics, sport and fashion, church and state. In each of these areas we are led either in terms of the kingdom of light or the kingdom of darkness, obedience or disobedience. As Danie Strauss has noted, "It is impossible to speak of a neutral sphere within so-called common grace, where the total antithesis, for or against Christ, does not radically apply."[29] In all aspects of life, in every activity, institution, and discipline, we will be either for or against the Lord.

That the man Christ Jesus, the suffering servant who went to the cross, is Creator and Redeemer, Lord and King, ruling and reigning over all life, so that His Word is law and so that as God, He is the proper object of all worship, possessing total power and dominion, constitutes a radical offense to the spirit of the world. As Kierkegaard puts into the mouth of an unbelieving philosopher, "'If this insane thing were possible, that an individual was God, then logically one must worship this individual. A greater philosophical bestiality cannot be conceived.'"[30] It is this offense that tempts us to be offended at Him, to seek the honor that comes from men rather than that which comes from God. Here we are enticed to synthesize our message with the world, with the religious desires of our culture to make the pill go down more easily. A Christ disjointed from the real world, confined to a privatized "spiritual" domain, His authority limited to one institution, one subject, His Lordship relevant only for another place in another time, is no threat or offense to sinful and apostate people. Such a message is a replica, a mock-up with a facsimile of Christ that will prove powerless to reproduce life of itself.

I am very fond of seedless grapes; they are sweet and very easy to eat with no bitter bite or hard to chew pips. Originating naturally by a mutation

---

29. Strauss, "Scholasticism and Reformed Scholasticism," 11.
30. Søren Kierkegaard, *Training in Christianity*, trans. Walter Lowrie (New York: Vintage Books, 2004), 52.

from the original, and now produced by cutting and splicing, they have been propagated by clever human intervention—by a synthesis. But left to themselves they have no generating power within them. If they fall to the ground, they die and can pass nothing on. In the history of Christian faith, errors, like mutations, have arisen naturally because of the fallibility and sin of human beings. But if those errors are picked up and harnessed because they seem appealing and then spliced with the original, they continue only as invasive entities, synthesized with the original, borrowing its life and root. They exist only because the real life and generating power is in the original.

Christ and His unadulterated Word of a life encompassing Creation, Fall, and Redemption are the original—the root and seeded grape. The constant temptation for us as Christians is to allow imitations to persist because we think they make our witness more appealing, our faith less offensive, the gospel more palatable. So, we splice them in. We propagate the error by our ingenuity. But what the synthesis produces has no generating power. It looks similar and may go down easily, but once consumed it dies and can pass nothing on. If the bite is taken from our message, if the seed of offense is removed, if we splice other worldviews onto the Christ of Scripture, the fullness and power of the kingdom message is removed and our restorative potential withers away.

Reformational thinking holds that at the deepest level of our humanity, at the *heart of our existence*, all of life is a *continuous response* to the *Word of God* (Rom. 12:1). All the laws and norms Christ Jesus has ordained and revealed for created reality, standing above us, yet binding us, call us to conformity and joyful obedience. It is by a faithful response to the imperishable seed of the Word that we grow, bear fruit, and pass that life on to the next generation. The matchless beauty of the gospel is that Christ's Word is true life and His total kingdom one of righteousness, peace, and joy in the Holy Spirit.

CHAPTER 2

# *Think Christianly About Christ*

*For in him, all the fullness of God was pleased to dwell and through him to reconcile to himself all things, whether on earth or in heaven, making peace by the blood of his cross.*
— *Colossians 1:19-20 (ESV)*

## Christ or the Idols

TO ASK WHETHER A PERSON believes in God is, in many respects, a serious misunderstanding of the most important issue at stake in human life. The Bible is clear throughout that the central question for every person is not *whether* you believe in God, but *what* or *who* is your God? In the scriptural world-and-life view, unbelief is not presented as the *absence* of belief, but rather a misdirected belief in a false god or idol. This is because human beings, created in God's image, are inescapably religious creatures (*homo religiosus*) directed by a given faith, and so we require an ultimate point of reference for our thinking and doing. To reject one religion or god is only to do so in the name of another.

In the previous chapter we saw the central importance of placing Jesus Christ, our Lord and our God (John 20:28), and His Word-revelation, at the foundation of *all* our thinking and doing, and we observed some of the ways in which humanistic and pagan assumptions consistently threaten to undermine the distinctive character of the Christian life and mind. It should come as no surprise that the battle for a truly Christian mind began early in the life of the church, in its confrontation with the spirit of the world which sought to deny the true identity of Christ by fashioning Him into another idol. The outcome of that early struggle would have monumental significance for human civilization. What we believe about Jesus Christ, in the final analysis, will determine everything, and so the Christian must truly think Christianly about Christ, or else face shipwreck.

The apostle John reminds us emphatically of the identity of our Lord:

Jesus told him, "I am the way, the truth, and the life. No one comes to the Father except through Me.

"If you know Me, you will also know My Father. From now on you do know Him and have seen Him."

"Lord," said Philip, "show us the Father, and that's enough for us."

Jesus said to him, "Have I been among you all this time without your knowing Me, Philip? The one who has seen Me has seen the Father. How can you say, 'Show us the Father'? Don't you believe that I am in the Father and the Father is in Me? The words I speak to you I do not speak on My own. The Father who lives in Me does His works. Believe Me that I am in the Father and the Father is in Me (John 14:6–11).

In the beginning was the Word, and the Word was with God, and the Word was God. He was with God in the beginning. All things were created through Him, and apart from Him not one thing was created that has been created (John 1:1–3).

This defining foundation of the Christian faith, once for all delivered to the saints (Jude 3), is utterly unique amongst all the religions of the world and the philosophies of human history, and its transformative power for human culture is unequalled. There are two principal reasons for this. *First,* the Bible reveals to us that the infinite personal God was manifest *in history* in the Lord Jesus Christ—Son of Man (Luke 12:8) and Son of God (Matt. 16:16). The various myths of demi-gods, sons of the gods, avatars, or manifestations of impersonal divine being in heroic figures or animals in the pagan religions are fables and philosophical speculations, categorically distinct from the Christian confession. The incarnation of the living, eternal God in Christ is historical and completely singular. The Christian thinker Søren Kierkegaard put it this way, "If the by-nature eternal comes into existence in time, is born, grows up, and dies, [this] is a break with all thinking."[1]

*Second,* non-Christian religions are primarily socio-political systems of thought with various societal objectives. The goal of their gods or divinity concept is the realization of some form of socio-political vision. This is true of ancient paganism, Hinduism, Islam, and even Buddhism—the teachings of the Dalai Lama being a good example.[2] But this political orientation is not limited to the so-called world religions. As Whale points out:

> There are other faiths to which men give themselves. The *mystique* of racial destiny or imperial mission takes many forms, as the pages of de Gobineau, Dostoievsky or Kipling testify. Political ideologies evoke and sustain the devotion of the elect Party and, through it, of the disciplined multitude; either assuming an explicitly religious character, or using quasi-religious ritual forms and philosophies of history. Fascism, Nazism, Communism, Japanese *bushido* and Emperor cult are modern versions of the immemorial "religious" secularism which would virtually deify the State or Society by giving it an absolute character. The omnicompetent State absorbs the sacred rights of the individual; it repudiates the unique status

---

1. Murray A. Rae, *Kierkegaard's Vision of the Incarnation: By Faith Transformed* (Oxford: Clarendon Press, 1997), 41.
2. See Dalai Lama, *Beyond Religion: Ethics for a Whole World* (Boston: Houghton Mifflin Harcourt, 2011).

of the human person with cynical ruthlessness, prescribing not only how he is to live from the cradle to the grave, but how he is to think and what, in fact, he is to worship. Nationalism becomes the chief end of man. The parade-ground is its symbol; the ant-heap its working model. Right and wrong are no more than tiddly-winks for political opportunism to play with. Truth has no transcendent, absolute. Meaning... [that if] there be no living God, the sovereign Creator and Redeemer in whose image man is made, why should the individual take precedence over the mass; over Party or Nation or Race?[3]

In other words, in *all* forms of non-biblical faith, the essential nature of religion is the effort to impose a pattern or abstract *ideal* upon history, invariably through various forms of societal compulsion and frequently by the force of the state. By contrast, for Christianity, true religion is the *historical* manifestation of the transcendent *Kingdom of God* in a person, the sovereign Lord Jesus Christ—a Kingdom that moves in terms of His purpose and direction and for which he speaks and acts with total authority. God's total Word, therefore, and not man's idea, simultaneously frees and governs all of life.

Here we have come to the root of the offensiveness of an orthodox Christian mind. A faith where *exclusive divinity* is assigned to an historical person is a roadblock hindering progress toward the goal of man-made religion to impose its own idea upon history, and in a very real sense, realise man's own godhood and plan for salvation. This essential distinction between Christianity and humanism is important for understanding both the development of the Western world and the historic confession of the church in the formation of the Christian mind. The ecumenical creeds which preserved the truth of Christ's identity proved to be far more than theological summaries of orthodoxy; whether their framers realized it or not, they were effectively blueprints for the future.

---

3. John S. Whale, *The Protestant Tradition: An Essay in Interpretation* (Cambridge: Cambridge University Press, 1955), 264, 266.

# The Roots of Controversy

The crucial battle over the true nature of God the Son, manifest in Jesus Christ, began early. In the first and second centuries the ideas of a movement know as Gnosticism threatened the faith of the church. The noted scholar, Adolf Von Harnack, in his *History of Dogma* referred to Gnosticism as, "the radical Hellenization of Christianity," with Greek philosophy an important factor in its development.[4] The Gnostics were people who in many cases claimed to be Christian and made their way into the churches, but influenced by pagan thought, denied any exclusive divinity to Jesus—seeing his "deity" as of a kind common to the potentiality of all people. In the Gnostic "trinity," the Father becomes an unknown God, the Holy Spirit the source of deity for everyone, and Jesus, one among many people who gains divine status. In this humanistic view, salvation was not by faith in Christ's finished work, but by means of self-knowledge and the realization of one's own divinity.[5]

It steadily became necessary, then, in the life of the early church, that definitive summaries of Christian orthodoxy rooted in the Scriptures be hammered out as the people of God confronted both pagan unbelief and heresy within their own ranks. This began in earnest in the fourth century. However, the earliest pagan writer we know of to oppose biblical Christianity with his pen was Celsus in his book, *The True Word*—the first known comprehensive critique of Christianity appearing in the second century. In the third century, this work was refuted by the church father, Origen, in his book, *Contra Celsus*. It is clear that Celsus, an eclectic follower of various Greek thinkers like Epicurus, Plato, Aristotle and various Stoic philosophers, is offended by the worship of the *exclusive* God-man, Jesus Christ:

> If these men worshipped no other God but one, perhaps they would have a valid argument against the others. But in fact, they worship to an extravagant degree this

---

4. See Frances M. Young, *The Making of the Creeds* (London: SCM Press, 1993), 17.
5. Rousas J. Rushdoony, *Foundations of Social Order: Studies in the Creeds and Councils of the Early Church* (Nutley, NJ: Craig Press, 1968), 10.

man who appeared recently, and yet think it is not inconsistent with monotheism if they also worship his servant (*Contra Celsus*, VIII.12).[6]

The pagans were deeply irritated and affronted by the fact that Christians would not join in the traditional cultic celebrations of the Roman Empire. Instead, these people preached that the revelation of the one true God, and what he required, was *finalized* and *universalized* in the life and teaching of Jesus Christ. As Young tells us, Celsus was happy to agree:

> [T]here was one ultimate divine being, along with most respectable philosophers of his day, Middle Platonist and Stoic, but the general consensus was that this supreme divinity delegated the day-to-day running of things to many lesser divinities, gods and demons, and *the safety and prosperity of the state* depended upon keeping the gods favorable... couldn't Christians behave like everyone else?[7]

The sticking point was always the same—the unique *divinity of Christ* as the incarnate God, Savior, Lord, and King. This new faith was seen as a threat to the unity and stability of the ancient pagan state, and what's more, it stifled the aspirations of great men to become gods.

As Christians began to engage with these various threats and defend the faith once for all delivered to the saints, two factors became increasingly relevant in the story of an emerging need for summary statements of the faith: first, the evident risks involved with utilizing Greek philosophy and its categories in arguing with pagans for the truth of the gospel; and second, the improving fortunes of Christianity politically with the ostensible conversion of the emperor Constantine and therefore the explicit involvement of the state in doctrinal disputes.

With respect to the use of Greek philosophy, when Christians were preaching throughout the Roman Empire in the early centuries the good news that the *one true and living God* had been made manifest in Jesus

---

6. Young, *The Making of the Creeds*, 33.
7. Young, *The Making of the Creeds*, 33; italics added.

Christ, they were frequently thought of as atheists who denied the gods. In responding to this scurrilous charge, some of the educated Christians and early apologists sought to show that many respected pagan philosophers also taught that there was an ultimate and supreme being above the whole cosmos. In their concern to reach unbelievers however, some argued that this god of the philosophers, whom the pagan intellectuals regarded as an impersonal first cause, was in fact the God of the Bible. Church historian Justo L. González points out:

> [T]his was also a dangerous argument. It was possible that Christians, in their eagerness to show the kinship between their faith and classical philosophy, would come to the conviction that the best way to speak of God was not that of the prophets and other biblical writers, but rather that of Plato, Plotinus, and the rest. Since those philosophers conceived of perfection as immutable, impassible, and fixed, many Christians came to the conclusion that such was the God of Scripture.[8]

The obvious problem with this is that the immutable, impassible, and fixed being of classical philosophy[9] does not speak, does not enter into covenant with man, and does not enjoy personal fellowship with its creatures as the God of Scripture does. The divine principle of *being* in Greek thought was aloof from the world of *becoming*—there could be no direct point of contact between the changeable material world and the Hellenistic concept of the divine. And so, with a strained and erroneous application of allegorical methods of interpretation, some apologists suggested that biblical passages

---

8. Justo L. González, *The Story of Christianity: Volume 1, The Early Church to the Dawn of the Reformation* (New York: HarperOne/Zondervan, 2010), 159.
9. The term *immutable* refers to the concept of God's unchangeability, and the idea of *impassibility* comes from the Latin meaning 'not able to suffer.' It conveys the notion that God cannot experience pain or pleasure or any emotion in relation to the actions of others. It these terms are carefully qualified, Christians can legitimately speak of God's unchangeableness in terms of his nature, dependable character and purposes, but the concept of *impassibility* is totally foreign to the Bible, since the Scriptures speak plainly of God *responding* to his creatures.

which did not fit this philosophical idea of God were not to be understood in the plain sense in which Scripture speaks.

Christian leaders like Justin, Clement, and Origen, deeply influenced by Greek thought, nonetheless recognized that an *unmodified* classical view of the divine was unacceptable from a biblical perspective, and so embraced a *compromise* through a particular idea known as the *doctrine of the Logos* which did not strictly deny Christ's divinity, but subordinated Him as inferior to the Father. González explains:

> According to this view, although it is true that the supreme being—the "Father"—is immutable, impassible, and so on, there is also a Logos, Word, or Reason of God, and this is personal, capable of direct relations with the world and with humans. Thus, according to Justin, when the Bible says that God spoke to Moses, what it means is that the Logos of God spoke to him.[10]

Clement of Alexandria's version of this was derived from the Hellenistic Jewish thinker Philo. Clement sees the Logos as the rational law of the cosmos and mediator between God and the world. Moreover, in clearly pseudo-Gnostic terms, the faith of simple believers is ranked well below that of the Christian "sages"—superior believers whose access to the Logos (divine reason) uniquely equips them to understand God's Word through allegorical interpretation of Scripture.[11]

From a truly scriptural standpoint, this attempted compromise is unacceptable, but in the Eastern, Greek-speaking part of the church, these views had become both widespread and popular, and provided the vital historical and philosophical context for what church history knows as the Arian controversy, leading directly to the formulation of the Creed of Nicaea at the church synod known as the Council of Nicaea in A.D. 325. This creed was

---

10. González, *The Story of Christianity*, 161.
11. Dooyeweerd, *Reformation and Scholasticism in Philosophy*, 76.

revised and clarified at the Council of Constantinople in A.D. 381, giving us the Nicene Creed in the form we have it today.[12]

## Origen, Arius, and Arianism

Origen is an important figure in church history (c. 185–254)—though, as we shall see, given his profound impact on Arius, his influence was of mixed quality. Born in Alexandria into a Christian family, he later studied philosophy with a Platonist teacher. His speculative theological system was an attempt to bring together biblical teaching with the Greek philosophical school of Platonism, and included the ideas of creation going on eternally, the pre-existence of souls, and the subordination of the Son. Herman Dooyeweerd's comments on the thinking of Origen are highly instructive and worth citing at length:

> Origen was the first to incorporate the Jewish-Hellenistic *logos* theory, in combination with Neoplatonic elements, in a systematic exposition of Christian doctrine, which in his hands was turned into a theological-philosophical system of grand dimensions. Like Clement, he regarded Christian doctrine merely as the perfection and completion of what the *logos* had already disclosed in Greek philosophy. Origen thus saw pagan wisdom as a preparation for Christianity, even though his judgment of it still remained rather reserved.

> In complete conformity with the philosophical theology of both Philo and the later Neoplatonists, Origen taught that God, in the truest sense of the word, is the absolute *unity* (ἑνας and μονάς), exalted above the *nous* (the thinking mind) and *being* (ἐπεκείνα νοῦ καὶ οὐσίας). This God in the highest sense of the word is the Father, the origin and goal of all created things. The Son or *Logos* has been generated from eternity from God the Father as an emanation of the divine light.

---

12. A. N. S. Lane, *The Lion Concise Book of Christian Thought* (Oxford: Lion Hudson, 2002), 30.

The Son does have a commonness of being (ὁμοούσια) with the Father, but this *homoousion* is merely relative in nature and implies nothing more than Plotinus' commonness of being between the divine unity and the *nous*.

Origen's *logos* is an archetype that proceeds from the Father, but it is of lesser divinity. It is a second God (δεύτερος θεός) of lower rank, who has the same relationship to the Father that the Christian has to him. In relation to the cosmos this *logos* is the original type, the image of the invisible God. By him all things are created, and they are made in his image alone, not in the image of the Father. As the first-born of the Father the *Logos* is the principle of all rationality. Seen from the point of view of the creation he is God, but seen from God's point of view he is a creature. As the divine unity unfolds into a multiplicity, the *Logos* is the first member and the Holy Spirit is the second. This Spirit is even less divine than the *logos*, and it stands the closest to the creation cosmos.[13]

It was this philosophical and theological background that would shape the controversy leading to Nicaea.

Arius (c. 256–336), the spearhead of the attack on biblical orthodoxy, was a presbyter in Alexandria, and a divergent pupil of Origen. He pushed Origen's philosophical speculations to the point where he eventually overtly concluded that the Father alone is truly God. It is at this point that public controversy began to erupt. Though Arius looked to Origen, Origen himself had remained biblical insofar as he viewed the Father-Son relationship as *intrinsic* to the divine being and Godhead; they were at least co-eternal. Arius, however, differed with him by regarding the *coming forth* of the divine Word as a service to the inferior created order:

> He reasoned that the Lord who was physically born of Mary, grew in wisdom, suffered dereliction and death, must be less than the unbegotten, impassible, deathless Father. God is beyond Jesus.... The theological implication is that the Son must be somewhere midway between the Creator and the contingent creation now

---

13. Dooyeweerd, *Reformation and Scholasticism in Philosophy*, 5/2.77.

in need of redemption. Arius therefore clashed with a principle strongly stated by Irenaeus: "Through God alone can God be known."[14]

In short, Arius held and taught that Christ was a *created being*, not eternally existent and therefore not of the same essence with the Father, nor equal to the Father. The practical result of his theology was that the church was really worshipping Christ as a creature, not as the living and eternal God. Arius stated his position in his *Thalia*:

> The Unbegun made the Son a beginning of things originated; and advanced Him as a Son to Himself by adoption. He has nothing proper to God in proper subsistence. For He is not equal, no, nor one in essence with Him.... Thus there is a Triad, not in equal glories. Not intermingling with each other are their subsistences... It follows at once that, though the Son was not, the Father was God... For the Son does not know His own essence, for, being Son, he really existed at the will of the Father.[15]

Under the guidance of classical Greek philosophical speculation, including the schools of Plato and Aristotle, this was a brazen attempt to import humanism into the apostles' teaching, subvert the Apostles' Creed (the "Old Roman Creed" from the second century), and turn Christianity into a religious philosophy. Here, Christ as the Son does not even truly know the Father, because for Arius, anything that has a beginning cannot truly grasp or know that which has no beginning. The *Logos,* declared Arius, "is only called Logos conceptually, and is not Son of God by nature and in truth, but is merely called Son, he too, by adoption, as a creature."[16] The Arian motto concerning Christ became, "there was, when he was not." Clearly contradicting the apostle John, for Arius the Word was *not* true God, just the first of all

---

14. John McManners, ed., *The Oxford Illustrated History of Christianity* (Oxford: Oxford University Press, 1990), 56.
15. Arius, cited in Rushdoony, *Foundations of Social Order,* 11.
16. See Jaroslav Pelikan, *The Emergence of the Catholic Tradition (100–600)*, vol. 1 of *The Christian Tradition* (Chicago: University of Chicago Press, 1971), 196.

creatures. As John Frame notes: "[I]n the end they regarded the Word as a lesser being than the Father, worthy of a lesser degree of worship. He may be called 'a god' (*theos*) but not 'the God' (*ho theos*)."[17] Originally, "the God" was alone as a bare monad. The Father God, who was "simple" and without personal distinctions, could not create "matter" by Himself because it would defile Him, which is why he *became* a father, by creating the Word before time began, through whom he would then create the world. With the *production* of the Son, we now have a Dyad. Inevitably, the Holy Spirit was an even lesser being, further subordinate and *produced* by the Dyad, so Arianism ends up with a triad, but not the Trinity. In essence, when drawing a line between God and creation, Arianism would put Christ, the Logos, on the side of creation. The implications of this for the meaning of salvation and for human society are far reaching—a subject we shall address later.

## The Story of the Council of Nicaea

Arius was not a lone voice in the wilderness in his time; he had support from several prominent bishops in the Eastern part of the Roman Empire who had been students with him at Antioch, and he also enjoyed some popular support from the people of Alexandria. These Arian ideas were spreading and becoming a significant concern for the orthodox faithful. To address this, Alexander, the bishop of Alexandria, held a regional council in Antioch in the early part A.D. 325, where they drafted a statement of faith affirming Christ as divine and anathematized those who think, say, or preach that the Son of God is a creature who was brought into being, rather than truly begotten. The statement did not mention Arius by name, but it included citations from Arian theology and there was no doubt about its target. Affirming the orthodox view of the Father and the Son as the true apostolic dogma of the church, the council proceeded to excommunicate the three men who

---

17. John M. Frame, *A History of Western Philosophy and Theology* (Phillipsburg, NJ: P&R Publishing, 2015), 105.

refused to sign the statement—including Arius.[18] This, however, was not the end, but the beginning of the protracted Arian controversy. Arius appealed to various bishops who wrote their letters of objection, local demonstrations ensued, and the Eastern church found itself on the brink of major division.

At this point the same year the emperor Constantine, in the providence of God, and recognizing the threat to the peace and unity of the Empire, decided to intervene. After sending an ecclesiastical adviser to investigate and try to reconcile the parties in Alexandria, he realized that a great council or synod of Christian bishops from all parts of the Empire was going to be necessary to resolve this important dispute. So, in A.D. 325, in the city of Nicaea in Asia Minor, the first great Ecumenical (universal) Council of the church was gathered at the financial expense of the leader of the Roman Empire—a mighty realm that had until recently viciously persecuted believers. There were probably 318 bishops in attendance, mainly from the Greek-speaking part of the church in the East; but others also came from the Latin-speaking West, including presbyters representing the aging Bishop of Rome.

The scene was awe-inspiring as Christian leaders from around the known world, some of whom had been physically scarred by their persecutions and torture and who had heard of each other only by reputation, saw for the first time in the history of the faith, the universality of the church in person. The historian Eusebius of Caesarea, who was amongst them, in his *Life of Constantine* records:

> There were gathered the most distinguished ministers of God, from the many churches in Europe, Libya [i.e., Africa] and Asia. A single house of prayer, as if enlarged by God, sheltered Syrians and Cilicians, Phoenicians and Arabs, delegates from Palestine and from Egypt, Thebans and Libyans, together with those from Mesopotamia.... Even from Spain, there was a man of great fame [Hosius of Cordova] who sat as a member of the great assembly.... Constantine is the first ruler of all time to have gathered such a garland in the bond of peace.[19]

---

18. See Pelikan, *The Christian Tradition*, 200–201.
19. See González, *The Story of Christianity*, 162–63.

The council addressed a number of issues relating to the life of the church at the conclusion of a protracted persecution, but its primary purpose was to deal with the Arian controversy. Bishop Alexander led the anti-Arian party and with him was one of his deacons, who was not a member of the official council, the young man Athanasius. Arius himself was not a bishop and so was not allowed to sit with the council either, but he was represented by the Bishop of Nicomedia (called Eusebius). Expecting his speech articulating the Arian views to be warmly received, he was shocked to discover that when he claimed the Word or Son was only a creature, he was met with angry cries of "Blasphemy," "Heresy," and "You lie!" The vast majority of the council then agreed that it was necessary for the purpose of clarity, and to overcome the Arian twisting of Scripture, to agree to a creed which expressed the unified faith of the church, whilst simultaneously condemning Arianism.

It may seem arcane, overly exacting, or scrupulous to modern ears and to the theological novice, but at this great Council, a battle was being waged over two similar Greek words, *homoousion* (being of *one* essence or substance) and *homoiousion* (of *like* essence or substance). Was Jesus Christ really *one* with the Father, or a great and noble creature of the Father? The Council's answer was emphatic for the apostolic faith. Here was their formula as recorded by Eusebius of Caesarea:

> We believe in one God, the Father Almighty, maker of all things visible and invisible.
>
> And in one Lord Jesus Christ, the Son of God, begotten of the Father, Only-begotten, that is, from the substance of the Father; God from God, light from light, Very God from very God, begotten, not made, Consubstantial [*homoousios*] with the Father, by whom all things were made, both things in heaven and things in earth; who for us men and for our salvation came down and was incarnate, was made man, suffered, and rose again the third day, ascended into heaven, and is coming to judge living and dead.
>
> And in the Holy Ghost.

And those who say "There was when He was not," and "Before his generation he was not," and "he came to be from nothing," or those who pretend that the Son of God is "Of other *hypostasis* or substance [ousia]," or "created," or "alterable," or "mutable," the Catholic [universal] and Apostolic Church anathematizes.[20]

This formed the basis of the most universally accepted Christian creed. Only a few bishops refused to sign, including Arius' representative, Bishop Eusebius of Nicomedia; they were declared heretical and deposed. But the sly Bishop of Nicomedia was an able politician and reputed to be a distant relative of the emperor and so, though it was hoped that the Nicene Synod would be the end of the controversy, the battle was in fact to drag on for another fifty years. Arius was soon recalled from exile and was to be restored to full communion on the authority of Emperor Constantine. History records that just before the time of Arius' triumphal procession back to the church to be publicly reconciled, Bishop Alexander was praying prostrate before God that he would pity his church, lest heresy enter again, and petitioned the Lord to take Arius away. En route to the church, Arius left his procession suffering with gastric pain. They waited a short while and then went to look for him. They found that he had collapsed and died, falling headlong into an open latrine. The orthodox declared it an act of God.[21]

Bishop Alexander himself died three years after the Council, and was succeeded by the great Athanasius, whose protracted struggle against Arianism continued with little relief until a synod gathered in Alexandria in A.D. 362, where most of the churches rallied again in support of the Council of Nicaea. The small, dark-skinned Bishop, mocked by his opponents as "the black dwarf," fought the good fight, often against daunting odds. Having been present as an assistant to Alexander at the Council of Nicaea in his youth, he now carried the torch of biblical orthodoxy through a very dark time.

At one point, by the plotting of Eusebius of Nicomedia, and on the orders of Constantine, Athanasius was exiled and banished as a troublemaker,

---

20. J. Stevenson, ed., and W. H. C. Frend, ed., *A New Eusebius: Documents Illustrating the History of the Church to AD 337* (Grand Rapids, MI: Baker Academic, 2013), 345.
21. See Rushdoony, *The Foundations of Social Order*, 17.

like most of the other Nicene leaders by that point. Yet, by the Spirit and grace of God, truth prevailed. Athanasius, who in his heart knew Arianism could be defeated, was eventually allowed to return and died in Alexandria in A.D. 373. He did not get to witness the final triumph of orthodoxy at the Second Ecumenical Council at Constantinople in A.D. 381, where the Nicene theology was refined and fully ratified. This was the revised version of the Creed that they affirmed:

> I believe in one God the Father Almighty; Maker of heaven and earth, and of all things visible and invisible.
>
> And in one Lord Jesus Christ, the only-begotten Son of God, begotten of the Father before all worlds [God of God], Light of Light, very God of very God, begotten, not made, being of the one substance [essence (*homoousios*)] with the Father; by whom all things were made; who for us men and for our salvation, came down from heaven, and was incarnate by the Holy Ghost of the Virgin Mary, and was made man; and was crucified also for us under Pontius Pilate; he suffered and was buried; and the third day he rose again, according to the Scriptures; and ascended into heaven, and sitteth on the right hand of the Father; and he shall come again, with glory, to judge both the quick and the dead; whose kingdom shall have no end.
>
> And [I believe] in the Holy Ghost, the Lord and Giver of Life; who proceedeth from the Father [and the Son[22]]; who with the Father and the Son together is worshiped and glorified; who spake by the Prophets. And [I believe] one Holy Catholic and Apostolic Church. I acknowledge one Baptism for the remission of sins; and I look for the resurrection of the dead, and the life of the world to come. Amen.[23]

---

22. The Western church later added the clause, "and the Son" in the famous *filioque clause*. By doing this, any lingering element of subordinationism of the three persons was eliminated. This revision contributed to the division of the Eastern and Western churches in A.D. 1054.
23. Philip Schaff, *The Creeds of Christendom, with a History and Critical Notes*, 3 vols. (Grand Rapids, MI: Baker Book House, 1877–1882), vol. 2, 59.

## The Relevance of Nicaea for Today

The significance of the triumph of the Nicene Council continues today, as evidenced in its ongoing regular use in church liturgies, and more broadly, because of its ecumenical protection against error in the global church. The clear affirmation of the creed is that Christ is *co-essential* with the Father, the true God-man, and therefore Arianism is not true Christianity. The Nicene Creed maintains within the universal church the rightful place of Christ as the Lord of life and eternal Word of God, made flesh. Historian Phillip Schaff thus rightly called the Council of Nicaea "the most important event of the fourth century, and its bloodless intellectual victory over a dangerous error is of far greater consequence to the progress of true civilization, than all the bloody victories of Constantine and his successors."[24]

This brings us to the abiding relevance of Nicaea for the Christian life and a scriptural world-and-life view today. The preservation of a uniquely biblical perspective on reality, salvation, and culture would have been very difficult to envision without this Council, and heretical views could have taken much deeper root. When thinking about heresy, we often limit its scope to narrowly religious beliefs about God and questions of personal salvation within the life of the church as an organization. But the fact is, what we believe about Christ impacts every sphere of life and thought, and both the bishops and the emperor showed an awareness that what we hold to be true about Christ has ramifications beyond the ecclesiastical sphere. The doctrinal disputes of the West have indeed shaped the course of civilization for that very reason.

A number of important lessons from this period are immediately apparent for Christians today. The *first* is the ever-present danger of turning Christianity into a human philosophical system. The powerful influence of Greek philosophy upon many Jews in the time of Christ, on various early pseudo-Christian sects and, as we have seen, even on diverse scholars defending

---

24. Philip Schaff, *History of the Christian Church*, 8 vols. (Grand Rapids, MI: Eerdmans, 1910–1915), vol. 3, 631.

Christianity, is undeniable.[25] The Council of Nicaea helped to break the philosophical pretentions of both Gnosticism and Arianism—movements which had deep roots in the Hellenistic thought of men like Philo of Alexandria and of various forms of Platonism. Both these early heresies, shaped as they were by Greek concepts of the material world and the nature of the divine being, denied that Jesus Christ was the eternal Son of God, truly made flesh. Instead, Christ was a creature, a demiurge, or superior angel, less than God, but bringing man wisdom, knowledge and a moral example to emulate—in short, Jesus was a divinized philosopher-teacher. Though the Greek language proved helpful in clarifying biblical orthodoxy, the primary thought forms of the classical world remained a threat to a faith based on revelation rather than on philosophical speculation. By the grace of God, the Council preserved Scripture's teaching about the mystery of the Godhead manifest in Christ, and hindered the progress of these dangerous movements.

Although the councils of Nicaea and Constantinople greatly weakened the influence of Greek philosophy on Christian life and doctrine, they certainly did not crush it. Again and again the West has faced distortions of biblical truth because of attempts to synthesize biblical Christianity with the thinking of the pagan Greek philosophers. The influence of Neo-Platonism on the Christianity of the early Middle Ages was profound, even on Saint Augustine, and it led to a world-denying asceticism and monasticism in parts of the church that rejected many clear teachings of Scripture—including the goodness of creation and the blessing of marriage and human sexuality.

With the High Middle Ages came an attempt to blend the thought of Aristotle with scriptural revelation. Thomas Aquinas' overt intellectualism and his effort to meld Christianity with Aristotelianism served to forge his defence of the papal theocracy, and with the tools of Aristotle's *Politics*, Aquinas developed a vision of social order deeply indebted to classical Greek thought.[26] During the seventeenth and eighteenth centuries, the Cambridge

---

25. See Dooyeweerd, *Reformation and Scholasticism in Philosophy*, 5/2.68–78.
26. See Eric Voegelin, "Saint Thomas Aquinas on History, Politics, and Law," in *Collected Works of Eric Voegelin*, vol. 11, ed. Ellis Sandoz (Columbia, MO: University of Missouri Press, 1999).

Platonists undermined evangelical Puritanism in England. And in the nineteenth century, Greek philosophical thought undergirded the popular Deism and Unitarianism attacking the church, which were discernably revived forms of Arianism. Modern liberal theology in our own time, which typically denies the full deity of Christ, is likewise a continuation of Arianism, leaving us an unknown God and mythic Jesus.

The *second* lesson of Nicaea for today concerns the ongoing threat to the doctrine of salvation that is present whenever a biblical Christology is in any way compromised. Without the clarification of Nicaea, the implication of Arianism is that the Christ of Scripture simply morphs into another pagan mythological demi-god. According to Arianism, the *Logos*, not being true God, had to *choose* to be good and seek to maintain that goodness, despite his changeable nature. Supposedly, God the Father foreknew that Christ would resist temptation and remain good and so was able to give to Him a name and glory *in advance* of Him attaining goodness by his own virtuous living. Pelikan explains the consequences for the truths of salvation:

> The Logos became the "pioneer of salvation" by first enduring in his own name and then enabling those who followed him to do likewise. "By his care and self-discipline" he had triumphed over his mutable nature. His "moral progress *[προκοπή]*" had won for him the title Son of God..., The ultimate outcome of the Arian system was [that]... God was interpreted deistically, man moralistically, and Christ mythologically.[27]

Thus, Arianism is nothing more than the humanism that preaches salvation by works. Christ merely points the way by modelling moral progress and goodness as the first of the creatures. We too can triumph over our material mutable nature by following his example. The outcome is pure moralism that is very much like modern liberal Christianity and every other world religion that believes man saves himself by good deeds. This means that Christ does not accomplish our salvation as both God and man,

---

27. Pelikan, *The Christian Tradition*, 198.

redeeming us for Himself from God's just wrath against sin, but he simply models how we also might become sons of God by self-discipline. Once again, man becomes a god by his own efforts and saves himself.

A *third* lesson of Nicaea for our era is the way it deepens our understanding and ability to address the various cults that have arisen in the course of time. It is remarkable how many of them have an essentially Arian foundation. We can even include Mohammedanism (Islam) among the late Arian cults in this regard. Mohammed was concerned to denounce the eternal Sonship of Christ as a form of polytheism (which was the charge of Arius against the orthodox). In fact, the Christian theologian St John of Damascus, who lived in the eighth century, regarded Islam as a late pseudo-Christian heresy. Griffith tells us of John of Damascus, "[H]e speaks of Muhammed as having been one who, 'having happened upon the Old and New Testaments, likewise having probably been in conversation with an Arian monk, contrived his own heresy.'"[28]

Similarly, both the Mormon and the Jehovah's Witness cults are Arian to the core and cannot be understood apart from their anti-Nicene heritage. For the Jehovah's Witnesses, Jesus was the first son *brought forth* by Jehovah—a kind of god, but not the eternal Son of God. Openly rejecting the Council of Nicaea, they reduce Christ to the status of a creature. According to Mormonism (the so-called Church of the Latter Day Saints), which has both Gnostic and Arian overtones, Jesus was the firstborn of many spirit children of a heavenly father (and possibly mother), and *becomes* a god, inheriting the powers of godhood. This paves the way for the divinization of his siblings—that is to say: all people, being sons and daughters of the divine, can become gods!

These claims necessarily imply the rejection of Scripture as the *final* Word of God. It is noteworthy that all three of these cults—Islam, Mormonism, and Jehovah's Witnesses—each require either new or modified texts as their Scriptures, whilst simultaneously claiming their foundation in the Bible.

---

28. David H. Griffith, *The Church in the Shadow of the Mosque: Christians and Muslims in the World of Islam* (Princeton: Princeton University Press, 2008), 42.

The Jehovah's Witnesses have the *New World Translation* which manipulates the Greek text to make it comply with their anti-Nicene commitments. The Mormons must add the *Book of Mormon*, first published in 1830, to ground their false doctrines. And Islam has the *Quran*, which nonetheless appeals to the "People of the Book" and the previous revelation of the Bible to claim authority. Since the god of Arianism (a bare monad) cannot be known or declared, even by Christ as a mere creature, it is not possible for him to reveal himself clearly or with finality in any person or text. As such, any number of creatures might bring *further* mystical insight into this indeterminate and unknowable God. True revelation is thus destroyed by all cults.

Finally, a *fourth* lesson for our time is the implicit resistance of Nicaea to statism and the claim that man can stand in for God. The concern of Arius was to return to a pagan emphasis on *unity* and the Greek conception of the divine as a bare oneness. This facilitated the idea of the unity of the empire and the special place of the emperor. The Council of Nicaea, by contrast, affirmed one God in three persons and therefore their equal ultimacy as both one and many. This meant that the man Jesus Christ was also "very God," and so total divine authority belonged to him! No other man could claim to be the living God, only the Lord Jesus Christ. It is no surprise, then, that pagan statism preferred Arianism. The emperors invariably favoured the Arians, and Arius himself, with influential friends, quickly convinced Constantine to reinstate him after the Council.

Because Arianism was humanistic, it was also statist. Rushdoony's conclusion is telling:

> It was a popular faith with rulers, in that it made possible the continuation of the pagan exaltation of the state as the divine-human order and politics as the way of salvation. The emperor, Constantine the Great, with his essentially Roman concern for religion, turned soon to Arianism for support.... For the empire, the door was open to Jesus as the great *creature* of God, but also open to many other divine creatures, all serving to unify the Roman Empire as the divine-human order. The Arian bishops were thus inescapably statist in their orientation and

faith. For them, the empire was God's true order, and the emperor God's present manifestation and power on earth.[29]

In the West, as we have turned again to humanism and statism, we have succumbed once more to the temptation to 'be as god' (Gen. 3:5). The state as man enlarged once again plays God in an effort to 'stand in' for Christ as the source of truth, law and meaning. The unity, good, and salvation of society is sought in the *political life* of the state. Jesus is acceptable as a good man, a great teacher, and quite possibly the greatest of all God's creatures, pointing the way to the truly moral life, but he is not Lord, God and King. As a result of our apostasy, just as Rome collapsed, we are seeing the hopeless decay of our society. Far from unity under the humanistic state, we have inherited disorder, disunity and decay. Unity in diversity through Christ being denied, the statist order becomes authoritarian, desperate to hold itself together, but in so doing only furthers its demise. As such, the biblical truths of Nicaea must be retained, treasured and reasserted against all Gnosticism and Arianism in our age. What Young says of the implication of Gnosticism is equally true of Arianism:

> Without the elimination of Gnosticism, Christianity would have become a mystical escapism.... There would have been no Christendom, no *Christian* civilization.[30]

The Nicene Creed is thus as relevant as ever. If we are to see a recovery of Christian faith, culture, and civilization, we must return to the Christ of that great Council. For, as Hebden Taylor faithfully pointed out, the Christ of Scripture, of the apostles, and of the church fathers is the risen and ascended Christ, the One who

> has been entrusted by God the Father with the great task of transforming not only individual lives but all cultural, legal, political, scientific, and economic life. As the

---

29. Rushdoony, *Foundation of Social Order*, 14; italics added.
30. Young, *The Making of the Creeds*, 32; italics added.

Lord of history and of time and space, Jesus Christ can be satisfied with nothing less than a Christian organization of human society as a whole.[31]

We must again think Christianly about Christ for all areas of life.

---

31. E.L.H. Taylor, *The Christian Philosophy of Law, Politics & the State* (Nutley, NJ: The Craig Press, 1969), 24.

CHAPTER 3

# *Think Christianly About Church and Kingdom*

*After He had suffered, He also presented Himself alive to them by many convincing proofs, appearing to them during 40 days and speaking about the kingdom of God.*
— *Acts 1:3 (HCSB)*

## The Mission

**THE MISSION OF GOD'S PEOPLE** is ultimately the faithful worship of the triune God in every aspect and sphere of life—as individuals and as families, neighbourhoods, communities, cities, nations, and cultures. Human beings are made "to glorify God and to enjoy Him forever."[1] The task of God's people is thus intimately tied to the purpose for which we were created. The mandate of the body of Christ does not

---

1. *Westminster Shorter Catechism*, Q&A 1.

then restrictively refer to the practice of churches sending missionaries to other parts of the world (one legitimate aspect of the mission) but to the comprehensive calling and purpose of God's people to build His kingdom on the earth. This is clearly a broader and more foundational application of the traditional term mission, one that includes global missionary work, but which focuses on understanding the way that Christians, as God's vice-gerents, live out the fullness of the gospel in every area of life as our act of worship (cf. Rom. 12:1–2).[2] This finds expression in every dimension, sphere and department of life and the way we think about that mission says something important about our understanding both of the nature of worship and of God.

The decline of a robust, comprehensive, vital, and applied Christianity in the West is clearly evidenced in our society's preponderance of ungodly laws, apostate educational practices, secular-humanistic political outlook and overtly neo-pagan arts and entertainment, to name just a few areas. As I hope to show in this chapter, Christians have allowed, and sometimes even been instrumental in furthering, this decline. An impoverished understanding of our calling has increasingly led us to either abandon these key areas of life and culture in the name of *piety*, or to uncritically adopt and synthesize them with our faith in the name of *relevance* or even wisdom. In either case, we have tacitly accepted an unbelieving view of the world as normative, and are in urgent need of fundamental redirection and reformation.

Following a squandered lead and brutal defeat in the 1960 NFL Championship Game, Green Bay Packers' head coach Vince Lombardi implemented a training regimen focused on first principles. "Gentlemen," he told the three dozen professional athletes gathered around him, "this is a football."[3] If Western Christians would have any hope of again impacting and transforming our society with the truth, freedom and beauty of the gospel

---

2. I say "vice-gerent" instead of the more common expression "vice-regent." Regency carries the sense of ruling in the place of another, whereas a gerent is one who rules alongside of, and subordinate to, a sovereign power.
3. David Maraniss, *When Pride Still Mattered: A Life of Vince Lombardi* (New York: Simon & Schuster, 1999), 274.

of Jesus Christ, we need to recollect where we are and what we are here for; we are on a cosmos-sized field of conflict, not for a game, but a battle between the kingdom of light and the kingdom of darkness. As such we must be prepared, by God's grace, to get to the root of what our mission is, and if necessary, radically reorient our lives and ministries accordingly. This is not a cause for despondency, but for hope. Because of the power of the gospel and omnipotent working of the Holy Spirit, there is every reason for confidence that God will win our nations back to Himself. But again, means matter, and in God's eternal wisdom He has called and commissioned us, His people, as ambassadors of the kingdom, to make disciples of the nations, teaching them to obey all that He has commanded (Matt. 28:18–20). This is our mission, this is true worship, and we must urgently recover the full extent of its power, scope and glory.

## Churchianity or Christianity

Despite undeniable decline, the impact of the Christian faith upon the cultural development of the West is inescapably visible all around us. From the church buildings on every Toronto city block, to the spires at the centre of every English village, the geography of town and country is testament to a once-vital faith. Indeed Christianity's formative religious power is not just around us to observe in buildings and monuments; it continues to actually inhabit the *people* of the Western world, even when they are unaware of it, embedded in their language, customs, and common assumptions. From some of the greatest works of art, literature, music, and architecture that the West ever produced, and which can still thrill the heart, to the names of our hospitals and schools—in fact, embedded in the mottos of some of the most prestigious universities—the cultural vestiges of Christianity are ubiquitous.

And yet it is no longer controversial to assert that the Christian church has, for the most part, ceased to be a truly moving force in the affairs of Western civilization. As the Christian philosopher Calvin Seerveld has put it:

> A foreign dynamic and the neo-pagan spirit of the Renaissance is shaping the culture of the world at the moment....
>
> [B]ut because God and the church are dead to the world there has inevitably come an all-encompassing, frustrating loss of order, certainty and security in the world, and that is disturbing even to those who suppress the truth in unrighteousness.[4]

In recent decades, with this clear abandonment of a Christian vision for culture happening at a rapid pace all around us, and the insecurity it has produced, some Christians have been waking up to the fact that there is a pressing and vital question to be asked: What is the nature of the relationship of the gospel of Jesus Christ to the society in which we live? To state the question in a slightly different way: What is the relationship of God's Word-revelation to the Christian's life in the world? It is a sign of hope for the church that there are those who have begun to consider carefully again the character of the relationship between the gospel and culture—perhaps with a degree of urgency not seen in many years. It is a prescient issue, because the conclusions Christians reach will determine the *essential character* of the mission of God's people in our day.

I say this *renewed* interest is a sign of hope because, generally speaking, and admitting of notable exceptions, this subject is one that Western evangelicals have *not* pursued with focused seriousness for several generations. As a result of this revived concern, a fresh line of thought is opening up, calling forth an essentially new specialization within theology—*cultural* theology.[5] My colleague Andrew Sandlin ably explains the expanding opportunity:

> An emerging specialty in theology is cultural theology. It is defined as the study of what God's full revelation teaches about culture and applying that teaching to

---

4. Calvin G. Seerveld, *A Christian Critique of Art and Literature* (Toronto: Association for the Advancement of Christian Scholarship, 1968), 3.
5. Although some would say these issues come under the theological rubric of missiology, contemporary missiology has not given sufficient attention to the specific application of Scripture to contemporary cultural and civilizational challenges.

pressing cultural issues. Because the issues of our time have become specialized, the study of revelation must include a special(ized) concern for culture. Of course, culture has been around as long as man has, and therefore cultural theology is not a specialty whose need has only recently evolved. However, dramatic developments of culture in modern times (in, for example, ideology, technology, jurisprudence, medicine, economics, and the arts) press serious Christians for a coherent grasp of godly truth to address and govern them. For instance, what does God's revelation have to say to the political views known as socialism, liberalism, conservatism, or libertarianism? Or ideologies like Marxism, feminism, Islamism, transgenderism, and white privilege? What about new technologies like stem-cell research, genetic manipulation, cloning, transhumanism, and surrogate motherhood? Consider theories of law: originalism, progressivism, sociological law, utilitarian law, and natural law. These developments, contemporary or traditional, and many others require a distinctly Christian evaluation.[6]

This need for Christians to turn to God's Word-revelation for clear guidance in such complex matters belonging to the world of everyday cultural experience simply expresses another aspect of the constant necessity for believers to be both *in*formed—that is, inwardly guided from the center of their being—and *re*formed, or reshaped, by God's Word when our attitudes and thinking in any area of life are found contrary to that Word.

## The three interrelated senses of the "Word of God"

To speak in this way about the Word-revelation of God is to confess that in every area of our lives, we are *subject* to that Word. That confession addresses three primary realities. *First*, we are subject to the *creation Word* of God which called all things into being and holds all things together (Col.

---

6. P. Andrew Sandlin, "Introducing Cultural Theology," *DocSandlin*, last modified July 12, 2017, https://docsandlin.com/2017/07/12/introducing-cultural-theology/.

1:17). We daily encounter the power and glory of God's Word for creation. Creation is a concretization or instantiation of the powerful Word of God. In it we discern laws and norms that God has established for all creation from the very beginning. The mediator of that creation Word is the eternal Son (John 1:1–5). *Second,* Jesus Christ is the *incarnate Word* of God. As the second person of the godhead, He is the historical manifestation of the Word through whom all things were made. And *third,* the Bible holds a central place in the Christian life because it is the *inscripturated Word* of God that tells us of the person of Christ, His creative and redemptive work in history, *republishing* the norms of the creation Word so as to make crystal clear in a fallen world what God requires of us.

All three of these manifestations of the *Word of God* are involved in each other, presuppose one another, and cannot be artificially divided or separated from one another as we address the relationship of God's Word to culture; in fact they cannot be properly understood except as a *unity* within a coherence of meaning established for creation by God. For example, we see in all forms of false teaching that a Christ separated from His creative work and the authority of the Scriptures produces an imaginary Jesus in the likeness of sinful man's desires. Equally, the Bible abstracted from the concrete world of creation and history, or from the living and resurrected Lord, is reduced to just another piece of human literature. And in the same way, a cosmic order separated from the eternal Son of God and His inscripturated Word is reduced by philosophers and scientists to a mass of sensory data (or "brute facts") and formal abstract ideas impervious to true interpretation without unity or coherence of meaning. To properly understand God's *world* we need both the Word *incarnate* and *inscripturated,* otherwise the criterion for true insight into the meaning of all things is lost. The unity of God's Word to us in creational and redemptive revelation speaks volumes about the *undivided character* of our calling in the world in terms of that Word.

# The Need for a scriptural Theology *and* Philosophy of Culture

Because the *Word of God* is of this creative, formative and unitive character, it is that which must constitute the foundation of *all* truly Christian thought for each area of life. This is crucial because many of the questions being raised by *cultural* theologians are different from those of the more familiar disciplines like dogmatic or systematic theology. But I would suggest that the questions dealt with in theology and philosophy cannot be neatly separated from each other into hermetically sealed domains that never touch or overlap. This is because theology will always be carried out in terms of underlying concepts and categories of thought that have a philosophical and religious character. Underlying both disciplines—theology and philosophy—is a fundamental *religious orientation* and faith perspective that for the Christian must be controlled and directed by the Word of God. Moreover, it is a grave mistake to think that it is only the professional theologians who can have genuine access to the truth of the Word and be permitted to apply it to the world.

Philosophy looks at the *totality* of reality, and asks about the true nature, origin, and relationship of all things and events. Scripture declares the fundamental *answer* to that question which must govern Christian thought in philosophy. At the same time, Christians need to grapple with all the particular challenges within culture from a robustly *scriptural* standpoint, and so must examine the biblical material as the authoritative *starting point*. And so in a very real way, the task before God's people is one of developing a faithful cultural *theology,* because we are dealing with our *faith*, the *teaching of Scripture*, and our *confession of Christ* as these relate to the culture around us. Christian theology and philosophy need to work together, in submission to God's inscripturated Word, in this endeavor. So, whether we characterize this task as working out a scriptural cultural *theology* or *philosophy* is less important than articulating clearly for the church in our time the relationship of God's Word and gospel to culture itself. Until we do that there will be confusion in the church about the Christian mission and an ongoing decline of the impact of our faith on society.

## Two Dominant Tendencies Regarding the Mission of God's People

It should come as no surprise that something is amiss amongst modern evangelical churches, whether Reformed, episcopal, charismatic, Pentecostal, Lutheran, Baptist, or any other stripe. They are generally not providing an adequate or biblically consistent response to the challenges of an increasingly anti-Christian culture. On the whole, evangelical leaders seem poorly prepared to equip God's people for the pressing task of applying scriptural truth to all of life in an often hostile cultural context—indeed part of the problem is that not all are agreed whether we *should* apply scriptural truth to all areas of life and thought.

I discern two common tendencies in response to the question of the gospel's relationship to culture, and by extension, to the mission of God's people who declare and live that gospel in the world, and these inclinations are linked by common root problems. These tendencies in the church today can be seen first in those who greatly overrate the place and role of the *institutional church* and its offices—thus neglecting or even rejecting the idea that other spheres, institutions, and forms of cultural life are realms subject to God's Word. Second, there are those who greatly overrate the role of the *state* (or political life in general) and its responsibilities and functions in working out the kingdom purposes of God in history.

In the first case, the visible *institutional church* is essentially identified and conflated with the city and kingdom of God, and so what develops, despite a common insistence that they are "gospel centered," is a radically *church-centered* faith—what I am calling *churchianity*. This group is at best disinterested in Christ's *manifest* Lordship over any other sphere of life or institution, and at worse they are hostile to it. Those in this camp are normally biblically orthodox in soteriology (the doctrine of salvation) whilst pietistic and often retreatist when it comes to culture. In general they want little or no engagement with society, the arts, and civil government from a *distinctly* Christian standpoint—especially in the areas of law, politics and education—and any talk of redeeming or transforming culture is seen as out of bounds.

To the extent that these leaders do engage culturally, their involvement is usually described as being for the purposes of "evangelism" rather than for any broader kingdom purpose or cultural good in its own right. At the very least, such non-ecclesiastical activities are carefully distinguished, such that they do not involve "gospel issues." For these believers "the gospel" essentially refers to a narrow set of affirmations about the cross, the new birth, the justification of individuals, and their escape from hell. The immediate result is the truncation of the Christian mission to the task of getting more people saved and *into the church*, so that they can go to heaven. Such believers tend to reduce the Christian life to personal evangelism, personal piety, personal growth, and personal blessing. The Christian calling to seek first the kingdom of God, His righteousness (Matt. 6:33), and the *reconciliation of all things* to Him, is conspicuously diminished in this paradigm. There are obvious elements of truth in this position regarding the importance of justification, the new birth, and God's final judgment on sin, and this obviously *includes* the salvation of individuals; but is it really a full-orbed and robustly biblical Christianity?

This pietistic, broadly theologically conservative worldview frequently produces immature believers, attending churches where they can remain unchallenged week after week, calling on God for personal blessing or to increase their faith and obedience, but with little or no conception of the scope and grandeur of the gospel or the transforming power of the kingdom of God for all of life. Christians in this context can remain spiritual infants all their lives. The birth of a baby is a wonderful thing, but it would be a tragedy if a baby did not mature over the years into an adult. Such church communities are often marked by frustration and cultural impotence, where congregants are endlessly urged to "be holy" and do evangelism whilst waiting for the *parousia*. Yet the average congregant has little or no idea of how to *relate* his faith in Christ the Lord, and the Scriptures, and the call to holiness (i.e. to sanctify life to God) to his marriage and family, his children's education, his vocation, recreational pursuits, or civic responsibility—in short, to culture. Salvation, he is told, is for his soul and his inner life, whilst the kingdom of God is something that is coming at the end of the world and thus belongs to another age. As a result, the institutional church is progressively viewed as the *only place* where God's rule and Christ's lordship are expressed in the earth, especially in the form of the spiritual disciplines of individual Christians, congregational worship, and liturgy. Furthermore, on this view, to genuinely serve God completely or be "in ministry" means either being a pastor, holding office in the institutional church, or being involved in some activity governed and prescribed by the church. Supposedly, only pastors and missionaries are in "full time Christian service." As such there is a glaring and radical sacred/secular divide running through the whole life of such Christians.

At the other end of the spectrum, in the *second* grouping, we have a growing tendency within professing evangelicalism, especially amongst the young, to greatly *underrate* the importance of the institutional church and its administration of the sacraments, the preaching of God's Word, diaconal care, and church discipline. Here, respect for church's confessions, historic teaching and governing authority is dangerously minimized or set aside in favour of a free-wheeling antinomian approach where the church's institutional role, teaching, and discipline in the Christian life is seen as unnecessary or outmoded—nothing but a patriarchal religion of life- and freedom-sapping formalism.

These professing Christians rightly detect a problem with cultural abandonment and retreatism in the churches in which they often grew up, perceiving that the gospel must involve more than the salvation of "souls" for heaven, being present for worship on Sunday, getting the liturgy right, and attending the Wednesday night Bible study for personal discipleship. They believe that God's kingdom must be broader than the walls of the church, one's personal prayer life and piety, and that it must impact the world for the good in the here and now—in this they are quite right!

At the same time, however, the tendency amongst these believers, in questioning whether a pious and retreatist gospel is big enough, is to shift the locus of hope and focus of life from the *institutional church* to the institution of the *state* and its powerful apparatus: its civil laws and civil rights legislation—that is, to a political enactment of "social justice." Under the guiding influence of humanistic philosophy, social action, or what has been dubbed a "social gospel," starts to replace the centrality of Christ's atoning death, resurrection, and transforming, life-giving power.

As a consequence, the kingdom of God is increasingly identified with persons, movements, and institutions pursuing social and economic "equality," so that a kind of politicization of salvation occurs, with the state functioning as *de-facto* high priest in bringing about a secularized deliverance from oppression. Moralism and social action thus gradually eclipse reconciliation with God in restored relationship, justification by faith in Christ through grace alone, whilst a God-centered inward renewal producing outward transformation is replaced by external political coercion as the route to the kingdom. The institutional church, its teaching, discipline, and sacraments, then become almost peripheral to the so-called "main task" of saving abstract political identity groups like "the poor" and ending abstract social evils like "inequality" for the oppressed and other alleged victims of discrimination or exploitation—including the planet itself.

Stewardship, dominion, and care for the creation, service to people in genuine need, and a heart for those oppressed by injustice are of serious concern in Scripture; however, the underlying philosophy that informs a syncretistic drive for "social justice" is *not* scripturally rooted, resulting in a revised version of the Christian lexicon, where the same words are imbued with very different meanings. Thus these Christians regularly drift in a theologically liberal direction—as witness the now mainstreamed Emergent Church movement—the label no longer being used because it is no longer needed. In extreme cases the gospel of Christ becomes directly identified with egalitarian and identitarian progressive political philosophy where God's law and Christ's Lordship in terms of Scripture play little or no part. Instead of a familial, ecclesiastical and moral commitment to voluntary charity and social responsibility, we see political controls, punitive laws of confiscation, as well as judicial activism toward social and sexual liberation put forward as the answer for realizing "the kingdom of God." In fact for some, the gospel becomes practically indistinguishable from the neo-Marxist, utopian vision of "humanization" for the biosphere by politics.

Both of these bifurcating tendencies in modern evangelicalism—one identifying God's kingdom with the institutional church, the other identifying

God's kingdom with the political life and social planning of the state—share common root problems. The *first* is a failure to rightly identify the *foundation* of the Christian hope, which is neither the institutional church itself nor the state and its activity, but the salvation and lordship of Jesus Christ *Himself* over the *totality of life* as the one mediator between man and God. Both the church and the state are institutions with offices placed under God, which limit their role, power, and function. The very concept of an office in human culture presupposes service to a broader purpose and higher authority.

The *second* problem is a mischaracterization of the nature of the church and the state, and thereby of the church's mission. The institutional church cannot be directly identified and conflated with the kingdom of God, and therefore the Christian's calling extends well beyond the ministry of the institutional church. To limit the kingdom of God to the church is to surrender culture to the enemies of God. As the Christian thinker S. U. Zuidema put it, 'He who ecclesiasticizes God's covenant makes the kingdom of God, insofar as he is able, sectarian because he restricts it to a section of life.'[7] At the same time, however, the church is an important *part* of the kingdom. It cannot be made peripheral to the kingdom by reducing it to a servant or chaplain of the humanistic state, doing its bidding, where scientific socio-political planning and engineering is confused with the kingdom of God. Instead the church must witness scripturally and prophetically to political power. When it becomes a handmaiden of the state and an advocate of liberal progressivism (social justice) rather than biblical righteousness, it has forsaken its true character. Likewise, the state overreaches and violates its delimited role and office when, in parts-to-whole fashion it seeks to absorb other spheres of life as departments of state, subject to state planning, control and manipulation.

A *third* problem, which has been with the church from the time Greek philosophy impacted its theological development in the early centuries, is an implicit and destructive *dualism* that slices up reality into matter and spirit, nature and grace, secular and sacred, natural and supernatural, time and

---

7. S. U. Zuidema, *Communication and Confrontation: A Philosophical Appraisal and Critique of Modern Society and Contemporary Thought* (Toronto: Wedge Publishing Foundation, 1972), 43.

eternity, higher and lower, with one area perceived as lesser or evil and the other as higher and good. This tendency has resulted in a radical separation of creation and redemption (where redemption is essentially for the higher story of existence), spiritual life and historical-cultural development and mutually reinforcing pattern of *subservience* to non-Christian culture (nature/secular), on the one hand, and the *abandonment* of Christian culture-building (grace/sacred) on the other. Both tendencies emphasize a part of this artificial duality.

Surely to truly grasp who Christ is, as the root of all truth and meaning, is to grasp the universal lordship of Christ and His marvelous call to His people to participate as co-workers with Him in the restoration of all things to God—since we are now in Christ and have been given a ministry of reconciliation (2 Cor. 5:19–20). As Seerveld has put it:

> *[T]he totality of creation's meaning lies singly in Jesus Christ and His body.* And this idea, that the meaning of the individual and universe, lies beyond both in the Son of God, that everything is meaning-less, aim-less, vain unless it be set in Jesus Christ, that the crown of creation, humanity, because justly commanded by God to love the LORD with all our heart, all that is in us, that humanity is meaning-full only if at work in the covenantal community of believers serving the realization of God's plan, re-creation, reconciliation of all to God through Christ: it is this idea... [which shows] that the struggle of history is between a newborn *civitas Dei* and the age-old dragons, *civitates mundi*.[8]

Given the clear biblical teaching concerning the person of Christ as the one from whom, through whom and to whom all things exist (Rom. 11:36), and knowing that He is reconciling *everything* to God the Father (Col. 1:16–20), why is it that Christians seem to struggle to reach agreement about the mission of God's people?

The message of the gospel is clearly centered in the declaration that this Jesus Christ is Lord and King over all the earth, over all cultures, peoples and

---

8. Seerveld, *A Christian Critique of Art and Literature*, 15.

lands (cf. Matt. 28:18–20), and that He is calling all people to repentance and to joyful obedience, to the coming kingdom of God.

## An Example of Churchianity

In this chapter my primary concern is to address not the advocates of social justice (which I have considered in detail elsewhere[9]), but the pietistic cultural retreatism amongst those who are largely theologically orthodox and who are advocates of a kind of *churchianity*—which I want to contrast with scriptural *Christianity*.[10] For the sake of clarity it will help us to begin the discussion of *churchianity* with a typical and representative example of how this problem manifests itself when the calling of Christians and the church in the world is discussed. In an interview entitled "On the Mission of the Church," the popular American pastor, Mark Dever, attempts to articulate the essence of the Christian's gospel-centered calling in the face of the challenges in today's culture.[11] The program is very instructive as an illustration of what I have called *churchianity*.

In a series of pithy statements, the sincerely evangelical Dever declares that the sum total of the Christian's calling is to "make disciples" and "build churches." The term "church" is not clearly defined in the discussion, nor is the actual nature and scope of disciple-making. Dever is clear, however, that the central calling of the Christian is *evangelism*, by which he means telling people about Jesus so that they can be forgiven, saved from hell, and join the church. No distinction is made between the life and work of the institutional church and the biblical conception of the kingdom of God. According to Dever, "Christianity goes forward by pastors raising up other pastors and

---

9. See the lecture "Recovering the Foundations of Social Justice," at https://www.ezrainstitute.com/recovering-the-foundations-of-social-justice/.
10. In *The Mission of God: A Manifesto of Hope for Society*, I deal extensively and critically with the social justice movement within modern evangelicalism.
11. Jonathan Leeman and Mark Dever, "On the Mission of the Church," *Pastors' Talk*, Episode 25 (podcast audio, 9Marks, October 31, 2017), MP3 audio, accessed June 2025.

sending them out." Well and good for pastors, but where does this vision of Christian mission leave parents and families, schoolteachers and truck drivers, business leaders and politicians, lawyers and doctors, housewives and farmers, scholars and architects, musicians and artists, cooks and builders, in the biblical calling to advance the gospel, other than with the suggestion that they attend church services, be a "witness," and go to Bible study?

Given Dever's implicit identification of the institutional church with the kingdom of God, Christians, he argues, are certainly allowed to *pray* about "life issues" and for "local schools," etc., but their real work as God's people is evangelism and discipleship. Dever suggests he is all for parents being involved with the lives of their children and supporting marriage, but that does not mean he assumes we can work to impact social problems like suppressing gambling and other vices, or reducing divorce rates. In any case, if the pastor devotes his time to these latter activities, then, he asks, who will preach *the gospel*?

When Dever is specifically asked whether he would ever use the language of "redeeming culture" or "transforming the city," he answers forcefully, "No!," for that would only discourage people, he argues, since Dever sees no indication in the Scriptures that cultural transformation is promised when Christians embody and live out the gospel. This is an incredible assertion for any student of Scripture to make. The following Scriptures warrant a serious consideration in regard to the transforming impact of God's Word in our lives and in cultural life: Genesis 1:26–28; Psalm 2; 8; 110:1–4; Isaiah 9:7; Daniel 2:46–49; 3:26–30; 4:34–36; 6:18–28; Jonah 3:5–10; Habakkuk 2:14; Matthew 28:18–20; Luke 13:18–21; John 12:20–32; 2 Corinthians 5:17–21; Ephesians 1:10, 15–23; Colossians 1:15–20; Hebrews 2:6–13; Revelation 1:4–6. These illustrative texts concerning God's sovereignty, the calling of the covenant people, and Christ's authority, power, and expanding kingdom, clearly lead us to expect (as has been seen in the past) great cultural impact when believers are walking in obedience to God and serving the purposes of Christ's reign which culminates in the consummation of His kingdom (Rom. 8:22–23; Rev. 21:5).

Following his denial that the Bible teaches that cultures will be transformed by the gospel, it is disappointing to hear Dever and Leeman engage in disparaging the venerable Abraham Kuyper and the vision that he articulated of the Lordship of Christ transforming all of life. Dever asks what good these teachings ever did the Netherlands during Kuyper's tenure as Prime Minister. This is an astonishingly short-sighted attitude toward Kuyper's remarkable and influential legacy; Dever appears to believe that because there are lots of Christians being faithful in various places, who do not yet see big changes in public cultural life, therefore cultures aren't changed by the gospel. This belief is a non-sequitur and lacks insight into what is happening at the religious *root* of life when a person's heart is reoriented by the Holy Spirit to serve Christ with all their being. Is the open hostility to a faithful Christian politician (and theologian) like Kuyper the result of Dever's restriction of the gospel to a limited section of life? Zuidema is to the point: "An integral Christian politics, an integral Christian view of the state, and an integral Christian political party which as such play up to neither the ecclesiasticization nor the secularization of life outside of the church—these are a thorn in the flesh for the ecclesiasticized church-man and the politicized politician."[12]

The inescapable reality is that human beings are religious beings and cultural creatures. Everything we do in and with God's creation is a work of culture-making, and therefore the salvation of an individual and their subsequent faithfulness to God in their personal and family life *does* effect an immediate change in culture as they live in the world. The culture of the home is altered when a man surrenders his life to Christ. The culture of a business begins to change when its leader orients his heart towards God's Word. The culture of a school or political party begins to change when the head teacher or party leaders turns to Christ and are directed by the Scriptures. Indeed, everything in which the true believer is involved, as they live out the truth in terms of God's Word, is powerfully impacted. Yet Dever states with satisfaction that he has had political figures come to him at his Washington D.C. church saying they thought they had come to the capital to impact politics as Christians, but they had since realized at Dever's

---

12. Zuidema, *Communication and Confrontation*, 42.

church that they really had been brought to Washington to learn about *being church* and a good disciple. The *church-restricted* or *ecclesiasticized* character of Dever's understanding of the gospel is thus reinforced in the starkest terms. This is logical because

> [t]he ecclesiasticizing of religion necessarily calls into being the profaning of the non-ecclesiastical area.... The ecclesiasticized church calls into being a secularized "world" which cannot rest until it in its turn has subjected to itself this ecclesiasticized church; until it has subjected the ecclesiasticized Bible use to a secularized Bible use which rejects the ecclesiasticized authority of the Bible and *therefore*, in its opinion, fundamentally rejects all authority of the Bible....
>
> The ecclesiasticizing of religion on the other hand always has the tendency to identify the instituted church and its membership with the life in the Kingdom of God, just as the profaning of life outside of the church constantly tends to reduce the authority of God's Word to an authority of and for the church; it tends to banish the immediate relevance of the Christian religion for life outside of the church and persecutes this immediate relevance as separatism, as a violation of national solidarity, as world estrangement and as life enslavement.[13]

Dever certainly affirms Christ's Lordship as a theological *idea*, but materially and practically, for everyday life outside of the church, it fades from view. This is because, as far as Dever is concerned, he can simply cooperate and collaborate with non-believers in all the "ordinary stuff" of life, since he sees no directional distinction in what believers and non-believers are doing in their everyday activities. Thus, for Dever, there is no need for, nor indeed is there any such thing as, Christian media companies, Christian universities, or Christian trade unions, etc., and there is certainly no need for Christian political parties and institutions. Naturally he also argues that it is simply wrong to say that the true way to educate children is *Christian*

---

13. Zuidema, *Communication and Confrontation*, 42.

education. The goal of *Christianizing* anything, according to Dever, is badly misguided—though he never actually clearly explains why.

There is a profound irony in American pastors using their pulpits and religious freedom to attack the Christianization of culture and the application of Scripture to the totality of life, given that the American nation was effectively founded by evangelical Puritans and was radically shaped throughout its history, in all its public institutions, by Christianity—with the words of Moses himself being engraved on Supreme Court buildings. In fact, it was the Christianized nature of American culture, however imperfect, that gave men like Dever their freedom to be pastors and to witness to the gospel without legal hindrance. Moreover, there is a disturbing presumption and arrogance that attends church leaders identifying the institutional church with the kingdom of God. Zuidema's challenge here is profound and searching:

> The sin of the identification of church with the kingdom of God, of church with Covenant, of church with heart religion, whereby for all intents and purposes this church as it were coincides with itself and Christ coincides with the church, is all the more serious since it once and for all blocks the Christian's freedom and the free reign of God's Word over the ecclesiastical offices. Humanly speaking, nothing is so stubborn and so hopeless, so tyrannical and so anarchistic, because nothing is so pious seemingly as this ecclesiasticizing of the Bible and religion.[14]

Despite the privilege of a remarkable Christian heritage in the United States, Dever piously argues that the future will surely be dark, like the days of Noah. Instead of speaking of cultural transformation he says, "I wish you would just share *the gospel* with that person on the bus." In this statement we see the appearance of a radically truncated gospel and clear question-begging regarding the nature of the gospel mission—which is in fact the matter in question. It is certainly true that the calling of the church is centered in the gospel. But what is the nature and character of the gospel of the kingdom,

---

14. Zuidema, *Communication and Confrontation*, 43–44.

and what are its implications for us as God's people? Do they go beyond personal evangelism and adding people to the institutional church?

Dever's conclusion regarding the mission of the church is that we don't redeem and transform anything cultural. Thus, his objective is to spend time and resources to *establish churches* that will do witnessing and discipleship. Again, these are no doubt critical tasks for Christians. But for Dever *this alone* is what advances Christianity. We have in this interview, then, a very good example of what I am claiming to be modern and popular evangelical *churchianity*. Calvin Seerveld's caution is telling:

> Many Christians have been content to *witness to* the world, vigorously preaching Christ crucified but holding back from involvement in the culture because it is so immoral and demoralizing.... Yet it is not the full gospel. It has the ascetic reticence of John the Baptizer who preached repentance from sin and counseled moral rectitude in whatever profession you were in, but stopped there. John the Baptizer's disciples fasted, and Christ did not condemn it; He just commanded His disciples who freely ate and drank to fashion new wineskins.[15]

Seerveld goes on to note that while we may be tempted to settle for such an introverted, pietistic Christianity—and it is an easier answer for the older and wiser believers—it is not the Reformed tradition. Which is to say, such a perspective is not found at the root of the scriptural faith emerging from the most consistent stream of the Reformation. Moreover, the culture around us *cannot be helped* by such distortion of the biblical mandate. None of this is an appeal to politicize the gospel (as though salvation were by politics), because a politicized gospel is as great an evil as an ecclesiasticized faith. However, to divorce religion from politics, or from culture in general, is a sheer fiction and can no more be done than separating religion from the church.

---

15. Seerveld, *Christian Critique of Art and Literature*, 4–5.

## What is the Church?

An important question that arises from all this is, what is the church? And with reference to the question of cultural theology and philosophy, what philosophy is at work in the thinking of those who limit the kingdom of God and direct rule of Christ to the institutional church and its activities—who advocate churchianity?

In the Scriptures the people of God are identified as those who are called out by the Spirit, gathered together as a body and *appointed to a task*. With the dispersion of the Jews, the synagogue became the center for worship and instruction for the covenant people—a pattern that was carried over into the Christian era with the local church. In the Newer Testament the people of God are called the *ekklesia*: a called-out and renewed people likewise appointed to go and bear fruit (John 15:16). Biblically then, the church is clearly a *people* whose lives in their totality are oriented toward the gospel of the kingdom—this life is evidently much more than the buildings, liturgies, and structures of the institutional church.

In late-medieval Roman Catholic theology, or what is often called *scholastic* theology, the institutional church and kingdom of God basically coincide. The church cathedral was called a *basilica* (from the New Testament Greek term for "royal" or "king") and was thought to be the realm of Christ, where the church hierarchy was regarded as the means by which Christ exercised His rule and authority. In this line of thinking, which is still very much with us, no clear distinction is made between the church as *organism* (i.e., the body of Christ) and the church as an *institute*. This results in the ecclesiasticizing of the entire life of the Christian community, clericalism, and the spiritual ideal of "holy orders" and asceticism, which were common phenomena in the medieval world.[16] It was not until the Reformation era that a clear distinction was again made between the church functioning as organism and as institute. Abraham Kuyper crystalizes that distinction:

---

16. In spite of this, the medieval church was more interested in broader cultural activities than Dever is now.

> The conception of the *instituted Church* is much narrower than *the Church*... when taken as the *body of Christ*, for [the latter] includes in itself all the powers and workings that arise from re-creation.... The instituted Church finds her province bounded by her *offices* [italics original], and these offices are limited to the ministry of the Word, the Sacraments, Benevolence and Church government.... All other expressions of the Christian life do not work by the organ of the special offices, but by the organs of the re-created natural life; the Christian family by the believing father and mother, Christian art by the believing artist, and Christian schools by the believing magister.[17]

In fact, the boundaries and limitations placed by God upon the *institutional* church reflect the outward-facing purposes served by the Sabbath church *service*. Because Christ Jesus in His resurrection life and power is the head of a new race and the founder of re-creation (renewal of creation), the day of rest (resurrection Sunday), opens up the new week so that Sabbath teaching and worship is directed toward the kingdom work of the six days ahead. The word "liturgy" literally means "public work." Public worship prepares us for the very public cultural task ahead. The worshipping community on a Sunday is not directed only toward personal piety and getting the faithful to glory. Rather it is the place where God's people are prepared for the liturgy of life in all creation (Rom. 12:1). As such the *institutional* church is established so that the church as *organism* (a living body) can live out its kingdom life in the world.

The church institute is *service to this purpose,* and it is not to be a power center existing to serve, expand, and enrich itself. Consider that in the Older Testament the tithe was paid to the *Levites*, who had a varied social and educational function in the cultural life of the Hebrews (cf. Num. 18:21–26), rather than to the *priests*. This biblical scenario reveals that those responsible for the institutional worship of the people received *a tithe of the tithe*, restricting both the size and power of the priestly office. The institutional church

---

17. Abraham Kuyper, *Principles of Sacred Theology* (Grand Rapids, MI: Eerdmans, 1954), 587–88, italics added.

is not an end in itself and does not exhaust the scriptural understanding of the kingdom.

The church therefore has two clear modes of existence. The church is manifest in temporal reality as both institute and organism. It is a worshiping community—an *institute* with various offices and ministries—and it is an *organism*—a living *body of believers* engaged daily in the non-ecclesiastical areas of life in service to Christ. We can certainly say that the church is a *unique* body, instituted by Christ, of which He is head. The Lord Himself gave it an organizational expression in the apostolic office and the sacraments.

This body of Christ is first the *invisible church*. Then it is also the *visible church*, which is the historical manifestation of the invisible body, seen organically in every area of life. Finally, the *institutional church* is the local organisation and expression of that body of believers in a worshipping community with its functioning offices. The visible church thus embraces more than any particular church denomination; it is found wherever God's people are living faithful Christian lives in each area of life. Moreover, and critically for the purposes of this discussion, the body of Christ is manifest across the full range of societal relationships, of which the local institutional church is but one manifestation.

Although the institutional church is of a special character, the kingdom of God and the visible church are clearly not identical. In fact, Christ and His disciples were found preaching the gospel of the kingdom, and people were entering into it, long before any local churches were established and before there was any institutional expression of it in terms of church government. Nor are the *invisible* church and kingdom of God identical, because the rule and reign of Christ, the ruler of the kings of the earth (Ps. 2; Rev. 1:5), is not limited to those who love and obey Him. That rule cannot be restricted to Christian people in their personal relationships but extends to the entirety of created reality and all that believers do and form within God's world. Kuyper famously said that "there is not a single square inch of the entire universe of which Christ the sovereign Lord of all does not say 'This is mine!'" In view of this, and over against Mark Dever's truncated view of discipleship, Gordon Spykman writes,

It is our obligation to honor this claim [i.e., of Christ's total Lordship and sovereignty] and to press it whenever and wherever possible. This calls for political discipleship, academic discipleship—in short, for all sorts of cultural disciplines. This constitutes a truly staggering agenda.[18]

Such an agenda for discipleship seems startling to modern evangelicals nurtured on churchianity. The notion that the Christians should respond to systematic *unbelief* in culture with systematic and comprehensive *belief* is simply foreign. This is in large measure due to a fundamental doubt in the evangelical mind that a specifically Christian view or approach to anything in culture in general is really necessary, or even possible. After all isn't "common grace" enough? This idea is usually vague enough to mean that the vast majority of things in life, from education to politics and art, can be dealt with on their own, apart from the Christian world-and-life view—that is to say: in a neutral way.

This idea is not only wrongheaded, it is impossible. Men and women, believers or not, cannot think of themselves as disconnected from God's world. By virtue of creation and being made in God's image, human beings are compelled to deal with the real world as God has made it, even in their apostasy; and this means that we may often find ourselves in broad agreement with non-Christians in a variety of areas. Common Grace, or better *Creation Grace*, simply means that even after the Fall, the creational structures in which we continue to live and find meaning remain valid in order to maintain creaturely existence. Laws which govern motion, growth, thought, sexual distinctions, and so forth persist despite sin. The entrance of sin, however, has misdirected people's lives—their sexual acts, thought acts, acts of motion, and so forth. So, the Christian response to the radical *misdirection* of the Fall must be a comprehensive *redirecting* Christianity—the permeation of Christ's saving grace, into every area of life. Just because unbelievers do not all suppress the truth to the same degree and, while acting in orderly ways graciously preserved within the creation ordinances, often

---

18. Spykman, *Reformational Theology*, 474.

stumble upon many wonderful secrets of the creation, this does not mean that Christians are excused from systematically manifesting the redeeming and reconciling grace of Christ in each area of life. Sadly, the conserving gift of so-called Common Grace is all too often made into a complete *dis*-grace by Christians who refuse to obey the gospel of God by bringing all of life into subjection to the Word of God. Once again, Seerveld has said it well:

> [God's conserving work] does not permit the newborn Christian to be satisfied with a common grace culture christianized. For then the Christian would be denying that the good news has the power to set radically right what sin has misdirected and unbelievers are prostituting, however honorably. The Christian would then be selling the peculiar birthright we share as children of Christ, the right to be the proper lords of creation's development, if the Gospel was not allowed to shed its full light for time-bound re-creation as well as for eternal salvation.... It is a regrettable mistake to think that because our gracious God's cosmonomic theatre allows all humanity to act coherently that this absolves the [C]hristian community from our special calling to praise God ourselves, wholly, unreservedly, in the bonds-bursting power of the Holy Spirit.[19]

What Seerveld is rightly resisting here is the synthesizing motive of churchianity which wants to use robbery from anti-Christian culture as a synthetic solution to the Christian life—to regard the institutional church as the only distinctly Christian sphere of life, and simply adopt the world's way of doing politics, medicine, law, art, education, and much else besides, in the name of common grace, with the saving grace of Christ perhaps sprinkled here and there as a sort of condiment. This is indeed a dis-grace. But it appears acceptable when we do not recognise that all the life-dimensions in which we function as human beings must be permeated with the Christian life principle by the power of the Holy Spirit and in terms of God's Word. The body of Christ, the universal and organic covenant people of God, can reject this requirement to make all things holy to the Lord only if we view the

---

19. Seerveld, *A Christian Critique*, 18–19.

earth as completely destitute after the Fall and simply a stage for the institutional church to battle through its "spiritual" life as pilgrims on the way to somewhere else. But this is surely not the biblical picture. As Kuyper wrote:

> The world after the fall is no lost planet, only destined now to afford the Church a place in which to continue her combats; and humanity is no aimless mass of people which only serves the purpose of giving birth to the elect. On the contrary, the world now, as well as in the beginning, is the theater for the mighty works of God and humanity remains a creation of His hand, which, apart from salvation, completes under this present dispensation, here on earth, a mighty process, and in its historical development is to glorify the name of Almighty God.[20]

If this is the scriptural position regarding God's sovereignty over all humanity and all history, and I believe it is, what is the fountainhead of the idea that the institutional church and its work are essentially identical with the kingdom of God, reducing the Christian calling to church attendance and to the sole task of "witnessing," and providing discipleship for the believer's "personal spiritual life"? What led to the view that planting more churches essentially exhausts the mandate God has given to His people? In short, what is the religious root of churchianity?

## The Philosophical Foundations of Churchianity

We saw that according to scholastic theology, the institutional church coincides completely with the kingdom of God, giving rise to the ecclesiasticizing of all of life, a view and practice ubiquitous in the medieval Roman Catholic view of reality. However, as we will see, the churchianity that persists amongst many evangelicals in our age posits an even more radical ecclesiasticizing of life, where the link between creation and redemption, which scholastic thought struggled to maintain, has been all but severed.

---

20. Abraham Kuyper, *Lectures on Calvinism* (Grand Rapids, MI: Eerdmans, 1931), 162.

In both cases, beneath this dualistic perspective actually lies a *non-Christian* philosophy of life. The scholastic tradition essentially sought to Christianize the pagan Greek view of nature (composed of form and matter), in order to forge, via this synthesis, a meaningful connection between the "credible" philosophical views of the ancient world (especially in the thought forms of Aristotle) and the gospel.

According to the ancient Greek view, nature was composed of two ultimate and uncreated elements, form—spirit or idea—and matter. Nature itself was the product of impersonal divine reason that gave form to matter; these two poles stood over against each other. In this dualism, matter was the lower realm and spirit, idea, or form was the higher, superior realm. Consequently, for many Greek thinkers, the body was a prison for the soul, from which one ought to seek escape. Early Gnostics, and Marcionite heretics in the early church, expressed this dualism both by denigrating the body and creation—some claiming that the material world was created by a lesser god or demiurge—and by driving a wedge between the Older and Newer Testaments, between law and gospel, between creation and redemption. The former belonged to the lower realm of matter, and the latter belonged to the higher realm of idea and spirit.

Eventually, in this accommodation to pagan thought, a theological trend developed that we might call a psycho-creationist anthropology. This paradigm asserts that with each new life, God permits the implanting of an indestructible soul substance into a body from without—the body being prepared by an organic life principle. So instead of maintaining the biblical unity of the human person, what emerges is the uncomfortable assemblage of two independent substances—body and soul. The flesh (non-divine earthly matter of the body) is viewed as a shell for the noblest "part" of man, which is the immortal soul which escapes the corruptible material flesh at death. The rational soul is regarded as a spiritual complex of particular functions (i.e., thinking, feeling, willing, etc.), the seat of true light, natural reason, and spirituality, whilst the body is implicitly or explicitly denigrated in terms of lower desires and carnal appetites. Predictably, sin's root is then supposedly located in these "lower" fleshly desires. This teaching obviously entails the problematic notion that God creates and inserts sinful souls into each new body—hence the need to shift the seat and root of sin to the body's "lower" capacities. This unequal yoking of biblical creation with paganism helps account for the rise of the medieval ascetic ideal—a vision of monastic life as manifesting the fullest expression of devoted service to God.

When certain Christian philosophers like Thomas Aquinas tried to harmonize Christianity with Greek thought, on the basis of an unfallen reason, they began with the Greek view of nature as *form and matter*. With the intellectual soul understood as absolute form, man's knowledge and understanding of reality in terms of independent reason was fine, as far as it went, i.e., for all the ordinary stuff of life—for philosophy and education, science and art, politics and government. However, for "spiritual life" and the way of salvation, that is, for the realm of faith, man needed the addition of grace—a *super*natural addition. In this way the scholastic tradition sought to *maintain a bridge* between the gospel of redemption in Christ, and a philosophical view of nature that had been inherited from Greek philosophy.

This sacred/secular dualism provided the institutional church with the roles of the mediator of salvation in the *sacred* realm (the church or kingdom of God) and the "spiritual director" of society when playing the role of chaplain to a *secular* government which went about its common tasks in terms of the dictates of reason. At times, nature and grace, or emperor and pope, battled it out for supremacy in terms of who anointed whom.

The Protestant Reformation did much to restore biblical worship within the church, and to vindicate the claims of Christ and Scripture over all of life; however, this work was not fully accomplished in the Reformation era, and even the most august names of that age were not wholly free of this Thomistic dualism – a subject we will return to in later chapters. And although we rightly associate the Reformation with Martin Luther, the Lutheran and Calvinistic views of the relationship of the gospel with culture, of creation and redemption, and consequently of the mission of God's people, developed in very different directions. Luther continued Ockham's sharp distinction between *natural* life and *super*natural Christian life. It is no surprise, then, that we do not find in Luther an intrinsic connection between the Christian faith and one's earthly life.

Accordingly, redemption was seen as the *death* of nature rather than its renewal and rebirth. It is certainly the case that Luther rejected monasticism, but he is radically inconsistent. Following the scholastic thinkers and despite famously calling reason a whore, for Luther, reason remained the guide for the realm of *nature* and there was no clear point of contact between this reason and the revelation of God's Word. In the vein of Ockham, he regarded secular government, social order and justice as belonging to the domain of reason, not revelation. Although Luther was not thoroughly consistent, and clearly saw a place for God's commandments in society because of the context of Christendom he inhabited, nonetheless, a radical sacred-secular dualism remained in Luther's thought, where ecclesiastical life was identified with the kingdom of God. What was proper to the distinctly Christian life was the realm of grace, expressed in Word and sacrament in the church, but justice, beauty, and the like belonged to the realm of the sinful nature.

Like many Christians before him, Luther did not recognize that the totality of a person's life and thinking *in every area* arises from a religious root. The result was that in Lutheran thought, a divide ran through the centre of reality. Worldly life belonged to the realm of nature and law, and lived in a constant and inner tension with the gospel of love that belonged to a higher *super*natural realm. This tension remains entrenched in the thinking of many modern evangelicals who oppose law to grace or gospel, and who regard most of secular life as religiously neutral and governed by principles other than the Word of God. There is no intrinsic point of contact for most evangelicals today between their vocation or cultural life and the Word of God—these belong to virtually sealed domains. Moreover, creation itself is consistently viewed as something to be finally escaped; at the very least, it is a devalued realm destined to be destroyed. This produces an insoluble tension in the lives of modern evangelicals, between the sacred call to holiness given by the church, and their life everywhere else. Creation and redemption are essentially separated from each other, with the worship of the Christian church increasingly resembling a mystery cult disconnected from the real world.

Many modern theologians, notably Karl Barth, went on to develop a perspective that openly opposed the scriptural idea that there is no neutrality (cf. Romans 1; Acts 17), that in fact a *religious antithesis* is found in all aspects of life in the world.[21] As a result, Barth and others who shared his neo-orthodox convictions rejected the notion of Christian politics, Christian scholarship, and Christian education, which resulted in ecclesiasticizing and privatizing the Christian life. Barth pressed the logic of Greek dualism and argued that the Word of God is *wholly other,* with no point of contact between nature/creation and grace. Life in the world is then viewed exclusively in terms of the Fall. As the doctrine of creation recedes from view, knowledge of the ordinances of creation is lost, and creation and redemption are separated in a way that divides God's will as creator and God's will as redeemer. Consequently, in place of God's law is established a vague and seemingly abstract command to love.

All this has led to modern evangelicalism's denial that the totality of God's revelation is relevant to *every area of life,* and consequently that there is any such thing as a Christian view of education, law, art, politics, economics, scholarship, etc. Most of today's Protestants and evangelicals have imprisoned the body of Christ, the organic church, and indeed kingdom of God, within the walls of the institutional church—its offices and ministries. As a result, the gospel itself is redacted to one small element of its full and glorious scope. This intellectual lineage reveals that well-intentioned pastors and leaders who have strongly influenced contemporary evangelicalism, like Mark Dever, are still in the grip of Greek thought as it has come down to them via scholasticism, Lutheranism, pietism, and neo-orthodoxy.

## Retreatism, Pietism, and Churchianity

Piety is an important quality of the Christian life. It denotes reverence toward God and sincere devotion. But pie*tism* is the tendency to restrict the meaning of the Christian life to personal devotional disciplines and

---

21. Cornelius Van Til, *The New Modernism: An Appraisal of the Theology of Barth and Brunner* (Philadelphia: Presbyterian & Reformed, 1946), 83.

inward spiritual growth. Pietism, which has so afflicted all stripes of modern evangelicalism, was a movement that began in German Lutheranism, with theological foundations in medieval thought, that quickly spread to the English-speaking world. The pietists tended to see biblical orthodoxy as dead religion, and boasted a more spiritual faith focused on the new birth and various devotional exercises. Emphasis was laid on emotion and feeling, because doctrine was considered dry and intellectual. There are significant evangelical church movements today that won't sing hymns for this very same reason—they are allegedly too intellectual and get in the way of emotional engagement with God.

All dualism since Ockham, especially the dualism expressed in pietism, has had the cultural effect of weakening the church and strengthening the state. With its retreat inward, pietism was completely unable to combat the forces of the Enlightenment, just as Lutheranism was found powerless against the rise of the Third Reich. The Enlightenment perspective saw the state, not the church, as the truly universal institution; the church was the area of *private* faith, whereas the state was the realm of *reason*. The state would therefore assert itself as the new arbiter of order. Given pietism's primary concern with "spiritual" life, it did not contest this claim. The same is true of modern evangelical pietism. It has allowed the state to move into and control most areas of life, and most of that ground has been surrendered without a fight. While on the one hand emphasizing the church and spiritual life, pietism actually allows the church to become an essentially peripheral institution, irrelevant to life in the world.

Pietism also typically derides pleasure in life and the world, viewing this present world as comparatively unimportant. Pietists often refused to enjoy good food and drink, marital sex, beauty, and indeed life's many joys, with clear parallels to medieval asceticism. Out of such a distorted view of reality, pacifistic ideals also emerged, according to which being killed by thugs assaulting you in the street or being slain by invading military forces is preferable to killing one of the attackers, since the pietist knows he is going to heaven, but the hoodlum may not know Christ and would therefore go to hell. This kind of sentimentality is commonplace in today's evangelical world, where God's law is neither known, nor regarded as important. The salvation of individuals from hell is seen as the preeminent concern for the pietist, not the glory, justice, and kingdom rule of God. From its inception, pietism was implicitly antinomian, seeing no role or function for God's law-Word. And yet, modern pietistic evangelicalism is divided into numerous groups, denominations, and communions that are all too ready to condemn one another for not being holy or spiritual enough, too charismatic or too Reformed and doctrinal, rather than focusing on bringing every area of life and thought into captivity to Christ.

An immediate offspring of this dualism and pietism is retreatism. Modern churchianity seems to overlook many of the clear demands of Scripture. In Matthew 10:8 we are told, "The kingdom of heaven is at hand. Heal the sick, cleanse the lepers, raise the dead, cast out demons. Freely you have received, freely give." In 1 Corinthians 6 believers are told to establish courts of arbitration to judge God's people in terms of God's Word. In the book of Acts, we also see believers caring for the poor, widows, and orphans. The early church quickly launched hospitals, care homes for abandoned children, schools, homes for the elderly without families, and much else besides. It was not a church in retreat from the world, but an organic body determined to live out the life of the kingdom, teaching and discipling all the nations in terms of everything Christ commanded. Long before the church was permitted to own buildings for worship, it had established a variety of institutions to meet human needs. R. J. Rushdoony has incisively commented:

> The personal impulse, and theologically grounded faith, that we have an obligation under God to minister to human needs, to bring *every* area of life under Christ's dominion and God's law, and the duty to make God's earth His Kingdom, all this has been abandoned as the church has retreated into the position of a mystery religion or cult. All the world is surrendered to evil, and only a little corner, the church and the people in it, represent Christ's domain. How will Christ the King treat a church that hands His world over to His enemies...?

It is amazing how many people there are who actually believe they are holier and purer because they have surrendered one area after another to Christ's enemies.[22]

Because the *institutional* church is rightly limited in its role and jurisdiction in the Christian life and in human society, whenever and wherever an unscriptural dualism reigns, where artificial separations of nature and grace, law and gospel, creation and redemption are propounded, God and his Word become theoretically imprisoned in the church, and Christ's reign is faithlessly limited to one sphere of life.

## The Recovery of Christianity

If the institutional church is identified simplistically with the body of Christ and with the kingdom of God, then clearly the rule of Christ is possible only within that single institution and sphere. Moreover, the gospel itself becomes entirely church-oriented—saving people for heaven and securing them safely within the worshipping community until Christ returns.

But Christianity, the true gospel of the kingdom, cannot be locked up within a single institution any more than it can be corralled into the enclosure of individual salvation from the consequences of sin. For salvation, which implies total wholeness and restoration, is also *deliverance* from the power and corruption of sin. The scope of salvation is as broad as the scope of the Fall. Clearly then, the faith of the gospel is centered in and focused upon Christ Himself, not in an institution. This is why we are called *Christians* and our faith *Christianity*, not churchianity. As Willem J. Ouweneel has pointed out in his criticism of Darryl Hart:

> As long as we do not see the difference between the calling of the [institutional] church and the calling of individual Christians, we will not make any progress in

---

22. Rousas J. Rushdoony, *An Informed Faith: The Practice of Christian Scholarship* (Vallecito, CA: Ross House Books, 1992), 385.

these things. For instance Hart tells us that the Bible "is the guide for church life," and not "for political life." This is a fundamental mistake. The Bible is the guide for *Christian life*, which is a far wider notion than just church life. Would Hart deny that the Bible is a guide for *Christian* husbands and *Christian* wives, and for *Christian* parents and *Christian* children? And why not for *Christian* employers and *Christian* employees (cf. Eph. 5:25–6:9)? And why not for *Christian* politicians, or *Christian* businesspersons? ...[T]he Bible is our starting point for developing a *Christian worldview* in which we investigate the creation ordinances for marriages, families, schools, companies, and so on.... [F]or non-church life, we do not rely only on reason and prudence, as he (following good scholastic traditions) asserts..., but on Scripture, as well as a Christian worldview rooted in Scripture.... The church is *not* the "special community that renders *worship* to God" [contra David VanDrunen]. *Christians* render worship to God at all times, in all circumstances.[23]

Within a large segment of the evangelical community today, *churchianity* has replaced Christianity. It is only in Christianity that believers are living out, applying, and asserting the Lordship and salvation-victory of Christ within every area of life, rooted in the Scriptures.

The gospel is the wisdom and power of God, according to the Bible, for Christ is the wisdom, the glory, and the power of God made manifest. His kingdom and rule are unlimited and extend over all the cosmos—over things visible and invisible, in this age and the one to come (see Col. 1; Eph. 1). Such wisdom in Christ and the gospel cannot be restricted to the institutional church any more than the meaning of the reconciliation of all things to God can be limited to the souls of individual believers. God's wisdom is for all people and nations, and it is being manifest to all for the good of all. Surely the manifestation of this wisdom and grace must be the deepest desire of every Christian who loves the Lord with all his being. Seerveld asks the pertinent question:

---

23. Willem J. Ouweneel, *The World Is Christ's: A Critique of Two Kingdoms Theology* (Jordan Station, ON: Paideia Press, 2017), 260, 262.

> [H]ow can you live openly in this world, God's cosmonomic theatre of wonder, while the graciously preserved unbelievers revel in music and drama, painting, poetry and dance, with a riot of color, a deafening sound raised in praise to themselves and their false gods, how can you live here openly and be silent? Are you satisfied with bedlam for God? Where is our concert of freshly composed, holy stringed music? Our jubilant dance of praise to the Lord? What penetrating drama have our hands made...? Human existence is not absurd: we glory in the image of God! The world is not a curse: it is good creation, struggling under sin toward final deliverance...! [W]e as a Christian community must serve up the new wine.[24]

The time has come to be done with the retreatist, pietistic, and syncretistic gospel of *churchianity* that has led to the radical decay of our culture, the collapse of the Christian calling, and the impotence of an institutional church that refuses to bring the Word of God to bear on all of life. A new generation of Christians must, in the power of the Holy Spirit, take up the task afresh of being Christian lords in the development of creation and in the direction of culture as Christ Jesus intends. For this we need true grace and wisdom, not only in our churches but in our marriages and families, schools and civic associations, universities and businesses, political parties and guilds. We need the truth of the Christian gospel to permeate family, church, and state, and every dimension of life, as leaven permeates the dough. We must boldly proclaim and apply, in detail, the wisdom of God for every domain of life, regarding not only the way of personal salvation, but regarding the entirety of our lives, for the reconciliation of all things to God. Only in this way will the gospel be unhindered, and the wisdom and renewing power of God be effectively released again in our time.

---

24. Seerveld, *Christian Critique*, 21–22.

CHAPTER 4

# Think Christianly About Law (Part 1)
## The Meaning of Law, Natural Law, and Politics

*As far as the principle of the natural man is concerned, it is absolutely or utterly, not partly, opposed to God. That principle is Satanic. It is exclusively hostile to God. If it could, it would destroy the work and plan of God.*
— Cornelius Van Til

## The Law-Word

WE HAVE SEEN IN PREVIOUS chapters that the significance of the word-revelation in Scripture cannot be *reduced* to simple "moral" guidance for limited areas of a so-called "spiritual" life, or "religious" instruction for personal salvation—as though it were possible to separate the creative and redemptive Word of God and our most fundamental faith commitments from our everyday activities in the world. Rather, what we see given in the Scriptures is the religious *direction* for *every* area of life, grounded in the person and work of Christ, the living Word of God, through the transforming power of the Holy Spirit. This direction-giving for the believer is not based upon knowledge of the science of theology as an academic discipline, but upon biblical revelation itself and the world-and-life view that emerges from it. The Bible reveals that God has placed the *entire cosmos* in all its dimensions and structures under His law and ordinances (Job 38–39; Psalm 119:129–130, 160). This includes, but is more than, the Decalogue (Ten Commandments) and its meaning as explained and applied in the wisdom literature and prophetic instruction of the Bible. It encompasses *all* the universal ordinances that form the *structural principles* for the existence of all differentiated things. God's law is literally the *condition of life* in all its varied dimensions, for "in Him" all things consist or hold together (Acts 17:28; Col. 1:16–17).

The law for creation therefore functions as a *boundary* between God and the cosmos which His Word maintains, ensuring the distinction between the Creator and the creature. God alone is above law, everything else is *subject* to His law *for* creation. Thus, creation has a law side and subject side—i.e., the law that holds for all things, and all that is subject to the law. This unequivocal Creator/creature distinction is vital for a Christian understanding of reality. God Himself is not to be conflated with His law—for *temporal law* is not something *eternally existing* in God—but neither is law apart from God. Instead, our loving and gracious God binds Himself to His creation law in covenant faithfulness (Gen. 8:21–22). In short, Scripture gives us a three-factor worldview regarding God and His relationship to the world:

A. The Triune God
B. His mediating law-Word

C. The cosmos, where the law-Word of God is both the *boundary* and *bridge* between the Creator and the creation.[1]

This is the *general* sense in which we can understand the biblical teaching concerning God and creation as a law-order subject to His decrees and ordinances (Ps. 11:7–10; 119:13–16, 18–21, 30–32; 136).

More *specifically*, in the Bible, God's law is something that is revealed and disclosed to man. The word *torah* is usually translated as 'law,' and its basic meaning is *instruction*, which is reflected in various contemporary translations. The English word *instruction* reminds us that we are *in-structure* in God's creation, which is to say, our lives are to be ordered by God's law-Word (Ps. 1). As Herman Bavinck explains:

> The Christian worldview holds that man is always and everywhere bound by laws set forth by God as the rule for life. Everywhere there are norms which stand above man. They find a unity among themselves and find their origin and continuation in the Creator and Lawgiver of the universe. These norms are the most precious treasures entrusted to mankind.... To live in conformity to these norms in mind and heart, in thought and action, this is what it means most basically to become conformed to the image of God's Son. And this is the ideal and goal of man.[2]

In terms of our subject of law in its specific *juridical meaning* in this chapter, the implication is that, like the moral and logical dimensions of life, legal reality is not *founded* in man's reasoning nor subjective consciousness, nor the science of law itself, but in the very Word of God. We can therefore provide a working Christian definition of law as: *A complex of norms, regulating the relations between people and human institutions by means of the balancing of their interests in conformity with God's creation order and His revealed Word.*[3]

---

1. Spykman, *Reformational Theology*, 75.
2. Bavinck, cited in Spykman, *Reformational Theology*, 94–95.
3. I have adapted this definition from E. L. Hebden Taylor, *The New Legality: In Light of the Christian Philosophy of Law* (Philadelphia: Presbyterian & Reformed Publishing Co.; Craig Press, 1967), 13.

## Law and Religion

Bavinck's reference to worldview in his discussion about the law is not incidental. Only the most superficial of thinkers today would assert that the *foundations* of law and legality can be explained or addressed without reference to overarching worldviews—in short, to *religion*. As Albert Wolters points out:

> A worldview is a matter of the shared everyday experience of humankind, an inescapable component of human knowing, and as such it is... *prescientific* in nature. It belongs to an order of cognition more basic than that of science or theory.... *[L]egal theory presupposes a fundamental notion of justice...*, a pretheoretical perspective on the world.[4]

The idea of law in its full juridical sense cannot be *reduced* to the commands of a sovereign authority, to a system of legal rules recognized by legislative enactment and then applied in the courts. This is because law is inextricably bound to the *moral* dimension and religious direction of human society. It is occupied with ultimate ends, not just means, with the ideas of justice, obligation, duty, and the legitimation of authority. These are inescapably *religious matters,* or we might say, questions of ultimate concern.

From the standpoint of the Christian worldview, the apostle Paul uncovers the religious nature of humanity when he addresses a fundamental problem for human beings in addressing matters of law and justice—the rebellious suppression of the voice of God at the religious root of our lives since the Fall of man:

> For God's wrath is revealed from heaven against all godlessness and unrighteousness of people who *by their unrighteousness suppress the truth*, since what can be known about God is evident among them, because God has shown it to them. For

---

4. Albert M. Wolters, *Creation Regained: Biblical Basics for a Reformational Worldview*, 2nd ed. (Grand Rapids, MI: Wm. B. Eerdmans Publishing Co., 2005), emphasis added, 10.

His invisible attributes, that is, His eternal power and divine nature, have been clearly seen since the creation of the world, being understood through what He has made. As a result, people are without excuse. For though they knew God, they did not glorify Him as God or show gratitude. Instead, their thinking became nonsense, and *their senseless minds were darkened*. Claiming to be wise, they became fools... (Rom. 1:18–22).

For Paul, there is clearly no religiously neutral thinking, no "view from nowhere," and no sphere of life where our faith response to the revelation of God is not determinative. This includes the realm of law. Critically, St. Paul does not tell us that only some narrowly defined "spiritual" truth has been supressed, leaving man's unaided thinking as a reliable and trustworthy guide for most areas of human life and culture. Instead, he tells us that the human mind, because of sin against our better knowledge, has become senseless and darkened to the point where the law for life and the very concept of the divine is sought *within* creation itself—eliminating the all-important Creator/creature distinction of Scripture. This, the apostle explains, is an exchanging of truth for a lie and leads to the radical distortion of human relationships (Rom. 1:24–32). The French Christian philosopher, Jacques Ellul, draws the theological implications precisely:

> When man takes the fruit of the tree, he separates himself from God. Consequently his knowledge of good and evil is a knowledge in separation from God, in sin and in death. Man does not know the good except in sin. He does not know the good except as static and separated from the love of God. This is to say that he has not the slightest idea of what the good really is and that, separated from God as he is, he has not the slightest idea of justice, which is conformity with the will of God. Biblical teaching affirms beyond question that natural man, man by himself, does not know what justice is.[5]

---

5. Jacques Ellul, *The Theological Foundation of Law*, trans. Marguerite Wieser (Garden City, NY: Doubleday, 1960), 87.

Without genuine submission to the law-Word of God, which is possible only by the work of the Holy Spirit (Rom. 8:4–11), man in his sins does not truly know what justice is because he will not submit in his heart to God's law. The apostle Paul never impugns the truth or authority of this law for, "the law is holy, and the commandment is holy and just and good" (Rom. 7:12), but he denies man's ability to love and do it from the heart, "because natural wisdom is at enmity with God, not submitting itself to His law; it is impossible that it should" (Rom. 8:7, Knox Bible). Thus, the way man understands law is rooted in a spiritual ethos—his pistic (from the Greek word *pistis*, belief) response to law as *homo religiosus*, whether believing or unbelieving.

## Greek Thought and the Law

This uniquely revelational and Christian conception of law and its relation to the human condition was a radical break from the religious and philosophical milieu of the Greco-Roman world. Perhaps most important here in the Western tradition was the thinking of Aristotle via his teacher Plato. For Aristotle, there could be no *revelation* to human beings in creation or Scripture, because there is no such thing as creation, and no infinite-personal-relational God to speak to man in lingual form. In his works *Physics* and *On the Heavens*, he clearly teaches that the world is eternal, because the abstract principles of *form* (idea or law) and *matter* are uncreated. The "god" of Aristotle's thought is certainly not the Creator God of Scripture, distinct from nature, but a philosophical limiting concept, an abstract cause. Secondly, for Aristotle, the human mind is not darkened through rejecting divine revelation, because for him the intellect itself *is* something divine. This notion is related to Aristotle's faulty conception of the divine as *pure intellect*, a view he set forth in his works *On the Soul* and *Metaphysics*. Here, "god" is literally "thought thinking on itself"![6]

---

6. Aristotle, *The Basic Works of Aristotle*, ed. Richard McKeon (New York: Random House, 1941), 879–80.

Because of his unscriptural views of both man and God, Aristotle believed that when one thinks, "intellect thinks by actually taking on the form of what it thinks about... the intellect is potentially everything."[7] This absolutizing and divinizing of thought clearly implies that law and justice is not something *revealed* by God in creation or Scripture. Instead, it is a product of divine "reason" reflecting on the *goal* of man's life; a life reaching its true fulfilment and perfection in the *legal order* of the state as a political community.[8] Nature, which for Aristotle included the natural political life of man (since man is a political animal), far from being a *fallen realm* that cannot be normative, was taken as the standard for social, political and legal norms:

> Aristotle did not think in terms of a deity who authored nature; nature itself was divine. He is therefore very exposed to the skeptical view that "natural" and "unnatural" are synonyms for "usual" and "unusual" or for "morally good" and "morally bad."

> Throughout his *Politics* it is taken for granted that nature is the ground of social norms. When Aristotle asks whether there are slaves "by nature," he wants to know whether there are persons whose proper place in the world is to serve as slaves to others. If there are, it explains *both* why there is slavery *and* why it is good for (natural) slaves to be slaves. Discovering what is "natural" uncovers both the way things are and how they should be.[9]

The force of Ellul's previously cited biblical contention is seen here in its radical light: fallen, sinful man does not know either the good or true justice, for he does not recognize its ground as the will of the living God.

---

7. Peter S. Adamson, *Classical Philosophy: A History of Philosophy Without Any Gaps* (Oxford: Oxford University Press, 2014), 280.
8. Herman Dooyeweerd, *Time, Law & History: Selected Essays*, Collected Works, Series B, vol. 14 (Jordan Station, ON: Paideia Press, 2024), 230–31.
9. Alan Ryan, *On Politics: A History of Political Thought: From Herodotus to the Present* (New York: Liveright Publishing Corporation, 2012), 76.

## The Legal Crisis in Modern Culture

In the West, we are currently returning to a humanistic faith in a self-generating, ostensibly infinite (in some form) and evolving universe; such a perspective clearly precludes any standard of law *above* nature. This also indicates that the law of the state (as a product of nature) is beyond criticism by any transcendent source of authority—for there can be no such thing as a *transcendent* source of authority and law in such a worldview. This means further, that state law is inescapably *totalitarian law*, which is to say, there is no right, no realm of justice, no source of law beyond or above what the state enacts. As such, the modern state steadily seeks to unite *total power* and *total jurisdiction* with a growing claim to *total competence*. As the *source* of law, the humanistic neo-pagan state claims to stand above the law as the new god of being, engineering, planning, and ruling over every sphere of life. This is the idolatry of statism and a revival of paganism: "[I]t is a reductionist vision of mankind and society, i.e. a vision that absolutizes—and therefore idolizes—one aspect of the created order above other equally legitimate aspects of Creation that exist independently of the state."[10]

In the name of secular psychology, anthropology, and sociology, our era is experiencing a reversal of biblically derived law for man's so-called "rational law"—that is, sociological law and social-scientific planning. This has created the modern crisis in law and politics and fomented people's growing disillusionment and increasing disregard for the validity of law and justice as propagated by the modern secular state.

It is possible to identify several key trends that have shaped this "progressive" revolutionary spirit in the West today. *First,* whether or not God exists is seen as basically irrelevant. Either way, functionally, God is dead for us because there is allegedly no *identifiable* and *authoritative* revelation from God. As a result, anything is potentially permissible in the context of an elastic social contract which may be updated according to the "general

---

10. Stephen C. Perks, *The Politics of God and the Politics of Man: Essays on Politics, Religion, and Social Order* (Tonbridge, UK: Kuyper Foundation, December 1, 2016), 49.

will." There are no abiding norms or standards which bind people from above—any acceptable social restraint must be horizontal in character, not vertical. All we have available to work with is our relative cultural history, and a "rational" analysis of legal systems within an evolving social reality, leaving law floating in mid-air without a truly objective criterion.

*Second*, since man is now enlarged in the form of the state and effectively made sovereign over the world, having become the *source* of his own standards and values, people should not be compelled by law to obey an *external* authority like the Ten Commandments or the moral teaching of Christ within society. Any such imposition of moral and jural authority from the outside, implicitly denying an open universe, especially a morally open universe, must be rejected as heresy and treason against the new god of state.

*Third*, traditionalist holdouts in society, those still enslaved to the archaic notion of God's *revealed* Word, must be made to realize that the scriptural ideas of creation, fall, redemption, and the consummation of all things in the man Jesus Christ are a myth. Human beings are not image-bearers of the living God, nor are they fallen creatures that need to be cleansed and redeemed from sin, regenerated, and redirected at the root of their being. Rather, man is his own god in the process of saving himself from political, cultural, and planetary ruin by his creative reason, activism, and social engineering. In practice, this means that in the name of the common good, the law of the state exists to serve all human wants and desires, passions, and lusts. Sexual satisfaction, in particular, is an absolute value needing no higher justification. Christians must be educated into the reality that modern people live *over*, not *under* the law, and will not be disciplined or restrained by God's law revealed in the Bible.

It is evident then, that the law of the new society is inescapably *utopian* law. Godless legality means the de-facto established religion of the political community in neo-pagan society is a form of *scientific humanism*—a common faith in the power of man's thinking, language and technique to re-create reality and save humanity by social planning, manipulation, and control through legislation. This drive for total control and total jurisdiction by the modern state has brought the West to a point of crisis and profound instability, with reactionary movements emerging on every side.

## The Meaning of Law

In responding to this crisis, the essential question that confronts the Christian is that of the nature and *meaning* of law in its juridical sense. This is contested because there have been a variety of views of law (jurisprudence) in modern Western thought that seek to compete with the scriptural perspective. Some older schools of thought seek universal validity for normative principles, while others deny constant and universal starting points for human thought and action which is recognized as changeable. From the secular humanistic standpoint, and at the risk of oversimplification for the sake of brevity, there have been two main approaches to jettisoning God and His Word from the realm of law and legality in the contemporary context.

The first is a "Pure Theory of Law" (analytical jurisprudence), in which the question of whether a law is good or bad, just or unjust, is thought not to be the concern of jurisprudence. This model holds that *moral judgments* cannot be defended by rational argument. As a consequence, morality is not inextricably bound to law. Rather, we are confronted in jurisprudence with various normative *situations of fact*, operating in a variety of legal systems based in diverse constitutions. Each constitution is a kind of hypothesis, and legal rules are simply deductions from this hypothesis. The academic discipline of Law is therefore reduced to *the structural analysis of positive rules within these various systems*. It is concerned only with the *actual* and not with the *ideal*. This means that "every arbitrary content can be law. There exists no human action for which, according to its quality, it is excluded from being the content of a legal norm."[11]

The second main theory of law emerges as the "Sociological School," in which law and juridical life are considered a social institution based in an experimental science. This science has the task of *satisfying human desires and wants* that are constantly changing. The sociological view of law is not concerned with logical deductions from first principles, whether biblical or

---

11. Kelson, cited in Danie Strauss, *The Philosophy of Herman Dooyeweerd*, (Jordan Station, ON: Paideia Press, 2021), 70.

constitutional. As such, "human interests" are the true subject of the law. The goal of juridical life is the smooth operation of a societal machine in terms of various social interests—law is therefore merely instrumental to a particular end. On this supposition, law is simply *what the courts do and decide*, and is therefore reduced to a form of *legal behaviorism* where we "scientifically observe" the way courts act in various cases to determine what law is.

Whether sociological or analytical in emphasis, both of these schools conceptually reduce law to the relative and subjective command-word of human beings, and the purpose of law is degraded to the purely pragmatic. Law is merely descriptive, ultimately, of whatever "works" for a given society or community. If most people obey societal laws in a given context, then those laws are deemed valid. The ultimate ground of *authority* and *validity* is sought, not in God's Word-revelation, but in human culture and experience. Critically, one can also see that on this basis, there is no discernible relationship between law, morality, and justice. This is because faith and revelation, truth and justice, are being radically disconnected from law and legality. As an inevitable consequence, *objective* legal norms and values are abandoned as mythological (since this would require accepting an external authority), with God and His law-Word excluded at the very outset. From this humanistic standpoint, human beings are left to find out the meaning of law, how they should behave, and what justice is, solely from the social practice of their society which, inevitably, will reflect ever-changing desires.

The scriptural vision, which forms the paradigm for the Christian mind, is radically different. From the biblical point of view, law in its juridical sense is not concerned with *prescribing* (either on the basis of rational deductions from constitutional hypotheses or observations of the way in which courts behave), but with *discovering* the creational meaning of the concept of justice and its implications for human society in the light of God's revealed Word.

It is relevant to note here that the juridical norms of law are of a different kind than those governing the natural sciences which explore other dimensions of God's creation-order. When considering the meaning of law and justice, we are not just dealing with *descriptive observations* of regular and unvarying states of affairs, but with truly *normative criteria* for human life—criteria which can be obeyed or disobeyed and applied rightly or wrongly— whereas a rock is not able to disobey the laws of gravity or motion. This does not mean people are any less conscious that there are jural norms. In fact, as creatures of God, people manifest an everyday awareness of both jural and moral creational norms when we experience a *sense* of injustice, *demand* that justice be done in a particular situation, and when we unavoidably *invoke* normative criteria like truth, fairness, right and wrong, just deserts and equity within legal societal relationships. We will return to the core significance of law in its juridical meaning when we consider the central meaning of *justice* as retribution (tribution) and the *Lex Talionis*.

## The Origin of Natural Law Theories

Having determined that the meaning of law in the biblical worldview is something *discovered* by man as a revelation of the will and purpose of God for human societal relationships, the question remains: How is this to be discerned or ascertained? How are we to know what justice is? Where do we find the foundation of valid law within the Christian frame of reference?

So far I have argued that human understanding, bound to God's creation, is in no position to *prescribe*, but must *discover* the laws and norms for reality empirically revealed in the created order and in Scripture. God's revelation in the creation Word, incarnate Word, and inscripturated Word is one *unified garment*, the threads of which cannot be rightly grasped in isolation from one another, and which, properly interpreted, do not contradict each other. Jesus Christ as the Word of God, the mediator of creation, is also the mediator of redemption. "He is God's first, middle, and last Word for the world. All God's dealings with the world—creation, preservation, judgement, redemption, consummation—are through Christ."[12] Within this garment, the scriptural thread has *epistemic priority* through the work of the Holy Spirit, so that we might comprehend who Jesus Christ really is and might properly read creational law. Spykman is to the point and worth quoting at length:

---

12. Spykman, *Reformational Theology*, 84.

The full sweep of cosmic history stands under the holding and healing power of God's Word.

There is no inner tension or contradiction between the creational Word, the inscripturated Word, and the incarnate Word. His Word, with and for creation from the beginning was "trust me, love me, serve me." The same call to obedient living constitutes the heart of biblical revelation....

Epistemologically, therefore, it all comes down to Scripture..., the hermeneutic key for our knowledge of the enduring norms of God's creational Word in its holding power for our life together in the world. Given our present human predicament, only in the light of that redeeming and liberating Word in its lingual form can we gain insight into the meaning of created reality.

The creational Word remains God's first Word for the world. It is also His lasting Word. God has not withdrawn it. It stands firm and will endure to the end.... The trouble lies on the response side. Therefore, though that first Word is still sufficient for its original intent and purpose, it is no longer sufficient for our present need. So, thanks to God's condescending grace, that first Word is not God's last Word. He reiterates His creational Word in His Word of redemption.[13]

Christian thought and scholarship, including jurisprudence, must therefore discern God's creational norms for their various fields, self-consciously directed and illuminated by the Word in Scripture. As responsible creatures, human beings are required by God to apply His *instruction* to an endless variety of concrete situations, including *positivizing (formulating and encoding) valid law* for this life. These laws are necessarily *temporary* in nature, anchored in the present world-order. The challenge in the arena of law, as in every area of life, is that because of man's fallen and ruined state of sin (total depravity), he may fail in discovering, accepting, applying, and obeying God's normative law-order properly. In fact, there is a directional antithesis

---

13. Spykman, *Reformational Theology*, 86–87.

between how the believer and the unbeliever will each see and apply the meaning of law and justice.

In an effort to overcome the religious cleavage involved between believer and unbeliever, theories of universal natural law have, in the course of time, been adopted by Christians in hope of providing a criterion for discovering valid law *equally accessible to all people* and a potential basis for a religiously neutral and rational jurisprudence. The essential concept of natural law, which can be a very murky and confusing idea, is succinctly summarised by H. J. Hommes:

> Natural law in its traditional sense is the totality of pre-positive legal norms (not brought into existence through a human declaration of will in the formation of law) that are immutable, universal and per se valid, as well as the eventual subjective natural rights and correlating duties, based upon a natural order (whether or not traced back to a divine origin), such that the human being can derive it from the natural order aided by natural reason.[14]

Natural law theories, contrary to the more contemporary views of law addressed earlier, rightly recognise a law-*order for reality* as something given. Here we can rightly say "one cheer for natural law." There is a genuine desire in natural law theories to take seriously normative standards of justice which transcend subjective individual opinion, social convention, the historical moment, and tradition. As such, these theories frequently have an attraction for Christians as a potential solution to relativism and subjectivism in law by an appeal to natural justice and right reason, without having to make a distinctly Christian and scripturally grounded case. Difficulties arise, however, when looking at the *idea of law* for human society inherent in natural law theories. The natural law ideal has an ancient provenance in pagan Greek thought and was advanced by various philosophers of the classical world who believed they had discovered a rational criterion for law and justice. To

---

14. Hommes, cited in Strauss, *The Philosophy of Herman Dooyeweerd*, 68.

understand the concept properly, the religious root of natural law needs to be examined.

Although there were early theories of natural law that were materialistic and posited that whatever was found in nature was right and lawful, the versions that came to dominate Western thought were idealistic—that is, based in the conception of eternally existing *ideas or forms*. In much of classical Greek thought, various philosophers held that there was *one reality* (i.e., one concept of existence, which excluded a Creator/creature distinction) subsisting on two levels—a transcendent part and non-transcendent part. There was *form* (transcendent part) and *matter* (non-transcendent), a higher and lower principle, corresponding to perfection and changeableness.

This ontology was most famously advanced by Aristotle and Plato. The forms were the eternal ideas or laws that determined the nature of all material reality which was constantly coming and going in its being. For example, Aristotle—who differed from Plato in how the principles of form and matter were related—saw man as having a rational soul existing in the *form* of the *material* body, both of which comprise a unity of substance. Man's reason (a rational capacity which could function independent of the body) was believed to *participate* in the higher reality of form which man was able to intellectually contemplate. "God" was a principle of *pure* form/reason (the unmoved mover), uncontaminated by material reality, in which everything else *participated* to a greater or lesser degree. For Aristotle, because the essence of a thing (its form) is present in the object itself—everything in this sense having a kind of soul, including plants and animals—justice, as an aspect of his catch-all concept of virtue, is discovered by rational reflection on the essence of *human nature*. As a result, if you know what man is, you can determine by *natural reason* how he ought to act, because ostensibly virtue is a constitutive part of the nature of man. Thus, laws are good if they contribute to the realization of man's true being and bad if they don't.

So how does man realise his true being and the goal of his existence? Just as there were higher and lower levels of reality, which also co-existed in the human person (form and matter), so too human society was strictly hierarchical. The philosophers' self-conscious cultivation of reason and awareness of natural law equipped them, they believed, to rule society. The *form* of the state was natural, and man was primarily a political animal, meaning that his social nature is realized only in the state. Specifically, *natural law* was the *form* of the state and provided the rules of man's social relationships as understood by human reason. So strong was their belief that the state was the humanizing institution, that for some Greek thinkers, the *barbaroi* (those outside the Greek city-state) were not fully human, "This view became characteristic for the entire classical theory of state and law."[15] Aristotle saw the life of the state as having a specific and unique *moral* task beyond the *jural* task of public justice, "for he assumed that the laws of the *polis* ought to be obeyed for the sake of the *moral end* of the state: the perfection of the life of its citizens into a good and beautiful life."[16] This involved a hierarchy of values,

> where the household—which he defined as limited to the satisfaction of the lower needs of life (as demanded by the "matter" in human nature)—is seen as being a lower part subordinated to the *perfect total community of the state* and serviceable to the higher rational-moral needs of man. Only in this way does man acquire a good and beautiful life.[17]

It becomes clear that the Aristotelian concept of natural law is really a subdivision of state law. The so-called natural law, the actual content of which is not clearly elaborated by Aristotle, is not a set of objective norms in his thinking, but an abstraction that serves to answer an *ethical* question regarding how one must behave in order to achieve happiness and natural perfection.

Because the state is viewed as the institution which takes the ethical perfection of the political animal as its primary goal, there is no intrinsic limit on the power and jurisdiction of the city-state to achieve its end. As a result, we are confronted with a *totalitarian conception* of the state. In fact,

---

15. Herman Dooyeweerd, *Time, Law & History: Selected Essays*, Collected Works, Series B, vol. 14 (Jordan Station, ON: Paideia Press, 2024), 212.
16. Dooyeweerd, *Time, Law and History*, 213.
17. Dooyeweerd, *Time, Law and History*, 229; emphasis added.

Aristotle's restriction of the validity of natural law to the state sphere shows that he does not acknowledge any inviolable natural right for family, marriage, or business and economic life. This all means that the nature of the state, itself a *product* of natural law, is not actually *juridically qualified (limited)* at all—which is to say, its ultimate purpose *stands outside* of the jural meaning of law. Instead, the purpose of state law is oriented to the humanistically conceived goal of the perfection of the individual, not justice as retribution in the establishment of a harmony of public *legal* interest. This is why the state's law and competency is implicitly *both* totalitarian for the common people, and yet potentially entirely superfluous to the superior man, since Aristotle claims in his *Politics* that a person who is without equal in surpassing others in virtue and skill ought not to be subjected to the law that holds for these other people, for such a person is a law unto himself.[18]

In the perfect community of the state, Aristotle distinguished between *natural law* (absolute law of unchangeable content) and *statutory law* (arbitrary law). The natural law, which he presupposes to be directed to what is morally good, is thought to be immanent in rational human nature which, participating in the realm of *form*, belongs to *immutable* being. Although natural law can be taken up and utilized by statutory law, it does not become statutory law. Statutory law is of a conventional nature and can be relatively arbitrary in content (such as the level of a ransom payment, or taxation levels). This sharp division helped give rise to the separation of natural law and positive law in modern legal positivism. Ultimately, as Dooyeweerd points out:

> This opposition between a natural law and a purely conventional law reveals an intrinsic dualism in the Aristotelian conception of law. In the final analysis, it is rooted in the irreconcilable dualism in the Greek ground-motive of form and matter.[19]

---

18. Dooyeweerd, *Time, Law and History*, 256.
19. Dooyeweerd, *Time, Law and History*, 257.

Although schools like that of the Stoics had slightly different versions of natural law, what is common to them all is the idea that man does not need to look outside of himself and his environment to know what is right and just, he can know these things without God and His revealed Word. A vicious and flat circularity is inherent in this concept, because man's idea of himself is his *own referent* for what is right and just: what is good is what is natural; what is natural is what is found in man's immutable rational nature; what is found in man's rational nature is good!

It is evident, then, that the Greek idea of natural law is not remotely similar to the biblical doctrine of the revelation of God's law-Word in creation, Christ, and Scripture. As Dooyeweerd summarizes the matter:

> Aristotle... assigned to his "natural law" an absolute and immutable character because he assumed it was based on the *immutable rational ontic form of human nature*, just like the state community to which it was necessarily related. Whoever understands the religious background of the Greek form-matter motive that gave birth to Aristotle's separation of natural law and statutory law, can no longer hold the opinion that this conception of natural law can be taken over by an intrinsically Christian view of law.[20]

The Greek philosophers thus attempted to flee from God and His Word to the universe, to nature, in order to seek there an eternal law, a rational law also inherent in their own divinized nature, by which they might justify their desires, control the masses, and fortify their politics.

## Christianizing Natural Law

The venerable antiquity of any idea does not make it true. Contemporary vague appeals to "The Great Tradition" among some Protestant natural law advocates are hollow unless they can show from the Word of God that

---

20. Dooyeweerd, *Time, Law and History*, 263–64; italics added.

the elements of the tradition to which they refer are firmly grounded in and subject to the authority and teaching of Scripture. Without such a perspective, there could be no reformation in the church nor progress in society—tradition itself would be the final criterion of truth.

From the early centuries of the life of the church, with notable exceptions like Tertullian and Tatian, critical biblical reflection on the philosophical inheritance of classical culture amongst the church fathers was minimal. Augustine in his classic, *The City of God*, makes a solid start, but the focus for Christians in the late Roman Empire was, understandably, restraining the worst excesses of pagan culture rather than a thoroughgoing reformation of it in terms of a radically biblical starting point. As a result, though biblical law gained significantly in appreciation, something we will explore in the next chapter, Christian thinkers typically attempted a synthesis of Christianity and classical culture with the use of pagan concepts like natural law in their efforts to relate the gospel of Christ to cultural and political life. The Greek word *logos* was particularly utilized in this regard. The early Christian apologist, Justin Martyr, for example, immersed in Greek philosophical thought through his schooling, considered the "Word" (*logos*)—referred to in the first chapter of St. John's Gospel as having been made incarnate in Jesus Christ—as the same *principle of reason* which had ruled the thinking and actions of people like Socrates and the Stoics. Since such men lived in conformity with "reason" (*logos*), they must have been unconsciously guided, he concluded, by the pre-incarnate Christ! As such they could be rightly regarded as Christians before Christ had come—much like the Older Testament saints.[21]

A truly dazzling synthesis was finally achieved in medieval scholasticism by the famous genius Thomas Aquinas (c. 1225–1274). Aristotle was, at this point, also effectively adopted as a kind of proto-Christian saint when Aquinas (the apogee of the scholastic movement) was tasked by the Pope with interpreting Aristotle for the Roman Catholic Church, providing Latin Christianity with an ideology of law and power. Thomas' attempted synthesis

---

21. Downie, "Natural Law and God's Law: An Antithesis," *The Journal of Christian Reconstruction: Symposium on Politics*. Vol. 5. Vallecito CA, Chalcedon Foundation, 1978, 82.

of "the Philosopher" (as he called Aristotle) and the Bible, meant that from the start he was working with two conflicting sources of authority—the Greek ideas of reason and nature found in Aristotle, and the revelation of Scripture. And so, as E. L. Hebden Taylor points out:

> Just as Aristotle had tried to answer his Sophist critics by trying to prove that the existing institutions of the Greek city-state, such as slavery and the exploitation of women and the working classes, were natural and reflected the very order of the universe, so now Aquinas tried to show that such feudal institutions as serfdom, the monarchy and papal theocracy were also natural, and arose out of the very nature of things.... With Aristotle's help he tried to prove that the feudal state was grounded in nature rather than in sin, as Paul and Augustine had supposed.[22]

Plato and Aristotle had both believed that their political reasoning represented a true rational order and therefore the natural law, and so in Aquinas, a powerful Greek revival was taking place. The Greeks had rejected the biblical doctrine of creation for that of *participation* and Aquinas tries to utilize this idea, without rejecting creation—a contradiction he never clearly overcomes. He therefore sees the natural law as essentially "right reason," with God and man existing in a continuity of being for, "all beings apart from God are not their own being, but are beings by participation".[23] Following Aristotle, he regarded the intellectual principle as the human soul, which, participating in the forms, is incorruptible.[24]

---

22. E.L. Hebden Taylor, *The Christian Philosophy of Law, Politics and the State: A Study of the Political and Legal Thought of Herman Dooyeweerd of the Free University of Amsterdam, Holland as the Basis for Christian Action in the English-Speaking World* (Nutley, NJ: Craig Press, 1966), 158.
23. Thomas Aquinas, *Summa Theologica*, trans. Fathers of the English Dominican Province, *First Part*, Question 44, Article 1, in *The Summa Theologica of St. Thomas Aquinas*, 2nd ed., 1920 (New York: Benziger Brothers, 1947), 19:238.
24. Thomas Aquinas, *Summa Theologica*, Part 1 of the Second Part, Question 85, Article 1, in *Great Books of the Western World*, vol. 20, edited by Robert Maynard Hutchins (Chicago: Encyclopaedia Britannica, 1952),

For Aquinas, therefore, as in Aristotle, God becomes identified with *pure form* (pure reason/intellect) and therefore with the law itself. In fact, God's essence is law, and in that sense, God *is* the law.[25] God's being is conceived as the *exemplar* of all composite things containing the *form* of all created things, which means, for example, that God has the *proper form* of a plant, or horse, or crocodile in Himself. These *archetypes* are then manifest in all created things. In essence, by knowing Himself, God knows and determines all reality. The forms are regarded as pre-existent in Him immaterially from all eternity and flow out from Him in creation before returning to Him. This Aquinas calls the *Divine Law*. One can see immediately how this idea seriously blurs and threatens the vital biblical distinction between Creator and creature.

With *form* and *matter* (the immortal and temporal, higher and lower, transcendent and non-transcendent) as a two-story metaphysical worldview of existing reality, the *Divine Law* is reflected in human reason as the *Natural Law*. Man, as a rational soul, mysteriously *participates* in divine providence itself and therefore in divine reason. This sharing in Eternal Law by rational man is Aquinas' idea of the Natural Law. Human reason therefore becomes an analogue of divine reason. Aquinas writes:

> Therefore, since all things subject to divine providence are ruled and measured by the eternal law, as was stated above, it is evident that all things partake somewhat of the eternal law, in so far as, namely, from its being imprinted on them, they derive their respective inclinations to their proper acts and ends. Now among all others, the rational creature is subject to divine providence in the most excellent way, in so far as it partakes of a share of providence, by being provident both for itself and for others. Therefore it has a share of the Eternal Reason, by which it has a natural inclination to its due act and end; and this participation of the eternal law in the rational creature is called the natural law.... [T]he light of natural reason, by which we discern what is good and what is evil, which is the function of the natural law, is nothing else than an imprint on us of the Divine light. It is therefore evident

---

25. See Van Der Walt, *Thomas Aquinas and the Neo-Thomist Tradition*, 50–51.

that the natural law is nothing else than the rational creature's participation of the eternal law. [26]

As a consequence, law is simply *the rule of right reason*. A valid law is thus whatever reason defines to be the good for man and the state. Obedience is required, and law finds its compulsory legitimacy in the fact that law is somehow the command of reason. These principles of reason, supposedly imprinted on the rational, incorruptible soul are thereby self-evident; the dictates of which, imposing themselves on the will, are the Natural Law as the ground of justice. Because human reason is here considered an analogue of divine reason, man's thinking can be confidently relied upon—follow right reason if you want to follow God. Taylor summarises what is happening:

> By means of his doctrine of the eternal law, with its subjective counterpart in the natural law, Thomas Aquinas sought to accommodate the Greek form-matter motive [worldview] with the biblical ground-motive [worldview] of creation, the fall into sin, and redemption in and through Jesus Christ in the communion of the Holy Spirit. Through the natural law the creation, in its essential nature, has a subjective part in the eternal law of God's world plan.[27]

This view inevitably leads to an incoherent dualistic concept of law with poles that cannot be readily reconciled—metaphysical *natural law* (as an analogue of divine law) and *positive law* (changeable human law).

Several problems with Aquinas' view of the law from the biblical standpoint are now apparent, which we can summarize briefly. First, as discussed already, the identification of God's person(s) with an abstract eternal law in His own being, expressed in and determining the cosmos, blurs the all-important Creator/creature distinction so central to the scriptural worldview which distinguishes biblical faith from paganism.[28] Second, by

---

26. Aquinas, *Summa*, 20.209 (*Summa Theologica*, Part I of Second Part, Q. 91, Article 2)
27. Taylor, *The Christian Philosophy of Law, Politics and the State*, 152.
28. Plato and Aristotle themselves oscillated between pantheism and a blank, contentless monotheism. New Testament scholar and specialist in pagan thought, Peter

identifying following right reason with following God's law, we encounter an absolutizing (deifying) of the *logical function* and dimension of human life and a failure to appreciate the limitations and fallibility of human understanding, not to mention the noetic impact of the Fall of man. Third, instead of *discovering* and *acknowledging* God's law, command, or instruction for human social relationships, human reason ends up inventing and articulating supposedly unchanging principles of human conduct thought to be valid everywhere and at all times. Fourth, inculcating and giving credence to abstract, unchanging legal rules and principles—as opposed to divine command and instruction to be positivized by man in his historical-cultural circumstances—is a radical underestimation of *historicity*. Both Aristotle and Aquinas, in the name of such unchanging principles, defended the unjust order of their time as natural—absolutizing slavery, feudal serfdom, and the Inquisition, respectively.[29] Fifth, Aquinas' thought soon led men to rely on reason without reference to revelation for the source of law, which always turns into rank speculation as the "right reason" of fallen men differs and descends eventually, into secularization and relativism. At which point, man's reasoning (analytical capacity) becomes a barrier to the proper knowledge of God. Sixth, like all the natural law thinkers before and after him, Aquinas does not identify the specific content of an abstract body of 'natural law' existing apart from God's revealed Word which can supposedly be grasped by some innate power of reason.

As the fulcrum of Aquinas' understanding of man and society, his natural law idea thus combines Aristotle's false doctrine of virtue, pursued in terms of rational ends, with the Stoic doctrine of the law of Reason and Nature. The nomism of Aquinas is summarized pointedly by Van Der Walt:

> Aquinas' whole hierarchy of being, therefore, is none other than a hierarchy of law! Not only is God regarded as law, but also the angels (as separate intellectual

---

Jones, has detailed the centrality of the Creator/creature distinction for Christianity over against paganism in numerous works, including *The Other Worldview: Exposing Christianity's Greatest Threat*.
29. Taylor, *The Christian Philosophy of Law, Politics and the State*, 175.

substances) and the human being (in whom the intellect is compounded with matter). Plato's laws (ideas and numbers themselves) existed in the intelligible world. But Aquinas' laws lie in the world that the senses can observe (the evident influence of Aristotle).

Plato's realism viewed laws as real things (the law has been cosmologised). In Aquinas, we find the opposite: things were turned into laws (the cosmos has been made into law). Summed up: (1.) according to Aquinas, the law for creatures exists *ante rem* (*before* the things) in God. (2.) God creates these archetypes *in rebus* (*into* the cosmic things). (3.) The law also exists through rational abstraction *post rem* (*after* the things) in the intellect of human beings.

The above concludes that Aquinas' ontology or doctrine of reality is a type of nomology (a view of the law). His philosophy tends towards nomism or an absolutization of the idea of law. As a result of this idea, Aquinas' nomism even determines the being of God. Aquinas, consequently, turns God into a law-god. The same happens with the cosmos: he turns it into law things.[30]

The thinking of the traditional natural law school followed by many Christians therefore absolutizes and eternalizes the legal principle. But biblically speaking, creational norms are significant only within history and for history (Matt. 5:17–18). Legal norms are not based in an abstract eternal-divine reason in which man's mind participates (Isa. 40:28; 55:8–9; Jer. 10:23; Rom. 11:33; 1 Cor. 2:16), but are part of a created structure of which *historical development* is an important dimension. God's created norms must be realized, positivized, and applied in historical-cultural circumstances, just as the Decalogue was given within history and was applied in case laws for Israel's situation. Biblical law is often called the Law of Moses even though the Ten Commandments were written by the finger of God as a republication

---

30. Bernie Van Der Walt, *Thomas Aquinas and the Neo-Thomist Tradition: A Christian Philosophical Assessment*. Jordan Station, ON: Paideia Press, 2021, 50–51.

of creation law, because their being made valid law (i.e., being enforced and applied) required the human element. As Danie Strauss has written:

> The legacy of natural law discerned an element of the underlying (universal, constant) structure of our legal experience, but it distorted its meaning by assuming that those underlying principles have already been made valid (enforced) for all times and all places. Yet no principle in this fundamental ontic sense is valid *per se*. Every principle requires *human intervention* in order to be made valid, i.e., no (pre-positive) ontic principle holds by and of itself. Only human beings are able to *enforce* them and only human beings can give a positive form or shape to them.[31]

This does not mean history is the *source* of law, God is. But history shapes the *forms* of law in which legal rules originate—this is the intertwining dynamics of constancy and change. The authority and binding character of law are based on the legal principle (the invariant created norm), and the validity of the law is manifest when enforced through the juridical formulation in a given historical situation. This does not mean that a God-given norm or command can become unsound and discarded; it means that at different times it may require a different formulation. One example is the change in the application of the sabbath law between the older and newer forms of the covenant. A contemporary illustration in law would be the *Lex Aquilia* (no liability without fault) no longer being applicable in every tort case of modern law, because with modern technology and in the case of a mass collision of motor vehicles, for example, it is no longer always possible to assign fault to one person.

## Natural Law and the Problem of Sin

Finally, we cannot conclude a discussion of natural law theories and their inadequacy without saying something about the doctrine of man. Under the

---

31. Strauss, *The Philosophy of Herman Dooyeweerd*, 69.

pagan influence of Aristotle's concepts of nature and of God, Aquinas and the Christian natural law theorists who follow him have not given due weight to the problem of sin and the Fall. This is largely the result of a faulty view of the human person. Aquinas' philosophy, in its synthesis with Aristotelianism, implies the recognition of the existence of a purely natural sphere of ethical and rational values to which right reason has access. This yields an ostensibly religiously neutral concept of the *animale rationale*. With human reason supposedly participating in eternal *forms*, man's capacity to grasp the dictates of natural reason pertaining to right and wrong, good and evil, just and unjust, remains essentially intact. Here, sin has *not* affected man's access to a realm of *natural* ethical values in which the state, in its political and legal relations, finds its *raison d'etre*.

Certainly, the Thomists would argue, sin took from man particular *supernatural* gifts (a higher realm of grace and faith), leaving him in a state of "privation." But man's essential nature, the *image of God* located in his intellectual reason and free will, though weakened, was left largely unaffected. It was only his *likeness* to God rather than the *image* of God which was distorted.[32] By this device, Aquinas had creatively worked around the biblical teaching that by his sin, man had not simply been deprived of a "supernature" (*donum superadditum*, a superadded gift of grace), but had lost the image he was created to reflect in righteousness holiness and dominion (which scripturally was part of his created nature, not a supernaturally added gift), rendering him "unnatural, inhuman and demoniac."[33] Indeed, Aquinas argued that the essential constitution of human nature is neither destroyed nor diminished by sin. In particular, the rational powers of the intellectual soul are undiminished, which is the part of man able to grasp the meaning of justice and virtue. Though the *gift of original righteousness or justice* was totally lost through the sin of our first parents, the natural inclination to virtue as part of man's essential nature is only *somewhat* diminished by sin.[34] As such,

---

32. Perks, *The Politics of God and the Politics of Man*, 155–69.
33. Taylor, *The Christian Philosophy of Law, Politics and the State*, 159.
34. Aquinas, *Summa*, 20.178.

for Aquinas and all his scholastic followers, "grace does not abolish nature but perfects it."

The tragic consequence is that, despite his sincerity and towering genius, Aquinas effectively empties the biblical doctrine of the Fall of its radical meaning, because, in this dualistic worldview, redemption is for the supernatural realm, restoring the lost gift, and not for the realm of nature, which is simply *perfected* through grace by bringing it to its proper goal. Instead of man being truly dead in trespasses and sins (Eph. 2:1–2) so that he needs to become a new creation to think and act in terms of true justice (Rom. 8:6–7; 2 Cor. 5:17); instead of a ruined world needing to be totally healed, purified, and cleansed because of the pollution of man's wickedness (Dan. 12:8–10; Luke 12:49; 2 Pet. 3:10–13); instead of a creation under a curse awaiting re-creation, redemption, transformation, and liberation from its bondage to corruption (Rom. 8:19–23; Rev. 21:1–6), both man and creation require only the addition of a perfecting principle.

Yet the Bible does not teach a distinction between so-called *natural* and *supernatural* spheres of reality in which we are now deprived of specific supernatural gifts without grace. The biblical distinction is not between *nature* and *grace* at all, but between *sin* and grace—the way of grace or the way of rebellion. The human problem is one of direction, not structure. Sin is not a *metaphysical* problem of privation, but a religious problem centered in the rebellion of man's heart—the root unity of his being. Grace, as Herman Bavinck wrote, "does not serve to take man up into a supernatural order, but to liberate him from sin."[35]

In contrast to the Thomistic error, Cornelius Van Til expresses clearly the scriptural and reformational teaching about the effect of sin upon the human person:

> This doctrine of the *total depravity* of man makes it plain that the moral consciousness of man as he is today cannot be the source of information about what is ideal good or about what is the standard of the good....

---

35. Bavinck, cited in Spykman, *Reformational Theology*, 69.

It is this point particularly that makes it necessary for the Christian to maintain without any apology and without any concession that it is *Scripture, and Scripture alone*, in the light of which all moral questions must be answered. Scripture as an external revelation became necessary because of the sin of man. No man living can even put the moral problem as he ought to put it, or ask the moral questions as he ought to ask them, unless he does so in the light of Scripture. Man cannot of himself truly face the moral question, let alone answer it.[36]

Thus, true knowledge of law and justice must now be received from the Scriptures:

Originally, man found in experience the manifestation of and the spontaneous response to the law of God, but since the entrance of sin there had to be given an objective manifestation of, and a renewed response to, the law. Scripture as a concomitant to Christ gives the objective manifestation of absolute law and the Spirit of Christ gives to man the renewed response when the law is seen.[37]

## Implications for Law and Politics

Aquinas' failure to recognise this state of affairs, a failure implicit in all natural law theories, meant that the reality of sin could have no part in justifying or explaining the necessity of the jural civil power of the state—especially since Scripture justifies the function of the state to restrain evil (Gen. 9:5–8; Rom. 13; 1 Tim. 1:8–10). This is because, following Aristotle, political obligation is seen as *inherent* in man's original nature. One cannot conceive of man without the state because it is only *through the state* that he can fulfil his earthly end.

---

36. Cornelius Van Til, *The Defense of the Faith*, 3rd ed. (Philadelphia: Presbyterian and Reformed Publishing Company, 1967), 54.
37. Cornelius Van Til, *The Ten Commandments* (Phillipsburg, NJ: Presbyterian and Reformed Publishing Company, 1974), 5.

Taylor clearly sees the implication of this for Aquinas' view of politics, law, and culture—a purely natural and rational explanation could now be offered for all human social institutions:

> Because his basic presupposition about human nature is biblically false everything else he builds upon it is false and shot through with error, no matter how eloquently and logically argued. If human nature is really such as Thomas supposes, what need had man for God's grace and help at all? Why bother bringing God into the human picture at all, if man is already perfectly rational and capable of achieving his own destiny and realizing his own potentialities in this world?[38]

As far as law, politics, and culture are concerned, Christ and His *revealed* Word are largely made redundant. There is no need for a *distinctly* Christian philosophy of anything; no demand for a uniquely Christian world-and-life view; no requirement to *think Christianly* about all of life. Unknown to Thomas, the seeds needed for producing a secular order and the "churchification" of the Word of God were being planted. In fact, from this point of view, "Thomas may well be considered the first modern liberal humanist in respect to his political and sociological thought."[39] As a result, Rushdoony observes,

> The revival of Aristotle made the Enlightenment inevitable, because the Enlightenment simply took over these concepts of right reason and natural law and carried them to their logical conclusion. Christianity and the church were very quickly seen to be excess baggage.[40]

As biblical law was gradually deemphasized during this period to make way for right reason and natural law, Deism and Romanticism quickly followed and, on their heels, liberal theology. The postmortem of Taylor on the

---

38. Taylor, *The Christian Philosophy of Law, Politics and the State*, 159–60.
39. Taylor, *The Christian Philosophy of Law, Politics and the State*, 160.
40. Rushdoony, *An Informed Faith*, 532.

legacy of the attempt to christen "The Philosopher" in the search for law and justice is telling and challenging:

> The Thomistic attempt to synthesize the wine of the Gospel with the oil of Aristotelianism has been the most misguided effort in the history of human thought. Far from baptising Aristotle into Christ, as he thought, Aquinas merely succeeded in opening the flood gates to modern humanistic apostasy, and the Leviathan godless state.[41]

Though the Reformation era had broken *in principle* from natural theology and the natural law tradition in its reassertion of biblical authority, widely expounding and applying the authority of biblical law when seeking to relate God's will to society, lacking an alternate philosophical *prolegomena* for their cultural theology, they fell back frequently onto the concept of natural law. As a result, for centuries, the Protestant church has all too often been caught up in a paralyzing and tragic contradiction between its ethics and its theological profession. A good illustration in this regard was the Christian philosopher, John Locke, whose thought impacted legal and political reality well beyond England into France and, via Rousseau, informed the French Revolution. The American colonies were also profoundly shaped by his thinking—the Declaration of Independence being deeply influenced by Locke through Thomas Jefferson and Samuel Adams. Downie's analysis of Locke is telling:

> He put into plain English, and he dressed in an English dress of sober grey cloth, doctrines which ultimately go back to the Porch and the Stoic teachers of antiquity. There is, he taught, a Natural Law rooted and grounded in the reasonable nature of man: there are Natural Rights existing in virtue of such law....
>
> Though Locke was a Christian, and attempted to derive his theories from Scripture, he was even then blinded to God's immediate rule of creation by this idea of

---

41. Taylor, *The Christian Philosophy of Law, Politics and the State*, 162.

an intermediate body of natural laws, innate to the nature of reasonable men. The tragic oversight of the impact of the fall on man's analytic capacity; the failure to perceive God's immediate rule of creation by His Word, were fixed in the minds of seventeenth-century Christians such as Locke because Christians had been shedding blood over doctrinal matters. These leading thinkers were driven *from* revelation by the conflicting appeals *to* revelation made by the ecclesia of the day while pursuing heresies with sword and faggot! The body of Christ had discredited itself in the management of public affairs. The present hostility of unbelievers as well as some Christians to "mixing" religion and politics can be traced to this period of history.[42]

This schizophrenic predicament continues as some amongst a younger generation of Protestant Christians, struggling in the decay of Western culture, cast about among the scholastics of the premodern world for resources to understand law, justice, and the state.[43] It is undoubtedly extraordinarily naïve, as Willem J. Ouweneel points out, to expect that both believing and unbelieving people, by means of an alleged "natural awareness" of principles and laws, "can construct a properly working nation state, society, judicial order, or economic order [when] this 'nature' is totally corrupt."[44] And yet, there is a perennial fascination with the idea of finding a basis for law and justice without the Scriptures and a direct appeal to Jesus Christ. But as Jacques Ellul notes, in order to know what is just, right. and true, man will do almost anything to avoid the necessity of receiving revelation:

> Every "Christian" view of natural law is placed in this framework. Man must be allowed to know of himself what is a proper regulation of society. Christians and non-Christians must come to an understanding on the lines of sound social and

---

42. Downie, "Natural Law and God's Law: An Antithesis," 81.
43. For example, in his book, *The Case for Christian Nationalism*, Stephen Wolfe attempts to patch together a political philosophy based on scholastic assumptions and natural law principles, without any meaningful engagement with Scripture or biblical theology. The "Christian" element is not essential to the project.
44. Ouweneel, *The World Is Christ's*, 89.

political order, based on capacities common to all men. They must be able to work together on this foundation and build the best human society. In the process God is considered more and more an outside factor. In all theories of natural law God appears more like a presupposition convenient for reasoning, like a hypothesis which is necessary as a point of departure, rather than as the living God, unique in three persons, at the same time creator, savior and revealer.[45]

And yet despite all their philosophical subtleties, one serious error of natural law theories is their failure to take proper account of the logical impossibility of moving from *observational data* (or hypotheses) to actual *ethical commands*. Which is to say, even if man's autonomous thought could penetrate reality to observe the existence of a natural moral and legal law in "nature," we cannot legitimately move from the observational "is" of abstract principle, to a moral "oughtness"—because ethical *obligation* can only arise by the command of a personal God. In short, "is" and "ought" are distinct categories. Just because there *is* a road sign saying "detour" doesn't mean I *ought* to follow the detour.

The great *danger* of all natural law theories is their tendency to *absolutize* that ostensible law in nature as an *eternal order* known by the natural fallen intellect, apart from the Scriptures and the illumination of the Holy Spirit. Law is shunted off to the heavens among the transcendent forms to be pondered and interpreted by the reasonings of the philosophers and intellectual elite. And yet nothing could be further from the tenor of the Bible, for God says through Moses:

> This command that I give you today is certainly not too difficult or beyond your reach. It is not in heaven so that you have to ask, "Who will go up to heaven, get it for us, and proclaim it to us so that we may follow it?" And it is not across the sea so that you have to ask, "Who will cross the sea, get it for us, and proclaim it to us so that we may follow it?" But the message is very near you, in your mouth and in your heart, so that you may follow it (Deut. 30:11–14).

---

45. Ellul, *The Theological Foundations of Law*, 11.

We have no excuse. God has revealed His law with clarity in His Word. But just as our first parents sought to hide from God and cover themselves by their own creative devices, so the essence of their error is repeated when we seek to use "nature" in false modesty to cover our own tracks, whilst usurping God's prerogative as lawgiver, by defining for ourselves good and evil, justice and injustice, virtue and vice. Indeed, it appears that "natural law is a fig leaf whereby man attempts to cover his moral and intellectual nakedness, and the attempt is a failure."[46]

---

46. Rushdoony, *An Informed Faith*, 529.

CHAPTER 5

# Think Christianly About Law (Part 2)
## Theonomy, History, and Messiah

*Fear God, and keep his commandments; this is the whole meaning of man. No act of thine but God will bring it under his scrutiny, deep beyond all thy knowing, and pronounce it good or evil.*
— Ecclesiastes 12:13–14 (Knox Bible)

## The Biblical Norm for Justice

WE HAVE SEEN IN THE previous chapter that unless, through biblical revelation, God Himself teaches us about His will and reveals to us His law-Word, we would not of ourselves, in our sinful and ruined condition, seek true justice or rightly apply His norms for legal life. In addition, we noted that because *jural* norms regulate relations between people and human institutions, law is concerned with the just balancing of human legal interests—that is, with giving people their due.

It is here that the Word of God, the law revealed in lingual form, gives us a clear criterion or jural principle. The biblical norm of *retribution* (or tribution) must be at the heart of the jural meaning of law if we are to think Christianly. In Exodus 21:24–25 we see an excellent example of this principle formulated in what is referred to in Latin as the *Lex Talionis*, the law of recompense or retaliation: "If there is an injury, then you must give life for life, eye for eye, tooth for tooth, hand for hand, foot for foot, burn for burn, bruise for bruise, wound for wound."

This important passage is sometimes used sneeringly by thoughtless skeptics who think they have identified barbarism in the Bible. First, however, it must be noted that reference to this principle always occurs in law court contexts and *not* in personal relationships outside the courts (something Jesus addresses in the Sermon on the Mount in Matthew 5–7).[1] Second, the norm expressed here is not that a judge is to order the burning of one who burned someone else, or bruise the perpetrator who has bruised a victim, rather it is concerned with the *jural principle* of restitution. Here, in the case of personal injury, the retribution must be commensurate with the nature and scale of the offense—in short, *proportionality* is view. The will of God is that justice be done through *retribution* and *restitution*, such that a harmony of public legal interests is maintained and punishments fit the crime. The principle of just retribution therefore prevents excessive severity or excessive laxity in the administration of justice by the magistrate.

Although man sins against his better knowledge without the renewing influence of the gospel, the central meaning of justice as *retribution* (which includes the principle of restitution) is grasped through *direct intuition* by God's creatures bound to His creation-order, which is why we can understand

---

1. Richard E. Averbeck, "The Law and the Gospels," in *The Oxford Handbook of Biblical Law*, ed. Pamela Barmash (New York: Oxford University Press, 2019), 409–23, 416.

the central religious *meaning* of the Decalogue, which republishes this norm. Man's jural norm-consciousness stems from the suppressed awareness that the judgment of God rests upon the lawless and evildoers individually and corporately (Rom. 1:18–32). It is an insight not deduced from something else, because the norm of retribution in the jural dimension of life is *irreducible* to another dimension of life and *indefinable* insofar as trying to define it leads only to using other words for the same concept.

## Justice and Love

It is critical to observe that this norm for legal justice does not conflict with the meaning of love in the moral sphere of life. Scripture reveals that the love of God lies at the religious root of God's relationship to creation and is covenantal in character (Zeph. 3:17; John 3:16; Rom. 8:37–39; Eph. 2:4–5; 1 John 4:9–10, 16). It is therefore important to see that retribution is the undergirding foundation of love in its moral sense. This is because legal norms are *presupposed* in the commandment to love God and neighbor— since you cannot love your neighbor while denying them what they are due (Rom. 13:8–10). The jural norms express the love of God and neighbor as the principles for *public order,* whereas ethical norms express the love of God and neighbor in our *personal lives.*

This is why not all sins are crimes, which means that not all ethical misdeeds have a jural penalty. And yet the *moral* commands of the Decalogue, such as "You shall not murder," or "You shall not steal," clearly appeal to the legal order, without which the concepts of murder and theft have no meaning. It is a marvel to see in this biblical structure that justice is the temporal foundation of love in that it protects the weak and the wronged and restores order when disrupted by wickedness. As such, we must not try to break down the crucial distinction between *legal* norms and the *moral* demand for love to neighbor, as though justice is somehow unloving—nothing could be further from the truth! Such reductionism produces great injustice and the coddling of criminals. Love certainly goes beyond justice, but not without justice as its foundation. To set love and justice in opposition to each other is a false dichotomy, an artificial contradiction, that leads to a world of tyranny by shattering the idea of justice itself.

This oppressive tendency is seen when the *goal* of legal justice is distorted. That goal is not primarily deterrence (though that may at times be a secondary benefit), neither is it moral education (though law does teach values). It is certainly not a form of "treatment" for a social illness. Crime is not a disease, but rebellion against God's law-order that demands retribution and restitution. If crime were a disease, then you might be cured by compulsion and "treated" for anything the state deems to be a sickness! C. S. Lewis' warning about humanitarian theories of justice is profound:

> The Humanitarian theory removes from Punishment the concept of Desert. But the concept of Desert is the only connecting link between punishment and justice. It is only as deserved or undeserved that a sentence can be just or unjust.... There is no sense in talking about a "just deterrent" or "just cure." We demand of a deterrent not whether it is just but whether it will deter. We demand of a cure not whether it is just but whether it succeeds. Thus when we cease to consider what the criminal deserves and consider only what will cure him or deter others, we have tacitly removed him from the sphere or justice altogether; instead of a person, a subject of rights, we now have a mere object, a "case."...

> But the humanitarian theory wants simply to abolish Justice and substitute Mercy for it. This means you start being "kind" to people before you have considered their rights, and then force upon them supposed kindnesses which they in fact had a right to refuse, and finally kindnesses which no one but you will recognize as kindnesses and which the recipient will feel as abominable cruelties. You have overshot the mark. Mercy detached from Justice grows unmerciful. That is the important paradox. As there are plants which will flourish only in mountain soil, so it appears that Mercy will flower only when it grows in the crannies of the rock of Justice: transplanted to the marshlands of mere Humanitarianism, it becomes

a man-eating weed, all the more dangerous because it is still called by the same name as the mountain variety.[2]

We can either retain the biblical legal norm of just retribution as the central meaning of justice, and therefore stand with the law of God, or be condemned to the control and "healing" of a pseudo-scientific elite.

The all-important biblical manifestation of the unity of love and justice is found in the work of the Lord Jesus Christ. At the cross, Christ has vindicated and proven the sanctity of God's law, and reconciled the righteousness of the law and divine love by paying the price for man's lawlessness (Isa. 53:5; Titus 2:14; 1 Pet. 3:18). There, He bore the retributive punishment for sin demanded by a holy and just God (that of death and eternal destruction) whilst manifesting His divine love (Rom. 5:8–11). The love of Christ and work of Christ established a new relationship between heaven and earth in the Newer Covenant in His blood. That relationship is bringing about the destruction of lawlessness as Christ sends out His people in terms of His Kingdom purposes till finally, He destroys the man of lawlessness at His unveiling:

> For the mystery of lawlessness is already at work, but the one now restraining will do so until he is out of the way, and then the lawless one will be revealed. The Lord Jesus will destroy him with the breath of His mouth and will bring him to nothing with the brightness of His coming (2 Thess. 2:7–8).

A strong delusion is at work in our antinomian Western culture, and behind it is the lawless one, drawing people to believe what is false among those who delight in unrighteousness but hate the truth. E. L. Hebden Taylor warned that without belief in God's sovereign law-order as the standard of justice, there remains no valid basis for the enforcement of law in a society moving headlong toward tyranny and ruin:

---

2. C. S. Lewis, "The Humanitarian Theory of Punishment," *Issues in Religion and Psychotherapy* 13, no. 1 (1987): 147–53, https://scholarsarchive.byu.edu/irp/vol13/iss1/11 (accessed February 2025), 148, 153.

When God and His laws and creation structures are rejected by nations then all defense against arbitrary power vanishes too at the same time. If Americans and Britons refuse to acknowledge God as their ultimate sovereign in this life they will finish up having tyrants as their masters because it is only God Himself who can subject the powers of politicians, judges, police and scientists to conscience. Without such a conscience enlightened by God's Word and God's Law there can be no abiding defense against injustice and tyranny.

It is therefore imperative that Christians realise the vital necessity for a constant witness on their part to the saving reforming and liberating power of the Lord Jesus Christ. Before they can hope to change the moral and legal direction now being taken by the nations of the English-speaking world they must reverse the present apostate religious direction. The Christian philosophy of life must not be allowed to hang in thin air but it must be brought down to earth in the hearts and consciences of the common people and in the concrete political, economic and legal situations of life.[3]

## Theonomy and its Emergence

The view that God's biblically revealed laws and creation norms for justice must govern human society rather than man's own arbitrary positive law has been relatively recently labelled "theonomy" by theologians. Though sometimes wrongly identified as a kind of *modern* "movement" because of a concerted restatement in the late twentieth century of the importance of biblical law among some reformed evangelicals,[4] an emphasis on the centrality of biblical law for the Christian life and for the life of peoples and nations has been ubiquitous from the inception of the Christian faith.

---

3. Taylor, *The New Legality*, 51.
4. For a detailed discussion of the origins and thought-leaders of the contemporary movement to reaffirm the abiding validity of God's law for men and nations, see this author's book, *The Mission of God: A Manifesto of Hope for Society*.

From the earliest days of the New Testament era, the law had a central place in the proclamation and *application* of the gospel for believers. In 1 Timothy 1:8–11, the apostle Paul writes concerning God's law:

> But we know that the law is good, provided one uses it legitimately. We know that the law is not meant for a righteous person, but for the lawless and rebellious, for the ungodly and sinful, for the unholy and irreverent, for those who kill their fathers and mothers, for murderers, for the sexually immoral and homosexuals, for kidnappers, liars, perjurers, and for whatever else is contrary to the sound teaching based on the glorious gospel of the blessed God, which was entrusted to me.

It is therefore perplexing to observe the antinomianism that has become rife in the modern church, since we learn plainly from the Scriptures that gospel (Good News) contains law and law contains gospel. St. Paul emphatically denies that the law is contrary to God's promises received by faith, "Is the law therefore contrary to God's promises? Absolutely not!" (Gal. 3:21). The Lord Jesus Himself taught us, "If you love me, you will obey my commandments" (John 14:15). And the apostle John was equally clear, "For this is what love for God is: to keep His commands. And His commands are not burdensome" (1 John 5:3). As Cornelius Van Til wrote:

> [I]t is not true that obedience to the law was an Old Testament requirement, while in the New Testament love has been substituted for obedience. Obedience is love and love is obedience and they alone can adequately respond to a spiritual law.
>
> ...[T]he very content of the Gospel is that Christ has fulfilled the law. Thus, the joy of the gospel is that man can in Christ know and obey the law and therefore live in the presence of God forever. There is no Gospel but that of the law. On the other hand the Gospel is law because all must obey it.[5]

---

5. Van Til, *The Ten Commandments*, 9.

The source of law is God Himself, and it is always according to the glorious gospel. As a result, any opposition between law and gospel is both artificial and impermissible for the truly Christian mind.

The inescapable choice before the Christian, and indeed before the whole of mankind, is very simply autonomy or theonomy. The word autonomy brings together two Greek words meaning *self* and *law*—to be a law to oneself. The term *theonomy* likewise combines two Greek words, *theos* and *nomos*, simply meaning "God's Law." Although the term theonomy has been historically employed in very general terms in writings like those of Paul Tillich as referring to "the state of culture under the impact of the Spiritual Presence"[6] its meaning in current theological and cultural discussion has a more definite and specific implication—that the revealed law of God, properly interpreted, has a binding force and significance today in every aspect of life. This is to say, in the age of the church and the working of the Holy Spirit, the commandments of God in *all Scripture* and their various implications for personal, familial, cultural and political life have lost none of their relevance or universal obligation (Matt. 5:17–20), for "He will not be disheartened or crushed, until He has established justice on the earth; And the coastlands will wait expectantly for His law" (Isa. 42:4). The implication being, rightly understood, the *principles* of God's law remain valid and in force requiring human positivization (i.e., formulation, application, enforcement) within the juridical sphere of modern life. This is the basic meaning of theonomy.

Obedience to the law of God—summarized by the Lord Jesus Christ and the apostle Paul as the essence of our *response* of love toward God and neighbor—is basic to the scriptural vision for social reality:

> And you shall love the Lord your God with all your heart, with all your soul, with all your mind, and with all your strength. This *is* the first commandment. And the second, like *it, is* this: "You shall love your neighbor as yourself." There is no other commandment greater than these (Mark 12:30–32).

---

6. Paul Tillich, Systematic Theology, 3 vols. (Chicago: University of Chicago Press, 1951), 1.83–86 and 147–50, and 3.249–75.

Owe no one anything except to love one another, for he who loves another has fulfilled the law. For the commandments, "You shall not commit adultery," "You shall not murder," "You shall not steal," "You shall not bear false witness," "You shall not covet," and if *there is* any other commandment, are *all* summed up in this saying, namely, "You shall love your neighbor as yourself." Love does no harm to a neighbor; therefore love *is* the fulfillment of the law (Rom.13:8–10).

The reformational theologian, Robert Knudsen, former professor at Westminster Theological Seminary in Philadelphia, in an important essay responding to the question, "May we use the term Theonomy?," answers in the affirmative. The meaning of God's law thus remains perpetually binding:

[T]he Scriptures teach that Christians are to obey the will of God and that this will is expressed in his law. Christ Himself joined love for Himself with keeping his commands. This is important to remember as we observe modern theologians refusing to say that love can be commanded or insisting that there is at best a tension-filled, dialectical relationship between love and law....

[I]t is also inconceivable that there will be any changes in the meaning of God's law as expressed in the Ten Commandments.[7]

## The Ancient World

Setting forth the abiding validity of the law is no novel opinion. It is noteworthy that the early church apologist Justin Martyr, who despite the influence of Greek philosophy upon him, boldly confronted paganism, employs the distinction of moral, ceremonial and judicial law (without negative remark on the judicial law)—a distinction utilized centuries later during the Protestant Reformation. Moreover, Julius Firmicus Maternus,

---

7. Robert D. Knudsen, *Roots and Branches: The Quest for Meaning and Truth in Modern Thought* (Jordan Station: Paideia Press, 2009), 95–96.

a Roman Christian apologist in the early fourth century during the reign of Constantine I makes an explicit appeal to the *judicial laws of Moses* in his argumentation.[8]

This historic turning to the resources of God's law among serious believers from the early centuries in the life of the church should be no surprise, because Christian life and thought, in the ongoing conflict with the myth of the pagan world, is not otherworldly, but concerned with the life of humanity in relationship to God and neighbor within human society. The Byzantine scholar and professor of early church history, John A. McGuckin, has pointed out in this regard that in the first two centuries of the church, "Mosaic Torah remains as a paradigmatic guide."[9] He affirms that from the earliest time Christians made a distinction between the ceremonial elements in the Law (liturgical rules, food regulations etc.,) and the moral prescriptions, "The moral laws are held by the Church to still be in force."[10] Though the older form of Sabbath observance, the covenantal mark of circumcision in the flesh and other outward distinguishing marks and practices were set aside for God's people, the meaning and applicability of the Law continued. As such:

> Christianity emerges as a religion with its eyes firmly fixed on society: a religion that has definite social aspirations despite its claims to be the eschatological community. It is a religion that wishes to build a civilisation, not one that is simply running to hide itself. Even if it has "seen" the New Jerusalem in another place, that very radiant vision makes the Church see the Earthly City in a new light...; that proximity between what is aspired to as the ideal *politeia* and what is presently experienced forms a tension that drives so much of eastern Christian political

---

8. J. Lecler, Toleration and Reformation, trans. T. L. Westow, 2 vols. (London: Longmans, 1960). On Martyr's distinction and attitude, see Marc A. Clauson, "The Mosaic Judicial Law in the Early Church" (unpublished paper, Liberty University, 1990), 7.
9. John A. McGuckin, *The Ascent of Christian Law: Patristic and Byzantine Formulations of a New Civilization* (New York: St. Vladimir's Seminary Press, 2012), 19.
10. McGuckin, *The Ascent of Christian Law*, 19.

theology. In no more than two centuries from this time, Christianity will assume charge of the whole empire of the Romans.[11]

The central difference between the pagan and Christian view of law concerned the *source* of law. In the ancient world, man arrogated the role of lawgiver to himself, especially as embodied in the king or head of state. Likewise, we noted in the previous chapter that for Plato, Aristotle, and the Greek philosophers, the source of law was human reason. Not human reason in general, but the rational insight of guardian philosophers should rule the state; any kind of *external law* to "hem in" the philosophical genius was anathema. This ideal of rule by philosopher-kings led naturally to the devaluing of the individual (since there is no concept of the equality of all before a transcendent law from God) and instead an emphasis on the collective—the state. But biblical faith introduced, in principle, a radical break with pagan thought with its invoking of a *theocratic* conception of law:

> By restoring a profound sense of an external *theocratically ordered* standard of justice (the scriptural and evangelical charter), Byzantine Christianity, paradoxically, restored to the social order a profound sense of the importance of the individual, the person, and in this alone it made a most radical critique of Platonic premises.[12]

As Christians began to engage with classical Roman law, successive *Christianized* emperors began to reform it in terms of the Bible and teaching of the church. By the time of the Justinian Code in the sixth century, which bridged the gap from the classical to medieval world, a new central principle was now at work, "society was bonded in common rights and obligations because of its primary bond under God."[13]

As R. J. Rushdoony has pointed out:

---

11. McGuckin, *The Ascent of Christian Law*, 25.
12. McGuckin, *The Ascent of Christian Law*, 34; italics added.
13. McGuckin, *The Ascent of Christian Law*, 253.

> As the early [church] councils faced problems, they set forth canons or truths and laws in terms of Scripture. True canon law is Biblical law. Canon law most certainly applied and applies to the church, but we miss a critical fact of history if we fail to see that Christians have always held that canon law applies also to nations.... During most of the church's history, the church has seen God's rule or canon as applicable to all men, institutions, and states. In fact, the justice pagans recognized in old Rome in the canon law led them to go to church courts with their cases. So much of the litigation by AD 300 was in the hands of the church courts that Constantine, on gaining power, gave bishops the status of Roman magistrates in order to give official status to the governing courts! To this day, bishops wear the garb and carry the insignia of Roman magistrates. For some centuries after the fall of Rome, canon or Biblical law was the only law of Europe....
>
> Canon or biblical law was [later] restricted to the church by the rise of natural law. The natural law advocates, in turning to the old Greco-Roman concept, did not realize what they were doing. Ostensibly, they found classical support for Biblical faith; in reality, they undermined it.[14]

Incredibly, this meant that Christian preaching and the permeation of biblical law into Roman law throughout the first few centuries had in large measure achieved the demise of slavery, the end of the blood-letting games of the Roman colosseum, the radical transformation of marriage and the family, the practical elimination of abortion and infanticide, and the transformation of certain political institutions of the Empire.[15] The law codes of Christian emperors Constantine and Justinian in particular (especially through the influence of Justinian's wife, Theodora), bear the hallmarks of Christian teaching in addressing the place of women, the condition of the poor, the treatment of slaves and prisoners, gladiatorial contests, marriage

---

14. R. J. Rushdoony, *An Informed Faith: The Position Papers of R. J. Rushdoony*. Vol. 2, Ecclesiology, Doctrine and Biblical Law (Vallecito, CA: Ross House Books, 2017), 2.534–35.
15. Jean-Marc Berthoud, *In Defense of God's Law*, trans. Molly Anderson Orr (Tallahassee, FL: Zurich Publishing, 2022), 141.

and family, divorce, adultery, property, inheritance, and criminal law.[16] This steady transformation was rooted, as McGuckin explains, in a new Christian anthropology that overthrew Aristotle:

> The position of the unfree woman or the slave, as the ancient Greeks would argue, however, is not negotiable, since they are unable, precisely because of their position, to argue the philosophical case for change. As non-free, unreflective agents they live the unexamined life. Aristotle's entire premise of this inbuilt vision of inequality will be challenged by Christianity's new anthropology. The unexamined life of the working man, woman or the slave, in ancient terms, is cast down root and branch by Christianity's understanding of the sacred and individual worth of all human souls as redeemed images of the divine.[17]

## The Middle Ages

By the High Middle Ages, Western medieval Christendom, looking for intellectual resources to combat Islam as well as to justify the traditional social order, was in the process of being shaped by the scholastic movement. This was powerfully expressed in the thirteenth century by the eventually dominant thought of Thomas Aquinas—the effective patron saint of Roman Catholic theology and the "doctor angelicus." And yet, despite the profound influence of Aristotle and natural law ideals of pagan origin in Aquinas' thought—Greek philosophy giving shape to his theological project—he nonetheless states plainly in his classic *Summa Theologica*: "The written law is said to be given for the correction of natural law... because the natural law was

---

16. For representative studies on this topic, see James Allan Evans, *The Empress Theodora: Partner of Justinian* (Austin: University of Texas Press, 2002), and Peter J. Leithart, *Defending Constantine: The Twilight of an Empire and the Dawn of Christendom* (Downers Grove, IL: InterVarsity Academic, 2010).
17. McGuckin, *The Ascent of Christian Law*, 36.

perverted in the hearts of some men... so that they thought those things good which are naturally evil, which perversion stood in need of correction."[18]

Again, because Aquinas was working with two sources of authority (the Bible and Greek philosophy), there is an unresolved tension in his affirmation of biblical law *and* an Aristotelian conception of natural law—a law he reasons must be perverted in the hearts of some people. Nonetheless, his use of biblical law was not a passing generalization without concrete application or civic sanction, but included a recognition that it is tyrants who legislate *contrary* to God's revealed law. Aquinas carefully differentiated the various types of law in the older testament and recognized that although the details may vary with circumstances, the *principles* remain entirely valid—the judicial precepts being required to maintain justice in the civil sphere. In fact, Aquinas cites numerous passages from the Pentateuch in support of his argument:

> We must therefore distinguish three kinds of precept in the Old Law: namely moral precepts, which are dictated by the natural law; ceremonial precepts, which are determinations of Divine worship; and judicial precepts, which are determinations of the justice to be maintained among men.[19]

The ceremonial aspects Aquinas sees as set aside because they are fulfilled in Christ's priestly office, but the judicial elements remain unaffected since they do not concern the restorative and priestly aspects of salvation but are there to regulate *external behavior*. In a ground-breaking lecture on "Theonomy in the Middle Ages," Professor Marc A. Clauson has argued persuasively from the source material that:

> Thomas follows the Mosaic judicial laws closely, justifying the various punishments without modification or criticism, including the comprehensive details

---

18. Thomas Aquinas, *Summa Theologica*, trans. Fathers of the English Dominican Province, rev. Daniel J. Sullivan, 2 vols., *Great Books of the Western World 19–20* (Chicago: Encyclopedia Britannica, 1952), II.I, q. 94, art. 5, Reply Obj. 1.
19. Aquinas, *The Summa Theologica*, II.I., q. 99, art. 4.

such as restitution for varieties of theft, wrongful death, negligence regarding animals, "man stealing," adultery, and even, surprisingly, the death penalty for a rebellious son....

In every case, he gives ample evidence that the judicial precepts are just as valid in his own day as they were for the Hebrew Commonwealth. This is not to say that Aquinas sought to *require* the adoption of the details of the Old Testament Mosaic judicial laws. On the contrary, he sees them as valid in principle. In other words, he advocates a "general equity" theory of Theonomy.[20]

Clauson shows that Aquinas, as someone who represented Medieval thought in the West, regarded the Lord Jesus as having placed the administration of judicial precepts in the hands of temporal authorities, and regarded the biblical judicial precepts as valid and their application appropriate though not necessarily binding, whilst the underlying principles remain both valid and binding on the civil magistrate.[21]

## The Reformation and Modern Era

When it comes to the Reformation era, we can observe that without apology, the Rhineland, Huguenot, Dutch, Scottish, Swiss, and Puritan commonwealths clearly founded their regional polities on the book of Deuteronomy. Martin Bucer, John Calvin, and Pierre Viret had led the way in holding high the law of God for all of life. Viret expounded the law at great length, and wrote in the preface to his commentary on the law:

> I have proposed to declare the law of God, which must be held as the rule of all others by which men must be directed and governed.

---

20. Marc A. Clauson, "Theonomy in the Middle Ages: The Case of Thomas Aquinas," lecture delivered at the American Political Science Association Annual Meeting, Washington, DC, 2005, 24, 26; italics added.
21. Clauson, "Theonomy in the Middle Ages," 26.

...God wanted Himself to give a law which would be used as a rule to all men of the earth to regulate mind, understanding, will, and affections, as much of those who must govern the other as of those who must be governed by them. And He has done this in order that, all together, they would recognize one God for their sovereign Prince and Lord and that they would recognize themselves as His servants and ministers.... [He] comprehended in that law all moral teaching necessary for men to live well. He has done this much better, incomparably so, than all the philosophers and all their books, those of ethics as well as of politics and economics, and than all the legislators who have ever been and those who are and will be, in all their laws and ordinances.... [T]his law could function for us as true Christian ethics, economics and politics, if well attended to.[22]

A similar perspective was adopted by the Reformers' heirs in England, the Puritans, who regarded and applied the equity of God's law very seriously to family, church, and state.[23] Perhaps more surprising, national *covenants* based on the Pentateuch were originally used in the founding of many colonies in British North America, again following the Puritans in England. Scholarly review of the relevant literature reveals that by the time of the American Revolution, the polemical political argumentation between 1765 and 1805 contained more citations from Deuteronomy than all the European political philosophers combined![24]

It is therefore very clear that from the time of the first codification of English law with Alfred the Great in the ninth century (which began with the Ten Commandments), to our present era with its steady *repeal* of biblical laws, the legal jurisprudence in the Anglosphere has for centuries developed in perpetual interaction with the revealed law of God.[25] In fact, biblical

---

22. This original translation from the French is taken from Berthoud, *In Defense of God's Law*, 143–44.
23. For a detailed study of the Christian impact on law in the Reformation and post-Reformation period, see Harold J. Berman, *Law and Revolution*, vol. 1, *The Formation of the Western Legal Tradition* (London: Harvard University Press, 1983).
24. Daniel J. Elazar and Stuart A. Cohen, *The Jewish Polity* (Bloomington, IN: Indiana University Press, 1985), 121–34, 137–45.
25. Berman, *Law and Revolution*, 65.

faith, not natural law, in several striking examples, is the sole reason for the abolition of man-theft and enslavement, polygamy, and infanticide in the West, which were all ubiquitous in the classical world.[26] Conversely, dechristianization in legal jurisprudence is the central reason for the scourge of abortion, no-fault divorce, pornography, prostitution, euthanasia, the advent of the legal fiction of "homosexual marriage," the legalisation and promotion of various forms of sexual perversion, the denial of human sexual identity as male and female, and the general decline of freedom.

## Law and Constitution

Sadly, the *historical* significance and formative influence of God's revealed law in the West tends to be missed or swiftly passed over by both unbelieving and Christian critics of a theonomic vision for the social order. It is regrettable that in contemporary culture, the past is often seen, even by many professing Christians, as something to be *transcended* rather than gratefully *inherited* and built upon—imagining that what is latest is best, whilst what has antiquity must be outdated and irrelevant. As a result, many become angry or upset when those concerned with a *recovery* of biblical law move beyond theoretical theological discussion or historical review, and challenge the socio-political status quo by speaking of the transformative power and importance of the law of God for *today* in the context of secular liberal democracies.

Whilst it must be granted as obvious that biblical Israel was constituted somewhat differently from the modern nation-states of Europe or America, that does not mean biblical law has nothing to say to these nation-states today. In fact, unknown to many, the law of God contains material that defines the legal status of persons and regulations for the exercise of governmental power. The Bible is in many respects a covenantal, and therefore

---

26. See Vishal Mangalwadi, *The Book That Made Your World: How the Bible Created the Soul of Western Civilisation* (Nashville: Thomas Nelson, 2011).

*public legal document,* that enables certain kinds of communities, polities, and civil societies to emerge under its guidance. As a result, *covenant* is a seminal *political* idea.

The constitution of the Hebrews is grounded in God's covenant Word which constitutionalizes His relationship to Israel. Through this special treaty, a people, individually and collectively, are "called out" to live in freedom under God with specific obligations. Jonathan Burnside explains that Deuteronomy 16:18–18:22 sets out a division and balance of power between judges or elders from among the people, the king, priests, and prophets, ensuring that power could not be concentrated in the hands of any single human authority, in marked contrast to the Israelite experience in Egypt under Pharoah and what developed later among the Babylonian kings and the Roman Caesars. In short, there was to be no divine-human configuration, no "imperial man."[27]

In the self-understanding of Scripture, which is self-attesting, the Torah as a whole forms the model constitution to be emulated by *all* the nations (Deut. 4:5–8). As Van Til appropriately reminds us:

> All men have disobeyed the law, yet all men must obey the law. The fact that the command comes directly to "God's people" only is due to the economy of redemption rather than to any difference of obligation between one nation and another. God deals with man generally and federally.... The several stages in the economy of redemption do not in the least affect the requirements of God's law.[28]

Indeed, a structure which sets all authority under the sovereignty of the King of all kings has proven itself compatible with various constitutional arrangements. Interestingly, rabbinic commentary claims that the Torah was given in the wilderness (and not later in Jerusalem, during a period of

---

27. Jonathan Burnside, "Old Testament: Torah and Constitutionalism," in *Christianity and Constitutionalism*, ed. Nicholas Aroney and Ian Leigh (Oxford: Oxford University Press, 2022), 33–57, 39.
28. Van Til, *The Ten Commandments*, 7

monarchy) precisely so that all nations could accept it as their own![29] Much of it consists largely of practical *case studies* regarding implementing justice in various circumstances, demanding that judges, who are chosen by ordinary people and are not political appointees (Deut. 16:18–19) "judge the people with righteous judgment" (Deut. 16:18). The goal of the covenantal arrangement is that righteousness and justice are done according to God's standards. This necessitates wisely applying (i.e., positivizing) God's instruction, whilst demanding real limits, not just on judges, but also on the king, to prevent the monarch from becoming like a pagan sovereign and turning the state into a totalitarian power center. These restrictions included limiting the stockpiling of weapons of war (Deut. 17:16), the contracting of multiple marriages with foreigners in order to consolidate power, and the control of economic life in terms of taxes, confiscation, and plunder (Deut. 17:17). The central positive duty required of the king is very telling indeed:

> When he is seated on his royal throne, he is to write a copy of this instruction for himself on a scroll in the presence of the Levitical priests. It is to remain with him, and he is to read from it all the days of his life, so that he may learn to fear the Lord his God, to observe all the words of this instruction, and to do these statutes. Then his heart will not be exalted above his countrymen, he will not turn from this command to the right or the left (Deut. 17:18–20).

Clearly, there was to be no *absolute* monarch, for the ruler is required to be a vassal king under God—to serve the law and the people in his sphere of authority. In particular, the king was not permitted to usurp the roles of the priests and Levites (1 Sam. 13:8–14; 1 Kings 21), a limitation that radically relativized his role and authority under God, separating the jurisdictional spheres of priesthood (church) and kingship (state).

The older testament "church," with its priesthood and prophets, was likewise radically limited—in the case of priests, through laws regarding land ownership (Deut. 18:1–2), and because the Torah was a public document that

---

29. Burnside, "Torah and Constitutionalism," 47–48.

was read and taught throughout Israelite society—against which the teaching of priests and Levites could be measured. A covenantally educated society produced accountability at all levels of government. In the case of prophets, who were frequently a constitutional check on wayward monarchs and independent of the priesthood, false prophets were weeded out by public tests of their integrity and veracity (Deut. 18:14–22). As the Scriptures say, "To the Law and to the Testimony! If they do not speak according to this word, it is because there is no light in them" (Is. 8:20, NKJV). If we were to hold political and church leaders to this standard today, what kind of a church and society might we enjoy?

Burnside helpfully summarizes the constitutional arrangements in biblical Israel:

> These include (1) a kind of separation of powers; (2) a "covenant" between ethnic or other groups as the basis for the constitution rather than the rights of the individual; (3) a focus on citizen obligations rather than rights; (4) a head of state that is under, and not above the law; (5) restraints on capital and land markets to protect family and community relationships; and (6) the importance of collocated extended families for the provision of welfare.[30]

Burnside's conclusion is poignant in arguing that theonomically oriented constitutional life, compatible with various political regimes, would take serious note of what biblical law teaches regarding "finance, avoidance of national debt, criminal justice, administration of welfare and health care, and a host of other areas...."[31] Since idolatry always leads to injustice (which is why the standards of pagan thinking can never be the measure of justice), so true worship and obedience will lead to justice and blessing upon the peoples (Amos 5:8–15, 24). We may rightly conclude that without a constitution faithfully administered under the living God and His law, decay, decadence,

---

30. Burnside, "Torah and Constitutionalism," 48.
31. Burnside, "Torah and Constitutionalism," 49.

and a loss of freedom will inevitably steadily follow (Prov. 1: 20–33; 14:34; Amos 6:8).

In sum, God's law is an inescapable aspect of His sovereignty and total authority over men and nations. Scripture gives no room for antinomianism and destroys the myth of human autonomy (cf. Ps. 2; Ps. 110). All legitimate human authority is only a *delegated* and *limited* authority, an office held at the pleasure of the ruler of the kings of the earth (John 19:11; Rev. 1:5). It does not originate with the individual, but comes from God so that people and nations might serve Him. The prophetic and paradigmatic deliverance of Israel from servitude under the totalitarian power of Pharaoh shows the eschatological direction of all history. The Exodus and the giving of the law constituting Israel as a nation signifies the liberation of all nations and political orders to become humble servants of Jesus Christ and His law-Word. (Rom. 13:1–10).

The law continues to address us as prophets, priests, and kings in Christ, directing us as Christians in our cultural calling. Whatever constitutional arrangements we live under, we are sent out to prophesy in His name, speaking the truth to power, holding all authority accountable to the absolute monarch and His covenant law. Because the gospel of the Kingdom is true, Caesar is not Lord, the modern state is not the ultimate sovereign authority—Jesus Christ is! This emphatically relativizes political life and the role of the state, and requires that we live, in each area of our lives, by every word that proceeds from the mouth of God (Deut. 8:3; Matt. 4:4). In the area of public life, this surely means the pursuit of a *covenantal politics* where law and gospel are a seamless garment bringing life and hope to the nations.

## Christ in Context: The Advent of the King

We have now considered the subject of law from philosophical, historical, and finally covenantal viewpoints as it came to expression in the constitution of ancient Israel. But it would be impossible to treat the meaning of law and justice adequately without focusing ultimately on the *living Torah*, the Lord Jesus Christ, the one in whom all authority in heaven and earth, as sovereign Priest and King, is concentrated (Matt. 28:18–20).

To gain proper perspective on the teaching and work of God the Son in relation to the law, we must go back to the very beginning of the Scriptures. At the dawn of time, in self-glorification, our first parents sought "to be like God" (Gen.3:5), shattering communion with the divine during the first light of world history, so that each human community which followed thereafter became an emergency structure built on ruined foundations. Because of that Fall, in an important sense, all history became a *history of guilt*, manifesting itself as a public, societal, and civilizational reality. At the root of all the striving for life in the pagan world before Christ—whether in frenzied battle, orgiastic fertility cults, blood sacrifices, or idol worship—was a religious yearning to appease the wrath of God (or the gods), restore fellowship with the divine, and bring about the renewal of paradise amidst the wearisome cycle of birth, growth, decay, and death. The unyielding pessimism and despair of ancient peoples was embedded in this mysterious and ineradicable sense of guilt in the face of divine justice, touching past, present, and future, which no ritual, rite, or struggle could evade or overcome. The ubiquitous practice of blood sacrifice, in particular, was a perpetual testament to this fact. As Rodney Stark has pointed out:

> Blood played a significant role in sacrifices in all of the ancient temple religions.... Even very primitive people realize that blood is the stuff of life, which suggests that blood and, indeed, life itself often were the fundamental aspects of sacrifice, being the "ultimate" sacrifices, as in the case of human sacrifice.[32]

And yet, "each new sacrifice on the altar is a proof that the previous sacrifice, all previous sacrifices, were inadequate."[33] All of this led to the *tragic* view of life. Tragedy is more than an art form exemplified by the Greeks. It

---

32. Rodney Stark, *Discovering God: The Origins of the Great Religions and the Evolution of Belief* (New York: HarperOne, 2007), 107–108.
33. Ethelbert Stauffer, *Christ and the Caesars*, trans. K. and R. Gregor Smith (Eugene, OR: Wipf and Stock, 2008), 39.

reenacts a deep-seated human perception of world history as guilt and curse because of man's lawless deeds.

Despite this powerful reality, tragedy was not man's final cultural word. Something new was to be introduced into history, something that, it was hoped, might bring blessing rather than curse. And so, the demonic delusion was born that if guilty man could establish his *own law and throne*, he could abolish guilt and realize life, freedom, and eternity. As Ethelbert Stauffer remarks, "Who is this man, this chosen one, who by his deeds is to refute the witness of tragedy? He is the statesman. And what is the work of blessing to which he is called? His work is Empire."[34] However, to truly abolish guilt, this ruler must be a child of the gods; a quasi-divine figure; a hero who will establish justice, peace, and law, and bring about salvation. Thus, "A daimon took hold of Xerxes and filled him with the greatest idea that a statesman of the ancient world ever had—to unite land and sea, east and west under *one* sceptre."[35] The politics of salvific empire required not just a politician, but one who would be lawgiver, priest, and savior. Here, the eternal and divine are conceived as *coalescing* with the human, overcoming guilt and alienation by self-acquittal as the giver of a *new law*. This coalescence in a political savior was more than a mystical and philosophical belief in the basic divinity of man and nature, something which Dodds notes was true of many of the Roman emperors:

> The old feeling of the divinely ordered unity of things is still alive and powerful in Marcus Aurelius, as where he speaks of 'one world containing all, one God penetrating all, one substance and one law'. And he reminds himself of his own unity with it: 'every man's mind is a god and an emanation from deity'; the man who cuts himself off from the City of God is like a rebellious cancer on the face of Nature.[36]

---

34. Stauffer, *Christ and the Caesars*, 21.
35. Stauffer, *Christ and the Caesars*, 19.
36. E. R. Dodds, *Pagan and Christian in an Age of Anxiety* (Cambridge: Cambridge University Press, 1965), 80.

It was a short and logical step from this state of affairs to the worship of man as the embodiment of the state. The emerging *emperor cult* of Rome, for example, went beyond common pantheism. Here in emperor worship was the new source of life, peace, justice and unity.

From Africa to Asia and Europe, man has succumbed to the same demonic temptation over and over. Typified in the pretentions of Pharaoh Thutmose III, when he scaled the steps of the throne and called an imperial assembly proclaiming, "The god of heaven is my father. I am his son. He has begotten me, and commanded me to sit on his throne, while I was still a fledgling,"[37] imperial man became the ideal for several thousand years, an ideal that reached its culmination in Augustus Caesar at the time of Christ. Though Julius Caesar had gotten himself elected *pontifex maximus* (high priest) as early as 63 B.C.,[38] Diarmaid MacCulloch explains the reverence paid to Augustus and his successors:

> He raised no objection to a system of honours in which offerings and sacrifices were made to his *genius*, the sacred force or guardian spirit which guided his personality and actions...; After Augustus's death, his successors in any case did declare him a god..., the consecration of a predecessor as divine gave the living emperor prestige and legitimacy as well as glorifying the dead. Some of Augustus's successors explicitly assumed the role of a god in their lifetimes... by the late third century it had become routine for emperors to claim divine status.... [W]hatever religion any individual emperor chose to favour would arouse the same set of associations *between politics and the world beyond* as the imperial cult encouraged by Augustus.[39]

With the Caesars gradually deified, inscriptions and coinage provided the official commentary of "good news" and began to appear with the words, *divi filius* (son of God) and "savior of the world." The emperor cult was thus

---

37. Stauffer, *Christ and the Caesars*, 37.
38. Stark, *Discovering God*, 123.
39. Diarmaid MacCulloch, *Christianity: The First Three Thousand Years* (New York: Penguin Books, 2009), 45–46; italics added.

established and sacrifices to the emperor were made in temples throughout the empire.

The related political eschatological theme of the *advent* and *appearing* of a semi-divine lawgiver and priestly savior to establish peace and justice is also important. The emperor Nero was the first to have the word ADVENTUS inscribed on Roman coins, but in the year 275, Aurelian was celebrated as "god and lord from birth"—though the very same year he was murdered. Many others followed with similar audacious claims.[40] But the classical advent philosophy, that God would become man, establishing justice and peace, is disappointed and frustrated again and again as each new leader fails and falls. Indeed, history shows that nothing really changed, justice and peace were not realized, sacrifices did not end. Guilt remained in cycles of recurrence till the burning out of Western paganism in the fourth century A.D. when finally, Constantine the Great, in the providence of God, put the name of Jesus Christ upon his battle standard.[41]

Caesar Augustus had died fourteen years after the true advent and epiphany—the birth of the Son of God, the Lord Jesus Christ, in an animal stable where He was laid in a manger, in the town of Bethlehem, part of a far-flung corner of the Roman Empire. His appearing spelled the coming end of an age-old misapprehension of a primeval promise:

> The dream of the classical age, that God would be incarnate in the emperor, that political man is of divine origin and can bring salvation, is at an end....
>
> The way was free for the revelation of the eternal Gospel.... The Advent of the One becomes the first date of a new reckoning of time, a new understanding of history. All previous history is the prologue to the Christmas history. All history since then is the pre-history to the *Parousia* of Jesus Christ at the end of time.[42]

---

40. Stauffer, *Christ and the Caesars*, 40.
41. Vivian Green, *A New History of Christianity* (Bridgend: Blitz Editions, 1998), 23–24.
42. Stauffer, *Christ and the Caesars*, 40–41.

When Christ, the true God-man and universal King, appeared and was confronted by Satan in the wilderness, He was subtly tempted by being offered "all the kingdoms of the world"—the very kingdoms He had come to claim and rule—if only He would bow down to the lawless one. But instead of acting autonomously and succumbing to the *daimon* of this world, like all before him, He responded directly from the law of God, "Go away, Satan! For it is written, 'Worship the Lord your God, and serve only Him'" (Matt 4:10).

God's covenant law, quoted by our Lord, opens with the greatest and most revolutionary words ever heard in the ancient world:

> I am the Lord your God, who brought you out of the land of Egypt, out of the place of slavery.
>
> Do not have other gods besides Me.
>
> Do not make an idol for yourself, whether in the shape of anything in the heavens above or on the earth below or in the waters under the earth. You must not bow down to them or worship them; for I, the Lord your God, am a jealous God, punishing the children for the fathers' sin, to the third and fourth generations of those who hate Me, but showing faithful love to a thousand generations of those who love Me and keep My commands (Exod. 20: 2–6).

Here we encounter a shattering polemic against the ancient demonic myth of the creature as divine, of man as lawgiver, because "The religious transfiguration of the creature is the *proton pseudos*, the first error of mythology, which is brought to light by the Decalogue."[43] The triune God is the only Lord and is Lord over all, the true Archimedean point for all truth and meaning.

The life and ministry of Christ reveal that history is not to be the endless recurrence of guilt, but has a future hope ordained by God, subject to His gospel, law, and judgment. In His covenant law the living God promises

---

43. Stauffer, *Christ and the Caesars*, 24.

faithful love and mercy—to end the *tragedy* of past guilt and to open the way to the future. This is the meaning and mystery of the incarnation of the Son of Man, the living Torah and the goal of the law. It is here that God answers the myth of the ancients by both subverting, fulfilling, and dissolving it. Yes, man is genuinely guilty. And yet, the universal empire of the true God-man can overcome guilt by establishing His kingly throne, upholding His righteous law, and by providing, as priest, endless mercy, the forgiveness of sins, by meeting the demands of justice in full—a final blood sacrifice once for all, the just for the unjust, to bring us to God (Heb. 10:5–13; 1 Pet. 3:18; 1 John 2:2). This is the gospel embraced by the believer with a truly Christian mind. Because of the victory at the cross of Calvary, tragedy is brought to an end. The gospel has conquered forever the cycle of guilt. Sin is paid for. The victorious King is risen and seated on His throne. And His righteous law is smashing the myth of self-deification from East to West, North to South, as His kingdom extends through all the earth (cf. Ps. 2):

> He will not grow weak or be discouraged
> until He has established justice on earth.
> The islands will wait for His instruction (Isa. 42:4).

## Following the Priest-King and True Teacher

As a result, when we ask, at the most fundamental level, what Christianity is, if we are to be scriptural, we must answer that it consists in knowing and following Christ Jesus, the long-expected priest-king and lawgiver. The true Christian does not simply affirm certain doctrines, recite confessions, or explore historical theology to engage in learned dogmatic dispute, but in the here and now worships and follows Jesus Christ the Lord. He is the Master, and the disciple is not greater than his Master (Matt. 10:24).

For those of us growing up in the Western tradition, we are less familiar with the ancient Eastern style of learning by literally attaching oneself to the teacher and learning his way of life and thought by *imitation*. We do speak of tutors and professors and even mentors, but these fall short of the ancient Jewish tradition of following a rabbi and his teaching, committing it to heart. When Jesus called the first disciples, it was not to an academy for a lofty exchange of philosophical ideas in Socratic dialogue; still less was it to have essays or exam papers marked and reviewed. When Christ called the disciples, it was to follow Him and devote their lives to Him, to live with and learn from Him, to memorize His sayings, witness His actions, hear His prayers, question Him about His parables, and walk the paths He walked. In short, to be a disciple of Christ meant, and means, to *imitate* Him in everything, to take up the cross and follow Him. As the apostle Paul wrote, "Imitate me, as I also imitate *Christ*" (1 Cor. 11:1).

Imitation, then, is the basic meaning of Christian discipleship. This is easily overlooked when we seek the function of God's law within a secularized and repaganizing culture that has deeply influenced the church. More often than not, the matter of God's law, the meaning of justice, is approached by Christians in a detached, theoretical way, as though they are personally uninvolved with the question. In other words, the issue of *theonomy* is regarded as a matter of theological polemics or of only theoretical dogmatic interest.

Sadly, it is not uncommon to find professing Christians who are overtly hostile to God's revealed law, treating it lightly, glibly, or even with a haughty disdain as though they were holier than God Himself. It is impossible to see the Lord and Master in such an attitude. And yet, to some professing Christians, God's law is regarded as a threat, an aberration, something parenthetical that has been and is now gone—even an unchristian blemish on the pages of Scripture that has, for all intents and purposes, been erased for the New Testament believer in favor of living as one personally sees fit or "feels led"—as though law and gospel are as incompatible as oil and water. But Jesus' relationship to the law as author, exegete, master-teacher, and Lord is profoundly significant for all true disciples. Jesus modelled what it meant to take the totality of the law seriously, and what matters to Jesus should matter to the Christian. In fact, as is clear from Christ's Sermon on the Mount (cf. Luke 16:16–17), "Jesus's main point here is that his proclamation of the good news of the kingdom of God does not eliminate the fact that everything in the law of Moses is still in effect until heaven and earth pass away."[44] What He taught we must believe, remember, and teach. What He did, we must emulate and copy. If we want to call ourselves Christian, we must be truly yoked to the one true Rabbi.

This is no easy task, and it does not come without a cost. For this attachment must take place in our rebellious age that wants to vanquish the justice of God, trumpet its nihilism, champion a grand levelling, and, through fear and intimidation, cow and terrify the faithful individual into quiet submission. Our time embraces and effectively deifies an unofficially established order in both state and liberalising church, whilst fear and trembling before a holy God and His righteous law are abolished. In a return to pagan premises, truth and justice are being made the province of man alone. As Søren Kierkegaard prophetically put it:

> If you are a student, then you can be sure that the Professor is the measure and the truth; if you are a parson, then the Bishop is the way and the life; if you are a scrivener, the Judge is the standard....
>
> The deification of the established order is the secularization of everything.... The established order desires to be totalitarian, recognizing nothing over it, but having under it ever individual, and judging every individual who is integrated in it. And "that individual"... who expounds the most humble, but at the same time the most humane doctrine about what it means to be a man, the established order desires to terrify by imputing to him the guilt of blasphemy.[45]

This is precisely what true Christians face today when proclaiming Christ and His law. We are implicitly accused of blasphemy against the progressive State orthodoxy, just as Jesus was accused of blasphemy by the Pharisees who neither knew the Scriptures nor the power of God (Matt. 22:29). Ours is a

---

44. Averbeck, "The Law and the Gospels," 412.
45. Kierkegaard, *Training in Christianity*, 77–78.

time where human beings have again sought to make themselves the gauge, the measuring reed, the canon, in place of God's law-Word.

The impact of this on the church has been very great because, in place of God's law, the new Pharisees, parroting the culture, have elevated to the level of articles of faith various human preferences, traditions, laws, and customs (often in the name of "the common good" or "natural law"), which conform to their desires and wonts. Following Jesus is no longer the measure. The established order of the world, infecting a rebellious institutional church like a virus, takes the place of Christ:

> So holy in fact had the Pharisees and scribes become, and so holy do men always become when they deify the established order, that their divine worship is a way of making a fool of God. Under the pretence of serving and worshipping, they serve and worshi[p] their own device, either in self-complacent joy at being themselves the inventors, or through fear of men.[46]

We cannot be ruled by the fear of man, but only by the Word of God. We must be attentive to our Savior who shows the Christian how to regard the law of God in a lawless world. Jesus said, "You call Me Teacher and Lord. This is well said, for I am.... [A] messenger is not greater than the one who sent him" (John 13: 13, 16).

## Jesus and Creation

Of first importance is recognising Jesus' relationship to creation itself as lawgiver from the beginning, for there is only one unified revelation of God in Christ (Rom. 11:36; Col. 1:16–17, 20). The apostle Paul writes that in Him God has been "making known to us the mystery of His will, according to His good pleasure which He purposed in Him for an administration of the fullness of the times, *that is*, the summing up of all things in Christ, things in

---

46. Kierkegaard, *Training*, 79.

the heavens and things on the earth in Him" (Eph. 1:9–10, LSB). As creator, whilst in His human tent (John 1:14), the Lord spoke to calm the waves of the sea, curse the fig tree, heal the blind and deaf, and raise the dead by the power of His Word. Yet Christians often begin the question of Jesus' relationship to law with an assumed *dualism* between *creation* (nature) and *revelation* (grace), which we have seen the Bible simply does not teach. As Willem Ouweneel explains:

> God's one and only revelation is *creational* revelation. This does not exclude Scripture, simply because Scripture is God's major creational work. Nor should we, conversely, limit revelation to Scripture (or to the person of Christ for that matter). On the contrary, God's revelation encompasses the totality of created reality, in which Scripture, as the creaturely-immanent form in which it pleased the eternal, transcendent Word to be inscripturated, constitutes the radiating and directive center.[47]

There is therefore an unbreakable cosmological relation between creation and redemption, between the *physical* and *moral* orders of creation (as there is between all the dimensions of one creation), clearly manifest in Jesus' life, works, and teaching, just as it is patently expressed in the Older Testament. For example, in some cases, when Jesus healed *physically*, He simply made a moral and redemptive declaration, "your sins are forgiven you" (Matt. 9:2). The connection between the moral law and created physical reality is seen here as utterly fundamental:

> Which is easier: to say to the paralytic, "Your sins are forgiven," or to say, "Get up, pick up your mat, and walk"? But so you may know that the Son of Man has authority on earth to forgive sins, He told the paralytic, "I tell you: get up, pick up your mat, and go home" (Mark 2: 9–11).

---

47. Willem J. Ouweneel, *The Eternal Word: God Speaking to Us. An Evangelical Introduction to Reformational Theology*, vol. 1, part 1, *Scripture: The Revealed Source for Theology* (Jordan Station, ON: Paideia Press, 2021), 216.

The moral law does not hover in some abstract realm of "reason" above earthly reality, but is embedded within it. Unlike the rationalism of Enlightenment thinkers like Immanuel Kant—who thought that moral norms exist in a separate world other than the cause-and-effect creation around us—in Scripture the Word of God speaks to *every aspect* of an integrated cosmos, to an integral existence. When the triune God created human beings from *physical* dust and breathed into them the breath of life, there were *moral* and *jural* obligations intrinsic to their existence, bound as the physical world is to all the other dimensions of God's order. This is why in the Bible, moral disobedience to God's Word had *physical effects* in the Fall of man. These included thorns and thistles, pain, disease and ultimately, death. It is also why the homosexuality and perversions of Sodom and Gomorrah ended with fire and brimstone raining down from heaven (Gen. 19:24–25). It is why St. Paul warns of 'receiving in the body' the due penalty of doing that which is contrary to the creation-order in Romans 1:27. It is why the land of the Canaanites spewed out their civilization (Lev. 18:28), and why Israel also was finally dispossessed and taken into exile (Deut. 28:58–64). Lawlessness always brings individual, social, biological, environmental, and cultural ruin. To act in a manner contrary to what God has established in His creational and inscripturated Word brings a curse. As Jonathan Burnside notes, "Biblical law operates 'beyond the confines of a historical past or single culture.' Instead, it is established 'in the bone and flesh of created humanity.'"[48]

All this points to the fact that biblical law does not just mystically appear on the scene with Moses, which Jesus then comes along to set aside in favor of a vague principle of love. Rather, moral law, the law of love to God and neighbour, is embedded into creation and *republished* in God's written law. When God created all things in the beginning with the "ten utterances" (Gen. 1), and when He later created Israel at Sinai with the "ten words" (Ex. 20), the law-Word was central and intended as a blessing to all peoples. Willem Ouweneel points out that "the law of Moses is a written positivization of the

---

48. Burnside, citing James K. Bruckner, *Implied Law in the Abraham Narrative*, 209, in *God, Justice and Society*, 77.

one central (transcendent) Law of Love, and covers all of human life...."[49] The written law is the *immanent* form of *transcendent* Torah that is manifest perfectly in Christ. So, when Jesus taught about God's law for marriage, He went back to His own *creation* and to the book of Genesis (Matt. 19:8).

It is no surprise to find in Genesis 6–7 that Noah and his family, as well as the animals with two of *each kind*, enter the ark as "married couples." There is no sign of a transsexual man or a transsexual elephant, because both the norm of sexual distinction and marriage are basic to God's law-order. As God's image bearers, awareness of these creational norms is inescapable, even for those who are without the revealed law of God, and these norms are a basis of divine judgment because, though the unbeliever cannot expound the law, the *work* of God's creation law is manifest in them and to them (Rom. 2:12–16).

We can truly follow the Master only if we recognize, as He Himself taught, that the law is abiding from the beginning of creation (Mark 10:5–9), will continue till the consummation of the ages (Matt. 5:17–20), and we thereby acknowledge Him as creator, lawgiver, and redeemer whom we must obey and serve with total fealty.

## Jesus and Satan

As noted previously, at the beginning of Jesus' ministry, after His baptism in the Jordan, He was led out by the Spirit of God into the wilderness for forty days (Luke 4:1–13). It is noteworthy that the birth, life, and ministry of Jesus recapitulate, to a significant extent, the life and journey of Israel. Israel was called out of captivity in Egypt, as was the Lord Jesus with His parents (Hos. 11:1; Matt. 2:15). He passed through the waters of baptism like Israel, and went out into the wilderness to be tested and tempted, not for forty years but for forty days (Mark 1:9–15). Shortly thereafter, like Moses, He went up on the mountain, not to receive the law but to teach, expound, and interpret

---

49. Ouweneel, *The Eternal Word*, 215.

the very law He had given to His servant Moses (Matt. 5:1–2). He began with a series of blessings (beatitudes) that correspond to the curses and warnings that came from Mount Sinai (Exod. 19:12–13, 20–24; Deut. 28:15–68).

During His time in the wilderness, He was confronted by Satan and tested. How the Lord responded is most telling. If Christians are to *imitate* Christ as true disciples, we too must learn to deal with testing and temptation with the law-Word of God, in the power of the Spirit. Jesus responded to temptation with three citations from the Torah, the context of which was the testing of Israel as to whether she would obey God's commands. In the *first* instance, just as the Israelites were hungry in the wilderness and received manna from heaven, the Lord Jesus was hungry and was tempted to speak to the stones and turn them to bread to prove His identity and address His near starvation. But Jesus responded with "It is written" and cites Deuteronomy 8:3: "Man must not live on bread alone but on every word that comes from the mouth of God" (Matt. 4:4).

In the *second* instance, Jesus was taken to Jerusalem to the pinnacle of the temple, the historic dwelling place of God, and tempted to prove His identity as God's Son dramatically, violating God's purpose of concealment in the form of a servant, by throwing Himself down only to be rescued miraculously by angels. This time, knowing the Lord's total trust in the truth of God's law-Word, to strengthen his case, Satan craftily quotes Psalm 91:11–12 regarding angelic protection—thereby showing us that God's Word can also be misused! Jesus' response again was from God's law in Deuteronomy 6:16: "It is also written: Do not test the Lord your God" (Matt. 4:7).

In the *third* instance, the Master was taken to a high mountain and was shown the splendor of the kingdoms of the world. In exchange for committing idolatry by submitting to the devil and bowing in worship, Satan offered Jesus all those kingdoms as a gift. In Luke's account, Satan correctly pointed out that he could give Him their splendor and authority, "because it has been given over to me.... If You, then, will worship me, all will be Yours" (Luke 4:6–7). This enticement to false worship was a very great temptation, for the precise reason that Christ had in fact come for all the kingdoms of world, to take back possession of them as the heir of all things, and to assert total authority as the ruler of the kings of the earth (Rev. 1:5). But the Lord knew this could happen only according to the Father's way, not by violation of the law, and so He again responds from the Torah (Deut. 6:13) and not with a quote from the philosophers: "Go away, Satan! For it is written: 'Worship the Lord your God and serve only Him'" (Matt. 4:10).

Because our Lord and Master wielded God's law, He was the authentic Israelite and the truly obedient Son, the greater Moses, and also the last and greater Joshua who would come into the full inheritance promised. As Scripture says, "The kingdom of the world has become the kingdom of our Lord and of His Messiah, and He will reign forever and ever!" (Rev. 11:15).

Jesus unquestionably regarded the written law of God as the only suitable tool for defeating Satan, for staying on mission, and for setting the example for us to follow. He recognized the power and authority of the law and confronted temptation with "It is written" and overcame temptation through the Word. It would be strange indeed if the very Word which vanquished the devil was now to be thrown aside by the believer in favor of human customs, reasonings, and vain imaginations. Since the disciples were not present to witness Jesus' temptation in the wilderness, it is clear that these events were related to them by the Lord Himself for both their instruction and ours.

We should also remember that the tempter Satan is referred to in Scripture as the "lawless one" (2 Thess. 2:8), and sin itself is defined as *lawlessness* (1 John 3:4). Jesus Christ has come to destroy the works of the devil and to restore His people to righteousness and, therefore, to obedience to His law. The logic of the apostle John in this regard is unshakeable: "Everyone who commits sin also breaks the law; sin is the breaking of law. You know that He was revealed so that He might take away sins, and there is no sin in Him" (1 John 3:4–5).

This is why the true disciple does not live a lifestyle of practicing sin (lawlessness), because to do so is to place oneself on the side of lawlessness and therefore with the devil himself: "the one who practices sin is of the devil; for the devil has sinned from the beginning. The Son of God appeared for this purpose, to destroy the works of the devil" (1 John 3:8, NASB).

## Jesus and the Pharisees

Another vitally important point to explore is Jesus' relation to the law in His public ministry—specifically as we see it in debates with the religious authorities who were the official interpreters of the law. Throughout the Gospels, we find Jesus in frequent dialogue and dispute with the teachers of the law who regularly challenged Him. He did this in order to demonstrate that He was not a violator of God's law in either His way of life or teaching, but rather He was its perfect fulfilment, fulness, confirmation, and completion. The Lord showed for all time that He put His law into practice completely and accomplished its requirements flawlessly. One of the serious sins of the scribes and Pharisees was not that they loved God and, with misplaced zeal, longed to obey the details of God's law, but that, in the grip of their unbelief in Christ as the Son of God and the living Torah, they were always seeking a way around obedience to the weighty substance of God's righteous law through their own sophistry and tradition. And yet Christ was explicit in tying belief in the teaching of Moses to belief and faith in Himself. "For if you believed Moses, you would believe Me, because he wrote about Me. But if you don't believe his writings, how will you believe My words?" (John 5:46–47).

The Jewish Talmud[50] carries on the tragic and rebellious unbelief of the Pharisees and has done for centuries. It forms a telling illustration of the kind of arguments that unbelief construes. Unbelief in Jesus leads to Pharisaic thinking and ultimately to a misunderstanding of their own Scriptures. As Gary North observes, "The Talmud is a giant exercise in finding ways to escape the Old Testament texts. The Pharisees were in rebellion against God's law, all in the name of God's law."[51] He goes on to cite David Weiss, who is a master of the Talmud, formerly an orthodox Jew, and then professor at the Conservative Jewish Theological Seminary, who devoted his academic

---

50. The Talmud contains the writings and opinion of thousands of rabbis as commentary on the Torah compiled over centuries. It is the central text of Rabbinic Judaism and the primary source of Jewish religious law (*halakha*) and Jewish theology.
51. Gary North, *The Judeo-Christian Tradition* (Tyler, TX: Institute for Christian Economics, 1990), 87.

career to a detailed study of the various versions of the Talmud. Here is how Weiss describes its effective use:

> With one hand you acknowledge God's existence. At the same time, you want to have some maneuverability. Studying critically is contending with God's writ—acknowledging it but using criticism to alter it. Man is powerless vis-a-vis God and powerful vis-a-vis His Torah. *There* he can assert his independence by offering an interpretation different from the one God intended.[52]

It was this "critical" approach to the law of God that Jesus publicly addressed. In essence, like many modern professing Christians, they didn't really believe Moses and so Christ's question echoes down the centuries, "But if you don't believe [Moses'] writings, how will you believe My words?" (John 5:47).

Some telling examples of the heart of the dispute are found in John 7–10 where, during the feast of Tabernacles, Jesus was engaged in an extended discussion with the Pharisees about His authority and identity. Not only did Jesus show that He is the fulfilment of the *meaning* of the older covenant feasts, but He clearly pointed to the authority of the law itself. In the course of His teaching in the temple precinct, Jesus said, "Did not Moses give you the law? Yet none of you keeps the law! Why are you trying to kill me?" (John 7:19). This statement invoked both the authority of the Decalogue and the prohibition against murder. Jesus had healed on the Sabbath, and for this work of restoration to wholeness (the central *meaning* of Sabbath), some of the Pharisees wanted to kill Him. They cannot agree about their interpretation of the Sabbath, and yet all the while they are seeking to violate God's law by murdering Jesus. This betrayed the life-giving purpose of the commandments, a purpose which the Master had come to fulfil when He defeated at the cross the one who was a murderer from the beginning, who did not stand in the truth of God's law but who is a liar and the father of all liars (John 8:44). All three synoptic Gospels deal with the Sabbath controversy (Matt. 12:1–14;

---

52. Weiss, cited in North, *The Judeo-Christian Tradition*, 89.

Mark 2:23–3:6; Luke 6:1–11) in which Christ explicitly declared His Lordship over the Sabbath principle instituted at creation as a gift to man. This staggering claim proved again the continuity of God's law-order and the fact that the Creator had come among men as their Redeemer. As Averbeck notes, "He proclaims His lordship over the Sabbath, but there is no indication he set it aside or resisted the basic principle of rest on the sabbath."[53]

In the fascinating account of John 8:13, the Pharisees then challenge Jesus' testimony about Himself as though it were invalid. The Lord, in His matchless wisdom, turned the argument against them and accused them of judging by man-made standards and not in accordance with God's law. He invoked the law of God, saying, "Even in your law it is written that the witness of two men is valid. I am the One who testifies about Myself, and the Father who sent Me testifies about Me" (John 8:17–18). Once again, Jesus proved that His witness was in accordance with God's law par excellence, and that He was not in violation of the principles of the law, but fully upheld it. The ultimate purpose of Jesus' teaching here was much more than simply dealing with a specific point of Jewish casuistry (whether one witness is enough or not); rather it was to show that the commandment to honor father and mother is exemplified in His relationship to His Father: "the reader is to perceive that the 'light of life' ([John] 8:12) available in Torah is available in knowing the one who keeps the law of Exod. 20:16 and Deut. 5:20 in association with the Father himself."[54]

This same point is then expressed in John 8:49, as Jesus responded to the charge that He had a demon, with a remarkable reference to the fifth commandment (Exod. 20:12) and honoring parents. The Pharisees deliberately insulted Jesus, and by extension His Father, but the Lord declared, "I do not have a demon.... On the contrary, I honor My Father and you dishonor Me." This is a prelude to Jesus' theme of glorifying the Father and the Father glorifying the Son later in the dialogue. Ultimately, by honoring Christ

---

53. Averbeck, "The Law and the Gospels," 420.
54. George J. Brooke, "Christ and the Law in John 7–10," in *Law and Religion: Essays on the Place of the Law in Israel and Early Christianity*, ed. Barnabas Lindars (Worcester: James Clarke & Co., 1988), 102–112,106.

Jesus the Son, a person honors the Father and thereby hallows God's name ,which *fulfils positively* the law of God prohibiting taking the Lord's name in vain (Exod. 20:7). And in John 10:30, where Jesus stunned His listeners by declaring His unity with the Father, saying, "I and the Father are one," the prohibition of the Decalogue, "You shall have no other gods before me," is evidently being stated positively.

Pivoting back to the Master's teaching in the synoptic Gospels, we see that several clear statements in dialogue with the Pharisees are most instructive for the true disciple seeking to *imitate* the Lord, seeking to learn and apply what He had to say. In Matthew 23:23–24, Jesus declared:

> Woe to you, scribes and Pharisees, hypocrites! You pay a tenth of mint, dill, and cumin, yet you have neglected the more important matters of the law—justice, mercy, and faith. These things should have been done without neglecting the others. Blind guides! You strain out a gnat, yet gulp down a camel!

What is everywhere implied in John's Gospel is here made explicit by Matthew. Notice again that Jesus takes issue, not with the law of God, cut by the very finger of God and placed in the Ark of the Covenant, but with the Pharisees' hypocrisy in regard to it. Jesus is never critical "of the law itself but of the way it was being taught by the Jewish leaders. His attitude to the law is not in question. He was fully supportive of its ongoing significance and application in the kingdom of heaven."[55] The Lord does not even criticize taking care to be faithful in the matter of tithing, but He distinguishes in this case the weightier matters of God's law-Word that come first. This was the constant rebuke of rabbi Jesus against the teachers of the law in His day, they lacked consistency and kept the parts of God's law that looked good on the outside to be performed before people, whilst the substance of the law and its meaning was neglected. This contradiction is also what makes Jesus' remark so humorous. To see a man straining a gnat from his drink but being happy to gulp down a camel perfectly expresses the sin of the Pharisee and their

---

55. Averbeck, "The Law and the Gospels," 414.

actual rejection of God's law-Word. This same thought is also pictured in the image of a person concerned to wash the outside of a cup and bowl, whilst the inside of the dish remains dirty, making the outward washing entirely pointless. In clear reference to the tenth commandment which prohibits covetousness, Jesus declares, "inside they are full of greed and self-indulgence! Blind Pharisee! First clean the inside of the cup" (Matt. 23:25–26).

At the center of the Lord's woe pronounced against the religious authorities is that it is possible to look clean on the outside when you are dead and dirty on the inside. It was *not* that the law of God was loved and obeyed from the heart by the religious teachers as the law itself requires (Deut. 6:6)—it was quite the opposite. Their outward conformity was a pretence, a sham, a piece of theater that lacked authenticity and the passion of true inwardness. Jesus is explicit, "on the outside you seem righteous to people, but inside you are full of hypocrisy and lawlessness" (Matt. 23:28). The Lord makes the same point in Matthew 15:18–20, with direct reference to the Decalogue:

> But what comes out of the mouth comes from the heart, and this defiles a man. For from the heart come evil thoughts, murders, adulteries, sexual immoralities, thefts, false testimonies, blasphemies. These are the things that defile a man, but eating with unwashed hands does not defile a man.

Contra the Pharisees, because of sin, salvation was *never* possible by obeying the law, for only Christ ever truly obeyed it. In fact, giving salvation was never the law's intended purpose or function. The law, the wisdom of God, was given as the *path* of life and blessing, not as its *source*. Only faith in the promises and blood of the covenant meant salvation and redemption, which is why instructions for the construction of the tabernacle were also given to Moses by God Himself. Obedience to God's commands was the expression of love and of gratitude for grace. Christ Jesus was and is the full realisation of the promises in His atoning sacrifice. Just as the true temple is in heaven where Christ makes continual intercession (Heb. 7:25–8:2)—the earthly copy being given to Moses—so the law, given with creation and inscribed in stone by the Lord at Sinai, is now written on the tables of our hearts in the newer covenant (Jer. 31:31–34; Heb 8:7–12). The priestly administration and location of the covenant law have changed, but the substance is unaltered.

One final encounter with the Pharisees recorded in Matthew 15 and Mark 7 is very relevant in understanding Jesus' attitude and example regarding the law. In this incident, the Lord is challenged as to why His disciples are not following the tradition of the elders by ceremonial washing of hands before eating. Jesus' response again directly quotes the Decalogue (Exod. 20:12; Deut. 5:16), but combines it with a case law from Exodus 21:17 that carries a penal sanction:

> He answered them, "And why do you break God's commandment because of your tradition? For God said: Honor your father and your mother; and, The one who speaks evil of father or mother must be put to death. But you say, 'Whoever tells his father or mother, "Whatever benefit you might have received from me is a gift committed to the temple"— he does not have to honor his father.' In this way, you have revoked God's word because of your tradition (Matt. 15:3–6).

Notice especially that Jesus does not say, "why do you break Moses' command?" or "Moses said, honor your father and mother," nor "you have revoked Moses' word." On the contrary, Jesus explicitly affirms that this is what *God* has said; that these are *God's* commandments; that they are revoking *God's* word. Again, at issue was the hypocrisy of the Pharisees who had scruples about ceremonially unwashed hands but excused a man from financially supporting his parents in their old age if he had made a substantial gift to the temple instead. Human teachings and traditions had been put in the place of God's law. In our own time, this kind of attitude is commonplace in many churches across the West where we neither know nor teach God's law as our Lord and Master taught it, but put in its place our particular preferences, customs, reasonings, and political ideas.

At the heart of Christ's rebuke is not just an affirmation of the righteousness and authority of God's law, but a warning against *replacing* God's law with man's own ideas, when He says, "they worship me in vain, teaching as doctrines the commands of men" (Matt. 15:9). In all these various interactions with the teachers of law, we see that

> Jesus and his followers had neither broken nor abrogated the law. Those Jews who remained unconvinced were caricatured as blind Pharisees descended from the devil.

> ...For those who desire wisdom they can now find her in the person of Christ, who is both the law-giving prophet promised by Moses and the very meaning and purpose of the law itself as he gives eternal life to those who believe in him and keep his commandments.[56]

## Jesus and the Mountain

We cannot complete a discussion of Christ and the law without reference to Rabbi Jesus' great Sermon upon the Mount. As previously noticed, coming in from the wilderness, our Lord went up on the mountain as the greater Moses to explain, teach and confirm the law. It is worth restating again at this juncture that the law did not *begin* to have relevance with Mount Sinai or with this paradigmatic sermon. As Vern Poythress has explained:

> The law of the Old Testament is not a mere datum or a mere code book, but the personal word of the great King of the universe. And who is this King? From eternity to eternity the Word was with God and the Word was God (John 1:1). The King is the trinitarian God, Father, Son, and Holy Spirit. God the Son was always at work from the beginning. The law of Moses is a reflection and foreshadowing of the absolute perfection and righteousness of Christ, rather than Christ being a reflection of the law.[57]

---

56. Brooke, "Christ and the Law in John 7–10," 112.
57. Vern S. Poythress, *The Shadow of Christ in the Law of Moses* (Brentwood, TN: Wolgemuth and Hyatt, 1991), 92–93.

All people, in all ages, have been obligated to love their creator and their neighbour—the *summaries* of the law reiterated by Christ. Since the law of God had such relevance and power *prior* to Moses, we would likewise expect that it would have no less force after the *passing* of Moses. Notably, the kings of Israel were especially required to read the law every day, and to make a copy of it for themselves (Deut. 17:18–20). We would therefore expect that the greater Son of David, the Messiah-King, would endorse and apply the law of God in its fulness as author and Lord of the law. This is precisely what we see in Matthew 5–7. Here, "he proclaims the coming of the 'kingdom of heaven' (Matt. 4:17; cf. 3:2; 5:3, 10, 19–20, etc.), and the Sermon on the Mount amounts to the proclamation of the 'law' of that kingdom."[58] Indeed, the Sermon on the Mount shows that Jesus *presupposed* the validity of the law and binding authority of the Word of God:

> Do not assume that I came to destroy the Law or the Prophets. I did not come to destroy but to *fulfil*. For I assure you: Until heaven and earth pass away, not the smallest letter or one stroke of a letter will pass from the law until all things are accomplished. Therefore, whoever breaks one of the least of these commands and teaches people to do so will be called least in the kingdom of heaven. But whoever practices and teaches these commands will be called great in the kingdom of heaven (Matt. 5:17–19).

Jesus is clearly referring to the totality of His law until the end of history as we know it. To *teach* and *practice* God's commands will mean being called great, not in some past dispensation, but in the kingdom of God. To break God's law and teach others to do the same will mean being the least. The meaning of the Word *fulfill*—which has been much discussed—is surely settled by the context of abiding validity and the presence of the kingdom of heaven, so at the very least the law's validity is being confirmed. It cannot mean an ending or setting aside of the law, or the entire Sermon becomes a self-contradiction. On the contrary, it means that the law and the prophets

---

58. Averbeck, "The Law and the Gospels," 413.

(prophets who called people back to obedience to God's law), which are not yet filled-out, Jesus Christ is going to make full.[59] Christ will bring righteousness to its fullest expression and teach and live it fully so that people will see what it means to live the law as one should.

Thus, rabbi Jesus was not setting aside God's law, nor adding something quantitatively to the law as a supplement, but giving it the *rightful measure* God had always intended. Herman Ridderbos is to the point: "Fulfillment [means] the effectual assertion of the demands of the law. The word suggests a vessel that is being filled. The 'vessel' of the law is given its rightful measure. For this purpose, Jesus has come."[60]

This means that when the Master in His Sermon repeatedly uses the expression, "You have heard that it was said... but I tell you," He is neither refuting nor correcting God's own Word, but 'filling out' its meaning by dealing with abuses and misunderstandings that had arisen. And He does so with total authority as well as originality as the Author of the law. In fact, the grammar of the Greek expression allows for the meaning, 'in agreement with that,' I say to you! So, the meaning of murder, adultery, divorce, oath-taking, just retribution, generosity and love of neighbor are all taken up and *filled out*. The practices of true worship, facing worldly cares, distinguishing between good and evil, following Christ and accepting His authority, are all dealt with in the Sermon in reference to the wisdom of God's law, and in so doing, rabbi Jesus gets to the root of our heart motives.

The Lord's climactic call to "Be perfect, therefore, as your heavenly father is perfect" (Matt. 5:48), echoes the words of God's law, "Be holy because I, the Lord your God, am holy" (Lev. 19:2). Discerning the way in which each aspect of the law is confirmed and 'filled out' in and through Jesus' life, redemptive work, and teaching involves the careful task of rightly dividing

---

59. See Jochem Douma, The Ten Commandments: Manual for the Christian Life, trans. Nelson D. Kloosterman (Phillipsburg, NJ: Presbyterian and Reformed, 1996), 376.
60. Herman Ridderbos, *The Coming of the Kingdom*, ed. Raymond O. Zorn, trans. H. de Jongste (St. Catharines, ON: Paideia Press, 1978), 294.

the word of truth under the yoke of Christ in the Spirit's power.[61] But there can be no question of abolishing or setting aside the law, as Richard Barcellos rightly explains:

> The law Christ expounded in the Sermon on the Mount and revealed in the epistles through His apostles includes portions of the very things Moses wrote, and sometimes without qualification.... Paul quotes the Decalogue in Romans 13:9 without any New Covenant contrastive qualifications....
>
> In Matthew 5 Jesus *is* indeed introducing a contrast, but not between the Law of Moses and the Law of Christ. Rather, the contrast is between a true understanding of the Law of Moses and the false understanding evidenced in the hypocrisy of the scribes and Pharisees.[62]

## Jesus and Disciple-making

A disciple is nothing without a master to follow and obey. If we really claim to follow Christ and desire to have the mind of Christ (1 Cor. 2:16), we "should fulfill the law the way he taught it because he was the one who filled it up to its full intent and potential."[63] Part of that intent of the law is manifest in what we call the Great Commission (Matt. 28:18–20). Here the Master makes plain that the commandments have an ongoing role in evangelism, disciple-making and the advance of God's Kingdom. Shattering the restrictions of national Israel (Matt. 21:43), the international people of God, both Jew and Gentile, now disciple all nations, which includes teaching the full content of God's law. "'Everything I have commanded you' naturally

---

61. Jonathan Burnside's discussion of "Law in the hands of Jesus" is, in my view, the gold standard for explaining Jesus' use of the law: See *God, Justice, and Society*, 404–25.
62. Richard C. Barcellos, *In Defense of the Decalogue: A Critique of New Covenant Theology* (Enumclaw, WA: WinePress Publishing, 2001), 75–76.
63. Averbeck, "The Law and the Gospels," 413.

includes the Sermon on the Mount, and within the Sermon it includes Jesus' statement about the continuing force of the law."[64] In addition, we are given the personal assurance of our divine rabbi that His everlasting presence will empower and accompany us in our mission. We are therefore to imitate Christ by teaching the law and understanding it through His life and work. As Greg Bahnsen points out:

> The Christian being condemned by the law, saved by Christ's obedience to the law, and sanctified by the Spirit in accordance with the law, is to propagate the Christian gospel *in conjunction with* pressing home the demands of God's holy law. Teaching the nations to observe the commandments of God is a definite obligation laid upon Christians by Christ.... [T]he Christian life and God's kingdom are theonomic through and through, as evidenced by both the Lord's prayer ("Thy kingdom come, Thy will be done") and the Great Commission.[65]

When all is said and done, to be a Christian is to walk with the Master. To truly be His disciple we must tread the same sod by honoring the same Father, loving the same law, teaching the same commandments and imitating His life of faithful obedience. As Ridderbos exhorts us, "The theonomy of the gospel is subjection to the law, and any attempt to eliminate the category of law from the gospel is frustrated by the continuous and undeniable maintenance of the law by and in the gospel."[66] This is confirmed by words of the Priest-King from His heavenly throne, the same Lord who engraved His law on the stone tablets at Sinai and expounded Torah on the mountain:

> But the cowards, unbelievers, vile, murderers, sexually immoral, sorcerers, idolaters, and all liars—their share will be in the lake that burns with fire and

---

64. Poythress, *The Shadow of Christ in the Law of Moses*, 271–72.
65. Greg L. Bahnsen, *Presuppositional Apologetics: Stated and Defended*, ed. Joel McDurmon (Powder Springs, GA: The American Vision, 2008), 254–55.
66. Ridderbos, *The Coming of the Kingdom*, 307.

sulfur, which is the second death.... Outside are the dogs, the sorcerers, the sexually immoral, the murderers, the idolaters, and everyone who loves and practices lying (Rev. 21:8; 22:15).

CHAPTER 6

# Think Christianly About Apologetics

*...and you are all partners with me in grace, both in my imprisonment and in the defence and establishment of the gospel.*
— *Philippians 1:7 (HCSB)*

## The Calling to Give a Defense

THE REQUIREMENT THAT WE TRAIN, equip, and prepare ourselves to give a *defense* for the hope we have in Christ is laid out memorably by the apostle Peter in the great *Magna Carta* of Christian apologetics:

> But honor the Messiah as Lord in your hearts. Always be ready to give a defense to anyone who asks you for a reason for the hope that is in you. However, do this with gentleness and respect, keeping your conscience clear, so that when you are accused, those who denounce your Christian life will be put to shame (1 Pet. 3:15–16).

How we are to go about the task of giving an *apologia* has long been a matter of debate and dispute. We certainly need to reflect carefully on the apologetic mandate because it is possible for believers to think about methodology in apologetics utilizing largely non-Christian assumptions—it is essential we think Christianly even about apologetics. That said, given the potential for misunderstandings and squabbles in this area, what is most important to keep in mind is the biblical priority of obedience to God, to glorify His name and extend His kingdom. Notwithstanding the critical importance of developing a faithful and effective methodology, our *primary* concern should be with giving an authentic witness to the gospel among the lost and strengthening the faith of believers, not winning arguments with other Christians over apologetic methods and strategies.

Christians are surrounded in Western society by people who do not yet know the Lord—often from many parts of the world. The ceaseless clamour and noise of our diseased culture seeks to distract those people from honestly confronting themselves alone, and so face their hopeless condition before a holy God. With gentleness and respect, the apostle Peter tells us, we are to offer a reason for our hope, even in the face of opposition, so that the quiet convicting presence of the Holy Spirit might still hearts before Him, and God's Word be heard. At the same time, our lives are to reflect the integrity of the gospel we preach, with our consciences clear, so that those who might accuse or defame us will be shamed by their actions.

Regrettably, amongst many Christians, the apologetic mandate is frequently misunderstood and misapplied, leading to either ambivalence, reticence, or even a hostility toward the calling to defend the faith. These misapprehensions tend to arise from being led to believe that apologetics should be principally concerned with *establishing* the truth of Christianity by the ingenuity of human "reason"—that is, by direct rational "proofs" for God and His Word, and through various forms of theoretical and scientific demonstration which allegedly *verify* Christian belief beyond a reasonable doubt when brought before the bar of human reason.

Unfortunately, this perspective both attempts far too much whilst accomplishing far too little. It places an impossible and unsustainable burden on fallen man's theoretical reasoning, whilst simultaneously failing to challenge unbelievers at the religious root of their willful rebellion against God. In the tradition of St Augustine, St Anselm, and John Calvin, the first modern Christian thinker to specifically identity this problem was probably Søren Kierkegaard—the great nineteenth century critic of rationalism and romanticism:

> If one were to describe the whole *orthodox apologetic effort* in one single sentence, but also with categorical precision, one might say that it has the intent to make *Christianity plausible*. To this one might add that, if it were to succeed, then would this effort have the ironical fate that precisely upon the day of its triumph it would have lost everything and entirely quashed Christianity... to make Christianity plausible is the same as to misinterpret it.[1]

This is because biblical Christianity cannot be made plausible to fallen human beings within any paradigm other than one for which *faith in Jesus Christ is itself the starting point*.[2] From the biblical viewpoint, the unbeliever does not simply make errors of intellectual judgment or entertain certain erroneous beliefs; the unbeliever *exists* in untruth. As such, the orthodox, rationalistic, and evidential account of apologetics to which Kierkegaard refers neglects to take proper account of what Scripture teaches about the condition of fallen human beings outside of the enlightening work of the Holy Spirit, the nature of creation-order under a curse, and the character of God's self-revelation in Jesus Christ, who fundamentally shatters the assumptions of human reason at their foundation. The traditional approach also tends to the elitist and entirely unwarranted assumption that before anyone can seek to defend their faith, their intellectual development and relevant knowledge base must be highly advanced and their capacity to follow and retain lengthy chains of reasoning tightly honed. I hope in this chapter that we can move past these misunderstandings that deter so many,

---

1. Søren Kierkegaard, *On Authority and Revelation: The Book on Adler, or A Cycle of Ethico-Religious Essays* (Princeton, NJ: Princeton University Press, 1955), 59.
2. Rae, *Kierkegaard's Vision of the Incarnation*, 136.

and be encouraged to give an account of the hope that is in us with boldness and confidence in our spheres of influence.

## Governing Assumptions of a Presuppositional Method

Before summarizing the particular apologetic challenge we must confront in our time, it is important to identify the basic governing assumptions of a reformational apologetic, of a distinctly Christian apologetic method.

The first is to notice that there is no such thing as a 'view from nowhere"—the vaunted autonomy and neutrality of human reasoning is an illusion. Human beings are religiously pre-committed in their hearts to a particular ethos. In the Bible, the *heart* supplies the root unity of the human person out of which everything else finds expression, including thoughts, desires, and actions (Prov. 4:23; Matt. 15:19)—and that heart is notoriously untrustworthy: "The heart is more deceitful than anything else, and incurable—who can understand it" (Jer. 17:9). The idea that the reasonings of a person's heart function in an independent, objective impartiality toward a holy God is for the birds.

Human understanding—what the Western philosophical tradition essentially deified as "reason"—is a *tool*, a valid function of the human heart that can cut in various directions: which is precisely why there are so many different schools of thought competing within all the various academic disciplines, all claiming to be logical and reasonable. Furthermore, the existence of laws for thought (even though they are God-given) does not ensure anyone's beliefs or assumptions are true. Deductive logic may help us reach valid conclusions and show the implications of various assumptions, but it doesn't supply the beliefs, hypotheses or premises with which to begin.

This means that "reason" is far from something neutral, independent, or absolute; it is neither a thought-framework nor a paradigm. Instead, it is constrained and directed by the world-and-life-view (also known as "worldview") and plausibility structure within which the individual is operating. Consequently, even on its own terms, "reason" cannot function as a final court of appeal for settling disputes between competing truth claims, because attempted justification of those claims happens from *within* a given paradigm. It is because of this that a reformational or presuppositional apologetic focuses on the *internal critique*[3] of unbelieving world-and-life views in order to show how they collapse under their own weight, and why only biblical faith has adequate explanatory power to account for the failure of competing perspectives whilst providing the truths that make the rich diversity of human experience intelligible from *within* the structure of Christian commitment.

The second governing assumption of a reformational apologetic, given the inescapable limitations of human reasoning, is the central importance of this concept of world-and-life view—something that traditional and classical forms of apologetics have typically ignored or denied. Simply put, a world-and-life view is a framework or basic structure of understanding (i.e., a paradigm), whether extensively or feebly developed, that rests on certain foundational beliefs and faith-commitments, thus having an essentially religious character—and no-one is without one. Non-Christian perspectives on reality would all regard the essential claim of Christianity—that the eternal and infinite-personal God, the Creator of all things, was fully revealed and manifest in temporal history in the man Jesus Christ, dying for sin, yet raised to life in power and glory—as "implausible." This is because in order for it to *become* plausible to human reasoning, a person's heart, and thereby worldview and thinking, must be transformed by the reality of Christ Himself, so that their epistemic position is entirely altered. In other words, a new faith commitment for understanding our life and the world is required. Without such a change, people simply take offense at Christ because they are constrained by various world-and-life views from which they must be liberated. As the late Christian apologist Greg Bahnsen pointed out:

---

3. An effective internal critique occurs when the assumptions, presuppositions, and structural features of competing worldviews are examined for coherence, when cogency, contradictions, and antinomies are identified, and when their failure to give an intelligible account of human experience is exposed.

> Each worldview has its presuppositions about reality, knowledge and ethics; these mutually influence and support each other. There are no facts or uses of reason which are available outside of the interpretative system of basic commitments or assumptions which appeals to them; the presuppositions used by the Christian and non-Christian determine what they will accept as factual and reasonable.[4]

This makes clear that the choice before all people is either/or, as Kierkegaard expressed it—there is a basic antithesis involved. From a Christian apologetics standpoint, either a personal God or an empty vortex lies behind all things as the central principle and *archē* of reality. Either God has indeed revealed Himself in Jesus Christ, or we disintegrate reality downward into a void. Critically, this does not mean that a world-and-life view is just a hypothesis to be tested by an ostensibly neutral human reason. Rather, it is where our thinking rests with a kind of pistic certitude. It is that *by which* ideas are tested. According to Kierkegaard, it is

> certainty in oneself won from all experience whether this has oriented itself only in all worldly relationships (a purely human standpoint, Stoicism, for example), by which means it keeps itself from contact with a deeper experience—or whether in its heavenward direction (the religious) it has found therein the centre as much for its heavenly as its earthly existence, has won the true Christian conviction "that neither death nor life, nor angels, nor principalities, nor powers, nor the present, nor the future, nor height, nor depth, nor any other creation will be able to separate us from the love of God in Christ Jesus our Lord."[5]

The transcendental standpoint (the Godward religious direction) granting a certitude rooted in one's union with Christ, is what both Kierkegaard and later Herman Dooyeweerd regarded as the *Archimedean point* for the Christian—a starting point for understanding life manifest in, and yet lying

---

4. Bahnsen, *Presuppositional Apologetics*, 15
5. Søren Kierkegaard, "From the Papers of One Still Living," in *Early Polemical Writings*, ed. and trans. Julia Watkin (Princeton, NJ: Princeton University Press, 1990), 76–77.

outside, of created reality in the eternal God. Only from this vantage point can we grasp the significance and meaning of life.

## The Collapse of the Christian Mind

The immediate difficulty for the believer, however, is that the Christian world-and-life view has largely eroded in our era, even in much of the church. This problem is so fundamental, it cannot be fixed by a few seminars from Christian apologists, let alone lectures on doctrine from academic theologians, who may lack a comprehensive scriptural worldview themselves.

Some years ago, I was speaking in California, in the Santa Cruz area, on the centrality of Christ for Christian apologetics. After my lecture, I was taken to lunch by a very pleasant young couple. One of the first questions they asked me with a smile was how long I had been an *apolo-jedi*—a very humorous remark, but which, on reflection, highlighted a typical misapprehension of the real need of the Christian church as we seek to defend the faith in our time and confront the many challenges facing our culture. Because in my judgment, the most significant problem the Christian community in the West presently faces is the near total collapse of the Christian world-and-life-view in the culture, and often amongst believers themselves; and so it is insufficient for the church to simply address better *strategies* for church planting, more creative *techniques* in evangelism, or cultivating *smarter* apologists to overcome tough questions, like elite Jedi warriors. What we need is a wholesale recovery and, in many respects, a fresh discovery of what it means to *think Christianly* and therefore to *be Christian* before a watching world. A Christian renaissance is the need of the hour.

The current reality is that the questions confronting believers in the West are qualitatively, not simply quantitatively, different from those we faced even twenty-five years ago, because there is no longer a shared understanding of reality that can readily undergird a common discourse; the former plausibility structure based on Christian foundations and biblical presuppositions has buckled and given way beneath us. For the first time in centuries, we find ourselves in discussion with ordinary people where our most basic religious assumptions about the nature of the divine, of human beings, and of created reality, are antithetical to one another. These differing religious starting points determine the kind of questions people deem relevant for addressing the existential, socio-cultural, and theoretical problems of life.

The pervasiveness of unbelieving worldviews in every aspect of our cultural life has had a profound and lasting impact on the contemporary church. A few cultural prophets saw this emerging problem back in the 1960s. Among them was the British thinker Harry Blamires, whose important book, *The Christian Mind*, was ahead of its time. He opens this short classic by recognizing the commonplace fact that the thinking of modern people has been *secularized*. Critically however, he goes on to point out that this disaster is *not* the primary catastrophe:

> Tragic as this fact is, it would not be so desperately tragic had the Christian mind held out against the secular drift. But unfortunately the Christian mind has succumbed to the secular drift with a degree of weakness and nervelessness unmatched in Christian history....
>
> There is no longer a Christian mind. There is still of course a Christian ethic, a Christian practice, and a Christian spirituality.... As a spiritual being, in prayer and meditation, [the Christian] strives to cultivate a dimension of life unexplored by the non-Christian. But as a *thinking* being, the modern Christian has succumbed to secularization. He accepts religion—its morality, its worship, its spiritual culture; but he rejects the *religious view of life*, the view which... relates all problems—social, political, cultural—to the doctrinal foundations of the Christian Faith, the view which sees all things here below in terms of God's supremacy....[6]

This being the case, it is clearly no longer enough to speak of equipping Christians to answer one-off or seemingly disconnected questions about their "personal faith," or an isolated Christian doctrine here and there—as

---

6. Harry Blamires, *The Christian Mind: How Should a Christian Think?* (London: SPCK, 1963), 3–4, emphasis added.

though all that is required is teaching people some canned answers to the five most popular objections to Christianity and all shall be well for the church. Instead, Christians need renewal and *reformation* in terms of a comprehensive scriptural view of reality, whilst learning to understand and respond to the underlying religious motives shaping our culture. This approach will enable a person to creatively *reformulate* the questions of our time by explaining the religious root and meaning of the unbeliever's own queries and difficulties—both real and imagined. But this kind of faithful Christian engagement can be developed and pursued only from the standpoint of a consistent and coherent biblical world-and-life view, as Blamires well understood:

> For there is something before the Christian dialogue, and that is the Christian mind—a mind trained, informed, equipped to handle data of secular controversy within a framework of reference which is constructed of *Christian presuppositions*. The Christian mind is the prerequisite of Christian thinking. And Christian thinking is the prerequisite of Christian action.[7]

In other words, effective Christian apologetics in our day requires a *total Christian view* of reality as rooted in the Scriptures—a cultural apologetic capable of confronting systematic unbelief with systematic belief, in every sphere of life. By this I do not mean working out a new elitist intellectualizing of the faith to try and impress the scholar or skeptic—a revitalized form of evangelical Scholasticism—but rather a relearning to think, speak, and live by the simple profundity of God's *Word-Revelation* in all life's dimensions; from human identity and sexuality, to marriage and family, law and politics, economics, philosophy, the arts, science, business, media, education, and all things besides, prepared and equipped us to give an answer in our own context.

---

7. Blamires, *The Christian Mind*, 43; italics added.

## Thinking Christianly

To some people, this kind of programmatic worldview apologetic for developing and defending a total Christian philosophy of life, might seem overly radical or simply unnecessary. As the American philosopher, Roy Clouser, once framed the question of the Christian believer skeptical of such comprehensive worldview thinking:

> While one can articulate a Christian view of God, a Christian view of how to stand in right relation to God, and a Christian view of ethics, why is it necessary to articulate a distinctly Christian view of *everything*?[8]

This seems like a fair question. After all, isn't the Christian faith we defend centred in the hope of heaven, life after death, and a final deliverance from this evil world? Isn't biblical faith fundamentally about my personal forgiveness and salvation and my private devotional life? If so, why must believers defend a distinctly Christian view of everything, since on this view of the matter, *everything* is just not really that important? Besides, isn't it only in the "religious" areas of morality and spirituality that Christians and non-Christians disagree? Surely the vast majority of life's vocations, disciplines, institutions, and activities are essentially neutral? Although many believers will agree that we certainly should think about "Christian" issues and themes, surely there isn't a distinctly Christian view of *everything*?

As we have already noted, to the extent that these questions embody assertions of neutrality and skepticism about uniquely Christian answers, these questions betray the collapse of a truly Christian mind and highlight the need for understanding and developing a full-orbed biblical cultural apologetic. The fundamental confusion in these objections, rooted in an underlying nature-grace dualism discussed in earlier chapters, is found in equating *thinking Christianly* with simply *thinking about Christianity* and

---

8. Roy Clouser, "Is There a Christian View of Everything from Soup to Nuts?" *Pro Rege* 31, no. 4 (2003): 1–10, 1.

its doctrines, or about the church and its activities. Blamires' clarification is instructive:

> To think Christianly is to accept *all things* with the mind as related, directly or indirectly, to man's eternal destiny as the redeemed and chosen child of God.
>
> You can think Christianly or you can think secularly about the most sacred things — the sacrament of the altar, for example. Likewise, you can think Christianly or you can think secularly about the most mundane things....
>
> There is *nothing in our experience*, however trivial, worldly, or even evil, which cannot be thought about Christianly....
>
> The fact that many people are writing about *things Christian* is in itself irrelevant to the question whether there is still a Christian mind.[9]

To establish this vital point biblically is important. How do we *know* there is such a thing as a Christian world-and-life view, a truly Christian mind? One essential teaching in Scripture, repeated in several places, is that "the fear of the Lord is the *foundation* of true knowledge" (NLT) or "the fear of the Lord is the *beginning* of wisdom" (HCSB; Ps. 11:10; Prov. 1:7, 9:10, 15:33). The word translated foundation or beginning, means literally the key or principal part. Jesus Himself makes the same point when rebuking erroneous and misleading interpretations of the law in Luke 11:52, "Woe to you experts in the law! You have taken away the key of knowledge!" Here, the key of knowledge is the knowledge of God, especially through the Son, as revealed in the scriptures by the Holy Spirit. This foundational heart knowledge is what Paul calls having "the mind of Christ" (1 Cor. 2:16).

The apostle Paul therefore directs us to Christ Jesus Himself as the one who alone gives true insight. The scope of that renewed understanding is comprehensive. He writes, "by Him you were enriched in everything—in

---

9. Blamires, *The Christian Mind*, 44–46; emphasis added.

all speech and all knowledge" (1 Cor 1:5). Clearly, what St. Paul is explaining here is that knowing God through Christ affects everything, including "all knowledge"—not some artificially restricted churchy or so-called religious or "spiritual" knowledge. A little later, in 1 Corinthians 3:20–23, the apostle goes on to discuss the contrasting Christless wisdom of the world that rejects the Word of God: "The Lord knows that the reasonings of the wise are meaningless... everything is yours and you belong to Christ, and Christ belongs to God." It would be easy to spiritualize this text into a mere pious sentiment, but that would be doing violence to the text. It clearly implies that every area of knowledge, in fact every area of life in all creation, belongs to those who belong to Christ. In short, truth and the meaning of life are not captive to the empty and meaningless reasonings of unbelievers. On the contrary, they refuse to know truth or life as they should.

The obvious implication of this is that, although unbelievers have a *partial* knowledge and insight into many things as creatures made in God's image, living in God's world, their understanding of *all things* suffers from a grievous shortcoming. As Clouser points out, "[T]here is some kind of mistake with respect to every kind of truth and knowledge that can't be avoided if one does not know God but can be avoided if one does know God."[10] There are key foundational elements to the unbeliever's edifice of knowledge, wisdom, and insight which are uneven, weak, and misplaced, skewing the structure of knowledge in the wrong direction—like the Leaning Tower of Pisa. The centre of gravity provided by God's law-Word for creation prevents apostate human knowledge from completely falling over (sometimes called common grace), but the defects remain critical.

What is *not* being said here is that if you want a distinctly Christian view of astronomy, quantum mechanics, the mating habits of the common cockroach, or the intricacies of human cardiology, you need only look up the relevant proof texts in the Scriptures. Any Christian headed to hospital for a heart procedure is going to be deeply concerned if, having entered the operating theatre, he finds the surgeon thumbing through the pages of a

---

10. Clouser, "Is there a Christian View of Everything from Soup to Nuts?," 2

Bible, desperately trying to find a text that will direct his scalpel for the next few hours! Heart surgery necessitates the diligent study of God's creational laws for human physiology, most especially the organ of the heart. It further requires the creative inspiration and discipline necessary for developing and mastering technologies and human techniques to make such surgery possible without killing the patient. The Bible, as the inscripturated Word of God, does not give us exhaustive or encyclopaedic data or knowledge concerning all creational aspects, structures, things, and disciplines—it does not intend to. Neither does creation come to us processed and microwavable or labelled "just add water," like instant coffee. That is, creation is not culture. Its ingredients must be measured, mixed, and turned into usable products— whether those products be thoughts, techniques, or objects. God ordains and mandates a learning and development process in history as we search out the depths of His revelation in the Bible and the created order. Part of the task given to human beings at the beginning of creation, according to Scripture, was to observe, discover, define, and name created entities and their functions, bringing out the potentiality of creation, by acquiring an understanding of created entities and God's laws for all aspects of reality in light of His spoken Word.

A distinctly Christian epistemology, worldview, and apologetic all rest, therefore, not on finding in the Scriptures proof texts for scientific theories like thermodynamics or medical hypotheses for treating heart disease, misusing God's Word with a form of anti-intellectual biblicism, but on recognising Jesus Christ as the *religious foundation* for all knowledge, taking full account of what the Bible says about God, His creation, His law, the human condition, and God's work in history, in all our observations, thinking, theorizing, and living—this is the critical starting point of a faithful Christian philosophy and apologetic. The Bible, as the Word of God, does not contain any theories or hypotheses. It is Truth (John 17:17). That total truth must form the foundation of all our thinking and living. As believers we will then aim to show the unbeliever that to reject the triune God and the creation, fall, redemption, consummation paradigm of the Scriptures is to make a tragic and perilous *religious* mistake that sets aside the principal part and critical foundation of all true knowledge, misdirecting one's total understanding and eventually reducing all of life to unintelligibility and meaninglessness.[11]

In view of this Christocentric starting point for knowledge, developing a truly Christian mind will equip the believer for the task of apologetics—which can be summarized as the work of articulating, defending, and translating the Christian mind, conscience, hope, and imagination with respect to all dimensions of life, so that the embodied Christian world-and-life view is set forth as true, satisfying, and full of meaning. This vision for a cultural apologetic integrated into the normal Christian life is part of our priestly service to God—the defence and confirmation of the good news of Jesus Christ as each area of life is brought into proper relation to the gospel (Phil. 1:7).

## Presupposing the Authority of God's Word Revelation

From a procedural point of view, the believer, thus equipped with a Christian mind and readied to defend and translate the faith, has truly set apart Christ as Lord in their heart (1 Pet. 3:15)—which includes a *total surrender* to the authority of Scripture. As such, God's Word in the Bible, which interprets what is set forth in creation, becomes their *ultimate criterion* of truth. If the reach of human reasoning or various forms of *external* evidence are considered or treated as more basic, reliable, or authoritative, and thus able to stand as "proofs" of the very Word of God, then it is human thinking and logical procedures which are elevated to the ultimate criterion, displacing the Word of God as the final authority.

The reality is that no-one directly *proves* their most basic assumptions or ultimate criterion, their Archimedean point—otherwise it would not be their ultimate criterion at all. All arguments, without exception, must begin with presuppositions and assumptions, and therefore it is impossible that

---

11. For a full discussion of the result of unbelief for knowledge and meaning, see the author's book *Why I Still Believe*.

all assumptions be based on arguments. The most fundamental and basic questions of life, the great boundary questions of worldview—origin, meaning, morality, destiny—always come down to a matter of faith and authority. Where does ultimate authority lie—with the living God as the author of all things, or with us? It is important therefore that Christians seek to defend the faith in a manner consistent with our fundamental beliefs about God and the teaching of His Word.

The very notion that the living God, the maker of all things, who destroyed the ancient world with a flood, delivered His people from Egypt with ten plagues and parted the Red Sea, who took up Elijah with chariots and horses of fire, and who walked on the water and raised Lazarus with a word, needs man's feeble efforts to prop Him up, is on the face of it absurd. We do not establish the reality of the one who establishes us. As creatures, we reason *from* existence, not *to* existence – contra Rene Descartes' famous maxim that "I think, therefore I am." The Holy Spirit, through the Scriptures, reveals to us the God of all truth whose Word is law, whose creation *is* meaning, and who knows the end from the beginning. The only kind of Word such a God can speak is a totally authoritative and infallible Word. Christ Jesus is thus the final Word as God incarnate. From the Christian standpoint, without such revelation from the all-conditioning God, there can be no ultimate objective truth, no absolute eternal reality, but, by definition, only human rationalisations applied to uncreated brute facts in a chaotic cosmos impervious to true interpretation—thoughts spinning like a wheel in mid-air and attached to nothing. All the facts of human experience then become like beads without a chain to link them in unity, and the task of gaining knowledge like a futile attempt to "sew without fastening the ends and without tying a knot in the thread."[12] Bahnsen said it well:

> For the Christian every fact is created, pre-interpreted, and divinely revelatory; the unbeliever holds just the opposite. Even their respective methodologies are

---

12. Gregor Malantschuk, *The Controversial Kierkegaard*, trans. Howard V. Hong and Edna H. Hong (Waterloo, ON: Wilfrid Laurier University Press, 1980), 74.

divergent: one begins with the Creator and approaches the world thinking God's thoughts after Him, while the other attempts to interpret experience by imposing abstract, formal, unifying principles on concrete, contingent, diverse facts.[18]

All this implies that the Bible's truth and explanatory power as the Word of God carries a *self-attesting* authority. The Lord Jesus never appeals to Greek systems of logic, human philosophers, or any human authority to support or prove His claims. He points only to the testimony of His Father, the Holy Spirit, the Scriptures, and His own words and works. It would be absurd for Him to point beyond Himself, as both God and King, the Word made flesh, through whom all things were made, to whom all things belong, and who declares, "before Abraham was, I am" (John 8:58), as though there were a source of authority greater than the triune God to which he could refer. The self-attesting and self-authenticating character of Christ's authority is what caused, and still causes, such offense.

Whilst the Christian engaged in apologetics may legitimately discuss the textual reliability of the Bible seen through the lens of historical and archeological investigation, point to the ancient and plentiful biblical manuscripts which show the accuracy of its transmission, answer the questions of those who ask about textual variants, and highlight scientific discoveries of all kinds as a means of focusing people's attention, none of this *proves* or demonstrates the Bible to be the Word of God and should never pretend to do so. This is because historical and scientific inquiry is also conducted in the context of changing worldviews and paradigms and can only ever produce varying degrees of confidence in any specific event. The world of immanent creation is in a constant state of change, movement or becoming, and no human mind, all of which are also developing and changing, can function as the north star for man's existence. Moreover, we do well to remember that sinful people in the grip of unbelief are no more inclined to be receptive to God's self-revelation in creation and history than they are to rejoice in the words of Scripture (cf. Rom. 1:18–32)

---

13. Bahnsen, *Presuppositional Apologetics*, 112.

Consequently, it is vital that believers place their faith and trust in the Word of God as the starting point for faithful apologetics, just as it is for the rest of the Christian life, not some other point of reference. Moving from the sphere of the family or church, we must not shift our ground to some other foundation or starting point when confronting unbelief in the culture, as though that were necessary to convince or have "credibility" with the unbeliever. Rather, we place our hope and confidence in Jesus Christ, not in the futile and empty reasoning of man, which results only in epistemic confusion. Boldly and unapologetically, the believer is to *presuppose* the truth of the Christian worldview, submitting *a priori* to the total dependability of God's Word in every part. We do not hold that the Bible is true and the Word of Christ trustworthy *after* we have analysed it and decided whether it is *logical* by our judgment, or *ethical* in our estimation, or sufficiently supported by external contemporary historical assessments of the expert"—the falsified theories of whom are scattered as plentifully as rotting driftwood floating on the waves of history. The Lord Jesus said in John 17:17 when He prayed to the Father, "Your Word is Truth." The psalmist in the great Psalm 119:142 declares "Your Law is Truth." This is the Christian's sure foundation. Prayerful reflection upon the Word of God through the power of the Holy Spirit is our *Archimedean point* of departure and starting point for our defense of the faith.

This approach clearly contrasts with traditional views of apologetics that seek to first directly "prove" God's existence with chains of human reasoning from allegedly self-evident ideas or concepts, and then the validity of God's Word with external evidences, before making any clear biblical truth claims or demands of man. Cornelius Van Til explains:

> The traditional method had explicitly built into it the right and ability of the natural man, apart from the work of the Spirit of God, to be the judge of the claim of the authoritative Word of God. It is man who, by means of his self-established intellectual tools, puts his "stamp of approval" on the Word of God and then, only after that grand act, does he listen to it. God's Word must first pass man's test of good and evil, truth and falsity. But once you tell a non-Christian this, why should he be worried by anything else that you say. You have already told him he is quite alright just the way he is! Then Scripture is not correct when it talks of "darkened

minds," "willful ignorance," "dead men" and "blind people!" With this method the correctness of the natural man's problematics is endorsed. That is all he needs to reject the Christian faith.[14]

It is precisely because of this that when the apostles are engaged in evangelism and giving a defense of the faith to the skeptic, they "reasoned with them *from* the Scriptures" (Acts 17:17). Notice they did not reason *to* the Scripture, as though they were establishing its authority, but *from* the teaching and worldview of the Scriptures. Clearly, this does not set aside careful thinking, philosophical engagement, or reasoned arguments, as witness St. Paul on Mars Hill in Athens. Nor does it require a mindless Bible-thumping by simply quoting Scripture passages at people. St. Paul on Mars Hill does not cite any particular Scriptural text, but his discourse is clearly an exposition of the biblical worldview and teaching. The apostles were all engaged in reasoning *with* the Scriptures and *in light* of the Scripture, not pretending to some imaginary rational neutrality by calling on the unbeliever to logically determine if God's claims in His own Word are valid. In all our evangelistic and apologetic efforts, it is imperative to remember that it is God the Holy Spirit who reveals Christ to people, and whilst the Christian may be used as God's instrument in a given situation, the power to change hearts does not lie with us. When Jesus asked Peter, "Who do you say that I am," and Peter replied, "You are the Messiah the Son of the living God," Jesus says, "You are blessed because flesh and blood did not reveal this to you, but My Father in heaven" (Matt. 16:17).

The Bible makes crystal clear that all people have a duty to acknowledge God's self-revelation in creation, Christ, and Scripture, and conform their thinking and lives to it (Rom. 1:18–32). The Christian's task is to witness to that reality, make clear Christ's unique claims, and give a reasoned defense for the hope we have so that every mouth may be stopped, and each one be confronted with their accountability to God (Rom. 3:19). The results of our

---

14. Cornelius Van Til, "My Credo," in *Jerusalem and Athens*, ed. E. R. Geehan (Phillipsburg, NJ: Presbyterian and Reformed, 1971), 11.

obedience in this area lie with God Himself. His Word is the *condition* of all life, and it is His Spirit that quickens the spiritually dead. God's holy Word we must take by faith and presuppose as the foundation of the Christian mind.

## Thinking Unchristianly

Those who reject Christ and the revelation of His Word obviously *do not* have this distinctly *Christian* view of things. We have already seen that this does not make them religiously neutral. It does not mean they lack a *faith dimension* in life or an essentially religious foundation for their thinking. Rather, unbelievers cling to something that *takes the place* and role of the living God—a God-surrogate. This fact does not eliminate the point of contact between the Christian and the unbeliever. As people living in God's revelatory world of total meaning, made in His image and likeness, human beings cannot escape their creaturehood and all that they have in common ontologically and psychologically. The Christian meets the unbeliever fully on the level of our shared humanity. But as Van Til has shown, the radical divergence comes about in the area of epistemology (i.e., the procedures of knowledge) because of the noetic effects of sin on the human mind and intellect—here a gulf separates the natural man and the regenerate man. In showing how Abraham Kuyper's writing pointed us in the right direction, Van Til notes:

> Kuyper has well brought out the fact that the natural man, working on the principles of his own adoption must, to be logical, deny all that Christianity stands for.
>
> It is this fact, that the natural man, using his principles and working on his assumptions, must be hostile in principle at every point to the Christian philosophy of life, that was stressed in the writer's little book, *Common Grace*. That all men have all things in common metaphysically and psychologically, was definitely asserted, and further, that the natural man has epistemologically nothing in common with the Christian. And this latter assertion was qualified by saying that this is so only

*in principle*. For it is not till after the consummation of history that men are left wholly to themselves....

As far as the principle of the natural man in concerned, it is *absolutely* or utterly, not partly, opposed to God. That principle is Satanic. It is exclusively hostile to God. If it could, it would destroy the work and plan of God.[15]

As such, the challenge we face in apologetic confrontation with those in the grip of unbelief is what we can call an epistemological sin of the heart—a refusal to acknowledge God's Word-revelation and then respond with obedience. This is how the apostle Paul describes the situation in Romans 1:18–24:

> For God's wrath is revealed from heaven against all godlessness and unrighteousness of people who by their unrighteousness *suppress the truth*, since what can be known about God is evident among them, because God has shown it to them. For His invisible attributes, that is, His eternal power and divine nature, have been clearly seen since the creation of the world, being understood through what He has made. As a result, people are *without excuse*. For though they knew God, they did not glorify Him as God or show gratitude. Instead, their thinking became nonsense, and their senseless minds were darkened.... They exchanged the truth of God for a lie, and worshiped and served something created instead of the Creator, who is praised forever. Amen.

All worldviews, not just the Christian faith, have their own religious starting point with a *presupposed* criterion of truth and ultimate explainer for reality. It is at this religious foundation that the truth is exchanged for a lie. The unbeliever's *explainer* for reality, when carefully examined, will always posit something that "just is," or is "just there," something that does not depend on anything else for its being, an unconditioned reality to take the place of God, a divine "per se." Simply stated, everybody either believes in the living God, or will give something created (i.e., the cosmos or some

---

15. Van Til, *The Defense of the Faith*, 169.

part of it), a God-surrogate, the status of divinity. This religious exchange the Bible calls idolatry, and it is this religious *foundation* that impacts all human knowledge and thinking, giving direction and shape to the non-Christian mind—its beliefs, theories, cultural expressions, and lifestyle choices. Over the centuries, the idol factory of the human heart has tried to give divine status to anything and everything: planetary bodies, emperors and states, angels and ancestors, numbers and ideas, logic or human reason, matter and energy, and much else besides. Clouser's explanation of this is instructive:

> Those who don't see the divine as the biblical transcendent Creator will make it some part of the world instead. And regarding anything in the world as self-existent will slant, guide and control the (deeper) content of every concept, including concepts of hypotheses....
>
> The name given to this way of explaining, the way that identifies *what part of the world* all the rest depends on, is "reduction." A reductionist explanation is one that claims to have found the part of the world that everything else depends on.... A Christian should say, "These are all wrong. They are all examples of regarding part of creation as the Creator. The ultimate explainer is no part of creation at all. Every one of these divinity candidates is real, but they all depend on God.... [T]he Christian would adopt a systematically non-reductionist approach to every sort of theory, every sort of knowledge, and every concept of everything.[16]

Idolatry can clearly take on remarkably deceptive forms, so that man's creativity in identifying God-surrogates can appear very complex and sophisticated. These idols then shape people's thinking and through them our society. For example, some people take the *physical* (sometimes coupled with the biological) aspect or dimension of reality and use it to explain everything else. This is done by attempting to reduce everything in creation to the physical. The physical dimension of reality is thought to be *truly real*,

---

16. Clouser, "Is There a Christian View of Everything from Soup to Nuts?," 6; italics added.

whilst everything else—the non-physical dimensions of creation like the numerical, sensitive, logical, aesthetic, lingual, social, juridical, moral, cultural, and faith dimensions are either illusory or simply by-products of what is really just physical. On this view, everything is made entirely dependent on and subordinate to the physical dimension of reality, and so every other facet of creation is diminished in status as much less important or less real. The importance of the physical dimension of creation is therefore vastly overestimated relative to everything that is said to be dependent on it. This is the nature of the kind of *reductionism* that characterizes the unbelieving mind. It performs a *grand levelling* of all reality as matter "leaps" from one dimension of existence to the next, as though the movement of atoms alone can account for the psychical, social, juridical, cultural, moral, and faith life of man!

By way of contrast, the truly Christian mind regards everything in all creation as equally real, equally dependent, and equally subject to God and His law-Word, so that no dimension of the cosmos, or combination of dimensions, generates or explains all the rest. The Christian mind has a *non-reductionist* worldview because it does not reduce the universe, in part or in whole, to one or more dimensions of the cosmos, or even to God. Neither can any entity within creation be looked to as the source or explainer for the world. There is a *Creator-creature distinction* unequivocally asserted by the Scriptures, denoting the dependency of all creation directly upon God, making every dimension and constituent of creation equally real, with no part reduced in its importance or role relative to the rest.

This is what marks out the *basic framework* of a truly Christian mind over against unbelief, and indicates the line of battle for a Christian apologetic as it internally critiques the worldviews that oppose the living God. Trying to stuff the entire cosmos into one dimension of it (such as the physical), is like trying to cram the entire contents of your shed into a small box—things will always stick out because they just won't be pressed into such a shape. As such, whenever religious idolatry is at work, *reductionism* manifests itself intellectually. And it always reduces human beings to less than they are. All forms of idolatry are dehumanizing, because they seek to remake man in the image of an idol rather than as he is: the image of God. As Nancy Pearcey has pointed out:

> The link is that idols always lead to a lower view of human life. The Bible teaches that humans are made in the image of God. When a worldview exchanges the creator for something in creation, it will also exchange a high view of humans made in God's image for a lower view of humans made in the image of something in creation. We could say that every concept of humanity is created in the image of some God.[17]

This is tragically seen in the real-world consequences of unbelieving thought, which is devastating when consistently applied. As just one example, evolutionary materialism (physicalism) helped to give the Western world both Nazism and Marxist-communism that sacrificed millions of lives to their idol in the twentieth century, regarding human life as a dispensable means to an end.

Perhaps the most popular idol of our own age is again, like ancient Greece and Rome, the idol of politics, where truth, morality, law, and meaning are the province of the State—the German philosopher Hegel's divine idea as it exists on earth—providing cradle to grave security as the new providential god and the arbiter of life. Here, justice and truth are what the state say they are. The crowd, the mob, the "democratic will" increasingly expresses this mutiny against the living God. The political idol of the West fights God and His claims tooth and nail, giving it a powerful demonic element. Interestingly, Søren Kierkegaard foresaw that atheistic and neo-pagan movements would make their appearance as political trends and then manifest their true religious identity:

---

17. Nancy Pearcey, *Finding Truth: 5 Principles for Unmasking Atheism, Secularism, and Other God Substitutes* (Colorado Springs, CO: David C. Cook, 2015), 44.

The future will correspond inversely to the Reformation: then everything appeared to be a religious movement and became politics; now everything appears to be politics but will become a religious movement.[18]

## Proof That Follows

In the apologetic mindset and method that I have described, I hope it has become clear that the *how* of the Christian faith, trusting in and following Christ and His Word, is as important as the *what*—because the *what* cannot be ascertained or established under the illusion of some universal capacity of autonomous human thinking. The attempt to do so will always end, as rationalism always has, in an *accommodation* of the Christian faith to the culture and to the gradual diminution of the gospel. We must never lose sight of the reality that human reasoning itself needs redemption and reconciliation to the truth, just like every other dimension of human life.

To *learn* the truth, the unbeliever must recognise and accept that they have, heretofore, lived in *untruth* and so acknowledge their dependency on the agency of God the Holy Spirit. It is only here that Christ, who is the Truth, becomes for us constitutive of a new paradigm—the Christian faith. We have seen that no higher human perspective can be invoked to bring Christ or His revelation into judgment. Faith in Christ is the Archimedean point.

The difficultly for sinners in believing this is not the reach of their reason, but the hardness of their hearts. It is difficult to believe, because it is difficult to obey. So, the Christian must invite the unbeliever to take a decisive step—to put on the lenses of Christ and the gospel of the Kingdom to look again at life and the world; to take up His Word and pray for insight; to surrender their illusions and so grasp the Truth. Ultimately, we must call the rebel to *follow and believe in order to understand*. It is only here that the rest of quiet certitude can arise:

---

18. Kierkegaard, cited in Malantschuk, *The Controversial Kierkegaard*, 73.

If someone wanted to be [Christ's] follower, his approach, as seen in the Gospel, was different from lecturing. To such a person he said something like this: venture a decisive act; then we can begin. What does this mean? It means that one does not become a Christian by hearing something about Christianity, by reading something about it, by thinking about it.... No, a setting (situation) is required—venture a decisive act; the proof does not precede but follows, is in and with the imitation that follows Christ.[19]

## The Apologist as Evangelist

Because of this distinctly Christian view of knowledge and the apologetic task, the defense and confirmation of the evangel, with all its varied implications, centres itself in *presupposing* the authority of the Lord Jesus, and therefore in the *proclamation* of the gospel of the Kingdom. It is only in truly *following Christ*, who is Himself the Truth, that we come to a right understanding and all of life is turned right side up. And so, in our apologetic labour, we must never lose sight of the fact that, first and foremost, we are evangelists. The evangelist is privileged to herald the *good news* of the reality of the Kingdom of God which appeared in history in the person of Jesus Christ, our Creator and Redeemer. By the power of the Holy Spirit, we are seeking to *call* people to Him and *show* them how to enter His Kingdom.

We have already seen that to do so is a challenging task in a context of *de-Christianization* in the West, because for people to readily understand each other requires a common language, a common discourse, a shared *framework* for understanding life in the world that rests upon a mutually accepted standard or authority. In this cultural moment, with the idols of our age as plentiful as they were in ancient Rome, the *foundation* for that common discourse has eroded beneath us—the biblical world-and-life view is no longer the directing principle of our culture. A once-shared understanding of reality informed by Scripture, one that enabled the gospel to

---

19. Kierkegaard, cited in Rae, *Kierkegaard's Vision*, 158.

be quickly grasped, has given way to a cacophony of competing ideas and voices that challenge and question our authority to teach, and even our right to speak at all.

When St. Paul first went to declare the gospel in idolatrous Athens he had to overcome a similar barrier to understanding. The common people called him a dabbler, a "seed picker"—someone who had picked up a variety of strange ideas, like many others in that city. In fact, Acts 17 tells us people often went to Athens just to say or hear something new. As such, some assumed the great apostle was speaking of two new gods, "Jesus," and "Resurrection" when he shared the gospel in the marketplace. Paul's subsequent opportunity to address the Areopagus led to his famous apologetic discourse on Mars Hill which required him to explain, defend, and declare the claims of Christ and the gospel to those ignorant of the living God and the Scriptures—people holding very different idolatrous worldviews. And yet, his message culminated in the audacious command to repent:

> God has shut his eyes to these passing follies of ours; now he calls upon all men, everywhere, to repent, because he has fixed a day when he will pronounce judgment on the whole world. And the man whom he has appointed for that end he has accredited to all of us, by raising him from the dead (Acts 17:30–31, Knox Bible).

Paul makes this declaration with an *emphatic authority* to sophisticated philosophers, as one called to do the work of the evangelist and who characterised his own ministry as existing for the *defense and confirmation of the gospel* (Phil. 1:7). In the twenty-first century cultural context of the West, we are similarly seen by a lost and ignorant generation as religious "dabblers" in a vast marketplace of spiritual ideas. And yet, we are called to declare and defend the gospel with a like apostolic authority.

## Romanticism and the Crisis of Authority

One of the key reasons for this loss of a common discourse and current resistance to the gospel goes back to a deeply religious philosophical movement known as *Romanticism* that profoundly impacted Western culture. Romanticism was the nineteenth century's spiritual reaction to the cold rationalism of the so-called Enlightenment. It was a time of religious upheaval and confusion in which another attempt was made to bring together Christian ideas and humanism in a new synthesis.

Romanticism wished to free the human person from the mechanistic picture of a scientific world of rigid law that dominated the rationalist philosophers and scientists of the previous century. But in the process of wanting to recover the freedom of the human personality from a deterministic view of the world, it rejected the notion of *universal moral law*. Instead, they looked for the rule of human conduct in the *individual* and their personal dispositions and feelings. The human personality was to be a *law unto itself*. This clearly implied a kind of *moral anarchy* with everyone doing whatever they felt was right for them, so Romanticism as an encompassing worldview needed some way to limit individual freedom in society. This was done by emphasizing human persons as members of an *embracing community*—a wider family, people or nation. The idea of being part of a wider, but nonetheless "unique" community with a particular spirit or ethos, was supposed to provide a sense of identity and viable limits for human expression in place of the law-Word of God. This ideal of Romanticism remains the dominant spirit of our present age in which we preach Christ. People are a *law to themselves* and seek their truth and identity in various discreet "groups."

In practical terms, this spiritual ethos wants no reality except the one it ordains by imagination. The mantra of romantism might be summarised, "*I desire, therefore, I am.*" If I want it or desire it, I must have it, and the world must adapt to service my desires and those of my unique group or tribe. Cultural theologian, Rousas Rushdoony, summed up this ethos effectively when he wrote:

> Romanticism wants the world of one's imagination, not reality. In fact, romanticism imagines that man can do things better than God, if only God would permit it! Not surprisingly, romanticism readily decays into occultism and Satanism....

The romantic refuses to accept God's reality and becomes enraged or grief-stricken when life frustrates him or her.[20]

Though according to the Bible we are fallen and ruined in sin, the Romantic ethos prefers to see people as *innocent victims* in the cosmos, where God's world is the problem. In a context where everyone wants to declare their own truth for themselves, imagine their own sexuality and gender, create their own self, and live their own lawless life, the Word of the gospel as something to be *obeyed* seems alien to the listener, and the apologist like a strange seed picker amidst the smorgasbord of spiritual choices.

## The Genius or the Apologist

This focus on particularity, where the rule for life is wholly individual, and where each one must "be themselves" as they imagine themselves to be, means that Romanticism promotes an *ethics of genius*. God's Word as carrying authority *for all* is seen as opposed to true *morality for the individual*.

The concept of *genius* has a pagan origin. The *genius* of a family, community, emperor or state was the guiding *supernatural spirit* that inhabited and took care of it and was therefore worshipped. Consequently, all faithful Romans worshipped the *genius* of Rome and that of Caesar as emperor, for it guided and protected both Caesar and Rome. Early Christians who refused to offer incense to the *genius* of the emperor were severely persecuted as traitors.

In the modern era, the intellectual, the scientist, the social planner, and the artist are widely regarded (and often see themselves) as the *genius* for the community—a new elite guiding the era and bringing out the spirit or zeitgeist of the age in their thought and work. By man's own "inspiration" he shepherds himself into the future without reference to the living God. As

---

20. Rousas J. Rushdoony, *Faith and Action*, vol. 1, *Authority, Humanism and Morality* (Vallecito, CA: Ross House Books, 2019), 428–29.

such, the world is not to be understood in terms of the Christian confession of faith and the Word of God, but by the *intuition* and *creative genius* of the heroic pioneer who charts a new path and makes a brave new world with a new truth, new morality, new society, and new sexuality. As Rushdoony observes concerning this development after the Renaissance:

> The artist, and especially the writer, began to see himself as a genius, producing for the ages. He was thus an *elite* man, but he was more than merely an elite man; the elite are the pick of society, the choicest part. The genius is much more than that: he is a supernormal and somewhat supernatural breakthrough into society and thus above even the elite....
>
> In the French Revolution, men who believed in their genius overthrew a social order and began the ruthless destruction of all things which ran counter to their "inspiration."[21]

This mentality inevitably becomes a war on the "normal" and a hatred of God's order for life and culture. The influential thinker Friedrich Nietzsche, for example, in a letter to his sister in 1888 wrote, "You have not the slightest idea what it means to be next-of-kin to the man of destiny in whom the question of epochs has been settled. Quite literally speaking: I hold the future of mankind in the palm of my hand."[22]

Over-against this apostate religious idea of the *genius*, the Bible places the *offices* of the apostle, evangelist and prophet who speak for God, declaring the gospel and fulness of God's Word-revelation. This important distinction between the Romantic, humanistic worldview and that of the Bible is vital for us to understand if we are to fulfil the apologetic task.

In the popular conception of the *genius*, we tend to think of highly gifted, original, or brilliant individuals in a variety of fields—thinkers, scientists, artists, musicians and so forth. In the course of history, certain outstanding

---

21. Rushdoony, *Faith and Action*, 1.441.
22. Nietzsche, cited in Rushdoony, *Faith and Action*, 1.443.

and talented people emerge who bring something fresh or new to human culture—a kind of *innate* originality. The Christian thinker Søren Kierkegaard posed the important question as to whether we can say the apostle Paul was a genius. He notes that when compared to Shakespeare or Plato, Paul was not a great stylist. However, though geniuses like Shakespeare and Plato do add something to their time and the story of human culture, what they produce is simply taken up in a history which assimilates their work and moves beyond them. Their life and contribution, however brilliant, can be adequately understood and relativized in the context of historical-cultural development which is a purely *immanent* frame of reference. But the apostle Paul, like all the apostles, is what he is not by mere natural endowment, but by *divine authority*, by *transcendent* calling. The message of the apostles cannot be just assimilated, *relativized*, and surpassed in the course of time. Kierkegaard highlights the difference this way:

> An apostle is not *born*; an apostle is a man who is *called* and appointed by God and sent by him on a mission.... By this call he does not become more intelligent, he does not acquire more imagination, greater discernment etc.—not at all; he remains himself but by the paradoxical fact [i.e., the incarnation of Christ and mystery of the gospel] is sent by God on a specific mission.... The apostle did not act as the person distinguished by natural gifts who was ahead of his contemporaries. Perhaps he was what we call a simple person, but by a paradoxical fact he was called to proclaim this new thing.[23]

This distinction is of inestimable importance. Many gifted people are *born* and, under God's providence (for He can create as many as He chooses), can bring something new to human culture that is gradually assimilated as a typical aspect of *historical* development. But the evangelist or apologist, like the apostle, is not, as the genius, simply *born*, but is *called* and commissioned by the transcendent God, to bring the good news of Christ whose

---

23. Søren Kierkegaard, *The Essential Kierkegaard*, ed. Howard V. Hong and Edna H. Hong (Princeton, NJ: Princeton University Press, 2000), 340 –41; italics added.

power and authority are from beyond history. The apologist defends and declares a message into a fallen world that is powerful and *always original* and transformative for the individual who receives it gladly, because it is not an idea, but *revelation* from the living God. The authority and the power of the evangelist-apologist's message are not a natural endowment, but a divine commission, carrying the divine imprimatur, because it involves the heralding of the very Word of God.

We can think about the difference in this way. A gifted person and the so-called genius are evaluated in terms of their art—it is an *aesthetic* assessment. Is their work beautiful, original, powerful, moving, and so on? The genius is admired, adhered to, or listened to purely on the basis of their unusually imaginative creativity or the profundity of their insight into a given field of human inquiry. But we do not listen to Christ because of his artistic creativity, or to St. Paul because of his brilliance—we listen because they have a unique *authority*. To ask if Jesus Christ is *profound* in the Romantic sense is a form of blasphemy, because it is to reduce Him to the level of every human being, to *assess Him* by our own criterion as we would an artist.

To listen to Christ over against the genius is like the difference between heeding the command of a King and the suggestion of a neighbour. One carries an unequivocal authority, the other does not. If my king in Great Britain were to issue me a command to take a message for him, and a passer-by on the street were to give me the *same command* using the *same words*, only the words of the king would have real authority standing behind them. It is, therefore, not simply the *form* or *content* of the words that grant authority to the evangelist-apologist, but their divine origin—it is the One who speaks through them. As Christians called to witness to the truth, we may not think ourselves the most gifted communicators or speakers, but this is irrelevant to the power and authority of our message.

Poor Aristotle was undoubtedly a brilliant person and what some would call a genius. He spoke much about his conception of "god," immortality, politics, and ethics, and though he thought a great deal of himself, he spoke with no true *authority*. He taught his *theories* about many things that were taken up, assimilated, surpassed, and corrected by subsequent generations. However, the good news of the Kingdom of Christ shared by the evangelist-apologist is not, like the work of Aristotle, a human philosophy, and the Scriptures contain no theories, for they are the very Word of God—the same Word that holds all things together.

Given this reality, it would have been absurd for St. Paul or Philip the evangelist to appeal to their brilliance, originality, or creativity to authenticate their message, as though they were simply gifted individuals with new ideas—it would destroy the truth and power of the gospel if they did. The question, when it comes to the Word of Truth in Christ, is not whether our hearers think us insightful, our presentation creative, or our ideas original, but only whether the hearer is ready to *obey* the gospel of God because we come commissioned with *divine authority* from the King of kings, in terms of the Word of God (Matt. 28:18–20)). The authority does not reside in our natural gifts, but in our *calling* to make known the *revelation* of God in the Lord Jesus. The unique quality of true *authority* is that it comes from above, irrespective of the aesthetic value of our evangelistic discourse.

It is easy to give lip service to this truth as Christians, but all too often we can be led astray by the world's *aesthetic assessment* of what is worth listening to. We can be so taken up with the creativity, subtlety, cleverness, or originality *of the telling* in our critical, Romantic age; we can so desire to *please our hearers* like an insecure artist, that we lose sight of the central message itself and forget that the *authority* and persuasiveness of our message lies solely in our *calling* to make Christ known, in the *power* of the Spirit. As St. Paul writes:

> When I came to you, brothers, announcing the testimony of God to you, I did not come with brilliance of speech or wisdom. For I didn't think it was a good idea to know anything among you except Jesus Christ and Him crucified. I came to you in weakness, in fear, and in much trembling. My speech and my proclamation were not with persuasive words of wisdom but with a powerful demonstration by the Spirit (1 Corinthians 2:1–4).

There is nothing wrong with seeking to be creative in order to be clearly understood, nor in being winsome. And yet the goal of winsomeness can become an excuse for our failure to fulfil our *calling* to declare and defend the gospel of the Lord Jesus Christ and the fulness of His law-Word. St. Paul did not go to the Areopagus on Mars Hill before the philosophers of the age to demonstrate his originality, genius, or rhetorical skill—attributes of an orator that were greatly admired by his hearers—but to call men and women to *repentance and faith* in the One who is to judge the world in righteousness.

The essential difference between the apostle Paul and the philosophers who heard him was not a *quantitative* difference in terms of natural ability, but a *qualitative* difference—divine authority as one entrusted with the gospel.

Because it is the very Word of the triune God that we declare, the matter of the Truth of our message is already decided. Some scoffed that day on Mars Hill. Others, intrigued, asked to hear Paul again. And yet some council members *believed*—for the gospel is not a matter of philosophical speculation (since no man can conceptually "think through" the eternal God incarnate in the man Christ Jesus); it must be *believed*. And that is why we preach Christ crucified, raised to life and seated at the right hand of all power and authority.

If the evangelist-apologist compromises the truth or plays with the Word of God in any way to ingratiate themselves, impress the critics, or "soften the blow" for their hearers, then they have lost sight of the fact that the gospel of Christ is not given to be admired, to be speculated about, or to provide entertainment; it is something to be *believed* and *obeyed*. In the same way, the gospel is not adorned or made more persuasive if it has powerful friends, the endorsement of celebrities, or the support of influential people, because the gospel of the Kingdom we proclaim as Christians is not a human achievement, a mere socio-political movement, a motivational self-help tool, or a school of thought for the brilliant to cogitate about. As soon as we implicitly reduce it to any of those things, we have undermined the gospel itself and made it about ourselves and our idea—we have reduced it to a *human work* of art. We have surrendered to Romanticism, propagating a truth "for us," placing the Lord Jesus and His apostles on the *immanent* level of the genius to be assessed by a sin-formed criterion, stripping the gospel of its *transcendent* authority.

## The Nature of True of Authority

We should reflect just a little more on this question of authority. As Christians, we make known the good news of the Kingdom, *in order to* glorify God and advance His kingdom reign. We have seen that we do so with divine authorization because we have been called and *entrusted* with this message by the King of kings and Lord of all lords. As such, evangelism comes down to *a question of authority,* and authority is an inescapably religious issue. In Matthew 28 and what we call the *Great Commission* we read:

> But Jesus came near and spoke to them; *All authority in heaven and on earth, he said, has been given to me; you, therefore, must go out,* making disciples of all nations, and baptizing them in the name of the Father, and of the Son, and of the Holy Ghost, teaching them to observe all the commandments which I have given you. And behold I am with you all through the days that are coming, until the consummation of the world (Matt. 28:18–20, Knox Bible).

As the ultimate sovereign power over all things in heaven and earth, several realities are inescapably implied in this final charge to the followers of Jesus. *Firstly,* Christ Himself is the source of all valid *law* and all legitimate commands. *Secondly,* He is the fountainhead of all true *authority.* Without recognising the living Christ, raised and ascended in power and glory, there is no abiding or valid law and authority. This reality is always reflected in culture. When Christ's authority is eroded in a society, a crisis of authority spreads from one area of life to the next, creating social decay everywhere. And *thirdly,* those sent and commissioned by Christ our sovereign Lord go out clothed in His *authority* and carrying His *presence*—go therefore; I am with you!

Notice that a peculiar authority was always the mark of the preaching of Jesus and the apostles. We are told in Matthew 7: "When Jesus had finished these sayings, the multitudes found themselves amazed at his teaching. For he taught them, not like their scribes and Pharisees, but like one *who had authority*" (Matt. 7:28–29, Knox Bible).

The Lord amazed His hearers not with brilliant oration, or subtle and skilled interpretation, nor by creative genius, but as one with unique authority. In like manner, those commissioned by the risen Lord will be bold and carry a unique authority: "Seeing the boldness of Peter and John, and discovering that they were simple men, without learning, they were astonished, and recognised them now as having been in Jesus' company" (Acts 4:13, Knox Bible).

Recognition of the believer's authority in the hearer is tied to both the *message* itself and the *messenger* as one *called* to do the work of the evangelist. When Christians are truly faithful, the Word of the gospel through us can penetrate to the very root of the person, *to the heart*, where the Spirit of God does His work of convicting, enlightening, and transforming (John 16:7–11). In fact, God's Word is clear that we are the fragrance of life to some and of death to others.

> I give thanks to God, that he is always exhibiting us as the captives in the triumph of Christ Jesus, and through us spreading abroad everywhere, like a perfume, the knowledge of himself. We are Christ's incense offered to God, making manifest both those who are achieving salvation and those who are on the road to ruin; as a deadly fume where it finds death, as a life-giving perfume where it finds life. *Who can prove himself worthy of such a calling?* We do not, like so many others, adulterate the Word of God, we preach it in all its purity, as God gave it to us, standing before God's presence in Christ (2 Cor. 2:14–17. Knox Bible).

This is remarkable imagery. St. Paul likens God's servants to *exhibits* of the victory of Jesus Christ, just as Roman conquerors displayed their captives and spoil to the public in triumphant processions into the city. Through us as believers the living God spreads everywhere, like a perfume, the knowledge of Himself. Unlike incense offered to the *genius* of (spiritual power behind) the emperor, we are *Christ's incense* offered to God, which literally smokes out those on the path to life and those on the road to ruin. We are not worthy of such a privileged calling. But Paul makes the central task clear—preaching the Word in all its purity as God has given it to us, not twisting, distorting, or watering it down to the liking of our culture, because we stand in Christ before the very presence of God in this task. Once the evangelist adulterates the Word, authority is lost!

## Romanticism or Repentance: The Price of Going with Authority

Entailed in the meaning of the Christian's calling is the reality that people are not a *law unto themselves*; the *zeitgeist* of our era is a deception. As such, confrontation with the neo-pagan spirit of Romanticism requires a willingness to battle the *genius* (i.e., spiritual lie) of the age—the *egalitarianism* that demands a leveling of all things, placing all people, ideas, truth claims, and cultures on a relativized playing field within the immanent frame. This makes the gospel of Christ and its *transcendent* source (with its claim to total authority) offensive to fallen man's sensibilities and religious preferences. And since the gospel of the Kingdom is not man's cultural idea or work of art, it is equally offensive to the spirit at work in each generation. It can never be merely subsumed within the historical-cultural process and transcended—it always stands in *paradoxical relation* to fallen men and women.

This means that everyone must pass *through* the offence of the gospel if they are to come to Christ—the alternatives are Romanticism or repentance, not both. There is no way around, over, or under owning one of these alternatives. No clever sleight of hand of the apologist can mitigate this offense. In our natural condition, fallen man is at enmity with God, hostile to Christ's authority and His claims upon us (Rom. 8:7–9). The message of the gospel in the God-man who possesses in Himself all truth and all authority, whose Kingdom is an everlasting Kingdom that cannot fail, and who redeems from sin, death, and the curse by His atoning death and resurrection, is foolishness and a stumbling block to those who are perishing. But to those who are being saved it is the power and wisdom of God (1 Cor. 1:18).

This encounter with *divine authority* through the Lord's sent ones means that as Christians we must be ready to suffer for our message because of the *genius* of the world. Jesus warned very clearly that if He was hated and suffered, though He is the very Word of life and truth and the bearer of absolute divine authority, then His *evangelists* are called to suffer also.

> If the world hates you, *be sure that it hated me before it learned to hate you*. If you belonged to the world, the world would know you for its own and love you; it is because you do not belong to the world, because I have singled you out from the midst of the world, that the world hates you. Do not forget what I said to you, no servant can be greater than his master. *They will persecute you just as they have persecuted me;* they will pay the same attention to your words as to mine. And they will treat you thus because *you bear my name*. (John 15:18–21, Knox Bible)

To bear the name of Christ in the task of evangelism and apologetics is to carry both His *authority* and His *reproach* in making the gospel known. The Christian must not be surprised or concerned if, in bearing His name and speaking His Word, we are rejected, slandered, mocked, or mistreated. Rather, we should be concerned if this *never* happens. The apostle Peter writes to the church:

> Rejoice when you share in some measure the sufferings of Christ; so joy will be yours, and triumph, when his glory is revealed. Your lot will be a blessed one, if you are reproached for the name of Christ... *it means that his own Spirit, is resting upon you* (1 Pet. 4:13–14, Knox Bible).

In evangelism and apologetics, we need not be geniuses, nor do we compete on the same human level as the expert, the polymath, or the prodigy in the defense and confirmation of our message. For by the gospel, the Lord takes what is weak and despised for His purposes.

> Instead, God has chosen what is foolish in the world to shame the wise, and God has chosen what is weak in the world to shame the strong. God has chosen what is insignificant and despised in the world—what is viewed as nothing—to bring to nothing what is viewed as something, so that no one can boast in His presence (1 Cor. 1:27–29).

In all our service and faithful efforts to declare and defend the faith once for all delivered to the saints, we are given this great assurance:

For it is written:

I will destroy the wisdom of the wise,
and I will set aside the understanding of the experts.

Where is the philosopher? Where is the scholar? Where is the debater of this age? Hasn't God made the world's wisdom foolish?

...because God's foolishness is wiser than human wisdom, and God's weakness is stronger than human strength (1 Cor. 1:19–20, 25).

CHAPTER 7

# Think Christianly About Science and Evolutionism

*In the beginning was the Word, and the Word was with God, and the Word was God. He was with God in the beginning. All things were created through Him, and apart from Him not one thing was created that has been created.*
— John 1:1-3 (HCSB)

## The Biblical Worldview

THE MAGISTERIAL BOOK OF GENESIS opens with these words:

> In the beginning God created the heavens and the earth. Now the earth was formless and empty, darkness covered the surface of the watery depths, and the Spirit of God was hovering over the surface of the waters. Then God said, *"Let there be light,"* and *there was* light (Gen. 1:1–3)

It is vitally important to notice here that the biblical view of creation involves a command-promise. There is first the *command* of God, "let there be." And using the metaphor of hearing, there is a *response* in all creation to God's omnipotent Word, "and there was." From the scriptural standpoint, because God's creation-Word is a law-Word, the cosmos itself includes God's laws *for* creation and the lawful response *of* creatures. For this reason, God's command-Word both calls all things into existence, and guarantees all entities and creatures "to be" according to their own nature, after their kind (Gen. 1:24). This means His command is, at the same time, a *promise* of coherence and continuance (Col. 1:17) such that everything which is, *exists as answering* to the voice of God. This profound reality is made crystal clear in Psalm 148:1–13:

> Give praise to the Lord in heaven; praise him, all that dwells on high.
> Praise him, all you angels of his, praise him, all his armies.
> Praise him, sun and moon; praise him, every star that shines.
> Praise him, you highest heavens, you waters beyond the heavens.
> Let all these praise the Lord; *it was his command that created them.*
> He has set them there unageing for ever, *given them a law which cannot be altered.*
>
> Give praise to the Lord on earth, monsters of the sea and all its depths;
> fire and hail, snow and mist, and the storm-wind *that executes his decree*;
> all you mountains and hills, all you fruit trees and cedars;
> all you wild beasts and cattle, creeping things and birds that fly in air;
> all you kings and peoples of the world, all you that are princes and judges on earth;
> young men and maids, old men and boys together; let them all give praise to the Lord's name.
>
> His name is exalted as no other,
> his praise reaches beyond heaven and earth; and now he has given fresh strength

to his people. Shall not his faithful servants praise him, the sons of Israel, the people that draw near to him? Alleluia.[1]

His *command* is the creational law-Word (v 5) that establishes everything in terms of a decree or *promise* of its abiding (v 6). This Word holds not only for the non-human creatures—where sun and moon respond to the command-Word in praise, and snow and clouds *fulfill His Word*—but also for kings and peoples, men and women, old and young. As such, the Christian worldview sees creation as lawful, purposeful, coherent, and abiding, upheld by the powerful Word of God that is entirely consistent and completely trustworthy.

## The Origins of Science

This vision of the world was vital for the development of the sciences. By "science" I mean the modern concern with general laws—the relations and structures that may be found to underlie particular phenomena in creation. The particular phenomena are the data for a given science, and the laws are what science seeks to uncover. Protestantism's focus on Scripture, in particular, played a decisive role in re-energising scientific endeavour with the dominion mandate of Genesis, simultaneously breaking the shackles of classical authorities like Aristotle, whose metaphysics had hindered greater development in this area.[2] In addition, the doctrine of man's radical fallenness taught by Protestant theology meant that scientific methods and techniques could be developed to help mend the damage done to man's understanding due to his rebellion.[3] The books of God's Word and Works

---

1. *The Holy Bible: A Translation from the Latin Vulgate in the Light of the Hebrew and Greek Originals*, trans. Ronald Knox (Baronius, 2012), italics added.
2. See Jeremy A. Thomas, *The Nation's Gospel: Spreading the Christian Faith in Britain Since the Reformation*, Vol 1 *(1516-1791) Reformation to Revolution* (Exeter: Wilberforce Publications, 2017), 131–34.
3. See Peter Harrison's important study, *The Fall of Man and the Foundations of Science* (Cambridge University Press, 2007).

(God's Word itself being one of His Works) had to be studied together because the unchanging nature of the triune God expressed in Scripture ensured that creation itself was lawful rather than arbitrary—an important precondition of experimental science. As Jeremy Thomas points out:

> The willingness to look at the universe anew led to new discoveries. Men like Kepler and Galileo believed that God worked according to mathematical models but, unlike Plato and other Greek philosophers, they did not believe that matter was an impediment to the implementation of those models in the universe. Others, such as Francis Bacon, publicised the benefits of learning, including that of the new science. Bacon criticized the "intellectualism of the Greeks, their neglect of experiments." It was the works of God that the scientist needed to study, not Greek rationalism.[4]

It cannot be seriously doubted today that the modern scientific method emerged from decidedly Christian, not pagan or atheistic, roots. Of the significant scientists of the sixteenth and seventeenth centuries, twenty-five percent were members of the clergy, sixty percent of the great scientists of the era were devout Christians, and the rest were conventional Christian believers. A mere two percent were skeptics. As the social historian Rodney Stark has noted:

> Clearly, the superb scientific achievements of the sixteenth and seventeenth centuries were the work not of skeptics but of Christian men.... The era of the "Enlightenment" is as imaginary as the era of the "Dark Ages," both myths perpetrated by the same people for the same reasons.[5]

Modern science was birthed in Christian Europe precisely because only Christian Europe believed things that promoted its emergence. Stark claims

---

4. Thomas, *The Nation's Gospel*, 132–33.
5. Rodney Stark, *How the West Won: The Neglected Story of the Triumph of Modernity* (Wilmington, DE: ISI Books, 2015), 310.

that "the basis of their belief was their image of God and His creation."[6] Even the English skeptic, process philosopher and mathematician, Alfred North Whitehead, acknowledged that Christianity was essential to the rise of science because of:

> the medieval insistence on the rationality of God, conceived as with the personal energy of Jehovah and with the rationality of a Greek philosopher. Every detail was supervised and ordered: the search into nature could only result in the vindication of faith in rationality.[7]

Despite some persistent and excessive rationalism inherited from Greek thought, Christendom believed a personal and *purposeful* God had created a world of law and structure that is both ordered and logically intelligible. An impersonal world of random chance, a cosmos ruled by capricious and warring gods, and irrationalist, fatalistic conceptions of the universe could not and did not conceive or deliver modern science—as the parallel history of the non-Christian world shows. However, when the mid-nineteenth century witnessed the rise of historicism, of philosophies of development and the emergence of Darwinism, the scientific community slowly began to turn on its Christian mother.

## The Evolutionary Story

Though the contextual background of modern science was Christian theism, humanistic secularization gradually pushed the biblical worldview to the periphery, and then out of the picture altogether. The evolutionary hypothesis was then leapt on as an ideal instrument for expelling God from the cosmos, or at the very least rendering Him an absent and irrelevant first cause. Over time, as much as a hypothesis in biology and paleontology,

---

6. Stark, *How the West Won*, 315.
7. Whitehead, cited in Stark, *How the West Won*, 315.

Darwinian evolution became at once a kind of theodicy, a totalizing philosophy, a way of seeing the world, and the zeitgeist of a new era well captured in C. S. Lewis' poem, "Evolutionary Hymn":

> Lead us, Evolution, lead us
> Up the future's endless stair;
> Chop us, change us, prod us, weed us.
> For stagnation is despair:
> Groping, guessing, yet progressing,
> Lead us nobody knows where.
> To whatever variation
> Our posterity may turn
> Hairy, squashy, or crustacean,
> Bulbous-eyed or square of stern,
> Tusked or toothless, mild or ruthless,
> Towards that unknown god we yearn.
>
> Oh then! Value means survival-
> Value. If our progeny,
> Spreads and spawns and licks each rival,
> That will prove its deity
> (Far from pleasant, by our present,
> Standards, though it may well be).

In Western culture, people's thinking about the nature of human life—its origin, meaning, purpose, and destiny—has been deeply impacted by this evolutionary perspective. For the most part, Darwinian and then neo-Darwinian evolutionary theory has been enthusiastically put into the service of atheism (naturalism), forms of deism, or radical skepticism. In fact, evolutionism is today the origins myth underlying the atheistic worldview with its continuity postulate—the philosophical idea of an eternal cosmos in continuous flux. In some quarters, the rhetoric of the ideological Darwinists is so vehement, shrill, and dogmatic, that it has been dubbed by some commentators as pathological atheism; the so-called New Atheists, like Richard

Dawkins, Christopher Hitchens, Daniel Dennet, and Sam Harris, are leading and obvious examples of evolutionary zealotry over the last couple of decades—though interest in them has waned dramatically in recent years. The aggressive evolutionary evangelism, as well as its waning currency, may be due, at least in part, to growing doubts about evolutionary explanations as to why paleontology has failed to substantiate the Darwinian account of origins. As one of the progenitors of neo-Darwinism, Ernst Mayr acknowledged:

> Following phyletic lines through time seemed to reveal only minimal gradual changes but no clear evidence for any change of a species into a different genus or for the gradual origin of an evolutionary novelty. Anything truly novel always seemed to appear quite abruptly in the fossil record.[8]

Nonetheless, naturalistic neo-Darwinian apologists typically claim that they have rejected Christianity because modern science (which they conflate with an evolutionary worldview) has supposedly explained and *demystified* the world for educated people.[9] The Bible's teaching about origins, the Christian confessions, or serious discussions concerning a transcendent God are simply irrelevant, even contemptible and not worthy of thoughtful people. Most especially, belief in Jesus Christ as Creator and resurrected Redeemer has been variously dismissed as a delusion, a brain virus, a mental illness, or even an evil and dangerous pathology. The empty hubris of such perspectives is on vivid display when, despite no scientist yet being able to tell us what a "natural law" or what "energy" actually is, never mind demonstrating from the fossil record the clear gradual evolution of one creature into the genus of another, the atheist philosopher John Searle has confidently declared: "The result of this demystification is that we have gone beyond atheism to a point

---

8. Ernst Mayr, *One Long Argument: Charles Darwin and the Genesis of Modern Evolutionary Thought* (Cambridge, MA: Harvard University Press, 1991), 138.
9. The ironies here are thick. Even the "scientific" consensus around the supposedly well-established Big Bang Theory is being challenged and looks set to be supplanted—see Sarah Knapton, "Big Bang theory is wrong, claim scientists," *The Telegraph*, https://www.telegraph.co.uk/news/2025/06/10/big-bang-theory-is-wrong-claim-scientists/, accessed June 13, 2025.

where the issue [of God's existence] no longer matters in the way it did to earlier generations."[10]

Such naïve, even comic declarations, apart from being a form of wishful thinking, are made because of the unwarranted *belief* that the scientific method, supposedly now bound to, or synonymous with, the naturalistic evolutionary hypothesis, has sufficiently explained the cosmos, its mysteries, and its origins (while no one was looking!) to be able to dispense with the need for God or revelation—for knowledge, meaning, and purpose that transcend human theories in the natural sciences.

## The Worldview Foundation of Evolutionism

This ideological scientism,[11] far from being the indubitable result of empirical investigation, involves a profoundly *religious* choice resting in a particular kind of *faith* that requires careful scrutiny.

To begin with, a closer look at the nature of human theorizing quickly reveals that there is no *proposition* without *presupposition*. All arguments must proceed from assumptions, so it is unreasonable to demand all assumptions be based on arguments, let alone scientific argument. This is especially applicable to the inescapable religious *choice* we face with regard to the origin and destiny of all things. Though our media and popular education, trading on peoples' ignorance, tries to present the naturalistic Darwinian story of reality as an established "fact of science," Thomas Nagel, noted philosophy professor at New York University, realizes the current orthodox account of evolution is "an assumption governing the scientific project rather than a well-confirmed

---

10. John Searle, *Mind, Language and Society: Philosophy in the Real World*. New York: Basic Books, 1998), 35.
11. Scientism involves an overestimation of the relevance, power, and insight of scientific tools and techniques for gaining knowledge and understanding. In philosophical terms, scientism espouses the view that the scientific method is the best or even the only way to render truth about the world and reality. It is important to notice here that scientism fails its own test, since such a metaphysical statement is not a conclusion deduced by the empirical scientific method.

scientific hypothesis."[12] In fact, the most influential philosopher of science in the twentieth century, the Austrian-British thinker, Karl Popper, once had the audacity to admit: "I have come to the conclusion that Darwinism is not a testable scientific theory, but a *metaphysical research programme*—a possible framework for testable scientific theories."[13]

The metaphysical and religious nature of this program becomes obvious when you consider the statements of some of evolutionism's most ardent public advocates. The media-hungry cosmologist, Laurence Krauss, for example, has confidently declared that "nothing can become everything" without a creator. He goes beyond garden variety atheism by saying, "I am an anti-theist. Maybe I can't prove there's no God, but I wouldn't want to live in a universe with one."[14] Nagel, being a more measured agnostic philosopher and critic of orthodox evolutionism, openly admits that his rejection of a personal God is based on "an ungrounded assumption of my own."[15]

Such personal faith commitments grounded in religious worldviews concerning origins inevitably go in several directions, not just skepticism, atheism, or rabid anti-theism. Reflecting on these worldview issues, the most famous scientist of the modern age, Albert Einstein said:

> I am not an atheist, and I don't think I can call myself a pantheist. We are in the position of a little child entering a huge library filled with books in many languages. The child knows someone must have written those books. It does not know how. It does not understand the languages in which they are written. The child dimly suspects a mysterious order in the arrangement of the books but doesn't know what it is. That, it seems to me, is the attitude of even the most intelligent human

---

12. Thomas Nagel, *Mind and Cosmos: Why the Materialist Neo-Darwinian Conception of Nature Is Almost Certainly False* (Oxford: Oxford University Press, 2012), 11.
13. Michael Ruse, ed. *Philosophy After Darwin* (Princeton: Princeton University Press, 2010), 167; italics added.
14. Laurence Krauss, "Something from Nothing," dialogue with Richard Dawkins, Arizona State University, February 4, 2012, https://dangerousintersection.org/2012/04/22/richard-dawkins-and-lawrence-krauss-discuss-something-from-nothing/.
15. Nagel, *Mind and Cosmos*, 12.

being toward God. We see the universe marvellously arranged and obeying certain laws but only dimly understand these laws. Our limited minds cannot grasp the mysterious force that moves the constellations.[16]

Einstein made no Christian profession, but he clearly considered a transcendent mind a metaphysical necessity and believed in an intelligent ordering of reality that was anything but the random chance world so frequently propagated by the popular worldview of neo-Darwinism. Again Einstein comments:

> Certain it is that a conviction, akin to religious feeling, of the rationality or intelligibility of the world lies behind all scientific work of a higher order.

> This firm belief, a belief bound up with deep feeling, in a superior mind that reveals itself in the world of experience, represents my conception of God.[17]

This statement might be described as a kind of vague theism or deism shared by numbers of physicists who find their work unintelligible without the recognition of intentional design and a rational law-order at the root of the cosmos. Quite recently, the once-notorious atheist philosopher, Antony Flew, wrote a controversial book concerning his change of mind on the subject of God:

> [T]he journey to my discovery of the Divine has thus far been a pilgrimage of reason. I have followed the argument where it has led me. And it has led me to accept the existence of a self-existent, immutable, immaterial, omnipotent and omniscient Being.

> ...[W]hat could happen next?

---

16. Max Jammer, *Einstein and Religion* (Princeton: Princeton University Press, 1999), 48.
17. Albert Einstein, *Ideas and Opinions*, trans. Sonja Bargmann (London: Souvenir Press, 1973), 262.

Someday I might hear a Voice that says, "Can you hear me now?"[18]

These various opinions demonstrate that it is not the so-called "hard facts of science" that are determinative for thought, but religious worldviews. Everyone is looking at the same universe, the same data, but even the scientists, as ordinary human beings, come to it differently. So, the vital question for Christian apologetics becomes: Which *religious starting point* truly accounts for and makes intelligible sense of human experience? In the case under consideration in this chapter, is it naturalistic evolutionism or Christian theism?

Recent surveys on this question make for interesting reading. Even though the data is not granular enough to tell us whether the broader philosophical question of atheism or theism is specifically involved, it is noteworthy that in the United Kingdom, despite generations of indoctrination through the education system, only twenty-five percent of British people claim to be convinced by evolutionary theory, a further twenty-five percent think it may be true, and the other fifty percent are strongly opposed to or reject it for various reasons—which was very upsetting to the establishment.[19] In the United States, with vociferous public indoctrination in evolution having been a reality for decades, especially on college campuses, those who believe in an evolutionary account of natural history still only account for just over half the population. And it is also very telling that these views about origins are increasingly tied to political conviction. Eighty-three percent of liberal Democrats, over against just thirty-four percent of Republicans, accept the evolutionary account of origins.[20] This again illustrates that much more is going on here than a cold analysis of so-called "hard facts."

---

18. Antony Flew, *There is a God: How the World's Most Notorious Atheist Changed his Mind* (New York: HarperCollins, 2007), 155, 158.
19. Riazat Butt, "Half of Britons Do Not Believe in Evolution, Survey Finds," *The Guardian*, February 1, 2009, https://www.theguardian.com/science/2009/feb/01/evolution-darwin-survey-creationism#:~:text=The%20poll%20found%20that%20 25,theory%20or%20confused%20about%20it (accessed July 2024).
20. University of Michigan, "Evolution Now Accepted by Majority of Americans," *Science-Daily*, August 20, 2021, www.sciencedaily.com/releases/2021/08/210820111042.htm

Divisions and differences over the status of the evolutionary account of origins are found among professing Christians as well. Theistic evolutionists, for example, attempt a synthesis between the biblical worldview and that of evolutionary theory. As such, Christian theists in the sciences differ over the *extent* to which a form of natural selection was involved in the development of our world; though all would agree that *micro-evolution*—variation (speciation) *within* the boundary of a distinct genus—takes place. Yet even amongst believers, it is philosophical commitments and beliefs about the nature of the biblical text and its teaching that shape the theoretical approach to such questions in both theology and the natural sciences. However, the popular account of neo-Darwinian evolution used to prop up anti-Christianity in our culture, that amoeba became antelopes and fish became philosophers—from the goo, through the zoo, to you—in an unguided and random process (macro-evolution), through mutation and natural selection, must be rejected by all orthodox Christians.

## The Nature of Science

One of the obstacles for the typical unbeliever in seeing clearly in this matter is an extraordinary lack of self-consciousness about the nature of a worldview and the role it plays in the development of theories, beliefs, and perspectives. The working assumption of many people is simply that if "science says" something is true (by which they mean particular kinds of experts called scientists), we should "follow the science"—as though science itself were synonymous with their favored perspective on the world, or that of the scientist or scientific theory they are referencing. The ubiquitous cultural myth of evolutionism thus frequently involves a basic confusion of the empirical *methods* of natural science (observation and testing), with the religious *worldviews* of atheistic materialism and naturalism. To illustrate the

(accessed July 2024).

misunderstanding, notice how Nobel Laureate, Steven Weinberg, regards "science" and evolutionary materialism as essentially one and the same:

> The *worldview* of science is rather chilling. Not only do we not find any point to life laid out for us in nature, no objective basis for our moral principles, no correspondence between what we think is the moral law and the laws of nature..., [but] the emotions that we most treasure, our love for our wives and husbands and children, are made possible by chemical processes in our brains that are what they are as a result of natural selection acting on chance mutations over millions of years....
>
> Living without God isn't easy. But its very difficulty offers one other consolation—that there is a certain honor, or perhaps a grim satisfaction, in facing up to our condition.[21]

We see here that Weinberg speaks explicitly, and erroneously, of *the* "worldview of science"—by which he actually means *naturalistic evolutionism*. However, the tools of the empirical method in the natural sciences do not themselves constitute a worldview—indeed, only the biblical worldview can consistently and coherently *account* for the reliable use of these tools. They are theoretical procedures for investigating measurable phenomena in a repeatable, testable way, to reach generalized conclusions which are always being updated and revised as new discoveries come to light. These procedures can and have been put into the service of supporting various worldviews.

The scientific method does not deal in certainties, but with *hypotheses* and *theories* interpreted within prevailing paradigms, and most definitely does not provide a world-and-life view as a certitudinal starting point for thought. Weinberg seems blissfully unaware that his religious worldview is causing him to confound the empirical procedures of science with his own philosophical views of the world. The nature of meaning, morality, love of

---

21. Steven Weinberg, "Without God," *The New York Review of Books* 55, no. 14 (September 25, 2008): 1–3; italics added.

family, and the existence of God, are simply not questions that physical experiments, tests, and other observational tools are either able or designed to address, anymore than a pickaxe is the appropriate implement for writing a letter. Scientifically observing that a given tree sheds its leaves in the autumn tells me nothing about the ultimate origin of the tree, the meaning trees have within human life and culture, why we consider them beautiful, the rights or wrongs of cutting down the tree, or why trees exist in such a marvelous variety. I might study *how* a tree develops and grows, but *what* a tree actually is and *why* it grows is a much deeper question.

In contrast to Weinberg, one of the great pioneers of quantum physics, Erwin Schrödinger, recognized that the empirical method, when treated like a worldview, is hopelessly deficient. Saying nothing about the deeper and ultimate questions of life, the scientific method is

> ghastly silent about all and sundry that is really near to our heart, that really matters to us. It cannot tell a word about red and blue, bitter and sweet, physical pain and physical delight; it knows nothing of beautiful and ugly, good or bad, God and eternity. Science sometimes pretends to answer questions in these domains, but the answers are very often so silly that we are not inclined to take them seriously.[22]

The reason I claimed that *only* the biblical worldview can coherently account for confident use of the scientific method for particular limited purposes, is that for any scientific investigation to be possible, all the sciences must *presuppose* the *givenness* of meaning in created reality—that is, the ordered, coherent world of our everyday experience, amenable to investigation and discovery, and intelligible to our minds, so that knowledge and understanding can arise. As the eminent English physicist, Paul Davies, has argued: "science can proceed only if the scientist adopts an essentially theological worldview.... [E]ven the most atheistic scientist accepts *as an act*

---

22. Erwin Schrödinger, *Nature and the Greeks and Science and Humanism* (Cambridge: Cambridge University Press, 2014), 95.

*of faith* the existence of lawlike order in nature that is at least in part comprehensible to us."[23]

This shows that, thankfully, the practice of anti-theistic scientists is inconsistent with their professed worldview. If they were consistent with what they professed to believe, they would abandon the work of science altogether.

The great blessing of the various sciences is that they can help deepen our understanding of how certain things function, and thereby advance our ability to work with and use the resources of creation to improve the life of human beings and the flourishing of living things. Some sciences build theories about everyday phenomena that can be employed in human technology, some sciences theorize about the past. We should notice here the important distinction between what we can call *operational* sciences (i.e., observable, testable, repeatable, experimental science) and *historical* sciences that try to construct a hypothetical picture of origins and the past which is neither repeatable nor testable in the same way.

The naturalistic, neo-Darwinian *belief system*—which includes the ideas that the universe *began* or exists without a cause (i.e., without a reason or purpose), that nothing generated everything, and that human beings are simply the product of cosmic stardust which coagulated into primordial slime and gradually evolved with consciousness, rationality, morality, and culture, by physical forces alone—is clearly a *religious worldview*, neither an operational science nor even a strictly historical science. The distinction between the operational and historical is well illustrated by the difference between *functional biology*, which is a useful operational science applied in, amongst other things, medicine, and *evolutionary* biology, which is a philosophical worldview research program masquerading as an operational science. In fact, Dr. Marc Kirschner of Harvard Medical School has admitted that "over the last hundred years, almost all of biology has proceeded independent of evolution, except evolutionary biology itself. Molecular biology, biochemistry and physiology have not taken evolution into account at all."[24]

---

23. Davies, cited in Flew, *There is a God*, 107; italics added.
24. Marc Kirschner, "Missing Links," in *The Boston Globe*, Oct 23, 2005, 77.

If the worldview and presuppositions of evolutionism were *necessary* for the practice of science, or constituted a *foundational* scientific truth, the incredible progress within the physical and life sciences would have been impossible without it, nor would scientists who reject evolution have been able to meaningfully contribute. Yet, as we have seen, since the modern scientific revolution was championed by Christian thinkers and researchers, and long preceded Darwin's theories, it is clear the evolutionary worldview is not only surplus to requirements, but also that it can be safely ignored. Whereas, in keeping with Paul Davies acknowledges above, the theological worldview positing law-order and design is indispensable for the sciences, even for the atheist who must borrow, usually without acknowledgment, from the resources of the biblical worldview to make his theoretical activities intelligible.

## Evolution, Divinity Beliefs, and Reductionism

Whether a Christian or naturalistic evolutionist, everyone believes that *something* has independent existence—a divine per-se. This divinity concept is a *religious* choice for every human being. Those who reject the God of Scripture revealed in Christ Jesus, go to the *cosmos* itself—which, interestingly, literally means a well-ordered whole—to find amongst its functions and properties a *substitute divinity* that might be said to have "given birth" to everything else and upon which, therefore, everything else depends either directly or indirectly. There have been numerous candidates proposed in human thought, such as number, matter/energy (i.e., the physical), motion, logical thought, or reason, will, or some combination.

In the case of naturalistic evolutionism, all reality is thought to have been birthed by self-existent matter/energy, and thereby the cosmos is essentially reduced to its *physical* function or aspect. All the *nonphysical* realities and properties of human experience (law, thought, feeling, love, justice, beauty, history, language, etc.) are necessarily reduced to being fortuitous by-products of matter in motion, wholly dependent on what is purely *physical* for existence. In this case, matter or energy is given quasi-divine status. Somehow, the *physical function* of reality *becomes* the arithmetical, spatial, kinematic, biotic, psychical, logical, cultural, lingual, social, economic, aesthetic, juridical, ethical, and faith aspects or dimensions of human experience, leaping over entire and irreducible spheres of law, as if by magic, to transform itself into completely new functions.

Consequently, the naturalistic Darwinian outlook is essentially the view that all phenomena we experience in the world can ultimately be explained purely in terms of *physics*. Christian philosopher Henk Geertsema explains the implications of this for living things and human beings:

> The explanation of living organisms is pursued in terms of an accidental organization of complex molecular structures. Mental phenomena are taken to be reducible to neuro-physiological processes. Religious faith and moral conduct have been explained as a form of behavior that exists because it conveys a selective advantage in the struggle for survival.[25]

Although there is increasingly a recognition in the sciences that one cannot reduce our *descriptions* of reality conceptually (at the greater levels of complexity), to the physical and remain true to human experience, nonetheless, argues Geertsema, "the conviction remains that all of reality ultimately is of a physical nature. The different levels with their specific properties are still seen as complex organizations of physical constituents."[26]

To put it differently, *ontological* reductionism persists as the religious choice, even if a veneer of *explanatory* non-reductionism is added in order to sound coherent. As such, underneath the colourful descriptions of a multi-functional world, everything is reduced to being merely physical, and the apparent distinctions between minerals, mice, and men, arise not from real qualitative differences, but from the accidental arrangement of entities with different levels of *physical* complexity. And yet, according to Stephen Meyer, as far as the doctrine of evolutionism is concerned,

---

25. Hendrik G. Geertsema, *Homo Respondens: Essays in Christian Philosophy*, ed. Govert J. Buijs and Perry Huesmann (Jordan Station, ON: Paideia Press, 2021), 239.
26. Geertsema, *Homo Respondens*, 239.

No undirected *physical* or *chemical* process has demonstrated the capacity to produce specified information starting "from *purely physical or chemical" precursors.* For this reason, chemical evolutionary theories have failed to solve the mystery of the origin of first life—a claim that few mainstream evolutionary theorists now dispute.[27]

Despite this, for many people in our culture, ontological reductionism to the physical seems plausible. The reason for this is that there really is a *physical aspect* or *dimension* to everything we experience in creation—there is a law for physical phenomena that is ubiquitous. It is this universality that gives a superficial persuasiveness to *physicalism,* making it an attractive candidate for a divine source of origin. However, with just a little reflection, we realize there is equal universality to other dimensions of the cosmos, such as the numerical, spatial, and kinematic dimensions in creation. And for human beings, the biotic, psychical, logical, historical-cultural and various other dimensions of reality are ubiquitous in our experience as well. So, the actuality of a *physical dimension* present in all phenomena is not a persuasive argument for *reducing* all reality to differing levels of complexity in the arrangement of elementary particles. It is important to notice, for example, that physics and physical theories have never made mathematics, geometry, chemistry, biology, psychology, logic, and various other core disciplines superfluous as curricular requirements in the university. In fact, these subjects continue to demonstrate considerable independence from each other, precisely because these dimensions of creation are irreducible to each other. Thus, for example, the biotic law-sphere simply cannot be reduced to the numerical sphere of law, and therefore, mathematics can never simply *replace* biology in the curriculum.

Given the abstract nature of this discussion, an illustration of the broader problem of reductionism is helpful. The inadequacy of this physicalist view can be illuminated with the example of an automobile built from

---

27. Stephen Meyer, *Darwin's Doubt: The Explosive Origin of Animal Life and the Case for Intelligent Design* (New York: HarperCollins, 2013), vi; italics added.

materials like metal, rubber, glass, and leather. On the basis of physicalism (materialism), an automobile is viewed as essentially the specific complex organization of physical materials into an object able to move with speed between given spaces. In itself, this bare observation is accurate. It is true that essential to the *being* of a car is the arrangement of its physical components. But if an automobile is *reduced* to this, we could never understand the full meaning or significance of an automobile referred to by its concept.

What a car truly "is," is not defined by the material parts from which it is constructed, but by the specific *functions* it has to serve—factors which in reality *determine* its construction. The *concept* of the car implies a specific structure built in such a way that it can transport people from one place to another, protected from outside elements and minor impacts, in a private space, at considerable speed. With advancements in technology, the car is now also a place for making phone calls, conducting business, consuming media, commuting to work, and transporting friends and guests in genuine comfort. The amazing variety of available cars exists to serve variations of the same basic functionality to maximize speed, or space, or innovation, or convenience, or comfort. The point is the *physical* materials with which a car is constructed are *subordinate* to the primary *functions* the car must serve.

This shows that the *rules* directing the organization of the materials for a car are more important and basic to what it is to be a car than the materials themselves—since those same materials could be used to make any number of other structures. Moreover, you could actually make a basic car out of many different types of material, so that "car-ness" itself is recognized by its design and *function*. Think, for example, of the numerous dimensions of reality in which a car performs its function. A car has *physical* parts, certainly. Yet one can *numerate* and differentiate those parts, which is a numerical reality, not a physical reality. It also takes up *space* and is able to *move*, so that it functions in a spatial and kinematic way as well. Some of its components are derived from *biological* organisms, like rubber and leather, but the biotic is much more than just the physical. Clearly then, a car's being and meaning cannot be reduced even to these diverse functions. A car is not simply a *physical* thing, but is constructed out of numerous naturally occurring elements, something that occupies space, and is able to move.

As objects, there is a very human *logic* required in the design, construction, and fashioning of a car. Cars are also *historical-cultural* artifacts with a long history of development stemming from the early invention of the wheel, and are shaped by the technological stage of advancement as well as the cultural fashions of their era—classic cars are collectible for that reason. Cars are also known by various names and brands which have become part of the common furniture of human *language*. A primary function of a car is *social* because it is a means of transport for various forms of human interaction (taking children to school, getting to work, traveling on vacation or to the golf course, etc.). Car racing has also become a means of social entertainment. Certain car brands and names can also confer a certain social status on the owner. This social function is closely related to the *economic* function of a car. Cars have a certain value, being expensive or cheap, and are a major investment for most people, second only to their house, and can be bought or sold. Cars are also *aesthetic* objects because people appreciate a good-looking and well-made car. Ugly cars are exposed to criticism and ridicule whilst beautiful cars are praised to the point that the car has become, in some cases, like a work of art. The car also has a *juridical* dimension because it is property owned by people; car theft is a major problem that frequently leads to legal charges as well as disputes over legal liability regarding their insurance. Cars also function in the *ethical* dimension of life because we are obligated to drive responsibly and respect other drivers. The car can be deadly if misused, so the moral obligation associated with their use is profound. This ethical dimension is expressed also when we lend our cars to help others in need or teach our teenager to drive in our precious car because we love our children. Finally, in some cases, cars become an obsession taking on a quasi-*religious* significance. There are people who religiously clean and polish their luxury or classic car every Sunday, and there are passionate enthusiasts who literally live for cars, car shows, or motor racing. All of this reveals that the meaning and function of a car cannot be reduced to its *physical* components.

This is equally true of the human person. It is accurate to say that a human being can be analyzed through the lens of physics and seen as a bi-pedal creature constructed of physical components that have a complex arrangement, which eventually becomes dust in the ground, deteriorating into a much less complex arrangement. But that does not mean that the human person can be *reduced* to a random collocation of atoms—that the concept of humanity is reducible to particle theories. In fact, we can go further and say that the very notion of *purely physical* particles is meaningless because it is literally inconceivable. As soon as we posit particles as entities, numerical (discrete quantity), spatial, and kinematic (motion) categories are involved, not just physical ones. The thought process itself involves abstract laws of thought (logical) that are not physical, and so forth.

In reality, it is simply impossible to *think* of any dimension of reality, physical or otherwise, in total isolation from all the rest, so as to propose that particular dimension as the generating source or root of all things. This is because all dimensions of reality appear together as an unbreakable unity in human consciousness and experience. As such, we cannot conceive of what it would mean for anything to be *exclusively physical* in isolation from all that is non-physical. Roy Clouser explains the extent of the conceptual problem with reductionism:

> What, for example, is left of the idea of sense perception when it is deprived of all connection to number, space, matter and logic? What, indeed, is left of logic if there is nothing nonlogical to which it can apply? Even its famous axiom of noncontradiction says that nothing can be true and false *at the same time in the same sense*. Thus it includes an essential reference both to time and to other "senses" (kinds of properties) to which it applies.[28]

The implication is that the cosmos is not reducible to any one or more of its dimensions to account for the origin of the whole, for these are simply *irreducible*– including the *physicalism* championed by evolutionists. To attempt to reduce reality to one or more of its dimensions destroys the intelligibility of human experience. If all that exists is just a materialist accident, why would any human brain—being part of that accident—be interested

---

28. Roy Clouser, *Knowing with the Heart: Religious Experience and Belief in God* (Downers Grove, IL: InterVarsity, 1999), 38.

or able to give a *correct account* of all the other accidents? If reality could be reduced to the physical and its "emergent properties," as many Darwinians imagine, then there are no truly *mental* states, but only *brain* states which as purely physical events can be neither true nor false.

Thomas Nagel has grasped something of the acute nature of the problem of reductionism and the metaphysical commitments involved. Describing the naturalistic evolutionary program and its lack of explanatory power he writes:

> It holds both that everything in the world is physical and that everything that happens in the world has its most basic explanation, whether we can come to know it or not, in physical law, as applied to physical things, events and their constituents.
>
> ...[T]he physical sciences will not enable us to understand the irreducibly subjective centres of consciousness that are such a conspicuous part of the world.[29]

As such, to speak of "pure physics" is simply nonsense. Scientific activity itself presupposes the *life* of the scientist, but as physical entities, atoms, molecules, and macromolecules are *not alive*. It is only plants, animals, and human beings that actively function in the biotic dimension of reality.[30] This is a vitally important point. Life cannot be identified solely with the physical dimension of reality, because elementary particles are not alive. So, then, what is life? The evolutionists cannot tell us. Materialist accounts of life are at this point entirely incoherent.

For example, we cannot actually deduce complex *biological* phenomena like reproduction and growth, controlled by our intricate DNA, from *physical* laws. In fact, merely describing them requires language and concepts that are not part of physics. The same is obviously true of our mental states, as noted above. Granted, mental states have a *physical basis* in the structure of the human being, but experiences like learning, expressing our will, or

---

29. Nagel, *Mind and Cosmos*, 41–42.
30. Danie Strauss, "What Happened to Evolution?" in *Discovering Dooyeweerd*, ed. D. F. M. Strauss (Jordan Station, ON: Paideia Press, 2023), 273–82, 273.

reflecting on our human intentions cannot be described in the language of physics. Consequently, the moves a chess player makes on a chess board cannot be accounted for solely in terms of the physical dimension of the cosmos, but are dependent on the rules of chess and the mental intentions of the player—and nobody has yet cut open a human brain to find a collection of intentions under the microscope.

The laws and structures for these different dimensions of being have a unique character of their own, meaning that diverse laws and norms determine the properties of different dimensions of reality. And these laws resist all efforts to reduce them to one another.[31] A human being functions in all the many dimensions of reality, including the physical, but can never be reduced to or summed up by any one of them. Take, for example, the experience of pain in the sensitive or psychical dimension of experience. Evolutionary theory, even when the biotic law-sphere (life) is combined with the physical dimension, has a real difficulty accounting for something as apparently simple as the human encounter with pain. From a medical standpoint, doctors know that pain has some kind of *physiological* basis, even if we cannot always track it down. Yet acknowledging a *physiological* element is not the same as saying the concept of pain can be accounted for and understood in purely physiological terms, because *consciousness* and the *ability to feel* are already presupposed in the concept of pain. Pain may be *rooted* in physiology, but it is clearly not *identical* with it. In many instances, the physiological traits of pain may in themselves be totally harmless yet be the cause of real suffering in the patient. As Geertsema explains:

> Pain cannot be described by physiological concepts alone. Neurophysiology can be helpful for the understanding of pain because specific neuro-physiological

---

31. This discussion is informed by the highly original reformational philosophy of the Dutch philosopher Herman Dooyeweerd, who developed a distinctly Christian cosmonomic law idea and theory of modal spheres (dimensions) as the created meaning-structure of reality. Each dimension of reality is both universal and irreducible. His genius is manifest in his monumental four-volume work, *A New Critique of Theoretical Thought*. The second volume deals specifically with his *General Theory of the Modal Spheres*.

structures are identified on the basis of their relationship to phenomenal pain. To discover these relationships, though, the concept of pain as such is basic. For that reason, physiological concepts, that as such lack the element of feeling, can never *replace* the concept of pain in which this element is essential.[32]

Once again we see that human beings cannot be reduced to their physical dimension or to their physiology, even when considering an ostensibly straightforward concept like pain. As the Christian philosopher Danie Strauss has pointed out:

> the foot, the hand or the leg of a human being is never *purely* physically, biotically or sensorially structured. The entire human personality, embracing all... interwoven substructures, is expressed in every part of the body. Therefore, it is impossible for medical and nursing practice to reduce a person to a purely *biotic entity*.[33]

Much more could be said about the unintelligibility of reductionism in the evolutionary worldview and its ruinous consequences for our understanding of reality. The key thing to remember is that *thinking Christianly* means recognizing that the laws and norms for the *totality* of human life in the world are established by and dependent upon God's creation-Word, and there is no true comprehension of the human person without taking into account the mystery of *creation* by a personal and purposeful God, distinct from the cosmos. The created law-spheres are the indispensable condition necessary for the existence and differentiation of all things. Whilst we can theoretically abstract them from each other to focus on a particular dimension of creation within a given scientific discipline (like physics focusing on the physical), in reality they are bound together in our experience as an indivisible unity. This clearly implies that the laws and norms governing the ways in which all things function are *not* a by-product of the physical function of the cosmos—as the evolutionary materialist worldview would

---

32. Geertsema, *Homo Respondens*, 244; italics added
33. Danie Strauss, *Soul and Body* (Jordan Station, ON: Paideia Press, 2020), 41.

have it—but are presupposed in the very existence and structure of all things. From the biblical perspective, all things exist only as answering to the law-Word of God.

## Darwinism and Human Values

The divinity belief presupposed by the naturalistic evolutionary account of reality obviously entails the logical denial of contrary beliefs. This gives it inescapable religious significance and shapes a worldview with profound implications for human values and society. But when the attempt is made to apply the laws of one dimension of reality to another, a procedure which is impossible, but made conceptually necessary by trying to reduce one to the other, failure and even disaster are the result. When people reject the transcendent God as the Creator Who holds all things together by His powerful Word, the false gods found in creation exact a heavy price.

Darwinism as a religious worldview must account for human values in the moral dimension of our experience—the things that matter most to us. Various attempts have been made at applying variations of Darwinian physicalism (materialism) to social ethics. Social Darwinism has a terrifying history in the twentieth century—a worldview that led tyrants to use the idea of *struggle* for survival (of the fittest) to justify war, inhuman experiments on children, eugenics, and a holocaust of millions of Jews in the context of a master-race ideology.

However, social Darwinism is not simply a matter of historical curiosity. Evolutionism applied to ethics continues to have a strong influence on contemporary issues we are wrestling with in Western society. The modern European historian Richard Weikart has argued that:

> Darwinism played an important role in the debate over the sanctity of human life, for it altered many people's conceptions about the value of human life, as well as the significance of death. Many Darwinists claimed that they were creating a whole new worldview with new ideas about the meaning and value of life based on Darwinian theory. Darwinian monists and materialists initiated public

debate and led the movements for abortion, infanticide, assisted suicide, and even involuntary euthanasia.[34]

In addition, Darwinism has been used to radically alter Western views of sexual identity and morality, including a near-complete overthrow of the traditional Christian teaching concerning sexual ethics, marriage, and family. As Helene Stöcker, a leading evolutionary thinker who sought to synthesize Darwin's and Nietzsche's philosophies, wrote in her essay, "On a New Ethics": "If one believes in the eternal Becoming in the flow of evolution, and holds struggle for the father of all things, then one can only see the moral task of humanity as seeking ever new, higher forms of morality."[35]

In popular science literature today, leading exponents of the evolutionary worldview, like the outspoken Sam Harris, continue to apply a naturalistic Darwinism to moral thought. Harris feels confident that we might well be able to "cure" evil (a moral category he cannot define), since it is essentially a physical and biological problem. He states:

> All of our behavior can be traced to biological events about which we have no conscious knowledge: this has always suggested that free will is an illusion.... [T]houghts and intentions are *caused by physical events and mental stirrings of which I am not aware.*
>
> Thoughts, moods, and desires of every sort simply spring into view—and move us, or fail to move us, for reasons that are, from a subjective point of view, perfectly inscrutable....
>
> From the perspective of your conscious mind you are no more responsible for the next thing you think (and therefore do) than you are for the fact that you were born into this world....

---

34. Richard Weikart, *From Darwin to Hitler: Evolutionary Ethics, Eugenics, and Racism in Germany* (New York: Palgrave Macmillan, 2004), 145–46.
35. Stöcker, cited in Weikart, *From Darwin to Hitler*, 132.

Where our intentions themselves come from, however, and what determines their character in every instant, remains perfectly mysterious in subjective terms.[36]

Harris admits, and rejoices in the admission, that the logic of his *reductionism* means that all retributive justice is called into question, which quite obviously is a denial of genuine human responsibility for moral action. Again he writes, "The men and women on death row have some combination of bad genes, bad parents, bad ideas, and bad luck—which of these quantities, exactly, were they responsible for?... In fact, it seems immoral not to recognise just how much luck is involved in morality itself."[37]

Harris appears to have overlooked the fact that if morality is merely a matter of chance, then there is no such thing as morality or ethics in any meaningful sense, any more than if human beings are just physical, bio-chemical events, there is any meaning in Harris' own fully bio-chemically determined reasoning process. His reductionism destroys both freedom and ethics simultaneously, rendering categories of good and evil, justice and injustice, empty and without meaning. There can be no *moral* values without *moral* actors and action—his evolutionism destroys the concept of both.

Harris' self-contradictory philosophical excursus would be laughable were it not so dangerous, for in his once-popular book, *The End of Faith*, life is so cheapened by his Darwinian reductionist mentality that he writes:

> The link between belief and behavior raises the stakes considerably. Some propositions are so dangerous that it may even be ethical to *kill people for believing them.* This may seem an extraordinary claim, but it merely enunciates an ordinary fact about the world in which we live.[38]

---

36. Sam Harris, *The Moral Landscape: How Science Can Determine Human Values* (New York: Free Press, 2010), 103–106; italics added.
37. Harris, *The Moral Landscape*, 109.
38. Harris, *The End of Faith*, 52–53; Italics added

From the orthodox evolutionary point of view, then, the idea of real objective values is like a wheel that spins without being attached to anything—totally superfluous. Nagel writes:

> So far as natural selection is concerned, pain could perfectly well be in itself good, and pleasure in itself bad, or (more likely) both of them in themselves valueless....
>
> From a Darwinian perspective, our impressions of value, if construed realistically, are completely groundless. And if that is true for our most basic responses, it is also true for the entire elaborate structure of value and morality that is built up around them by practical reflection and cultural development.[39]

This being the case, it is vital that the oft-heard and popular claim in our culture that "science" can determine human values should be subjected to damning criticism. The fact is that empirical methods for investigating and describing the physical dimension of reality cannot be used even to *define*, let alone *prescribe*, the moral norms for human life—in the same way that a scientific analysis of paintbrushes, oils, and canvas does not address the norms of aesthetic beauty manifest in a masterpiece.

## Darwin's Despair

It is not without significance that Charles Darwin's own evolutionary belief system rendered him a lonely and tragic figure. The Bible says that we become like the thing we worship (Ps. 115:4–8, 135:15–18). A reductionistic worldview will always lead to a dehumanizing of the individual, because the human person is degraded to less than what God created them to be. An emotional invalid and recluse from the age of twenty-eight, Darwin was practically confined to his home for nearly forty years. From his diaries which detail his various emotional conditions, we learn that he was diagnosed by

---

39. Nagel, *Mind and Cosmos*, 109.

authorities as suffering from agoraphobia and psychoneurosis.[40] His diaries included descriptions of

> fits of depersonalization, hallucinations, suicide thoughts, obsessive-compulsiveness, bizarre behavior, sadism (such as his inordinate love of killing animals), and evidence that he suffered from an anti-social personality disorder and an immature relationship with his children.[41]

He appears to have been completely unable to deal with death, and did not attend the funerals of either his father or his favorite daughter, who had died tragically at the tender age of ten. Throughout his life Darwin battled his doubts, worried about the implications of his theory, and struggled with his conscience. He felt caught between two opinions. Although most of his supporters have claimed him for atheism and naturalism, and he did have much to say about chance and purposelessness, he also wrote:

> [Reason tells me of the] extreme difficulty or rather impossibility of conceiving this immense and wonderful universe, including man with his capability of looking far backwards and far into futurity, as the result of blind chance or necessity. When thus reflecting I feel compelled to look to a First Cause having an intelligent mind in some degree analogous to that of man; and I deserve to be called a Theist.[42]

Raised within an heretical, unitarian, and deistic religious context, Darwin was educated in the "rational theology" of the so-called Enlightenment, which expected to find a perfect mathematical harmony in all of nature. This form of natural theology initially impressed him. But as a sensitive man, his heartrending encounters with deep personal pain, profound suffering in the animal kingdom, and the many evils in the world, left him truly perplexed by the apparent contradiction. If there is a good purposeful Creator, why

---

40. From Adler, "Darwin's Illness," in Bergman, *The Dark Side of Charles Darwin*, 97–98.
41. Jerry Bergman, *The Dark Side of Charles Darwin: A Critical Analysis of an Icon of Science* (Green Forest, AR: Master Books, 2011), 97–98.
42. Darwin, *The Autobiography of Charles Darwin 1809–1882*, 92–93.

all the pain, struggle, conflict, and suffering? The atheist philosopher Michael Ruse writes, "Most accurately, perhaps, Darwin is characterized as one who held to some kind of "deistic" belief in a God who works at a distance through unbroken law: having set the world in motion, God now sits back and does nothing."[43]

In this sense, Darwin's theory could be characterized as an attempted theodicy, i.e., a way of distancing and absolving a good God from all the trouble and evil in the world.[44] Unfortunately, it seems Darwin never really came to grips with the Christian worldview and gospel of the kingdom as revealed in the Bible. This worldview teaches us about a loving, holy, and righteous God and His good creation that fell into sin and ruin, a creation which, as a result, groans under a curse, with death, disease, and cruelty, but is now being redeemed by the incarnate Son of God, the Lord Jesus Christ. Through His death, resurrection, glorious ascension, and session at the right hand of all authority, all things are being made new and will finally be totally restored and released from their bondage to corruption (Rom 8:18–25). Here alone the apparent contradiction is resolved.

To place Darwin's very human quandary before the living God is to take away its despair, because it places all of life within the eternal frame of the gospel. The Kingdom of God points to the only escape from the reductionistic contradictions of our idolatrous lives, by transforming our minds through the reality of Christ's redemption. Only then can we truly understand all things through the conception of order and purpose, and so truly think Christianly about our God-given scientific task in His beautiful world.

---

43. Ruse, cited in Cornelius G. Hunter, *Darwin's God: Evolution and the Problem of Evil* (Grand Rapids, MI: Brazos Press, 2001), 131.
44. This thesis is worked out brilliantly by Hunter in *Darwin's God: Evolution and the Problem of Evil.*

CHAPTER 8

# Think Christianly About History

*Teach me Your way Yahweh, and I will live by Your truth.
Give me an undivided mind to fear Your name.*
— *Psalm 86:11 (HCSB)*

*Only the Christian can legitimately hold to the historicity of man; for Christianity alone views history as the unfolding of the eternal counsel of God. No other philosophy can offer certitude as to the unity of history.... [T]he Christian, on the other hand, is assured by Scripture that God has one plan for the race and that the historical process is the unfolding of that plan.*
— *Howard Evan Runner*

## Cultural Warfare and the Meaning of History

**W**ITH CHARACTERISTIC WIT AND INSIGHT, the Danish Christian philosopher Søren Kierkegaard highlighted the limits of the individual in any era:

> Each generation has its own task and need not trouble itself unduly by being everything to previous and succeeding generations. Just as each day's trouble is sufficient for the day, so each individual in a generation has enough to do in taking care of himself and does not need to embrace the whole contemporary age with his paternal solicitude or assume that era and epoch begin with his book.[1]

This is a humbling and sobering thought. Anyone who finds genuine delight in learning and in the wisdom of God (Prov. 2:6–10), as I have done throughout my adult life, knows not only that "of the making of many books there is no end" (Eccl. 12:12), but that "in much wisdom is much grief: and he that increases knowledge, increases sorrow" (Eccl. 1:17–18). This is never more apparent than when reflecting on the meaning of history, because a confrontation with the character of history is an encounter with the human condition—driving the wise into the arms of Jesus Christ, the Lord of all time and only hope for the ages. Amongst the urgent tasks facing this generation is surely confronting afresh the meaning and nature of history.

This raises a profoundly practical and relevant question for every society because the way human beings view their past and present directly impacts the rising and falling of nations in the unfolding of time (Jer. 19:3–8; Duet 24;18–22). The insight that "The most effective way to destroy a people is to deny and obliterate their own understanding of their history" has been attributed by some to George Orwell. Regardless of the accuracy of the attribution, we are seeing the truth of that saying play out in this generation. The reason for this is bound up with the deep connection that exists

---

1. Søren Kierkegaard, *The Humor of Kierkegaard: An Anthology*, ed. Thomas C. Oden (Princeton: Princeton University Press, 2004), 254–55.

between the past, present, and future in the character and consciousness of a culture—for in an important sense, who we are *is* who we were. If a people's *understanding* of their own history is radically altered, it will have a far-reaching effect on their present view of themselves and their cultural life; so much so that a profound change of historical perception can precipitate the eventual collapse of a dynasty—as witness Israel's fate under Jeroboam when he falsified Israel's religious history and thereby the meaning of its worship (1 Kgs. 12:25–33). It is important to note that it is not new discoveries or insights here and there regarding peculiar details of *events* in a people's history that transform a culture, but the alteration of their understanding of the *meaning* of their history. Such a shift is a fundamentally religious change.

To illustrate, in a penetrating article in the United Kingdom's *The Telegraph*, the prominent Canadian psychologist Jordan Peterson wrote quite movingly of his love and admiration for Great Britain. After describing his journey through some of the prestigious institutions of learning and corridors of power he writes:

> [T]he people of Great Britain have granted the world a gift whose power stands in permanent opposition to our most appalling proclivities as individuals and societies. That gift is the political expression of the sanctification of the word—freedom in speech, imagination and thought: freedom to engage in the very process that builds and rebuilds habitable order itself from the chaos that eternally surrounds us. And that freedom is expressed in many ways, small and great, in the British Isles: in the wit of its people, in the effectiveness of its institutions, in the beauty of its art and literature, in the political and psychological presumptions that guide private discourse and public conception and action.
>
> And that is most particularly why I love Great Britain. And that is why, people of that realm (and not only of that realm), you should love her too, despite her sins,

with your eyes lifted upward, your hope to the future, and the word of truth and faith on your tongues.[2]

Though presently under severe threat from Critical Theories based in a neo-Marxist worldview, this perception continues to form part of the historic self-understanding of the British and more generally the Anglo-American peoples. However, if the history of the British nation and its former empire is religiously rewritten and primarily understood, not as a variegated and complex story of the gradual emergence of free peoples and a commonwealth of nations from a great Christian land—in which freedom of thought and speech, commerce, governmental administration, technology, modern medicine, education, democratic institutions, rule of law, the principles of justice, Christian faith and morality were spread, fallibly and falteringly, through large parts of the world—but rather as a tale of unmitigated oppression, racism, slavery, exploitation, cruelty and war, then the cultural and moral confidence of a remarkable island people will be gradually shattered. The same issue faces those reflecting on the history of Canada and especially the United States in the twentieth and twenty-first centuries as it gradually took over global leadership from Great Britain. Winston Churchill (who was half-American) once perceptively described the American as the "Englishman left to himself." Has America's freedom-spreading Constitution, inherited legal tradition, cultural institutions, historically free markets, and broader role in the world been generally a force for good or evil, justice or injustice, when compared to other historic powers, cultures, and nations? How Americans understand their history will profoundly affect the cohesion of the people and nation, the vitality and survival of their culture.

It is for this reason that in Britain, much of her commonwealth, and in America, there is a desperate struggle going on about the meaning and significance of history. The contemporary phenomenon of a widespread self-hatred among the Anglo-American peoples—religiously catalyzed by a

---

2. Jordan Peterson, "Why I Love Great Britain," *The Telegraph*, December 14, 2021, https://www.telegraph.co.uk/news/2021/12/14/love-great-britain/.

spiritual uprooting of Christian commitment—is due in very significant part to a decades-long, self-conscious effort of radical "progressive" intellectuals in the West, especially in the institutions of learning, arts, and culture, to undermine and obliterate their historical self-understanding. This is visibly manifest in popular activist movements determined to rename educational institutions and streets; pull down monuments and the statues of those they disapprove; "purify" the books and films of the past through rewriting, censorship and "trigger warnings;" assault the cultural inheritance of productivity and industry; and overturn through law and politics the most basic institutions of Western cultural life—especially the Christian family, Christian law, Christian charity, and Christian education.

These social realities make the subject of the philosophy of history in the Christian worldview much more than a concern of the specialist. It is vital for all Christians and those sympathetic to a Christian worldview to grapple with this subject if we would understand, and reform, the decadent culture of our era. There is a war underway for the meaning of history. This is a war that God will most certainly win with His people in due time. It is therefore my contention that Christians need to take to the battlefield on the side of a scriptural historiography with confidence—the future is bound to it.

## The Nature of the Historical

Perhaps unexpectedly, people interested in the past are often those most concerned with the future. This is because, due to the influence of Christianity in Western thinking, we still tend to connect past, present, and future in a coherent unified relationship as goal-oriented, revealing important patterns and lines of significance—in fact this is the Western idea of history as fundamentally teleological (Rom. 11:36). As religiously responding beings (*homo respondens*), on this side of the return of Christ, we cannot help but think of history as moving toward some sort of culmination. For this reason, despite its mysterious character, we look for meaning and direction within history. In Christian theology we speak of this culminating process, the consummation of historical purpose, as *eschatology*. Eschatology is not simply about last things, but about first things as well. It is concerned with the overall *meaning* of history and humanity's central place in God's plan of redemption (John 1:1–5; Rom. 8:19–23, 28–30). As such, in this chapter, our concern will not be with the details of a specific period of history and its formative events—I am not a historian, and this is not an historical study. Nor will we take up a comparative discussion of the various theological views among Christians regarding the last things and the *parousia*.[3] Rather, our purpose is to reflect on the importance of a Christian view of history itself; we might say, a Christian *philosophy* of history.

We should begin by noticing that among the diverse aspects of human experience in God's creation, i.e., the ways in which we discover how reality *functions*—the historical-cultural dimension is one we can quickly identify. At the centre of this mode of experiencing life we find an essential, irreducible, and indefinable meaning-kernel of *formative power* (Gen. 1:28, 4:20–22). By this I mean that to varying degrees we all form and shape the things, events, and people around us through our presence, calling, creativity, work, and human technique (Gen. 11:1–4; Exod. 31:1–11; Acts 9:15; Eph 2:10). This cultural power does not mean *all* our actions within day-to-day activities are "historic." History is not simply "stuff that happened." Rather, that which is properly "historic" consists in those events in which the formative, cultural power of human beings, exercised in either faith or unbelief, is most clearly seen and manifest. Take the Bible, for example. Not everything in the life of the Patriarchs, the Israelites, Jesus, or the Apostles is covered and addressed—only particular periods, moments, or highlights. Because God's purpose was to unfold the history of redemption, very specific formative events were selected by the Holy Spirit for a special purpose; and because they were recorded in Scripture, these events are both historical and historic (cf. John 21:24–25).

We can illustrate the distinction between mundane things that happen and events which are historic by noting the obvious difference between a

---

3. For interested readers beginning to study this matter, I would recommend starting with Loraine Boettner, *The Millennium*, and Kenneth Gentry, *Postmillennialism Made Easy*.

person working through a Saturday morning job list—which includes replacing several burned out light bulbs in the house (i.e., stuff that happened)—and the American inventor Thomas Edison's *development* of the light bulb. Similarly, there is an important contrast between someone sitting down to watch a television program, and Edison's *development* of motion pictures. The former events are just mundane, everyday things that happened, whereas the latter are selected by human beings as truly *historic* because they were profoundly *culturally formative*. This is why we remember the name of Thomas Edison, but not the names of everyone who sits on the couch to watch television! Mundane events can of course become historic for a variety of reasons. Going out for a beer to the pub is common in Europe as a social activity, but some drinks enjoyed in public, like beer at the Bürgerbräukeller, can end up launching world wars! This was where Adolf Hitler launched what is often called the Beer Hall Putsch in November 1923, and where he later announced the re-establishment of the Nazi Party in February 1925.

Children begin to learn this important distinction in retelling the events of their day or week. Initially, children will go through a detailed blow by blow account of what happened during their day when asked. But as people mature, they learn (at least most do) not only how to summarize their account of events, but to identify the historical-cultural moments of importance *for them* and for those near to them, so that they pass over commonplace details as they move on to the significant things that shaped or were shaped by the happenings of their week: an engagement party, connecting with someone of influence, winning a scholarship, diagnosis with an illness, the gaining or loss of a job, an accident, the completion of a project, the birth of a new baby, etc. It is this distinction that differentiates the historical aspect from other dimensions of life and delimits the field of study for the historian. This insight overturns the assumption of *historicism* as a philosophy that aims to reduce *everything* in human life and culture to mere historical flux. If *everything* that happens *is history* in a proper sense, then there can be no such thing as a history *of* art or a history *of* language or a history *of* faith, because on this view, art, language, and faith are reduced to mere brute facts in a constant flux of historical eventuation—as purely historical phenomena. There could then be no normative law-order for art, or language, or faith, allowing us to identify and distinguish them. This shows that whilst all the happenings of our daily life *function* in the historical dimension of the creation order, only some especially *formative* events are the actual stuff of history and of potential interest to historians for their notable effect in shaping and influencing cultural life.

Human beings are totally unique in this regard. Mankind alone is a *historical-cultural subject* in all of creation because only human beings as God's image-bearers are truly *subject* to God's norms for history. In other words, only people can be obedient or disobedient to God and affect the course and development of history in a truly self-conscious way (Josh. 24:14–28). Plants and animals may be part of the story (Matt. 8:28–34; Acts 28:1–6), but they make no conscious formative contribution to historical-cultural development. How they function and what they do fits with creation law and instinct, but they are not *subject* to historical norms (Isa. 1:3; Matt. 8:20; 2 Pet. 2:12). Their behaviour is therefore predictable and largely consistent, but there is no *development* of culture, learning, or technology amongst animals—no symphonies issuing forth from a troop of gorillas. Animals are acted upon as *objects* within the historical dimension of creation in terms of the personal, accountable life of mankind in our faithful or rebellious response to the Word of God (Ps. 49:20). As such, human beings are the pinnacle of God's creation and the focus of its God-given meaning in history (Ps. 8; Rom. 8:19–23; Heb. 2:5–10).

It might initially seem strange to speak of *historical* norms—a divine law-order to obey for the way we move through time in our cultural life. But the universal ontic structure of reality means that these norms are the *preconditions* for the intelligibility of our experience. For clarity, as I am using the term from within the reformational tradition, a *norm* is a type of law *for creation* (not an eternal abstract law of "reason") which needs to be implemented and applied (positivized) by human beings in a particular time and place (Isa. 28:23–29; Ps. 119:33–36). The Bible everywhere *presupposes* the existence of these inescapable creational norms or ordinances; hence the many biblical references I have noted illustrating normativity. Unlike creational laws that govern the physical or biotic dimensions of created reality, such as laws for growth and digestion which regulate our existence constantly and involuntarily (Matt. 6:27; 15:17-20)—normative laws, like moral laws, can be obeyed or violated (Ezek. 33:10-11). We can act in either a normative or an antinormative way. We are certainly accustomed to thinking about other normative aspects of life, like norms of thought (i.e., logical laws for human reasoning (cf. Isa. 1:18; 2 Pet. 2:12); social norms of politeness and courtesy (1 Cor. 13:5; Eph. 4:29; 1 Pet. 3:3-4); aesthetic norms in the arts like beautiful harmony (Exod. 28:40; Ps. 96:9; Rev. 21:10-21); the moral norm of love to neighbor by doing to others as we would like them to do to us (Matt. 7:12); and the economic norm of avoiding wastefulness and being frugal (Prov. 29:3; John 6:12). Historical norms could initially seem more remote from daily life and may require a little more mental exertion in reflecting upon them.

From the Christian standpoint, it is helpful to meditate first on the normative principle of *historical continuity* (Gen. 8:22). When our first parents were placed in the Garden of God at the beginning of human history, they were given a specific task; there was a purpose and a goal in view, involving *cultural formation* under God's direction. First, they were told to rule and subdue the creation (Gen. 1:26-28). This implied bringing the creation under man's government as a vice-gerent and utilizing it to serve human purposes as God's image-bearers, exercising authority in all creation by bringing out the *potentiality* and wealth God had placed within it (Gen. 2:10-12). Secondly, Adam and Eve were required to dress, keep, and guard the creation (Gen. 2:15). This involved caring for, protecting, and *conserving* all that God had made, as His stewards. To fulfil this specific historical calling, Adam was given Eve as helper and partner in the task of cultural formation, which included multiplying and filling the earth (Gen. 1:28; 2:18, 21-25). There was to be growth and continuity of the human family, *conserving* God's order, as well as advancement and continuity in cultural *development*.

We see in these early chapters of Genesis two elements belonging to the normative principle of historical continuity—*constancy* and *change*. These elements are so intimately involved and intertwined that we cannot detect change without *presupposing* constancy. For example, in seeing an old friend after many years and telling them how much (or how little) they have changed, we would be unable to discern the change if there were not something constant about that person enabling us to recognize them. My dad as both a baby and now a grandfather has changed radically, but in an important sense he is the same person. At the physical level, most of the atoms in our body are replaced every 5–7 years, and yet we still retain a continuous identity. In a similar way, we may observe a beautiful tree in the garden changing continuously with the seasons over many years, yet there is nonetheless a *constancy* that allows us to identify it as *that* tree and not some *other* tree.

The reality of constancy and change in all of life gives us deeper insight into the God-given historical norm of *continuity* in cultural formation (Deut. 11:18–25; Matt. 21: 42–43; 1 Cor. 11:1; 2 Tim. 1:3–6; Heb. 8:7–13). This norm involves honoring both the principle of *preservation* (dress and keep) and *progress* (rule and subdue) which we see commissioned and required in the Garden of God for human history. In other words, the Christian view of history must discern a gradual and consistent *progress* (change) for cultural development in terms of *abiding* (constancy) laws and norms for creation established by God for the furtherance of His kingdom (Isa. 9:7; Hab. 2:14; 1 Cor. 15:22–28; Heb. 2:5–11). It is a beautiful thing to realize that the *abiding* structure of creation is what makes kingdom *progress* truly possible.

To put this in socio-cultural terms, there is both a *conservative* and *progressive* element within human history as God has ordained it. To violate God's kingdom norm for historical-cultural development results in two primary errors—for there is a chasm on each side of the road when it comes to what we might call *anti-historical* behavior, i.e., behavior that violates God's norm. The first error is to over-emphasize *constancy* or preservation to the point of excluding godly change and historical progress. This is a *reactionism* which, in rightly seeking to preserve good things from the past, at the same time wrongly holds on to those things that should be left behind, despite their antiquity, because they are either mistaken, antisocial, wasteful, morally wrong, destructive of harmony, unjust, or faithless.

A good historical example of this would be the cultural struggle to abolish man-theft and enslavement in human civilization (Exod. 21:16; 1 Tim. 1:10). In Christendom, this struggle occurred twice—once in the High Middle Ages, and again in the nineteenth century, led by evangelicals after the re-emergence of a slave trade with the so-called Enlightenment. Here, cultural tradition, which is so important for historical continuity, had to be forced to abandon an ancient and globally ubiquitous institutionalization of man-theft and servitude. In many non-Christian cultures, slavery persisted and still persists—with human trafficking for prostitution and pornography continuing to be a serious problem in the repaganizing West. This shows how the norms for the historical dimension of created reality are indissolubly bound by God to the moral and juridical dimensions of human life, and to God's laws regulating those dimensions. Without God's moral law of love to neighbour and God's law of retribution in regard to justice, regressive and progressive tendencies within history could not be discerned. In light of the biblical gospel of the kingdom, only Christian civilization was eventually able to see the need for *change* and thereby successfully quashed an inherited practice that was morally abhorrent.

The second error (anti-historical behavior) is basically the opposite problem and very much the dominant failing of our time. This is *revolutionism* which, instead of respecting continuity, emphasizes *change* to the point of denying any constancy. The revolutionary spirit seeks the abolition of the past, abandons all tradition, and seeks a new beginning in terms of one ideological principle or another. From a legitimate desire to overcome what are (rightly or wrongly) perceived to be bad things in society, many of the valuable, essential, and beautiful traditions, practices, and institutions end up being overthrown as well. This has been the result of all truly revolutionary movements seeking change outside the requirements of the Word of God (2 Thess. 2:15). The French Revolution ended in a terrifying bloodbath, with clergy and aristocracy as its initial victims, and it led to a violent and oppressive dictatorship. We have already noted that in the West today, ignorant youth indoctrinated by revolutionary neo-Marxists are anxious to signal their virtue as they tear down statues of great leaders who they think had any kind of direct or indirect connection to what they view as "racism" or "imperialism" and "colonialism." Recently, guards had to be placed around a statue of Winston Churchill in London, the famed Prime Minister of Great Britain during World War II and the European leader pre-eminently responsible for the crushing of Nazism, in order to prevent its total desecration.[4] Yet Churchill's heroic though fallible leadership and resistance against real tyranny did not stop progressives at St. Paul's Cathedral from describing Churchill on their website as a "white supremacist" and "unashamed imperialist."[5] The goal behind both the French Revolution and the modern neo-Marxist revolution was and is destroying and overturning the past.

Both these errors violate God's norm for historical development, and they have run wild in human thought, profoundly impacting culture. *Reactionism* tends to overlook the change and progress inherent within the biblical understanding of God's kingdom, insisting on perpetuating a status quo with ideas and practices from a given era or cultural situation which have been idealized in a reactionary way. This may be done with good intent and in the name of philosophical constructs such as "eternal law," "natural law," and even "creation order." Thomas Aquinas' adoption of Aristotle's economic theories of "just price," and arguably his defense of a papal theocracy and feudalism are good examples of justifying inherited and existing social preferences in the name of abstract "eternal laws" rather than holding up all cultural heritage to the Word of God for evaluation (Isa. 8:20; Ps. 19:7–11). Even Reformed Christians can inappropriately lionize the Reformation era with a kind of traditionalist primitivism, and thereby fail to see that the church must always be reforming according to the Word of God (Acts 10:1–15; 18:26; 2 Tim. 2:7; Heb. 4:12).[6]

By contrast, the latter error of *revolutionism* tends to reject the necessary and enduring constancy of God's creation-Word (Ps. 33:6–12; Isa. 40:6 –8;

---

4. Cheng-Morris, "Striking Image Shows Police Forming Ring Around Churchill Statue to Stop Clash Between Rival Protesters," *Yahoo! News*, https://uk.news.yahoo.com/police-guard-winston-churchill-statue-171822582.html (accessed June 2023).
5. Liz Perkins, "St Paul's Cathedral Branded Winston Churchill a 'White Supremacist' and 'Unashamed Imperialist,'" *The Telegraph*, June 24, 2023, https://www.telegraph.co.uk/news/2023/06/24/st-pauls-cathedral-winston-churchill-white-supremacist/.
6. Note well: *according to the Word of God!* Most commonly, this phrase is omitted by those using the Reformation mantra, so that it becomes simply a call to untethered change.

Heb. 13:8), the unchanging authority of the inscripturated Word (2 Tim. 3:16–17; 1 Pet. 1:25), and with it the continuity of any traditions, customs, or norms for the life of man. This is in clear contravention of God's Word (Judg. 21:25; 2 Thess. 2:15). Such revolutionism is brazenly on display in apostate Western churches where women are ordained as elders, bishops, and presbyters, and homosexuality, "gay marriage," cross-dressing/transgenderism, and lesbianism, which are all detestable to God (Lev. 20:13; Deut. 22:5; Rom. 1:26–27; 1 Cor. 6:9), are heralded as enlightened progress.

The Christian philosophy of history recognizes these two opposite dangers and tendencies as they come to manifestation in human culture due to sin; and the Christian philosophy of history instead maintains that under the providential and sovereign hand of God, history is the preserve of neither the reactionary traditionalist nor the revolutionary progressive. Rather, as the unfolding of God's counsel, history is to manifest the growth and *development* of the kingdom of God, in which the believer is called to preserve and apply to changing circumstances all that is good, right, and just in terms of the total Word of God, whilst steadily working against and seeking the removal of all that is unjust, evil, lawless, and rebellious in terms of that same Word (Isa. 9:7; Dan. 2: 34–35; Hab. 2:14; Matt. 13:31–33). As South African Christian philosopher Danie Strauss has pointed out:

> Reactionary movements cling to the status quo without any flexibility or willingness to face the challenge of *changing* historical circumstances. Revolutionary movements, by contrast, take such challenges so seriously that no room is left for any *historical continuity*.
>
> It is only when a sound application of the (constitutive) norm of historical continuity prevails that constructive *reformation* takes place, avoiding the historically antinormative extremes of reaction and revolution....
>
> Tradition, as the guardian of historical continuity, not only embodies the worthwhile legacy of the past, but also calls for continued reformation. But when an

accountable reformation takes place, it only causes *changes* on the basis of historical continuity and not at the cost of it.[7]

St. Paul brings together perfectly the historical norms of continuity, kingdom constancy and change, when he writes, "Do not be conformed to this age, but be *transformed* by the renewing of your mind, so that you may discern what is the good, pleasing and perfect will of God.... *Detest what is evil; cling to what is good*" (Rom. 12:2, 9). Godly tradition must never be despised: "Therefore, brothers, stand firm and hold to the traditions you were taught, either by our message or by our letter" (2 Thess. 2:15). Everything that opposes God's law-Word and the gospel of the kingdom is to be opposed (1 Tim. 1:8–11). Righteousness, truth, and faithfulness are to be advanced, and by the omnipotent power of the Holy Spirit, history will reach its goal when Christ consummates all things in the full realization of the kingdom of God (1 Cor. 15:23–28; Rev. 1:4–8).

When this Christian view of history is rejected and God's norm for historical development is set aside, culture becomes dominated by faithlessness and unbelief (Rom. 1:18–32). History itself is then perceived as a paradox and problem, a looming threat to be feared (Prov. 28:1). In denying the Word and Kingdom of the triune God, the unbeliever confronts a perilous threat in facing the world, namely, the problem of uncontrolled change.

## History as Threat and Dread

We have seen in the biblical perspective that God is the Creator and Governor of all things and as such has established the *meaning* of all events, having ordained *progress* and development within history in terms of His everlasting kingdom (Dan. 7:14; Hab. 2:14; Isa. 9:7; Rev. 11:15; Matt. 13:31–32). For biblical Christianity, creation *is* meaning with, in philosophical terms, a

---

7. Danie Strauss, *Philosophy: Discipline of the Disciplines* (Jordan Station, ON: Paideia Press, 2009), 316.

divinely ordered normative ontic structure. The eternal *unchanging* reality is not man, his ideas, nor anything in all creation, but God Himself, His being, counsel, and purpose. God's Word and work, from before the foundation of the world, establish the teleology of history, which has a beginning and an ordained conclusion in the counsel of His sovereign will (Prov. 16:1–4; Rom. 11:36; Eph. 1:11; Rev. 13:8).

Humanistic worldviews have no faithful God. Instead, "nature"—an impersonal cosmos of change—is *ultimate* reality with or without eternal "mind," "form," or "idea" in dialectical tension with "matter." In some pagan worldviews, change and movement in history are endlessly recurring cycles, making true progress and development impossible whilst emptying the concept of history of meaning altogether. In the dominant humanistic perspective today, the universe and everything in it emanates from primeval flux into a world of chance and change where possibility and potentiality are for all intents and purposes infinite. Simply put, since there is no infinite-personal-relational God distinct from creation, there is no supervening providence, no design-plan for history, and therefore no order or meaning that precedes or defines the existence of anything. Without the constancy of God's law-order there is only change and possibility. In such a world, how can there be any meaning or unity in the chaotic diversity of events? Can anything be permanent or abiding? How might human beings conquer a hopeless sense of blind fate?

Various attempts to overcome the false "problem" of change have been articulated in worldviews that deny the living God and His law *for* creation. Stemming from the classical world (especially in Plato, Neo-Platonism, and their intellectual offspring), an attempt is made to "solve" the problem of constant change in the world of our senses by positing an abstract, immaterial, and eternal world of forms or ideas to provide unity and constancy. Here, the "rational ideas" and ideals of philosophers become the permanent and the *truly real* over against the unstable environment of material change all around us.[8] Fast forward into the late eighteenth and early nineteenth

---

8. See Adamson, *Classical Philosophy*, 142–43.

centuries and we find the German philosopher, Georg Wilhelm Friedrich Hegel, one of the most influential thinkers who shaped the modern Western view of history, teaching that "the rational is real and the real is rational."[9] That is to say, world-spirit, idea, or mind is ultimate and truly real. History is a synthetic, dialectical process in which this world-spirit that pervades all things finally overcomes and resolves all change, when the mind and its content come to rest in the absolute. Then in Marxism, influenced by Hegel's idea of progress, the purpose of philosophy must now be to actively *change* the world, not merely reflect upon it. Marx conceives of man as his own creator through work. Here, humanity can overcome the oppression of a deterministic nature by changing the world through revolutionary action, altering the human environment by technique—the goal being the emergence of a final, structureless, and changeless social order.[10] And so with a recovery of ancient Greek views of reason and a planned society during the Enlightenment, biblical Christianity as the primary cultural force is steadily supplanted in the late-modern world, giving way to a psychological-religious understanding of reality. In the new religion, man is the new god over the changing environment, planning and remaking his own destiny in terms of his autonomous idea of himself. As Herman Dooyeweerd explains:

> Ever since the Renaissance, modern humanism has been driven by the proud *freedom motive* aimed at a new society, dialectically accompanied by the modern *nature motive*—i.e., the tendency to gain autonomous control of reality by means of modern science.... Modern man, uprooted, finds his "autonomous freedom" only in the existential possibility to plan his future in a mood of "concern," aware that this future ends ontologically in a "nothing," in "death."[11]

In this psychological universe of impending doom, some sort of order must be *imposed* upon a material history of *brute fact*—meaningless events

---

9. Cited in Rushdoony, *The One and the Many*, 305–306.
10. See Thomas Molnar, *Utopia: The Perennial Heresy* (New York: University Press of America, 1990), 98–100.
11. Dooyeweerd, *Time, Law and History*, 157.

not pre-interpreted by God. In theory, this imposition either can be a purely *existential* perspective for the *individual* who proudly stands at the abyss – where the "freedom" of the individual will is the will of "god" and all other wills which resist "my" will must be that of Satan (as in existentialist philosopher Jean Paul Sartre), or it will be a *collectivist* will, man's idea embodied in the state expressing the "freedom of necessity" which must be embraced by everyone. Either way, as far as cultural formation is concerned, God is abolished and meaning, sovereignty, and law are transferred to the human mind and will—individual or collective. Clearly, anarchy is implied in any societal realization of existentialism, making it an unworkable philosophy for the ordering of society. Ironically, for this reason Sartre could find no alternative but to support communism as a social theory, and even existentialist theologian Paul Tillich promoted socialism—for God is "being itself" that exists in all things, and no authoritative word from God has come to man through a resurrected Lord Jesus Christ! As a result, for the modern humanist, a form of *collectivism* is the only solution to the problem of change and the "threat" posed by human freedom.

Religiously, then, modern secular pagans see themselves as victims in a frightening world of unpredictability. As a result, they must defend themselves and the realm of public health by exercising *control* over the fearful world of *change*. This menacing environment of flux is viewed as constantly threatening to crush humanity. So in an effort to escape ruin and death, reality must have man's reason and technique imposed upon it to "arrest history" (which consists of unpredictability, change, and progress), creating out of the chaos a permanent, "sustainable," "equitable," "safe," and "changeless" order that ceases to jeopardize human well-being. Since there is no sovereign God, no norm for historical development, no kingdom of God in terms of which progress and change occur, humanity must provide an alternative kingdom—human reason and man himself must become the *substitute source* of permanence, security, and predestination.

It is relevant to notice that in the classical world, the humanistic cultural elite, the philosophers and orators, spoke often about the "freedom" of man whilst promoting a slave culture, whereas the early Christian church, with its teaching about the government, kingdom, and sovereignty of a personal

God, went on to actually birth socio-cultural and political freedom. Pagan thought has always required a powerful, totalizing, and priestly state to *save man* from his surrounding environment by means of the planned order of an intellectual elite; as witness Plato's *Republic* among the ancients and the cradle to grave welfare-state utopias of the modern world.[12] This is invariably done in the name of the *salus publica* (public welfare or public health), as Dooyeweerd has pointed out:

> [This idea was subordinated] to Wolff's natural law theory of the police State, to Hobbes' and Rousseau's natural law construction of the Leviathan State, to the classical liberal doctrine of the constitutional State (Locke and Kant), and also to the modern totalitarian political theories.
>
> For the sake of the "public interest," Plato and Fichte defended the withdrawal of children from their parents to entrust their education to the body politic. With a further appeal to the public interest, Plato wanted to abolish marriage and private property as far as the ruling classes of his ideal State were concerned. Aristotle wanted education to be made uniform in "the public interest"; on the same grounds, Rousseau wished to destroy all the particular associations intervening between the State and the individual. Wolff desired the body politic to be part of all human affairs.... The slogan of the "public interest" was the instrument for the destruction of the most firmly established liberties because it lacked any juridical delimitation.
>
> The universalistic political theories could conceive of the relation between the State and the non-political societal structures only in the schema of the whole and its parts. This is why they could not delimit the idea of the "public interest."[13]

Paganism and secularism today again talk a lot about freedom, the common good, and public interest, but don't really believe in it, whereas the truly

---

12. See Molnar, *Utopia: The Perennial Heresy*.
13. Dooyeweerd, cited in Strauss, *Philosophy: Discipline of the Disciplines*, 557.

Christian church speaks of liberty and the common good only in Christ, under the personal and all-wise government of God, and in that regard, has become the last defender of genuine liberty in the West. The conclusions of paganism in this matter are at least thoroughly logical. As we return full-circle and our culture rehashes these ancient ideas, the exhaustion and disillusionment of modern man amidst his futile social experimentation are increasingly manifest. Humanity has exhausted every avenue to return to paradise under its own strength, and so the same dead-end ideas are simply being recycled today in a different garment in order to appear new and "progressive."

## The Antithesis

The antithesis between the Christian vision of history and the humanistic one is now evident—it concerns our *ultimate environment* as human beings. In the final analysis man is historically conditioned either by the personal God of Scripture and His eternal purposes, or by "nature" i.e., an impersonal environment leading to the inescapable concept of fate. In the first instance, as the creature of God, man is *free* to be what he is created to be and as such is personally accountable to God. Here, freedom is found in the reality that nothing around man can coerce him to be other than what he is in terms of his response to the Word of God as His creature. In this biblical context, salvation and renewal are not found in a revolutionary transformation of the human *environment*, as though the environment is determinative for man's life, but in the transformation of the heart of man himself through the regenerating grace of God in Jesus Christ; only then can human beings go on to serve God in their environment to further His kingdom through continuity-abiding reformation. But in the case of pagan secularism, as the victim of a capricious and impersonal world, man can be "saved" only by a planning and controlling agency which acts to transform his environment by manipulating all of social reality. This ultimate *impersonalism* ends in the *depersonalization* of man and history itself because it destroys both freedom and ethics, good and evil. In such collectivist thinking, freedom and ethics steadily become irrelevant, as control, planning, and pragmatic concerns logically take their place.

Leaning heavily on the thought of ancient Greek philosophers, H. G. Wells in his 1905 novel, *A Modern Utopia*, sets out his eschatological views as a rational plan for the future. Though couched in a story, the book is really a philosophical discourse extolling the virtue of a world ruled by a small elite class. For Wells, history will culminate in the realization of a World State as one vast economic zone in whose hands all force and natural resources would be vested. The "undying organism" of the World State would be the sole landowner of the earth and the only producer of energy, yet the vast majority of people would still be happy! The miserable resistors would be exiled to isolated islands. In this ideal world, manual work would gradually disappear with the help of machine technology in every aspect of life; women would be sexually liberated; eating meat would be abolished; and cradle to grave welfare would be provided for all. The goal is leisure and pleasure in a labour-free world:

> The World State in this ideal presents itself as the sole landowner of the earth, with the great local governments I have adumbrated.... The State or these subordinates holds all the sources of energy, and either directly or through its tenants, farmers and agents, develops these sources, and renders the energy available for the work of life. It or its tenants will produce food, and so human energy, and the exploitation of coal and electric power, and the powers of wind and wave and water will be within its right. It will pour out this energy by assignment and lease.... It will maintain order, maintain roads, maintain a cheap and efficient administration of justice, maintain cheap and rapid locomotion and be the common carrier of the planet, convey and distribute labour, control, let, or administer all natural productions, pay for and ensure all healthy births and a healthy and vigorous new generation, maintain the public health, coin money and sustain standards of measurement, subsidize research, and reward such commercially unprofitable undertakings as benefit the community as a whole; subsidize when needful chairs of criticism

and authors and publications, and collect and distribute information. The energy developed and employment afforded by the State will descend like water.[14]

In some respects, these are laughable imaginations in the wake of two World Wars and the National Socialist and Communist terror that followed its original publication, yet the work has, nonetheless, been hailed for decades by progressive intellectuals as the most plausible utopia ever written and a blueprint for the modern welfare state. In the post-Covid lockdown era and an age of climate hysteria, it is even easier than before to recognize how contemporary these goals sound in the social democracies of the West—especially with the proliferation of the globalist bodies and their elite planners.

Indeed, much of what Wells imagined has been attempted over the past hundred years of our history. The massive growth of the welfare state; explosion of a regulatory bureaucracy; public ownership or state intervention in banks and industry; the growing control and manipulation of energy production; socialized medicine; state counterfeiting of fiat currency (quantitative easing); ensuring "public health"; control and censorship in the distribution of information; the control of media; state education; the subsidizing of research desired by the state; the so-called liberation of women through birth control and abortion on demand, and so forth. All this is being attempted and needs to be paid for. Remarkably, Wells anticipates the need for people to be permitted some property to use and trade but emphasizes there will be a "universal maximum" of individual freedom—it all sounds remarkably current and familiar.

Ancient or modern, the eschatology of pagan thought involves history culminating with a counterfeit "eternal security" provided by a god-like State which will deliver humanity from the burden of both work and freedom. The meaning of history is then realization of an essentially *static order* of sustainability in a cosmic-sized welfare program. But as Hendrik van Riessen

---

14. H. G. Wells, *A Modern Utopia* (Lincoln, NE: University of Nebraska Press, 1967), 89–90.

grasped during the emergence and growth of the modern welfare states of the West:

> [N]ow that the ideal is being put into practice, it is evident that nothing is behind it; the "happy society"—the welfare state—is in itself meaningless. Its meaninglessness is revealed by its very stability.
>
> For the fundamental meaning of all that exists is its dependence and dynamic concentration on the origin of all meaning, and this radical unrest disturbs any stability. No enduring situation exists on the way to death, or for that matter on the way to life. To the degree that the ideal of science is more fully actualized, the feeling grows that all is vanity, meaningless. If a person rejects God's law, eventually he will no longer see any guiding principles or perspectives. He will become a nihilist.[15]

The insight here is profound. If your worldview is faulty, if meaning is sought in the hope of imposing stability on an *impersonal* reality rather than in the dynamic dependence of all things upon Christ as the centre and concentration point of all meaning (John 1:1–5; Col. 1:15–20), then the failure of human technique to halt history or provide an artificial stability foreign to the nature of creation will produce only despair and feelings of hopelessness. Few things could be clearer than the fact that dread and hopelessness cling to this generation like mist in the morning hours.

Because the triune God is totally personal, not only are His image-bearers fully personal, but history itself, along with all else in creation, is part of a dynamic environment having personal significance. Just as everything in our homes is personal to us (each picture, piece of furniture, or child's toy), because it represents an event, decision or moment in our lives as persons, so *all things* are personal relative to God as their Creator, Governor and Sustainer (Col. 1:17). There is no aspect of creation or history that is hidden

---

15. Hendrik Van Riessen, *The Society of the Future*, trans. David Hugh Freeman (Philadelphia, PA: Presbyterian and Reformed Publishing, 1957), 63.

or alien, standing in impersonal relation to God. In this changing world that moves in terms of the eternal purposes of God, Jesus Christ clearly assures us, "Are not two sparrows sold for a copper coin? And not one of them falls to the ground apart from your Father's will. But the very hairs of your head are all numbered" (Matt. 10:29–30). This universe of total meaning under the all-wise providence of a personal and relational God is the antithesis of the nihilistic world of the scientific social planners for whom the arbitrary word of man in the state must become a word of totalizing power and authority.

# Thinking further about History with George Parkin Grant

The fundamental religious distinction between a Christian and secular-pagan view of the nature and *meaning* of history should now be abundantly clear. Not surprisingly, more than a few thinkers have recognized the disturbing implications of a view of history that sees culture culminating in a homogeneous, universal, egalitarian state—the product of intense political striving. As a result, it is not uncommon for those uncomfortable with either alternative to attempt to forge a *synthesis* of the pagan and Christian perspectives. In the process of Western secularisation, pseudo-Christian views of the historical-cultural life of man have been common; even Hegel considered himself a basically Christian philosopher and his view of history to be the "underlying" meaning of the Bible. On the one hand, there may be a rejection of the pagan dream of a totally *planned order* in terms of man's ideal by asserting a conservative view of tradition or freedom of the individual. But invariably there is also an abandonment of the biblical doctrine of creation and the cultural mandate. As such, all pseudo-Christian positions prove inadequate for overcoming or providing a valid alternative to the utopian delusions of a fallen world.

A powerful example of this synthesis thinking is found in the remarkable work of distinguished Canadian public intellectual, George Parkin Grant, who gave focused attention to the philosophy of history. I want to take some time to analyze Grant's work at this juncture, because his perspective draws upon a number of key thinkers in the Western tradition, making him representative of an important plank of pseudo-Christian thought. At the same time, interacting with Grant provides an ideal opportunity to address the key issues in developing a truly Christian philosophy of history. It also allows us to consider Canada in particular as a formerly Christianized nation in the West, losing its identity as it forfeits a Christian understanding of its history.

Grant was born in Toronto in 1918, the youngest of four children, descending from a Maritime family line of distinguished teachers and Presbyterian ministers. His father was a historian with a special interest in Canadian history, who taught at Upper Canada College, Oxford University, and Queens University during his career. Badly injured during the First World War, George's father returned to Canada in 1918 to become principal of Upper Canada College. The family context in which George was raised was a good example of a middle-class, liberal Protestant home, where a broad belief in Christian morality and conduct remained important—rooted in generalized notions of the existence of a higher being—but where the substance of the scriptural faith of their forbears no longer gripped their hearts or gave direction to their thinking.

Not surprisingly, George Grant attended Upper Canada College and then went on to Queens to study history and literature, hoping to enter law and then politics. He won a scholarship to study at Oxford University as the Second World War was just beginning, which interrupted his law degree. Initially a pacifist and conscientious objector, he enlisted in the ambulance corps. Later, under pressure to leave his pacifism behind, he enlisted in the merchant navy, was assigned a ship, but apparently deserted for several months to a farm in Buckinghamshire, England, where he had a spiritual experience that deeply impacted his life:

> At the worst stage of the war for me... I found myself ill, had deserted from the merchant navy and went into the English countryside to work on a farm. I went to work at five o'clock in the morning on a bicycle. I got off the bicycle to open a

gate and when I got back on I accepted God.... If I try to put [this experience] into words, I would say it was the recognition that I am not my own.[16]

He sometimes described this as a "conversion," but to my knowledge he did not unpack this event in anything more than very vague terms, and so it would be a misuse of the incident to regard it as a Christian conversion experience in any biblical-evangelical sense.

Suffering from tuberculosis, Grant returned to Canada to be nursed back to health in Toronto by his mother for the remainder of the war. Here he got involved in radio broadcasting with the CBC, bringing to this role a passion for educating the public about democratic citizenship. He returned to Oxford in 1945, but with a new mission of studying theology and philosophy, earning his doctorate in philosophy and becoming a university professor. He studied and wrote on the work of the Scottish theologian John Oman, with a particular interest in examining the relation between the natural and supernatural—a theme originating in Greek philosophy that remained important to Grant's thought for the rest of his life. He married in 1947 and taught philosophy at Dalhousie University in Halifax for eleven years.

Slowly, Grant began emerging as a public figure, no doubt in part because he emphasized the importance of philosophy for all sorts of people in their varied vocations in order for them to understand how their work relates to the general ends a society is pursuing. His style was fairly informal and often popular enough for the non-specialist to engage meaningfully with his writing. Manifesting a keen insight, he understood and attacked the complacent secularism and professionalism of academic philosophy, which promoted the illusion that their subject was "essentially a technique independent of theological dogmas of faith."[17] In 1958 he produced a series of radio lectures on *Philosophy in the Mass Age*, published in print in 1959, that set forth his basic understanding of philosophy. Moving to the Toronto area in 1960, he soon became head of the department of religion at McMaster

---

16. Hugh Donald Forbes, *George Grant: A Guide to His Thought* (Toronto: University of Toronto Press, 2007), 171.
17. Forbes, *George Grant,* 8.

University in Hamilton. This enabled him to focus his teaching and writing on thinkers he found interesting, unrestricted by the attitudes of the professional theologians and philosophers that irritated him. By all accounts he was unconventional, independent-minded, and an engaging teacher who enjoyed the freedom the new teaching post afforded him.

In his most noted early works, *Lament for a Nation* (1965) and *Technology and Empire* (1969), he secured a reputation as a kind of Red Tory and leading critic of modernity with a broadly nationalist vision for Canada—so he was not an uncontroversial figure! In *Lament for a Nation*, large segments of discussion are taken up with expressing approval toward the defeated Canadian Prime Minister, John Diefenbaker, and his resistance to certain American military demands, thus helping to reinforce a sense of independent Canadian identity rooted in a traditional British conservatism that he viewed as predating "the age of progress" and "the technological empire"—the vanguard of which he viewed to be the United States. His nationalism and the rather inequitable anti-American element in his writing nonetheless helped to build a loyal following for Grant across Canada. By the end of the 1960s he was not just a popular teacher but a prominent public figure with a fanbase outside university corridors—a significant achievement for an academic. Donald Forbes characterized him as "an odd mixture of the arrogance and pretensions of Canada's old anglophile elite and the rebelliousness of its counter-cultural youth."[18]

In the 1970s he began appearing on television and was involved in public debate, whilst his personal concerns broadened to include not only more abstract philosophical discussions regarding the thought and influence of Nietzsche and Heidegger or the liberal political theory of John Rawls, but also the practical outworking of liberal theory in the emergence of abortion on demand in Canada and the United States. For Grant, this social development was a sign that darkness now surrounded the idea of justice—abortion as "choice" was a poison chalice and the fruit of individualism gone mad. Not surprisingly this unpopular stance made Grant more controversial than

---

18. Forbes, *George Grant*, 11.

his soft socialism and Canadian nationalism had ever done, for here he was now well outside the acceptable consensus of elite opinion. Eventually, with failing health and in the wake of a bitter disagreement with colleagues at McMaster, Grant moved back to Dalhousie in 1980. His last book was *Technology and Justice* (1986). He died in 1988 at seventy years old and is buried in one of his favorite villages near Halifax.

Though dismissed by some today as a relic or incurable pessimist for his critique of late-modern social and political thought—especially the dangers of technology shaping that modern political spirit—Grant denied being *despairing* of the modern world, for "when a man truly despairs, he does not write; he commits suicide."[19] And Grant did write an impressive amount. I myself have profited from reading a number of his books and several works discussing his life and thinking. Certainly, his classic contribution to a specifically Canadian thought and context was *Lament for a Nation: The Defeat of Canadian Nationalism* (1965), which still deserves attention since the subject of Christian nationhood (or nationalism) has again become prominent in a decaying West.

In my judgment, Grant remains significant and fascinating because he was pre-eminently concerned with the historical-cultural life of man—especially the interrelationship of politics and morality with philosophy and religion. He wanted to trace political, social and cultural-technological developments back to underlying philosophical and religious ideas. It is this element that makes him a very noteworthy and interesting philosopher. However, he is also frustrating. Grant's approach is somewhat unsystematic and at times vague or elusive, typically raising more questions than providing coherent answers—which is a legitimate part of the philosophical task. What is clear, however, is that he regarded Canadian identity—and by extension, the broadly Christian identity of the West as a whole—as having gradually collapsed during the twentieth century. And he clearly recognized

---

19. George P. Grant, *Lament for a Nation: The Defeat of Canadian Nationalism* (Toronto: McClelland and Stewart, 1965), 3.

the utopian, collectivist, and statist character of the ideology now gripping Western culture:

> The confused strivings of politicians, businessmen, and civil servants cannot alone account for Canada's collapse. This stems from the very character of the modern era. The aspirations of progress have made Canada redundant. The universal and homogeneous state is the pinnacle of political striving. "Universal" implies a worldwide state, which would eliminate the curse of war among nations; homogeneous means that all men would be equal, and war among classes would be eliminated. *The masses and the philosophers have both agreed that this universal and egalitarian society is the goal of historical striving.* It gives content to the rhetoric of both Communists and capitalists.... Man will conquer man and perfect himself.[20]

As this far-reaching insight intimates, Grant perceived a significant crisis in late-modern Western culture. And Grant did call himself a Christian and regarded truth, beauty, and meaning as something that must transcend mere subjective human "value" judgments. As such, it is worthwhile for Christians to consider where this Canadian notable helps illuminate the historical-cultural crisis of our age.

## Grant's Lament

In lamenting with Grant where Canada and the West are generally, it is important for orthodox Christians to be mindful of several things. *First*, Grant rightly recognized that true "lamentation is not an indulgence in despair or cynicism. In a lament for a child's death there is not only pain and regret but also celebration of passed good."[21] When we lament, just as the prophet Jeremiah did over Jerusalem, we weep over the death or decline of something loved. Jeremiah declared regarding his city, "Her

---

20. Grant, *Lament for a Nation*, 53–54.
21. Grant, *Lament for a Nation*, 2–3.

uncleanness stains her skirts. She never considered her end. Her downfall was astonishing; there was no one to comfort her" (Lam. 1:9). Clearly such a lament presupposes the objective reality of good and evil, which can never lead to a despairing theatre of the absurd.

*Second*, from a scriptural standpoint, because all people must live in God's creation, subject to the governing and ordering authority of His law-Word for reality—which includes norms for human thought (whether people accept and believe this Word-revelation or not)—the fruits of serious and coherent intellectual labor from people with faulty religious assumptions can still contain many valuable *moments of truth* to be harvested. Grant's lament over Canada lacks sufficient hope and direction because he did not adequately grasp the explanatory power and truth of a consistently biblical world-and-life-view nor the might of the regenerating and transformative power of the Holy Spirit. As a result, scripturally directed Christians will not be able to agree with all Grant's religious presuppositions. Nevertheless, he did lament a nation collapsing under the weight of its own idolatry, even if he did not accurately recognize the root problem to be the apostasy of the Western heart from faith and trust in Jesus Christ as the Creator and Redeemer of all things.

With those caveats in mind, what are the main concerns in George Grant's lament? At the more superficial level, Grant is lamenting what he sees as the passing away of Canada as a sovereign nation—primarily via the loss of its particular and ultimately ancient Christian-conservative identity stemming from its British heritage. But even more important for Grant, this passing is actually a *symptom* of a broader and deeper problem—the religious character of the modern era itself. His idea of what Canada really was had been made increasingly redundant by the philosophy of the mass age which not only saw time as history,[22] but history as the theatre in which

---

22. Grant adopted an essentially ancient and platonic view of time as a "moving image of eternity" and rejected the biblical view of time as a finite creation by God moving from beginning to end in terms of God's active providence and redemption in history. This is one of Grant's most serious errors, and it leaves him without a viable source of resistance to tyranny in time.

man conquers both man and nature, and establishes a universal egalitarian order and value system by scientific technique. This vision was an expression of the religion of *historicism*—the belief that there is no eternal God and no transcendent law or reality that binds men and nations to something greater than human self-expression which arises in the course of history. True freedom from this perspective is man's autonomous prerogative to positivize his own values in time and create history so as to make all nature serve his self-centred ends.

## The Impossibility of Canada

Because in Grant's view, cultural striving in the West was now directed toward accomplishing this imperious historical purpose, the notion of "progress" or change meant that the *idea of Canada*—as a conservative and unique community in North America—was essentially obsolete. Gradually, Canada, like most of Western Europe, was being ideologically, politically and economically absorbed into a vast globalist vision, especially under the influence of its powerful southern neighbor with its dynamic progressive liberalism and rugged individualism. As a consequence, Grant laments the dying of Canada as a truly sovereign nation.

According to Grant, what was taken for granted back in the 1920s was that Canada was a unique nation with an ancient British heritage, deeply rooted in a *classical conservatism* that predated the age of "progress" or revolution[23]—an age of which he was deeply suspicious and indeed fearful, given its pretensions. The heritage he valued highly was more "communitarian" (self-giving) than merely "contractual" (self-interested) in its social outlook—a feature which he regarded, rightly or wrongly, as one distinguishing

---

23. There is no space here to discuss Grant's interesting reorganization of contemporary political labels. For example, he viewed American conservatism as actually old-fashioned eighteenth- and nineteenth-century liberalism. He doubted the future of American conservatism because he felt the USA was dominated by a vision of the age of progress.

aspect of essentially Canadian versus American political and social thought. However, Grant was not naïve, nor was he purely nostalgic. He was aware that the old aristocratic British conservatism of "throne and altar" was already a largely spent force. Even in Britain, Lockean individualism was taking over, so looking to Britain for clearer Canadian identity was no solution. Consequently, amidst Grant's enthusiastic opposition to *progressive* Western liberalism (in the modern sense), radical individualism, globalizing tendencies through massive corporations and the homogenizing of international political life, Grant unfortunately became reactionary and found himself defending a kind of socialism for Canada as "more conservative" than true economic freedom. This was a very dubious conclusion indeed, given that the emergence of the socialistic, interventionist welfare state is a late-modern phenomenon rooted in the progressive utopian ideologies and social engineering that Grant despised—but he had his political reasons for living with this tension, and he therefore embraced soft socialism.

From a scriptural standpoint we might observe that Grant was right to appreciate Britain's and Canada's historically communitarian, indeed, covenantal view of society, and to attack a reductionist contractual vision of social order that rejected tradition and did not wish to see beyond individual rights, capital gain, or personal autonomy and gratification. But like many professed Christian intellectuals, his not uncritical sympathies with Marxism and socialism were incongruent with his vision of a society rooted in *transcendent* norms and *voluntary familial community*, not to mention his opposition to an egalitarian homogeneous global order. Indeed, the British heritage and ancient traditions he looked to were aristocratic and monarchical in character, traditions that inherently resisted the leveling tendencies of both socialism and modern liberal democracy. Yet for what appear to be reasons of utility, Grant saw no practical alternative to a measure of planning and control from the seat of government in Ottawa in order to preserve a *nationalist vision* of the nation. He writes, "After 1940, nationalism had to go hand in hand with some measure of socialism. Only nationalism could provide the political incentive for planning; only planning could restrain the victory of continentalism."[24] From the scriptural standpoint this is a grave error, because no political philosophy can preserve the religious character of a nation.

There is a rather pragmatic type of reasoning at work here that obviously conflicts with his vision of natural law and eternal order. We may also be seeing the varied influence of Plato's *Republic*, British Fabian socialism[25], as well as Grant's failure to adequately consider the role of the Christian family, church, and private charity in building community. This misdirected him as he reached for a more communal understanding of social and political life than the modern technological world offered him. Whatever the primary force shaping his perspective, he deeply regretted the gradual perishing of Canadian community, and so the false hope of democratic socialism in a time of decline drew his gaze.

Essentially, Grant's lament for a dying Canada was rooted in his conviction that the nation had its foundations in a combination of Christianized organic conservatism, classical philosophical studies, and natural law—a view of life that urged self-restraint, with public order and tradition as guiding values as opposed to the emancipation of the passions in an individualistic, progressive society. A social order built on self-restraint had to be rooted in a recognition of a higher order. But his fear was profound that in our technological age, such a vision could not be recovered. Consequently, Grant lamented the loss of an original Romantic view of a Canada rooted in ancient tradition and a concept of eternal law, which had regrettably been replaced by a modern view of absolute freedom as man's essence—a freedom without limits.

The scripturally directed Christian can certainly see several moments of truth in this aspect of Grant's lament. The protectionist elements of his nationalism (which is not synonymous with patriotism) might be challenged

---

24. Grant, *Lament for a Nation*, 15.
25. Fabian socialism was a form of democratic socialism, originating with the British Fabian Society founded in 1844 that advocated for a soft socialism with a capitalist welfare state. They sought social change via gradual, incremental reforms as opposed to violent revolution.

as wrong-headed, and his rather unsympathetic and biased assessment of America's role in the world might be disputed, but it cannot be doubted that the familial, communitarian, conservative Canada he pined for had indeed been lost. Furthermore, this loss militates against many concerns of Scripture and should likewise be a matter of regret for every Christian. His critique of a radical and rugged individualism along with the demise of self-restraint in a technological age of so-called "progress" is also worthy of attention and should be taken seriously.

## The Killing of Canada and the West: Open-ended Progress

In Grant's view, then, the *proximate cause* of Canada's demise as an independent and unique nation in the Americas was the disappearance of an organic classical conservatism rooted in an appeal to transcendent reality through ancient tradition, a decline he claims was accelerated under the powerful influence of a technological, dynamic, and liberal southern neighbor. But his lament has a deeper underlying philosophical conviction concerning the *ultimate cause* for Canada's passing—the *religion of the modern age* itself. So, I want to briefly examine the broad contours of Grant's view of the modern age.

According to Grant, "Modern civilization makes all local cultures anachronistic. Where modern science has achieved its mastery, there is no place for local cultures.... Our culture floundered on the aspirations of the age of progress."[26] The basic idea here is that in the open-ended age of globalized "progress," where nature is conceived like an amorphous lump of clay ready for human formation, man *reimagines* the world as he wants it to be. Instead of inheritance, tradition and local customs shaping culture, the *mastery* of nature becomes an end in itself and the goal of history. Going beyond even the Marxist objective of recreating the world for the *perfectibility* of man, the

---

26. Grant, *Lament for a Nation*, 54.

truly free man is constrained by no particular concept of humanity, happiness, perfection or alienation, as he is in the materialist creed of traditional Marxism. Where man is fully self-conscious, *all* value judgments are purely subjective—the human good is simply what we choose for ourselves. Grant illustrates how this "freedom" increasingly operates in the social order:

> In the private spheres, all kinds of tastes are allowed. Nobody minds very much if we prefer women or dogs or boys, as long as we cause no public inconvenience. But in the public sphere, such pluralism of taste is not permitted. The conquest of human and non-human nature becomes the only public value....
>
> Liberalism is the fitting ideology for a society directed toward these ends. It denies unequivocally that there are any given restraints that might hinder pursuit of dynamic dominance.[27]

No preconceived notions of the good are now allowed to bind anyone, because such myths would limit the possibility of the future—the conquest and total reimagining of nature is the only public value. Consequently, for Grant, in an important sense, this was an age marking the "end of ideology" because here people just do whatever they want. Western civilization is "committed in its heart to the religion of progress and the emancipated passions."[28] Grant's critique of Protestantism's failure to curb this idolatrous spirit by allegedly encouraging greed through unrestrained acquisition is in my view both superficial, mistaken, and part of elite intellectual reaction against so-called "bourgeois" evangelical faith in mid-twentieth century liberal-protestant Canada. In reality, mainline Protestantism by Grant's time was firmly in the grip of liberal progressive theology anyway, was generally socialist, and in denial of the biblical view of man. In Grant's case his critique is particularly rooted in his unbiblical views regarding the nature of history (we shall return to this theme later). However, his lucid criticism of

---

27. Grant, *Lament for a Nation*, 57.
28. Grant, *Lament for a Nation*, 59.

the modern doctrine of "progress" via the emancipation of every restraint is plainly sound. And he clearly understood the trajectory of Western political thought from a classical view of nature and natural law to the modern concept of freedom that implied a progressive mastery of a malleable cosmos: "Man in his freedom was thought to stand outside nature, and therefore to be able to perfect it. We could interfere with nature and make it what we wanted. It is from this doctrine that the continuous revolution of the modern era has proceeded."[29]

This idea spread from Rousseau, through Kant, Hegel and Marx and has produced both communist and democratic totalitarianisms.[30] Moreover, Grant saw that modern state education had greatly helped to advance this secular vision of progress, whilst deliberately and purposefully denying the orthodox Christian view of man. He writes, "At the heart of modern liberal education lies the desire to homogenize the world. Today's natural and social sciences were conspicuously produced as instruments to this end."[31]

For Grant, because a residual Christianity had preserved some sense of the eternal in the West, it had so far been able to safeguard certain freedoms that were lost within Marxist tyrannies in the East. However, he recognized that a skeptical liberalism was now the dominant ideology of those who shape Western society, a liberalism whose goal is the mastering of nature and the reshaping of social order by means of man's planning and technology; this liberalism would sound the death knell for true liberty. In this regard, Grant is prophetic, anticipating the implications of radical queer theory and the climate cult seeking to homogenize the planet in the name of both freedom and science. He also foresaw today's crisis in conservatism, because in such a world, the "conservative" is reduced to being one who merely defends the particular structure of power at that time necessary for technological change. Grant saw that with only an *external human order* evacuated of norms transcending the historical aspect of life, a true conservatism had become

---

29. Grant, *Lament for a Nation*, 61.
30. See Polish philosopher Ryszard Legutko's interesting study, *The Demon in Democracy: Totalitarian Temptations in Free Societies*.
31. Grant, *Lament for a Nation*, 79.

almost unthinkable—as, I would add, has any meaningful concept of progress. In short, an ethic of virtue, true community, and self-restraint were incongruent with utopian movements pursuing an open-ended "recreation" of the world by man's free personality.

For Grant, this made the future appear very bleak because utopian philosophy committed to political, social, and economic universalism as well as unlimited technological advance, *cannot* take seriously a *transcendent order* by which human actions are measured, limited, and defined. Yet without such an order, conservatism is little more than a defense of property rights with a nostalgic appeal to the past. Thus, with a universal, homogenized order as the historical goal for modern elites, the *idea* of Canada, and by implication Great Britain or even of the United States becomes "a misguided parochialism."[32] Faced with such a philosophical and political juggernaut, one can easily understand why Grant turned for resources to ancient philosophy, classical notions of natural law and Canadian nationalism in an effort to arrest a seemingly irresistible march toward extinction. This is why he laments that Canada cannot survive as a sovereign nation, indeed has ceased to be a nation, in the face of utopian internationalism or globalism.

Though his tentative and overly pessimistic predictions of the gradual annexation or progressive political absorption of Canada into the United States have not been realized (and show little sign of ever being so, despite Donald Trump's invitation), his notion of Canada as increasingly a branch-plant satellite of American, liberal-democratic, technological progressivism has some merit. Canada's biggest corporate cities like Toronto and Vancouver are massive cosmopolitan centres that differ little from Democrat-run cities like Seattle or Los Angeles, and there is no denying the economic, social and political sway of progressives in the United States over Canada—its entertainment industry alone shaping the norms of Canadian youth culture. And ironically, with the collapse of conservative Canadian identity, Canada's rapid bureaucratization and social progressivism enshrined in its Charter of Rights and Freedoms has moved ahead of the religion of progress in the

---

32. Grant, *Lament for a Nation*, 85.

United States. There at least, a more traditional nineteenth-century classical liberalism (called conservatism in America) as well as a stubborn libertarian posture are still influential in various states with significant political counter-reactions to powerful elements of the progressive, homogenized global order championed by many of its elites.

Once again, without applauding everything he writes, the biblically faithful Christian can see several moments of truth in Grant's analysis of the religion of open-ended progress. From the scriptural standpoint, once man seeks to unhook himself from God's law-Word for creation—as though he can stand above and apart from it—he is on a suicidal course. The attempt to remake man and the world in terms of man's idea, constructing a homogenized society in defiance of God's kingdom-norm for historical development, goes all the way back to the Tower of Babel in Genesis 11 where God Himself reveals that man's pursuit of technological progress and global unification in one idolatrous order has to be undermined for humanity's own good:

> The Lord said, "If they have begun to do this as one people all having the same language, *then nothing they plan to do will be impossible for them.* Come, let Us go down there and confuse their language so that they will not understand one another's speech." So from there the Lord scattered them over the face of the whole earth, and they stopped building the city (Gen. 11:6–8)

Grant's lament over the pursuit of continental empires on the basis of a false *faith in historical progress* (before the EU became the political entity it is today!) is one that resonates with biblical concerns. For scriptural faith, a manipulative society governed by a desire to renew the world through man's autonomous power is a perverted parody of the biblical vision of the kingdom of God under Christ the king. It is because of its nature as *parody* that this pale imitation gains plausibility and power in historical-cultural life.

## Critiquing Grant: Inadequacy of Reactionary Traditionalism

Whilst many of Grant's insights are valuable and helpful in diagnosing today's context, his past-bound response to the religion of progress is wholly inadequate to the challenge of our age, and his strong tendency toward withdrawal and pessimism is testament to the fact that he was unconvinced of the historical usefulness of his own answers. Without insight into *continuity-abiding reformation* as God's norm for historical development (consisting of both constancy and change in terms of the kingdom of God), he confesses quite readily, "I do not know the truth about these ultimate matters."[33] He was even unsure as to whether, in the end, a universal and homogeneous state might not prove to be the better vision for social order![34] As a result he was left in doubt about the very propriety of his lament over the disappearance of a virtue-oriented Canada he and his forbears had known.

The problem is that, in the final analysis, Grant does not move beyond *appeal to tradition* and via tradition to *autonomous reason*, and a reaching back for the "alternative answers" of pagan thinkers for help with practical life. He wrote, "my lament is not based on philosophy but on tradition. If one cannot be sure about the answer to the most important questions, then tradition is the *best basis* for practical life."[35] Certainly, as I have already argued, the guiding and conserving power of tradition is vitally important; we could not have culture without it. But how could Grant make this value judgment if he had no certainty, no ultimate ground or criterion for knowing what is *best*? Indeed, how could we know that reaching back to ancient history and tradition is better for society than the liberal progressivism of our time? Consequently, though yearning to reach up for an eternal and transcendent order, he is unable to confidently connect such a rationalistic abstraction to the real world, to history. Grant is therefore unable to truly free himself from the grip of the historicism he resents. This is because when God's Word

---

33. Grant, *Lament for a Nation*, 96.
34. Grant, *Lament for a Nation*, 96.
35. Grant, *Lament for a Nation*, 96.

is set aside and man himself is made ultimate in the search for answers, reactionism, mysticism, skepticism and cynicism are the inevitable outcome. Out of his uncertainty modern man has turned to a faith in his own power to remake history for himself—that is, a mission not to *understand* the world as creation and to serve God's purpose, but to *change* it according to his own desires.

No one understood the predicament of modern man better than one of Grant's contemporaries in Europe, Herman Dooyeweerd:

> Historicism, sacrificing reality to its historical aspect, is the fatal illness of our "dynamic" times. There is no cure for this unwholesome view of reality *as long as the scriptural creation motive does not regain its complete claim on our life and thought*. Historicism robs us of our belief in abiding standards; it undermines our faith in the eternal truth of God's Word. Historicism claims that everything is relative and historically determined, including one's belief in lasting values.
>
> ...Above all you must be progressive, for then the future is yours.[36]

Grant did see the fatal illness of our dynamic times, but in the end, through his implicit appeal to the ultimacy of autonomous "reason" and explicit appeal to merely human "tradition," he unwittingly sacrifices reality to its logical and historical dimension—and in the process an idol is made of man's abstract ideas. In fact, in rejecting scriptural *revelation* as direction-giving for life, Grant looks to man and his philosophy to reformulate the very doctrine of God Himself: "Our doctrine of God will only become more adequate if a multitude of philosophers give their time to re-thinking in the greatest detail such concepts as 'purpose,' 'revelation,' 'progress,' 'time,' 'history,' 'nature,' and above all 'freedom' and 'evil.'"[37]

---

36. Herman Dooyeweerd, *The Roots of Western Culture: Pagan, Secular and Christian Options* (Jordan Station, ON: Paideia Press, 2012), 63–64.
37. George P. Grant, *Philosophy in the Mass Age* (Toronto: Copp Clark Publishing, 1959), 123.

Aside from the unabashed arrogant elitism in this perspective, there is on display a remarkable confidence in sinful man to arrive at true knowledge of the divine and of the world by "pure" theoretical thought. This is illustrated in the starkest terms when, citing the work of a German physicist seeking to bring together the idea of nature as something to *contemplate* as well as to *control,* Grant declares "with such people does our hope lie."[38] Grant's hope is finally in human intellectual culture and theoretical thought, not in Jesus Christ, the incarnate and redemptive Word of God. Quite logically he proceeds to overestimate and simultaneously greatly fear man's ability to manipulate and control God's world, to unfold "fate" on the basis of human judgments.

Understandably, Grant feels robbed by historicism of abiding standards and virtues, but he refuses to humble himself at the feet of Jesus and trust God's Word, whereby he would have rooted himself in the scriptural *creation motive* to discover those standards in God's Word-revelation. Whilst claiming to be a Christian philosopher, Grant's religious confusion and faltering tears remind me of the prescient words of Evan Runner around the time Grant was writing his first book:

> The weakness of the West is its inability to believe something. Unable to embrace any *integral Christianity,* the West, perhaps to a significant degree because of what yet is left of Christendom in the world, cannot with singleness of heart accept the faith of modern unbelief either. She is like Israel in the days of Elijah, limping between two sides, critically weak.[39]

Grant's unwillingness to embrace an integral Christianity, a failure grounded in his rejection of the Lordship of Christ and the biblical character of creation and history, consigns him to limping between the assumptions of Greek philosophy and Christian truth, between a rationalistic worldview

---

38. Grant, *Philosophy in the Mass Age,* 124.
39. H. Evan Runner, *Walking in the Way of the Word,* in *The Collected Writings of H. Evan Runner,* vol. 1 (Jordan Station, ON: Paideia Press, 2016), 127.

and a biblical one, making his lament for the nation spiritually toothless and inescapably gloomy.

## A Faulty View of History

It is impossible to properly understand the inadequacy of Grant's perspective without saying more about his view of history. Grant's view is a contradiction in this regard. His lament centers upon the impact of philosophical thought on *historical-cultural development* and he wouldn't have written his books without some desire for influencing history himself. Yet his view of time and history, in my judgment, results in his advocating a mystical *flight from history* to an abstract world of ideas, with human beings taking a *passive approach* to historical-cultural development in favor of a neo-Platonic life of metaphysical contemplation on eternal verities. His thought contains, at least theoretically, a fundamental rejection of historical progress as triumphalist and a rejection of man's role as the primary agent in the shaping of the world. Interestingly, this is a view shared by many modern evangelicals who similarly reject the cultural mandate, regard dominion under Christ as triumphalist, and discard the scriptural teaching that man's fundamental calling is to turn creation into a God-glorifying culture. This common evangelical error is grounded in some of the same philosophical missteps that plagued Grant.

Grant was caught in the dialectical character of the *nature* and *freedom* problem of modern thought—puzzling over how these ideas could live harmoniously together. By a form of "natural theology" he believed in a mysterious order to "nature" that should govern and guide one's thinking and living, but he equally wanted to believe in the "freedom" of the human personality. The reactionary and excessive rejection of that freedom was, he thought, the reason for the failure of Marxism. Like much of the Western tradition before him, Grant believed *nature* should be understood as the expression or image of an eternal order which impinges upon man—an order he thought was being foolishly jettisoned by purely pragmatic and instrumentalist concerns. However, at the same time, he assumed and desired the autonomy of reason or theoretical thought from "revelation," the outcome of which proved disturbing to him in its cultural effects. This deep anxiety is obviously connected to his critique of technology as an expression of man's desire to impose his "freedom" (his idea) on the world, and where Grant ends up primarily emphasizing the "nature" side of the nature-freedom dialectic.

It seems to me that, once again, in looking at the modern view of history, Grant was *partly* right in his assessment. He grasped the nature-freedom dialectical problem of modern thought, recognizing that contemporary man saw it as his role to impose a *limitless freedom* on nature or "substance" in history.[40] In this sense, Grant's lament was understandably troubled by the reckless pursuit of the expansion of power *as an end in itself,* and he even saw the coming of what today is called posthumanism and transhumanism:

> Will it be good for men to control their genes? The possibility of nuclear destruction and mass starvation may be no more terrible than that of man tampering with the roots of his humanity. Interference with human nature seems to the moderns, the hope of a higher species in the ascent of life; to others it may seem that man in his pride could corrupt his very being. The powers of manipulation now available may portend the most complete tyranny imaginable. At least, it is feasible to wonder whether modern assumptions may be basically inhuman.[41]

Given this insight, whilst he would have viewed them with genuine horror, Grant would clearly not have been shocked by recent revolutionary activities in our culture to redefine marriage or gender, manipulate human sexuality with hormone drugs and surgery, interfere with our genes, experiment with three-parent human embryos or replace human agency with AI in multiple fields. But for Grant, this technological and inhuman manipulation was *inevitable*, given the modern view of history.

Moreover, Grant saw that Protestantism, as an active faith historically concerned with the transformation of culture, when twisted and evacuated

---

40. Grant, *Philosophy in the Mass Age,* 119.
41. Grant, *Lament for a Nation,* 94.

of Christian theological content in the hands of secularists, had turned into a dangerous pragmatism and relativism that no longer aimed to obey God or follow the hand of providence, but sought to use nature for its own sinful purposes. Pragmatism exalted action over thought and thus refused to condemn any action as categorically wrong,[42] since all actions may be at some point "useful" to a given subjective purpose.

Once again, the scripturally directed Christian can agree with Grant's attack on the modern concept of history as the theatre for man to impose a limitless freedom on "nature." In biblical faith man is always regarded as a vice-gerent, bondservant and steward, called to pursue the kingdom purposes of God, not as a dominating dictator serving his own ends. Only in apostasy against God is man found seeking to *absolutize* his cultural calling for his own wicked purposes in the name of freedom. Thus, the faithful Christian can applaud Grant's assault on the iniquitous ideology of pragmatism which dominates even what passes for conservative political life today. However, Grant's *response* to this demonic urge is in error. Let's now examine why.

## Rejection of the Scriptural World-and-Life View

We can now approach what is the great disaster of Grant's "Christian" thought which prevented him, and so many like him, from discovering true answers: his tragic failure to embrace the pivotal scriptural religious motive of biblical faith, the kingdom of God. This can be summarized simply as Creation, Fall and Redemption in Jesus Christ by the consummating power of the Holy Spirit. Setting aside the Word of God, Grant dismissed a consistent and robust scriptural faith as "biblicism" and a rejection of philosophy.[43] In its place he wanted Christianity radically reformulated. In

---

42. Grant, *Philosophy in the Mass Age*, 105.
43. True scriptural faith is neither radically biblicist, i.e. narrowly interpreting all of Scripture with wooden literalism or limiting all valuable knowledge to that derived directly from the Bible, nor anti-philosophy. In fact many of the world's greatest

what is a high-sounding but essentially absurd rhetorical statement he said, "I have no doubt that Christianity is true, and therefore, I think it has to be reformulated."[44] Likewise, he said, "I can't look at Christ and say he is not the truth. I think many, many people in the East, for example, most followers of Vedanta, or what we call Hinduism, would look at Christ and say he is the truth."[45] Clearly Grant's understanding of Christ and truth are not that of Scripture and historic, orthodox Christianity.

Under the strong influence of the radical Marxist and religious mystic Simone Weil, as well as the neo-pantheist German philosopher Martin Heidegger, Grant shows great sympathy for both the polytheism of the ancient world and Eastern religions because his concept of *divine being* is vague at best and far from an orthodox Christian understanding of the infinite-personal God of Scripture revealed as Father, Son and Holy Spirit, providentially governing all creation. If Christianity has to be "reformulated," as Grant supposed, then biblical Christianity as received and taught by the church from the time of the apostles and early ecumenical creeds can't be true in any objective sense. So, what does it really mean for Grant to say he believes Christianity is true? That is not easy to clarify precisely because of a studied obscurity in his writing, but his definitions of faith and religious experience are surely illuminating in this regard. Religious experience for Grant is about a vague awareness of the supernatural and, following Weil, faith is "the experience that the intelligence is enlightened by love."[46] There is nothing remotely biblical about either of these definitions.

Not surprisingly then, like many liberal Protestants, Grant had a very low view of Scripture and viewed Christianity as locked in Augustinian forms or

---

philosophers from Augustine to Aquinas to Dooyeweerd have been Christian. The challenge is developing a distinctly Christian philosophy rooted in and directed by a total scriptural vision of reality.

44. David Cayley, *George Grant in Conversation* (Concord, ON: House of Anansi Press, 1995), 119.
45. Cayley, *George Grant in Conversation*, 119.
46. Forbes, *George Grant*, 209–210.

a "Western" interpretation.[47] Moreover, and of great import for all of Grant's thinking, this supposedly Augustinian and historic view of the Christian faith was the *underlying historical culprit* in bringing upon us the strange currents of thought that brought down conservative Canada and were pushing the West into a technological, utopian, planned society where man dominates and perfects nature. And yet this seems immediately counterintuitive. How could this be the case? Whilst Roman Catholic theology mistakenly speaks of grace perfecting nature rather than renewing and restoring it in Jesus Christ, how could scriptural Christianity be to blame for the decay of a conservative, communitarian and virtuous Canada into technological, liberal progressivism?

To answer that by brief overview, Grant essentially held that "the idea of creation," with its concomitant view of history, was at fault. This is a disastrous and erroneous line of thinking he gleaned from Weil.[48] The notion of creation was for Grant "an abyss in which our minds are swallowed up."[49] Whatever the precise meaning of this ambiguous statement, it is clear from his other comments on the subject that he is determined to deny the biblical doctrine of creation, and here lies the religious root of his error. Captivated as he was by the ancient Greek form-matter conception of nature, the biblical idea of creation was *excluded in principle*.[50] He then falsely characterizes the orthodox view of creation as an act of divine "self-expansion" and conceives of the scriptural doctrine as involving "the stamping proclamations of the creating will."[51] From this idea Grant concludes that the biblical doctrine of creation as a free act by a personal, relational and sovereign God led to

---

47. Augustine was in fact North African and followed the other Church Fathers in affirming the early creeds of the church. Moreover, the Eastern Orthodox churches uphold the same essential beliefs about the triune being of God, the person of Christ, divine creation, the meaning of time as history, and the presence of the kingdom of God. Grant appears to have been out of his depth in assessing historical theology and Augustine. If anything, Augustine failed to adequately ground the City of God in history and struggled to shake off his own Neo-Platonism.
48. Cayley, *George Grant in Conversation*, 35–39.
49. Cayley, *George Grant in Conversation*, 38.
50. See Dooyeweerd, *In the Twilight of Western Thought*, 30.
51. Cayley, *George Grant in Conversation*, 38.

the destructive concept of religion as the exercise or assertion of the will rather than the pursuit of knowledge. Grant not only artificially separates knowing and willing (since both gaining and sharing knowledge involve acts of will), but he also wants a "god" withdrawn from "nature," leaving man to his freedom. This freedom was both rationalistic and elitist; freedom was a gift of truth acquired through *right reason*.

Predictably, and again following the Marxist mystic Simone Weil—the thinker to whom Grant paid most frequent obeisance—it seems he regarded divinity or eternal being in essentially numinous and impersonal terms. God must be thought of as divine *absence* and not divine action and presence. Though Weil co-opts a Christian terminology, her thought-content is much closer to a kind of Hegelian Gnosticism. She (and it appears Grant), believed

> that the same truth that was manifest in Christianity had been manifest in all the ancient civilizations. "The children of God," she said, "should not have any other country here below but the universe itself, with the totality of all the reasoning creatures it ever has contained, contains, or ever will contain.... Christ has bidden us to attain to the perfection of our heavenly Father by imitating his indiscriminate bestowal of light.[52]

For Grant it was the Jews who first "discovered" and advanced the destructive idea of creation and history where time is finite, beginning with creation and concluding with a judgment at the end of the world. Moreover, biblical faith held that what happened in time was willed and governed by a sovereign and providential God with a definite goal or purpose. Grant wrote:

> By Biblical religion, is meant the Christian interpretation of the Old Testament and its culmination in the incarnation of God, Jesus Christ. That religion was unique in its absolute historicity. It was the Jews who discovered the very idea of history. More than anything else, what has made Western culture so dynamic is its

---

52. Cayley, *George Grant in Conversation*, 39–40.

impregnation with the Judaeo-Christian idea that history is the divinely ordained process of man's salvation. This is an idea utterly foreign to any other civilization.

...[T]he idea of a God of will, who acts in history, brings with it the idea of a final end or purpose towards which his acts are directed, to which history itself is directed.[53]

It was against this scriptural teaching that Grant strongly reacted. Such a conception of God and history, for both Weil and Grant, was the essence of the problem of the modern world with its technocratic drive for the dominance of nature. For Grant, the Platonic notion of time as the *moving image of eternity*—the ancient Greek notion of being and becoming—was the more healing vision. And so, scriptural faith in Christ as both Creator and Messiah, redeeming His people and establishing His kingdom, along with the spread of this biblical doctrine in the form of Augustinian Christianity was *the root* of modern historical man and "the deepest source of modern secular culture as a whole."[54]

In sum, the cultural problem in Grant's view was in seeing time as history—governed by a purposeful God. As we have been saying all along, time is expressed in *more* than the historical dimension of life, and so can't be reduced to history, but Grant wants an *escape* from history into mystical time. In addition, if man is made in God's image, as one who creatively shapes and forms, a vice-gerent called to turn creation into culture in terms of a particular teleology, then rather than passively withdrawing to intellectually contemplate being (like a Buddhist philosopher), man will seek to impose and dominate. Hence for Grant, here in biblical Christianity was the source of so-called technological domination which, when fully secularized, loses all connection with an eternal norm and becomes the naked drive for control.

---

53. Grant, *Philosophy in the Mass Age*, 56–57.
54. Forbes, *George Grant*, 92.

## Assessing Grant's Attack on a Biblical View of History

It is clearly true that biblical Christianity teaches a doctrine of creation along with a God-given cultural mandate for man to rule and subdue in history, and whilst it is undeniably the case that a dynamic, technological culture developed in the thoroughly evangelized West, Grant's charge that the modern relentless imperialism of the religion of progress is the *result* of biblical Christianity, is simply highly dubious. On the contrary, the Renaissance in the West was concerned with a "rebirth" of humankind that would revive the ancient religious ideas of the Greeks with which Grant was so enamoured. Indeed, with Enlightenment rationalism later developing this theme, the humanists were seeking a revitalized participation in Greco-Roman culture freed from its *accommodation* to Christianity.

Nevertheless, they did not want a simple return to an abstract philosophical world where reality is *anchored* in an invisible world of forms. Rather the *new humanists* asserted the freedom of the human personality as a law to itself. They sought a nature that was neither governed by the gods and fate, nor depraved by sin and the fall. Instead, nature began to be conceived as an arena of *infinite possibilities,* where sovereign man could achieve total mastery. That religious view of freedom and autonomy "did not permit scientific thought to proceed from a given *creation order*. The creation motive of the Christian religion gave way to faith in the creative power of scientific thought which seeks its ground of certainty only within itself."[55] It was this line of thinking, not scriptural *faith*, that gave rise to the notion of radical human autonomy and limitless freedom to impose man's idea on nature. Grant's assessment here was plainly wrong-headed.

Following the trajectory of all those impacted by humanism, whether of the ancient Greek, Renaissance or Enlightenment stripe, Grant had no patience for a realistic and historical view of sin. He rejected man's fallen condition, his need for regeneration and redemption in Jesus Christ, as well

---

55. Dooyeweerd, *Roots of Western Culture*, 151; italics added.

as his renewed calling to serve the kingdom of God on earth as in heaven (Matt. 6:10; 28:18–20). Instead, human purpose, in keeping with his notion of divine absence, is to *withdraw* from cultural work and to make one's "reason" receptive to "being." Time and history are not to be related in the scriptural sense. There must be no free act of creation where God governs by creation law and foreordains the coming to pass of His purposes according to the counsel of His will (Eph. 1:11). Neither can there be a God relating to man in terms of *historical covenant* with blessing and cursing for obedience and disobedience. There must be no interference in history from God. Rather, the ideal man for Grant is the contemplative *philosopher* who reformulates the doctrine of the divine as mystical absence, redevelops "Christianity" accordingly, and gives hope to man by resolving his modern philosophical antinomies.[56] In light of these things it is difficult to see how Christian "truth" ends up being any more than an existential leap into "being."

Following Plato, Weil, and Heidegger in denying a free creation ex-nihilo, Grant's ethereal and rationalistic view of time as a "moving image" of the eternal is both an attempted *flight from history* and finally a complete *absorption in being*—it is exactly where Greek philosophy ended up in Plotinus, in pure thought, an ineffable Oneness or unity. And this is the reason the ancients were fatalistic and disinterested in history as such and why Grant can put the *invention of history* down to the Jews. For many of the ancients, as for the Eastern religions, man was totally absorbed in *being* via an eternal process of *becoming*. Within earthly existence he is trapped in the wheels of determinism where the only hope is release and escape from the world of becoming by an ascent of the soul substance from the material world to contemplate the mystery of abstract being. It seems clear to me that this germ of Greek thought—this rejection of creation and history—was the *religious root* of Grant's mysticism, pessimism, and consequently of his suspicion, indeed fear, of *technology*.

The suspicion of technology, of development and change, was nurtured in Grant by the philosopher Martin Heidegger, whom he credits

---

56. Grant, *Philosophy in the Mass Age*, 111.

with teaching him its meaning: "what I have learned from Heidegger is the *meaning* of technology."⁵⁷ Technology was dangerous because it supposedly estranged man from "being." Egbert Schuurman has pointed out that Heidegger did not seek to appreciate technological development, but to draw back from it, "in order to command all devotion for the great *mystery of Being*."⁵⁸ Moreover, in Heidegger's opinion, Christianity "has abetted the advance of the destructive power of technology."⁵⁹ In fact history (in the Christian sense) is for Heidegger quite simply the history of technology (technique), such that technology becomes the hermeneutical key to history itself. Just as Marx reduced history to economics, Heidegger seeks to reduce it to technology, while simultaneously missing the specific *meaning* of technology as "freely giving form to material."⁶⁰

For Heidegger (who was both influenced by and critical of Hegel), man is caught up in the *destiny of being* in the midst of his technological life. He rises up in violence to subject everything to himself, yet at the same time has forgotten Being, "from which, by which, and unto which all that is, is; he has become a nihilist."⁶¹ Likewise, the Christian person (especially the Protestant, in self-assurance and self-interested in personal salvation) is seen as egocentric and consequently a major source of the modern problem. Human thought should instead be ruled by and directed toward "being." This idea supposedly "offers the perspective of escape from the turmoil, frenzy and destructive urge of modern technology."⁶² In such a view, victory over the destructive nihilism of modern culture cannot be achieved by any notion of *ruling being*—such a claim must be withdrawn. Man must be freed by "being," as thought and being become united in what is really a form of pagan mysticism. Only this road offers escape from man's suicidal course.

---

57. Cayley, *George Grant in Conversation*, 129.
58. Egbert Schuurman, *Technology and the Future: A Philosophical Challenge*, trans. H. Donald Morton (Jordan Station, ON: Paideia Press, 2009), 124; italics added.
59. Schuurman, *Technology and the Future*, 126.
60. Schuurman, *Technology and the Future*, 128.
61. Schuurman, *Technology and the Future*, 132.
62. Schuurman, *Technology and the Future*, 135.

The difficulties with these ideas are manifold. If, for example "being" is the mysterious source of all things and the end to which all things tend, then logically *being rules technology* through a self-conscious thinking being, which is man himself. In Heidegger's vision of being, human freedom appears swallowed up in the fatalistic destiny of being. How could and why should man halt his course with technology if he is caught in the wheels of the necessity of being, where thought and being are at root one? Schuurman states the problem this way:

> Heidegger becomes enmeshed in a dialectic. On the one hand there issues from Being the necessary destiny of Being... to which man is subordinate and because of which he is thus not free. On the other hand, Being must give man freedom. Heidegger's idea of Being is intrinsically contradictory.[63]

But Heidegger and Grant want to resolve these antinomies in their thought by speaking of the "mystery of being"—which is simply a non-explanation. Even if Grant believed that "being" is not completely self-sufficient (i.e., is not identical with the divine) and requires a "creator" (who for Grant is essentially unknown), this offers no help because "god" does not interfere in history nor reveal his specific will. Both Grant's and Heidegger's empty notion of "being" is simply a speculative product of would-be autonomous thought, leaving them with a great sense of powerlessness and hopelessness in the face of man's sinful domination of man.

The potent influence of Heidegger on Grant is very telling. Man now needs saving from his own creative technological development because it estranges or alienates him from true "being." So, let us suppose for a moment that Grant's view of history and technology became so influential that it was accepted by all—what does it really mean to be delivered from dynamic historical development? In the same way that his denial of "creation" implies a flight from history, surely this turning toward "being" to escape the turmoil of technology simply means the *end* of a cultural consciousness and

---

63. Schuurman, *Technology and the Future*, 141.

a cultural task. In sum, Grant's whole philosophy advocates a return to "nature," delivers people from the historical aspect of life centred in formative cultural power, relieves people of work, and denies them both responsibility and calling. Primitivism, decay, hardship, disease, poverty, suffering, and life in a world of permanent wilderness are implied and essentially legitimized in such a view. It is no wonder Grant was accused of pessimism.

## Grant, the Word of God, and Scriptural Diagnosis

Grant's life-long lament over the modern world certainly helped shed light on a serious problem in Western culture. He exposed the destructive nature of dynamic power exercised for its own sake—a demonic secularisation of the cultural mandate of the Bible; he highlighted a ruinous view of history in which time is made a theatre for the unlimited imposition of man's self-will; he drew insightful attention to the threatening development of a technocratic and bureaucratic elitism that sees its role as stage-managing the universe to realize man's utopian ends; and he attacked a pragmatism and subjectivism that denies objective truth whilst rejecting right and wrong as realities that transcend human desires. With these critiques and concerns the scripturally directed Christian has great sympathy.

However, we have also seen that Grant's critique is launched from a shaky and wholly inadequate platform—one without a truly transcendent foundation or viable criterion for truth. His turn toward abstract "being" and denial of the scriptural worldview left him with antinomies that are actually "non-problems" because they are the product of his idolatrous construct called "being." Grant's interminable vagueness and ambiguity throughout his work in offering real solutions for culture are not the product of "openness to being," but a consequence of his faulty religious assumptions. What we finally see in Grant, brilliant as he was, is a futile attempt to address the reality and challenge of sin—that is, man's disobedience to the law of God in asserting his own seditious and prideful will in historical-cultural life. The upshot is that Grant seeks to deal with man's rebellion and heal the ravages of sin by an *alternative act of disobedience*. He recognizes a problem with man's cultural activity, but then finally lays the blame for man's misuse of man and "nature" at the door of the living God and His Word for creation: in effect Grant says to God, "the *task you gave me* is the problem."

Grant is tragically wrong about God, creation and history because he denies the authority of God's Word-revelation. In so doing, he regards the biblical view of history as the *root* of the human problem and therefore the origin of the woes of the West. Yet the Word of God does not identify a philosophic estrangement from "being," the "Jewish idea" of history, or man's calling to freely form creation, as the source of our cultural problems. Robert D. Knudsen has clearly stated the scriptural diagnosis:

> Where all the strands of meaning come together in... the "heart," there is a fundamental religious taking of position *with respect to the origin*. Either one is rooted in the transcendent God as he is revealed in the Scriptures or he is related to an idol, worshipping what is a fabrication of his apostate and distorted imagination, namely, a myth. At any and every point one is turned in his heart either to the right or to the left, either to the true God or to an idol. Because it is of a central, radical kind, this orientation manifests itself in *all human activity*.[64]

Man is an idol maker, and it is a scriptural truism that man becomes like the idols he makes (Ps. 135:15–18; Jer. 5:21–31). If we reject the Creator God of Scripture, then we will create a false god of our own imagination. Because of Grant's unscriptural view of *origins*, his false and mythical god, who is indistinguishable from eternal "being," inevitably leads him to the creation of a false mandate, denying the cultural mandate assigned in God's Word. Grant's withdrawn, hidden and formless god who does not create or form by free act, nor command man to subdue all things in terms of a purpose, requires him to posit the "contemplative man," likewise hidden and withdrawn from freely forming creation for a purpose.

It is true that if historical life is seen only as a function of *human* self-will and dominion, with man as the absolute *ruler* of being, then man is gradually

---

64. Knudsen, *Roots and Branches*, 302; italics added.

robbed of freedom and identity and is pulled toward disintegration and death. The lawless imperial urge for limitless domination and control is certainly one of the roots of our lamentable culture in the West. The problems are indeed real, but Grant misconstrues and distorts them because he refuses to place Jesus Christ in the place of total authority and power. Schuurman's powerful answer seems tailor-made for Grant's perspective—one shared by many "spiritual" intellectuals in our time:

> What is essential is not a conversion to Being but a conversion to God, the Creator, the Redeemer in Jesus Christ. In this conversion there is no hint or shadow of flight, for man comes to stand once again in the place to which God originally appointed him—not at the center, not as the ruler of reality, not as man sufficient to himself..., but as a bondservant called by God to engage in the forming of culture, including the development of technology, and accountable to Him for every act of commission and omission. This confession is liberating in the face of the worshippers of science and technology on the one hand, and in the face of those who would flee science and technology on the other.[65]

The gospel of Jesus Christ is the only thing that can call man back from his apostasy to the humble service of God in creation. This task of service is not easy, and there are many temptations and challenges along the path of obedience to the cultural mandate and Great Commission. But the Christian answer to such challenges, obstacles, and anxieties can never be the *surrender of culture,* and thereby of God's good creation, to the apostasy of men and devils. When people's hearts are darkened so that they form the materials of creation in a manner that denies or distorts God's order, seeking to overturn his distinctions, norms, and boundaries, working to join what He has separated and separate what He has joined, the path of holiness and righteousness is the *cultural preservation of divinely ordained distinctions* and the differentiation and unfolding of God's purposes over against those of unbelief, sin, and death. We must not throw down our tools and implements

---

65. Schuurman, *Technology and the Future,* 144.

just because some men are ploughing in the wrong direction or freely fashioning an idol. Rather we must put our hand to the plough and sow the seeds of cultural renewal with the assurance that God will bring forth the harvest in due time. The Christian idea of cultural development, in the words of Herman Dooyeweerd:

> ...continues to observe the inner tension between sinful reality and the full demand of Divine law.

> This demand is terrifying when we consider how much the temporal ordinances labour under the destructive power of the fall into sin. Terrifying also, when it puts before us our task as Christians in the struggle for the power of cultural formation. For it makes a demand on us which as sinful human beings we cannot satisfy in any way. And it urges us, in the misery of our hearts, to seek refuge with Christ, from Whose fullness, *nevertheless*, a Christian can derive the confidence of faith to carry on the ceaseless struggle for the control of cultural development.

> ...That struggle is directed against the spirit of darkness who dragged us all down with him in the apostasy from God, and who can only be resisted in the power of Christ.

> As Christians we shall hate that spirit because of the love of God's creation in Christ Jesus.[66]

This great struggle must be rooted in the gospel of Jesus Christ and directed against the spiritual forces in heavenly places that war against us, or it will be futile and powerless. The Christian response to the false alternatives of *reaction* and *revolution* in history is that of constructive, continuity-abiding *reformation* in terms of God's Word and the power of His Spirit. As the Christian church we must say again to the Western nations, "For if the message

---

66. Herman Dooyeweerd, *A New Critique of Theoretical Thought*. In *The Collected Works*. Series A, vol. 2: *The General Theory of the Modal Spheres*, trans. David H. Freeman and H. de Jongste (Jordan Station, ON: Paideia Press, 1984), 2.364–65.

spoken through angels was legally binding and every transgression and disobedience received a just punishment, how will we escape if we neglect such a great salvation?" (Heb. 2:2–3).

CHAPTER 9

# *Think Christianly About Marxism*

*Beware lest any man spoil you through philosophy and vain deceit, after the tradition of men, after the rudiments of the world, and not after Christ.*
— *Colossians 2:8 (KJV)*

## Prophetism and History

**W**E HAVE OBSERVED IN THE previous chapter that in unbelieving philosophies of history, man appears fatally immersed in *historical time,* unable to identify any constancy, any abiding truth or value that transcends an endless flux. If no creator God stands behind history, then from a human standpoint it appears absurd—it is without meaning. Reflecting the implications of his worldview, the neo-pagan Goethe said that history is "twhe most absurd of all things," a "web of nonsense for the higher thinker."[1] The unintelligibility of past and present, including the life of all cultures and individuals (all being historically unique and "other") surrounds him.

We have also noticed that some philosophers have sought escape from this nihilistic immersion in historical time by borrowing and distorting elements from a Christian philosophy of history, either by asserting abstract transcendent standards in a supra-historical realm of being, or by proposing that man must impose himself on the constant change all around him—whilst historical actions and reactions are accounted for solely in terms of various material, social, and economic forces. In other words, "nature" may be deterministic, but somehow man must be made to transcend the flux of fate to *have a history*. We have discussed the first view (an escape from history) extensively in the thought of George Grant in the previous chapter. Now I want to turn to a specific consideration of the latter view as it comes to us in the secularized pseudo-Christian eschatology of Marxism—the most popular and recurrent secular view of reality in modern history.

The concept of history as we know it owes its origin to a biblical view of the world. We drew attention to the fact that the endless cycles of recurrence for the Greeks with their view of knowledge, as well as the nihilism of Eastern philosophy, could not and did not give rise to the idea of *historical progress and direction* that still shapes the mind of the modern West. Hermann Cohen's comment here is important:

> The concept of history is a product of prophetism.... What Greek intellectualism could not produce, prophetism has achieved. In Greek consciousness, *historein* is equivalent to inquiry, narration, and knowledge. To the Greeks history remains something we can know because it is a matter of fact [*factum*], that is, of the past. The prophet, however, is a seer and not a scholar; his prophetic vision has created our concept of history as being essentially of the future.... For this new future "the creator of heaven and earth" is not sufficient. He has to create "a new heaven

---

1. Cited in Karl Löwith, *Meaning in History* (Chicago, IL: University of Chicago Press, 1949), 53.

and a new earth." In this transformation the idea of progress is implied. Instead of a golden age in the mythological past, the true historical existence on earth is constituted by an eschatological future.[2]

The current cultural concern with being on the "right side of history," of a universal history involving *progress* toward a better and more just world is clearly bastardized from our Christian past, from the prophetic, messianic vision of Scripture. What shapes our Western cultural vision today, in the grip of unbelief, is a philosophy of history that tries to *secularize* biblical ideas to avoid falling back into a past-bound, fatalistic, or meaningless motion for history found in antiquity. The only choice remains either eschatological direction or cyclical motion. However, if man wants an actual history and therefore a future, whilst rejecting Christ and His prophets, then the apostate philosophers must themselves *create* the new heaven and new earth in which "righteousness" dwells. The contemporary view of history thus apes Christianity. It seeks to immanentize creation, incarnation, and consummation, for these must now emerge from *within* history rather than being from *beyond* history in the person of Jesus Christ. Man must somehow transcend himself, recreate himself, incarnate his idea and messianic vision, and bring his prophecy to consummation by his own socio-political power and technique.

## The Christian View of History

The biblical world-and-life view tells us that God's good creation fell into ruin due to sin, subsequently being subject to God's curse and thus placed under a *temporary* bondage to decay (Gen. 3:8–19; Rom. 8:19–22). However, according to the messianic covenant promise of God (Gen. 3:15; Ps. 2; 110; Isa. 9:6–7; Ezek. 21:27) from beyond history, the last Adam and truly obedient Son is to enter, in the flesh, the history over which He rules (Ps. 72:8; John 1:1–5; Rom 5:12–21). Christ Jesus, the heir of all things, is incarnate and

---

2. Cited in Löwith, *Meaning in History*, 17–18.

made manifest at the right time for our redemption and the reconciliation of all things to God (Heb. 1:1–4, 2:5–9; 2 Cor. 5:19). His power and authority to restore all things to the Father, renewing all that has been distorted by sin (1 Cor. 15:20–28; 2 Cor. 5:17; Rev. 21:5), was unveiled through the power of His Word, a Word which not only pronounced forgiveness of sins (Matt. 9:5), but healed disease (Matt. 4:23), calmed waves and storm (Mark 4:39), created new wine (John 2:9–10), and raised the dead (John 11:38–44). These signs pointed to the meaning and eschatological direction of history which culminates in the purging, cleansing, renewal, and restoration of heaven and earth (2 Pet. 3:13; Rom. 8:19–23; Rev. 21:5).

By His vicarious atoning death, resurrection from the grave, ascension, and session at the right hand of God the Father, now in the place of total authority (Mark 16:19; Acts 7:54–56; Eph. 1:20–23; Col. 3:1; Heb. 1:13, 2:8–11), the court of Christ's judgment is in session, for He must reign until He places all His enemies under His feet; the last enemy to be defeated is death (1 Cor. 15:25–26; Heb. 2:5–9; Rev. 6:2; 21:4–5). Now His salvation, rule, and reign are to be declared by His redeemed people through the gospel of the kingdom, as we pray and work for that kingdom to come on earth as it is in heaven (Matt. 6:10; 24:14; 28:18–20; Luke 19:13; Acts 28:30–31; 1 Tim. 1:8–11; Jas. 1:22–25). At a time known only to God the Father (Matt. 24:36), the last Adam and Lord of all creation shall return to consummate His kingdom purposes and release creation from its bondage to corruption, a liberation that will coincide with the resurrection of the body (Acts. 1:11; Rom. 8:19–22). Our renewed home will be even more glorious than this one, when the new Jerusalem comes down from heaven to earth and God makes His dwelling with men (Rev. 21:1–5).

This scriptural historical expectation, this biblical eschatology, forms the foundation of a Christian philosophy of history. It is easy to now see how *secularized copies* of the Christian vision have gained cultural force.

# The Legacy of Marx and the Idea of Progress

In all humanistic thought the focal point of "being" is autonomous man, not God in Christ. An apostate view of man as the centre of all things is closely linked to a secular philosophy of history. This popular philosophy no longer sees people under the absolute control of unchanging reason or a natural morality as earlier forms of rationalism had once done. Instead, there is at work a new "law idea" in which human beings are becoming, in the progress of history, increasingly "self-conscious" of their absolute freedom. In this sense "god" *potentially* exists as human self-consciousness unfolds itself.

The most consistent and culturally influential example of a philosophy seeking to plunder biblical resources whilst assaulting Christianity is Marxism—with us today in a variety of guises and modifications, including what is called progressivism or Cultural Marxism. Marx was enthralled in his early career by German Idealism, but this philosophy was not concrete or radical enough for him. For Marx, Hegel was still operating on the basic presupposition of the Christian religion—history being comprised essentially of B.C. and A.D. In fact, German philosopher Karl Löwith calls Hegel "the last philosopher of history," because he considered him the last major philosopher to be restrained by the Christian tradition.[3] Marx wanted *revolutionary* social change, not mere philosophical speculation. For him this was the proper goal of true philosophy which "does not simply interpret as all philosophies have done up till now. On the contrary, philosophy changes the state of affairs. Philosophy emancipates."[4] It was not enough to simply rebel against Christian teachings, because to Marx, Christian thought was a *result* of Christian *social order*. To destroy the former, one had to revolt against and alter the latter. This was a utopian idea, because Communist relations are supposedly free from antagonisms, since they eliminate, by "spontaneous love," the social conditions created by Christian civilization involving private property, retributive justice, and legal right.

---

3. Lowith, *Meaning in History*, 57.
4. Zuidema, *Communication and Confrontation*, 114.

Marx thus sought to absorb all history into an *economic process* which he taught was moving toward a final world revolution and renovation.[5] This involved the fundamental religious belief that there was no moral right to private ownership and control of production resources. Through the ideal of national economic planning and the demolition of wage-labor relations, Marx believed that he was realising the unity of reason and reality, of essence and existence—the rational was the real and had to be concretized. Some think of Marxism as concerned with justice, but this is a misunderstanding, for justice presupposes a world of juridical order and equality, a juridical community, with people as possessors of equal right before the law. As Will Kymlicka explains:

> Many Marxists believe that justice, far from being the first virtue of social institutions, is something that the truly good community has no need for. Justice is appropriate only if we are in the 'circumstances of justice'.... If, however, we could eliminate either the conflicts between people's goals, or the scarcity of resources, then we would have no need for a theory of juridical equality and would be better off without it.[6]

Rather than worrying about justice, "We should instead be concerned with transferring ownership of the means of production.... When this is accomplished, questions of fair distribution become obsolete."[7] So for Marxism, the philosophy which can meet the need of the hour has to be worldly, political, and economic—a new kingdom of God beyond justice.

Seeing mankind as essentially enslaved to a capitalist mode of production, Marx was clearly preaching his own form of regeneration, liberation, and salvation. Löwith wondered "if Marx ever realized the human, moral, and religious implications of his postulate: to create a new world by creating

---

5. Lowith, *Meaning in History*, 33.
6. Will Kymlicka, *Contemporary Political Philosophy: An Introduction* (Guildford: Clarendon Press/Oxford University Press, 1990), 171.
7. Kymlicka, *Contemporary Political Philosophy*, 170.

new men, a new kind of man."⁸ Unlike the grace and mercy we find in God's salvation in Jesus Christ, it is hard to see Marx's liberationist vision of regeneration for the proletariat as being motivated by love, grace, or compassion, because "Marx sees in the proletariat the world-historical *instrument* for achieving the eschatological aim of all history by a world revolution."⁹ The workers are the necessary cannon fodder for the revolution. As such, for Marx, history is a struggle not between the city of God and the earthly city of man seen in Scripture, between the kingdoms of darkness and light, but between the *oppressors* and the *oppressed*. Marx's new man was an ideal abstraction. All society must be liberated whether people realise and want it or not, and the "oppressed class" is simply a means to that end.

Marx's basic criticism of Hegel was that although he asserts the autonomy of man's reason, he fails to apply and realize the implications of this in history as the kingdom of man on earth. So, on the back of Hegel's rationalistic *secularization* of history, Marxism and the progressive neo-Marxists construct a philosophy where history is understood as both an inescapable *fate* or destiny toward liberation, and yet an arena where man is somehow *free* to remake himself—the paradox of the freedom of necessity. Dutch philosopher S.U. Zuidema points out that this constitutes:

> the secularization of the Biblical revelation of the providential guidance of God in history. In this philosophy of history the idea of a history-creating man and mankind, embodied in the proletariat, is a historicistic secularization of the Biblical revelation of the liberation through Christ, the lamb of God and King of kings.¹⁰

All of this makes the Marxist vision of history a profoundly religious enterprise—a new exodus and liberation from slavery with a new law and promised land to conquer. To justify the need for this secular emancipation, Marx and his contemporary disciples see exploitation, slavery and

---

8. Löwith, *Meaning in History*, 36.
9. Löwith, *Meaning in History*, 37; italics added.
10. Zuidema, *Communication and Confrontation*, 116-117.

oppression under every rock—even though their atheistic worldview lacks an objective criterion for such an ethical judgment. But this does not dampen their righteous indignation. As Löwith notes, "The *Communist Manifesto* is, first of all, a *prophetic document*, a judgment, and a call to action."[11] In Marx's own words, "We reclaim the whole content of history, but we do not see in it a revelation of God but only of man."[12] Consequently, the Marxist vision is transparently a secularized atheistic messianism; it holds a view of history born out of the religious root of Marx's own identity as an anti-religious and even anti-Semitic Jew. Whilst assailing a supposedly mythological Christianity, he borrows its categories of thought. His is an eschatological faith that apes the Christian philosophy of history in order to gain formative cultural power. So for Marx, true philosophy must emancipate and deliver man from all his "idols," beginning with the idol of the family.

## Cultural Marxism and Critical Theory

Although the focus of Karl Marx's philosophy of history was *economic* materialism, he well understood that you cannot have history-transforming world revolution without *sexual* revolution. Since he thought of social conditions as *determining* people's thinking, his logical concern was to change those conditions. The Christian concept of family was for him at the root of oppression, exploitation, and the evil of private property, and therefore became his central target. Above all, family was the wellspring of the religious opiate of the people—the myth of God. He wrote, "Thus, e.g., after the earthly family has been discovered as the secret of the holy family, the former must then itself be theoretically and practically annihilated."[13] This

---

11. Löwith, *Meaning in History*, 43; italics added.
12. Jacques Grandjonc and Karl Marx, *Editionsrichtlinien der Marx-Engels-Gesamtausgabe* (MEGA) (Berlin: Dietz, 1993), I. Abt. II, pp.426 ff.
13. Karl Marx, *Theses on Feuerbach: A New English Translation Based on the New Marx-Engels-Gesamtausgabe*, trans. Carlos Bendaña-Pedroza, 2nd rev. ed. (Bonn: International Marx-Engels-Foundation, 2022), 55.

sheds immediate light on the prevalent "spirit of the age" in our Western cultural moment where every basic assumption about the sexual order is being challenged and reality "remade"—from the binary distinction of male and female to the nature of marriage, family, and sexual morality. In truly Marxian fashion people are being "emancipated" from their humanity like a camel being surgically "freed" of its hump.

Following Marx, the contemporary mantra continues to divide participants in world history into oppressors and oppressed, whilst the newly expanded categories of people said to be victims of oppression involve not simply wage-laborers (the proletariat), but all those "victimized" by the Christian morality and social order of the past. This includes all who "transcend" male and female identity, reject monogamous marriage by living in various alternate sexual lifestyles, deny the authority of biblically derived law, and oppose the church as the institute sponsoring the historic oppressive arrangements. In short, all those who by religious persuasion, sexual practice, or social preference feel oppressed by traditional expressions of Christian faith in socio-political, cultural, and economic life. Furthermore, since the origins and cultural emergence of Christianity are misleadingly conceived as European and white (misleading because Christianity emerged in the Middle East and the great patristic theologian of the West, Augustine, was North African—though Europe quickly became the centre of Christian culture), every other people group or religious community is likewise alleged victims of the oppressive white Christian man and his middle-class family. All history, especially Western colonial history, must now be reinterpreted through this hermeneutical grid, and immediate revolutionary action must be taken to implement the social changes necessary to either convert or oppress the oppressor, casting them first into an immanent hell of social and cultural ostracism and then, if necessary, of criminal sanction. For neo-Marxism, just as justice is human, social, and communal, so too guilt must be human, social, and communal, so the individual character and behavior of the oppressor is irrelevant. Their crimes consists of "privilege" and resisting the inevitability of "progress." They belong to a condemned *class* with a secret history and intention not revealed by their actual words and convictions. This modern spirit "views culture in terms of unending historical development, rejecting all the constant, creational structures that make development possible."[14]

Today's progressive brand of neo-Marxism has thus pivoted from an *economic* to a *cultural-historical* focus, and it currently dominates the political landscape. As *cultural* Marxism, it is rooted in the twentieth-century development of Critical Theories. To adequately understand our historical direction and what is taking place in our cultural institutions today requires a firm grasp on the origin, meaning, and social significance of Critical Theory. Hidden beneath popular euphemisms like Political Correctness, Social Justice, White Privilege, Equality, Diversity, and Inclusion, Racial Justice, LGBTQ rights, Intersectionality, etc., is an ideological framework and set of concepts about which most people are ignorant.

## The Religious Foundations of Critical Theory

One of the essential characteristics of all non-Christian philosophical thought has been its *dialectical* character—always trying, but unable, to reconcile apparently opposing poles in human experience. As a result, like a pendulum it has swung between both rationalism and irrationalism, emphasizing constancy and then change, nature (determinism) and then freedom (indeterminacy). A period of rationalism in thought, with an emphasis on constancy and determinism, seems to lead inevitably to an irrationalist reaction with an emphasis on change, the freedom of the human personality and vice-versa. This is relevant because in many respects neo-Marxist Critical Theory grew out of disillusionment with the form of rationalism specific to the Enlightenment and the culture that emerged from it. It therefore claims to offer a new kind of emancipation: revolutionary social change and freedom from the structures and social order that allegedly oppress and enslave the human personality.

---

14. Dooyeweerd, *Roots of Western Culture*, 67.

Before we come to a brief analysis of the specifics of Critical Theory, it is vital to first note its *religious foundations*. One of the most important thinkers behind the development of Critical Theory was Max Horkheimer (1895–1973). Horkheimer was a German philosopher and sociologist amongst the key pioneers of the *Institute for Social Research*—a group of Marxist intellectuals who wanted to find a way to make philosophy truly "practical" (i.e., changing practices through which society realizes its ideals), thereby fomenting a social revolution in the Western world that traditional economic Marxism had failed to achieve. They believed this could be done by bringing philosophy and the social sciences together in the context of a materialistic worldview. By combining Marxian and Freudian thought (deconstruction in language being added later), they hoped to realize a new social reality.

In his *Critical Theory: Selected Essays* we find Horkheimer discussing his "Thoughts on Religion." As a Marxist, Horkheimer predictably denied that there are God-given norms and laws governing creation and social order—there is only the material existence of nature and society. Assuming rather than justifying the neutrality and authority of his "critical" posture, Horkheimer seems oblivious to his own religious worldview when he describes religion as "the record of the wishes, desires, and accusations of countless generations."[15] As with most twentieth century European intellectuals, the target of his criticism is Protestant Christianity in particular. For Horkheimer, God is neither the creator of earthly order (familial, ecclesiastical, civil, or economic normativity), nor the ruler of the course of history; there is no sovereign providence in the affairs of mankind. Although he reluctantly acknowledges the role Christianity played in earlier generations in challenging social injustice, nonetheless, "the productive kind of criticism of the status quo which found expression in earlier times as a belief in a heavenly judge today takes the form of a struggle for more rational forms of societal life."[16]

---

15. Max Horkheimer, *Critical Theory: Selected Essays*, trans. Matthew J. O'Connell et al. (New York, NY: Continuum, 2002), 129.
16. Horkheimer, *Critical Theory*, 129.

The struggle for a better world has thus thrown off its previous "religious" garb. Horkheimer embraces the Marxist theory that mankind inevitably loses "religion" as it moves through history. The church's current position in the Western world rested purely on the characteristics of the present social system—change that system and the church is finished. Its historic influence has rested "on the belief that absolute justice is not simply a projection of men's minds but a real eternal power."[17] This higher power Horkheimer emphatically denies. For him, absolute justice for humanity is an illusion ever on the horizon, but never to be realized. Bettering people's lives is a purely human project undertaken in terms of man's idea of liberty. In a telling example of the lack of religious self-consciousness in his philosophical thought, Horkheimer concludes, "In a *really free mind* the concept of infinity is preserved in an awareness of the finality of human life and of the inalterable aloneness of men."[18]

Appreciating this overtly *religious* foundation in approaching the topic is vital because it helps account for the development of various Critical Theories. They are built on an atheistic and evolutionary worldview which presupposes that mankind is unalterably alone; the present life and visible material world is all there is; there are no God-given laws and norms for people and society; no eternal God who is judge over all the earth; no government of God in history; no salvation or kingdom of God in and through the Lord Jesus Christ. For the cultural Marxist, this bleak situation *demands* that man's collective idea realizes a radical egalitarian equality (i.e., the new "justice" as far as possible) and implements it (i.e., makes it practical) in the *final court of appeal* which is now immanentized as *history itself*. By solidarity with wretchedness, man can now save and emancipate himself because human beings are become the self-creating producers of their own history.

---

17. Horkheimer, *Critical Theory*, 130.
18. Horkheimer, *Critical Theory*, 131; italics added.

## The Frankfurt School

Narrowly defined, Critical Theory identifies several generations of German, Hungarian, and Italian social theorists operating within the Marxian tradition of Conflict Theory, popularly known as the Frankfurt School, which was founded in 1923 at Frankfurt University in Germany as the previously mentioned *Institute for Social Research*. Along with Horkheimer, the group included several prominent European thinkers, such as Herbert Marcuse, Georg Lukács, and Theodor Adorno. These thinker-activists all advanced a variety of Critical Theories. It is important to note that they used the words *Theory* and *Critical* in a special way. The word *Critical* for their purposes refers not merely to social *criticism*, but to a specific practical and moral purpose—emancipation in the context of repression and oppression. As such, a theory is Critical only in so far as it brings about a liberating influence in history, helping to create a world satisfying human needs. This liberation is always liberation from God's order, so the true humanitarian is one denying any reference to what is supernatural. The discovery of *objective truth* is regarded as an impossible ideal because all knowledge reflects the interests and values of its producers—which obviously results in a radical relativization of all thought for Critical Theorists. In a similar way, the word "Theory" is not employed as an abstract noun referring to a model or hypothesis to be tested, but is used as a proper noun and is therefore capitalized. The word carries the freight of ethical ideas, methods, and modes of thought at the centre of a *worldview* defining Critical Social Justice.

Critical Theory is consequently much more than an analytical tool for academics; it is a philosophy and worldview to be applied to all of life. A Critical Theory is in fact adequate and authentic only if it is *entirely comprehensive*—explanatory, practical, and normative simultaneously. It will be *explanatory* because it must identify what is wrong with a given social condition; it will be *practical* because it will highlight what and who are required to change that situation; and it will be *normative* because it must provide a criterion for criticism with concrete and achievable goals for social transformation. Such theories aim at gradually *breaking down* all existing social ideas, norms, and structures that are oppressive—that is, hierarchical and not radically egalitarian and democratic. This democratization of all life and reality embodies the idea that all the conditions of human life should be the product of a *rational consensus*. It is easy to see how the central target of Critical Theory will be orthodox Christianity and the social order implicit within it, rooted in God's revelation with its order and structure for family, church, society, and all of life under the Lordship of Jesus Christ.

Several early Critical Theorists are important for our discussion. Georg Lukács, for example, was a Hungarian philosopher, the son of a wealthy banker, and one of the founders of the movement. The pioneer of what became known as "Cultural Terrorism," he began his political life as a Kremlin agent of the Communist International. His noted work, *History and Class Consciousness* (1923), aimed at the ideological subversion of the West and gained him notoriety amongst his contemporaries and cobelligerents. Like most Marxists he was deeply concerned with education and launched a radical sex education program in Hungarian schools which sought to overturn parental authority, Christian morality, and the influence of the church. He stated categorically, "Such a worldwide overturning of values cannot take place without the annihilation of the old values and the creation of new ones by revolutionaries."[19] He openly acknowledged that this required unleashing *diabolic forces* in history.

Another notable member of the Frankfurt School was Theodor Adorno. He made his way to America in the 1930s and coauthored the pivotal *Dialectic of Enlightenment* with Horkheimer (1939–1944), which has been described as "the most influential publication of the Critical Theory of the Frankfurt School, and one of its most compressed theoretical statements."[20] Allusive and obscure, it consists of five highly disconnected chapters with a collection of shorter notes. Adorno, in particular, sought to explain the idea of

---

19. Cited in Michael Löwy, *Georg Lukács: From Romanticism to Bolshevism*, trans. Patrick Camiller (London: NLB, 1979), 130.
20. Max Horkheimer and Theodor W. Adorno, *Dialectic of Enlightenment: Philosophical Fragments*, ed. Gunzelin Schmid Noerr, trans. Edmund Jephcott (Stanford, CA: Stanford University Press, 2002), 217.

*The Authoritarian Personality* (1950)—what is today popularly called "toxic masculinity"—as the counterpoint of the ideal revolutionary personality. The authoritarian personality was of course Christian, conservative, and capitalist, which is frequently equated by Critical Theorists with fascism. Like most of the Frankfurt luminaries, instead of recognizing the Nazi's National Socialism for the pagan, anti-Christian and totalitarian ideology it most certainly was, in order to disguise his own totalitarian ideas, Adorno identifies fascism with Western Christian civilization in need of liberation. This is why it has become popular to refer to genuinely conservative ideas and policy as "fascism," despite the fact that it was traditional conservatives who led the fight against fascism in the 1930s and 1940s. In fact, as the English philosopher Roger Scruton pointed out:

> It is testimony to the success of communist propaganda that it has been able to persuade so many people that fascism and communism are polar opposites and that there is a single scale of political ideology stretching from "far left" to "far right...."

> [We must] see through that nonsense, to perceive what it is designed to conceal: the deep structural similarity between communism and fascism, both as theory and as practice, and their common antagonism to parliamentary and constitutional forms of government. Even if we accept the—highly fortuitous—identification of National Socialism and Italian Fascism, to speak of either as the true political opposite of communism is to betray the most superficial understanding of modern history.[21]

Others in the movement openly attacked specific Christian doctrines as emerging from the *social conditions* of capitalism. For example, Erich Fromm, another social psychologist, came to American in the 1930s and blamed free markets for the emergence of Calvin's doctrine of predestination, which he

---

21. Roger Scruton, *Fools, Frauds and Firebrands: Thinkers of the New Left* (Croydon: Bloomsbury Publishing, 2015), 200.

argued involved the basic principle of human inequality. Positive freedom from such oppression required the *individual self* to be posited as the centre and purpose of life and as the highest power in history. They all shared the basic view of Antonio Gramsci (noted Italian Marxist and leader of the Italian Communist party) that Marxist intellectuals needed to take the lead in undermining and then reshaping the Western social order—for learning is wisdom and wisdom means the right to rule!

Because of the strong presence of Christianity in Western culture, the highly original Gramsci realized a sudden Bolshevik-type uprising would not happen. Rather what was required was a *long march through the institutions* of learning and culture to form a new Soviet man—this would lead to eventual political revolution and historic transformation. "Hence it was through culture—through universities, art schools, theatres and books—that the New Left had its greatest and most immediate impact."[22] Gramsci's goal was to reconcile a Marxist philosophy of history and society with a philosophy of political action, and as such he has been hailed as the true heir of Marx. He argued that historical development is as much the outcome of *political* will as it is of material processes. To understand the politicization of Western culture—where issues once thought to belong to the domain of the family, of the church, or the discipline of theology have now become the centre of *political* activism—is to see the profound influence of Gramsci. This new political revolution does not happen primarily by violence from below, but through a passive revolution that gradually replaces the ruling hegemony by capturing culture. Once captive to the Marxists, the society of the future in Gramsci's vision for history is one of contempt for all opposition, for "the purpose of politics is not to live with opposition, but to remove it."[23] One does not need to be a prophet to see the fingerprints of Gramsci all over today's progressive political goals and rhetoric.

---

22. Scruton, *Fools, Frauds and Firebrands*, 199.
23. Scruton, Fools, *Frauds and Firebrands*, 204.

# Critical Sexual Theory and Christian Morality

We have noticed particularly that *sexual* revolution is absolutely vital for Critical Theory and its largely successful "long march." Of particular importance here are Wilhelm Reich and Herbert Marcuse, who both left Europe to market their intellectual wares in America. Reich was the author of *The Sexual Revolution (1945)*, in which he attempts to bring together Freudian psychology with Marxist economic theory in a *sex-economic* sociology. For Reich, human beings were basically sexual animals repressed by Christian morality. The authoritarian character structure and "familial imperialism" of Western society is rooted in the embedding of sexual inhibitions and fear regarding sexual impulses. His solution, of course, is radical sexual liberation. If you can tolerate wading interminably through discredited psychobabble, frequently leading to conclusions directly opposite to demonstrable truth—for example, that the traditional family structure, sexual restraint, and parental authority lead to neurosis and sexual crime[24]—you find a deeply tormented man with a bitter hatred for the family and for God. His influence on later thinkers is, however, far-reaching.[25] In fact we see in Reich the foundations of almost all aspects of contemporary cultural progressivism.

Reich believed religiously in the total restructuring of man and idealized the dissolution of the family in the Soviet Union, which he saw as breaking the patriarchal link between economy and sexuality, producing instead a "work-democratic matriarchy" (workers collective) serving the gratification of all needs—especially the sexual.[26] At the same time, he understood that it was primarily the family which transmitted the conservative ideological atmosphere of his own society, disciplining the sexual impulse. In the family

---

24. The opposite is the case, as numerous studies have shown. Even non-Christian feminist writers acknowledge the issues. See Louise Perry, *The Case Against the Sexual Revolution: A New Guide to Sex in the 21st Century* (Padstow, Cornwall: Polity, 2022), 167–71.
25. Wilhelm Reich, *The Sexual Revolution*, trans. Therese Pol (New York: Farrar, Straus and Giroux, 1986), 82.
26. Reich, *The Sexual Revolution*, 161–62.

he *falsely* perceived a triangular structure in which the child generally loves the opposite sex parent while hating the other. Again and again, Reich rails against marriage, family education, fathers, and parental authority as destructive of *pleasure,* which he sees as the purpose of life. He writes, "The eventual dissolution of parental ties is *the* prerequisite for a healthy sexual life" (emphasis his!).[27]

The marriage relationship with its sexual restraint is, to Reich, an unbearable burden needlessly perpetuated in our offspring; a pattern they fall into mainly for "economic" reasons—thus maintaining generational sexual inhibition. It apparently does not occur to Reich that marriage might be pursued for its intrinsic goods of covenantal commitment, lasting companionship, sexual fulfillment and the way the family structure naturally leads to prosperity.[28] Like all Marxists he can view the family only as oppressive, in which any economic benefits are the product of mere authoritarianism and subjugation. He credits guilt feelings not to man's awareness of sin and culpability before a righteous and holy God, but to "the bottomless hatred the children have stored up over years of family living. If this hatred remains conscious, it may be turned into a powerful individual revolutionary drive."[29] His venom against the Christian view of family is unconcealed when he argues that the family's political function is, first, to reproduce itself by crippling people sexually. And second, by its maintenance of a "patriarchal structure" producing the "authority-fearing, life-fearing vassal."[30] With orgasmic sexual fulfilment as the real goal of life for Reich, any feelings of love, affection or family attachment are in actuality an unconscious superimposition concealing hatred.[31] Allegedly replacing an earlier clan solidarity, the family bond is therefore characterized by the "restriction of genitality" producing the first neuroses. This must be destroyed by the communist economic collective, because in the traditional family, "the naturally

---

27. Reich, *The Sexual Revolution*, 80.
28. Perry, *The Case Against the Sexual Revolution*, 170.
29. Reich, *The Sexual Revolution*, 81.
30. Reich, *The Sexual Revolution*, 82.
31. Reich, *The Sexual Revolution*, 164.

strong, self-confident biological organism becomes helpless, dependent, and God-fearing. The experiencing of nature in the orgasm is displaced by mystical ecstasy."[32] This is obviously ideological rage rather than the work of a careful scholar or scientist.

The fundamental goal of his thought is the making of a new man and a new history in total defiance of God and His order. The natural sexual urges of human beings must be given total freedom, something he considered present in primitive pagan religion that affirms sexuality through orgasmic ecstasy. Reich openly adheres to this religious worldview, consisting of nothing less than a neopagan sex cult as a life-affirming culture in which the orgasm and sexual pleasure are the central meaning of life itself.[33] He closes his work with these words:

> In the end man's natural forces will prevail in the unity of nature and culture…. The struggle for a "new life" is only now beginning in earnest…. He who is satisfied does not steal. He who is sexually happy does not need any "moral support" and his "religious experience" is true to nature. Life is as simple as this. It is complicated by a human structure which is afraid of life.[34]

One hears in these sentences the satanic lie that God is a kill-joy, "No! You will not die," the serpent said to the woman. In fact, God knows that when you eat it your eyes will be opened and you will be like God." (Gen. 3:4). For Reich, true freedom and happiness arrive when you can define life on your own terms and unfetter the libido. Religious experience true to nature entails primitive sexual gratification, and any structure that corrals or directs the sexual impulse is motivated merely by fear of life. Yet we might ask, if the orgasm is so powerful, healing, and transformative, why is it that the pornification of culture and vastly expanded sexual liberties of the past fifty years have failed to dissolve capitalism, destroy or discredit marriage, topple

---

32. Reich, *The Sexual Revolution*, 166–67.
33. Reich, *The Sexual Revolution*, 281.
34. Reich, *The Sexual Revolution*, 282.

the patriarchy (i.e., the family structure), or realise a sexual utopia despite all of Reich's ardent predictions to the contrary? The answer is simple: God's creation order and purpose for history cannot be overturned by man's sin and rebellion.

Rumors of Reich's therapeutic practices abound and are inappropriate for these pages. What is clear is that he was sex-crazed, seriously deceived, and deeply troubled by his past, in which his abusive father, enraged by his wife's unfaithfulness, drove his mother to suicide while Reich was still a child. His broken family experience clearly influenced his theories about and outrage toward both fathers and God. At once a pitiable and deluded man, he eventually claimed to have discovered the universal energy that animates all life. He called it "orgone" and created and sold wooden boxes for people to sit in to grow "orgastic potency" and release repressive forces. In a tragic end to a shattered life, Reich died of heart failure in jail, having been imprisoned for fraud. Yet the perceptive reader will detect in Reich the core doctrines of the ongoing "sexual revolution"—an expression he coined—currently undermining Western civilization.

The other vital figure in this movement who picked up Reich's mantle of *sexual revolution* was Herbert Marcuse, the "father" of the New Left. He also came to America to ply the intellectual chimeras of the Critical Theorists in the 1930s. Seeking the dissolution of American society, Marcuse was a social revolutionary committed to a subversive disintegration of the system from within. He targeted the universities and colleges. His book, *Eros and Civilization* (1955), was the guiding text for the 1960s sexual revolution in America. With modern industrial society seen as the enemy enslaving man in a one-dimensional world of technological rationality, his answer was to liberate the *erotic man*. War had to be waged against the white Christian male, with women's sexual liberation as the most vital front in the battle. Again, fathers and familial authority are seen as the root of guilt and of the "repressive tolerance" of a capitalist society. This "false consciousness" of the bourgeoisie had to be reformed by reflecting on its social origins.

For Marcuse the sex instincts are life instincts that need to be affirmed and liberated: "The 'struggle for existence' is originally a struggle for *pleasure*:

culture begins with the collective implementation of this aim. Later however, the struggle for existence is organized in the interest of domination: the erotic basis of culture is transformed."[35]

To resist the Christian conception of historical-cultural life—a slavish and repressive "performance principle" (over against a "pleasure principle') notoriously reflected in marriage and family—is styled by Marcuse as the "Great Refusal." This refusal to participate in the societal norms of Western cultural life is "the protest against unnecessary repression, the struggle for the ultimate form of freedom—'to live without anxiety.'"[36] Marcuse knows that his ideas expose him to the charge of utopianism, so he writes, "If the construction of a non-repressive instinctual development is oriented, not on the subhistorical past, but on the historical present and mature civilization, the very notion of utopia loses its meaning."[37] With Eros as liberation, the sexually free society is no longer a "no place" but a historical reality. The movement from historical animal man to a conscious rational subject indicated to him that, "The history of mankind seems to tend toward another turning point in the vicissitudes of the instincts."[38] The current norms and social structures are not for Marcuse objective entities, created by God, but constructed facts to be transformed by Critical Theories that liberate.

Reich and Marcuse thus helped to unleash the *unclean* spirit of Legion which possesses our increasingly deranged society—stripped naked, cutting at itself with an urge to self-destruction. No earthly power can subdue it. Only the mighty Word of the Master, the Son of the Most High, can leave us again clothed and in our right mind. Only there, sitting at the feet of Jesus, can our sanity be restored (Mark 5:1–20).

---

35. Herbert Marcuse, *Eros and Civilization: A Philosophical Inquiry Into Freud* (Boston: Beacon Press, 1974), 125; italics added.
36. Marcuse, *Eros and Civilization*, 149–50.
37. Marcuse, *Eros and Civilization*, 150.
38. Marcuse, *Eros and Civilization*, 150.

## Historical Roots and Fruits of Critical Theory

For all the Critical Theorists, Western Civilization, with its historically Christianized social order, is an oppressive yoke from which people need to be freed—a phase to be transcended in pursuit of a rational social order of individual and societal liberation. Here all hierarchies are to be broken down in a democratized equalitarian society of total consensus. Philosophically, it has strong ties to Romanticism. It styled itself from the outset as a rejection of the Enlightenment's *"disenchantment of the world."*[39] Yet there is an irony here because they speak of the need for a more "rational" order whilst at the same time rejecting rationality!

It is worth pointing out, however, that biblical Christianity *shares* the Critical Theorist's rejection of Enlightenment rationalism which seeks total mastery and control of creation/nature in terms of a totalitarian and technological reason. Horkheimer and Adorno point out that:

> What human beings seek to learn from nature is how to use it to dominate wholly both it and human beings. Nothing else counts.... On their way to modern science human beings have discarded meaning. The concept is replaced by the formula, the cause by rules and probability.... For enlightenment, anything that does not conform to the standard of calculability and utility must be viewed with suspicion.... It makes dissimilar things comparable by reducing them to abstract quantities. For the Enlightenment, anything which cannot be resolved into numbers, and ultimately into one, is illusion.... Unity remains the watchword from Parmenides to Russell. All gods and qualities must be destroyed.[40]

These observations about the tendency of Enlightenment in both rationalist and empiricist forms are surely legitimate. The abstractionism and theoretical reductionism of the scientific mentality in attempting to reduce everything to *manageable quantities* in order to master them are

---

39. Horkheimer and Adorno, *Dialectic of Enlightenment*, 1; italics added.
40. Horkheimer and Adorno, *Dialectic of Enlightenment*, 2–5.

successful for developing the combustion engine and nuclear power but hopelessly inadequate for understanding authentically *human* facts, such as the complexity of thought, culture, morality, justice, language, aesthetic value, social relationships, economic life, and the life of faith—indeed for the central human reality of meaning as a whole. However, in the pessimism and sense of meaninglessness engendered by rationalism's emptying the "external" world of qualities, and by extension ultimately of God, meaning is instead sought by a revolutionary *inward turn* to psychological, and radically personalized "meanings." Instead of scientific knowledge of nature being power, the *re-creation* of reality is revolutionary power. In rejecting one form of reductionism, the Critical Theorists simply embrace another. The idol of autonomous thought here simply rebels against itself and moves from taking refuge in lawful constancy (for mastering reality) to perpetual change (for remaking it). It pivots from the pole of nature (necessity) to the dizziness of freedom, from rationalism to a form of irrationalism. For these thinkers, the Enlightenment forfeited its own realization of freedom through the reason of man by its complicity in patriarchal, domineering power and an unholy alliance with Christian civilization with its confidence in a creation order (i.e., a given reality). Horkheimer and Adorno write:

> The fault lies in a social context which induces blindness. The mythical scientific respect of peoples for the *given reality*, which they themselves *constantly create*, finally becomes itself a positive fact... and degenerates in a compliant trust in the objective tendency of history.... Enlightenment... will only fulfill itself if it forswears its last complicity with them and dares to abolish the false absolute, the principle of blind power.[41]

Notice first, that the arrogant presumption of the Enlightenment is not really repudiated, but is merely accused of complicity and failing to go far enough in fulfilment of its potential. And second, that man is said to constantly *create* his own reality. Those who do not realize this are blinded

---

41. Horkheimer and Adorno, *Dialectic of Enlightenment*, 33; italics added.

by their social reality, for Critical Theorists alone truly "see"—implying that they somehow transcend social reality by their critical posture. The idea of true knowledge rooted in revelation in creation as a given, and the need for human conformity to it, are dismissed as a form of violent power and are therefore considered demonic. The present human situation is thus reduced to *conflicting power relations*. The ultimate source of blind patriarchal power is God Himself, reflected most overtly in marriage and the family structure and supported by the institutional church, *"which in the course of history has hardly missed an opportunity to take a leading voice in popular institutions, whether they be slavery, crusades or simply pogroms."*[42] The incurable recourse to special pleading in their work cannot be addressed in detail here, but suffice to say, no mention is made of the Christian West alone abolishing the institution of slavery, nor an effort made to understand the historical context of the crusades in resisting Islamic expansionism! Christianity is thus vilified as a force dressed up as the good to determine the course of history and finally to triumph—which is therefore an expression of blind power:

> In proclaiming power—even a benign power—they [Christianity and other philosophies of history] became themselves highly organized historical powers, and as such played their bloody role in the real history of the human species: as instruments of organization.[43]

Liberation therefore entails a rejection of creation (as ultimate patriarchal power), order, structure, and norms for the structureless freedom of the human personality—law is no longer the condition of life. Man is variously identified with his erotic urges that require unfettered expression. Destruction, rather than production, is the source of freedom. The idol of pure reason is replaced by the practical reason of social justice, deconstructing God's order as a man-made system of organized and institutionalized oppression.

---

42. Horkheimer and Adorno, *Dialectic of Enlightenment*, 206; italics added.
43. Horkheimer and Adorno, *Dialectic of Enlightenment*, 186.

In the process, the *cultural mandate* of Scripture to build families and take dominion by godly rule, work, worship, and service, tending creation as the theater of God's kingdom is rejected, with the injunctions of Luther and Calvin to work to God's glory dismissed as *"like mockery, the boot grinding the worm into the dust."*[44] Creation, Fall, and Redemption are reduced to cultural myths in service of the ruling class. Christianity thus stands accused of ringing in *"the modern bourgeois order by extolling work, which in the Old Testament had been designated a curse."*[45] That claim is, of course, completely false. Throughout Scripture work was not designated a curse but a blessing (Gen. 2:15; Eccl. 5:18–19; John 4:34; 5:17; Eph. 2:10; 3:9; Col. 3:23–24; 2 Thess. 3:6–12). Rather, the earth which man works is cursed, resisting and frustrating his efforts to fulfil the cultural mandate (Gen. 3:17–19). Regardless, for the progressives, this entire order must be abolished by social revolution, by a "Great Refusal" (Marcuse) rejecting all Western concepts, including that of hard work, demanding instead sexual revolution whilst promoting feminist and black revolution.

This new *methodology* of revolution means that we are now dealing with *cultural Marxism* as opposed to traditional Marxist mass uprisings. The current *modus operandi* is demoralization and moral subversion in every area of life. As such, Critical Theory has a multiplicity of applications, from literary analysis to economics. In a Critical view of economic life, for example, economic relations within a free market are recharacterized as "monopolism" and total domination, supposedly excluding the vast majority of human beings. This is dubbed the "racket pattern," which is now considered representative of all human relationships, even those within the working classes. The ostensible objective is the "racket-less" society, when a communist order has been realized through social revolution and the redefining of democracy. Raymond Raehn has therefore noted:

---

44. Horkheimer and Adorno, *Dialectic of Enlightenment*, 192; italics added.
45. Horkheimer and Adorno, *Dialectic of Enlightenment*, 192.

Critical Theory incorporated sub-theories which themselves were intended to chip away at specific elements of the existing culture, including "matriarchal theory," "androgyny theory," "personality theory," "authority theory," "family theory," "sexuality theory," "racial theory," "legal theory," and "literary theory." Put into practice, these theories were to be used to overthrow the prevailing social order and usher in social revolution based on cultural Marxism.[46]

As we have noticed, in these various theories of "liberation," Christian sexuality in particular is construed as repression, a reduction and hatred of the body, and the result of taboo—an expression of despising the flesh and nature. Again, Horkheimer and Adorno write:

> [The] repressed rebellion of despised nature breaks out. Its full hideousness is vented on the martyrs of love, the alleged sexual offenders and libertines, for sexuality is the body unreduced; it is expression, that which the butchers secretly and despairingly crave.[47]

Principled opposition to the sexual revolution against marriage (between a man and a woman) and family is here styled along the lines of Rousseau's thought as a form of rebellion against nature itself. The allegedly repressed—ironically showing by their resistance that they secretly crave promiscuity and homosexual acts—break out like deranged butchers in opposition to the self-sacrificing sexual pioneers who martyr themselves for "love." This deliberate inversion of morality and immorality seeks to turn tables and make the old "oppressor" the oppressed. Roger Scruton discussed the character of this sustained and withering attack on Christian culture (Western civilization) since the mid-twentieth century by the Critical Theorists:

---

46. Raymond V. Raehn, "The Historical Roots of Political Correctness," in *Political Correctness: A Deceptive and Dangerous Worldview. Its Pedigree, History and Practices*, ed. William S. Lind and Richard W. Hawkins, 16–29 (United States: Nehemiah Institute, 2020), 19.
47. Horkheimer and Adorno, *Dialectic of Enlightenment*, 196.

The left-wing enthusiasm that swept through institutions of learning in the 1960s was one of the most efficacious intellectual revolutions in recent history, and commanded a support among those affected by it that has seldom been matched by any revolution in the world of politics.[48]

The goal of this movement is nothing short of a complete *social subversion* and *cultural transformation* of the Western world. The "moral" justification for this revolutionary action centres around a reimagined concept of liberty:

> Two attributes of the new order justify the pursuit of it: liberation and "social justice". These correspond roughly to the liberty and equality advocated at the French Revolution.... It means emancipation from the "structures": from the institutions, customs and conventions that shaped the "bourgeois" order, and which *established a shared system of norms and values at the heart of Western society*.... Much of their literature is devoted to deconstructing such institutions as the family, the school, the law and the nation state through which the inheritance of Western civilization has been passed down to us.[49]

What the vast majority of Western people have historically seen as the normal and necessary structures of society and social order, the new left thinkers describe as *"structures of domination"* that must be subverted and destroyed. These poisonous ideas have forcefully made their way, not just into academic journals, galleries of abstract art, universities, and scholarly libraries, but into the courts, hospitals, parliaments, and senates, in fact, into the classrooms of the youngest and most vulnerable children in government schools. In this way, fraudulent and often unintelligible theories of language, identity, and social order are being passed off as the key to renewal and liberation within human society. One cannot understand modern Western culture without grasping this basic revolutionary motive.

---

48. Scruton, *Fools, Frauds and Firebrands*, 159.
49. Scruton, *Fools, Frauds and Firebrands*, 3; italics added.

## Assault on Meaning

The foundational idea of the revolution is that *meaning* is no longer something *objective* or *transcendent*—that is, something which transcends human signification (language), culturally conditioned perceptions, or social customs. This means that one should not look for objective meaning *as such* in the thinking and use of language among the revolutionaries, because that would presuppose reality has a pre-established givenness—a product of creation. For them, real meaning is simply in the chosen use—the way they manipulate language to reimagine a structureless and fluid reality. Language is no longer logocentric, referring to an actual existing state of affairs. It is merely a tool to *subvert* established meaning, because established meaning is pictured as oppression. Meaning as something *ontologically real* or objectively given is simply a Christian conspiracy. So, by the conjuring of the revolutionaries, new *language spells* are invoked to alter social reality. The alphabet soup of LGBTQ2SIA++ as well as the very public struggle over the use of pronouns is a central aspect of the artifice and subterfuge of the neo-Marxists to remake the world.

Scruton creatively called this assault on meaning and truth, the "nonsense machine." By a linguistic emancipation from accountability to the real world and Word of God, one eliminates real argument and reasoned engagement so that every question simply becomes one of shouting, power, and politics. Indeed, there is "[n]o need to ask what the revolution means or what you might achieve by means of it. Nothing means anything and that *is* the revolution, namely the machine to annihilate meaning."[50] The cry of "oppression" is sufficient for one to be classified as a victim of meaning and a heroic warrior in the cause of liberation.

One highly influential user of the nonsense machine is Critical Theorist Judith Butler. An American-Jewish lesbian and leading radical feminist, Butler influenced a whole generation of social theorists to regard the very idea of a binary distinction between man and woman as the mythical creation of

---

50. Scruton, *Fools, Frauds and Firebrands*, 174.

language repetition. What almost everyone in every culture through all of history has taken to be a real condition—that of being a man or a woman—is for Butler and those like her an imaginary formation. What ordinary mortals generally believe to be a real physical, biotic, and logical *direct perception* is for these radicals just a sophisticated illusion generated by language! Butler writes:

> there is no reason to divide up human bodies into male and female sexes except that such a division suits the economic needs of heterosexuality and lends a naturalistic gloss to the institution of heterosexuality.... [A] lesbian... transcends the binary opposition between woman and man; a lesbian is neither a woman nor a man. But further, a lesbian has no sex; she is beyond the categories of sex.... [O]ne is not born female, one *becomes female*, but even more radically, one can, if one chooses, become neither male nor female, woman nor man.[51]

The astonishing claim here is that the only reason our culture recognises a distinction between male and female, man and woman, is a socio-economic one—it simply suits the capitalist desires of heterosexual men (i.e., the Christian concept of family and private property), whilst *pretending* that the male-female distinction and relation is natural according to a givenness in creation, which is in fact an illusion. The fanatical feminist argument here is that the very *linguistic use* of the terms male (man) and female (woman) produces a culture that privileges heterosexuality and endorses marriage and family, which is oppression. For such theorists as Butler, the term female should not need to imply an opposite (male) and vice-versa. The pronoun farce current in Western society is a popular expression of this philosophical construct of gender fluidity.

We must go further, however, and note that on this view, "sex" is reduced to a political and cultural interpretation of the body. Human body parts are just a discontinuous set of attributes upon which the language of "sex"

---

51. Judith Butler, *Gender Trouble: Feminism and the Subversion of Identity* (New York, NY: Routledge, 1990), 153; italics added.

imposes an artificial unity. This artificial unity then becomes a "language regime" forming people's perceptions and forcibly shaping the interrelationships through which our bodies are then perceived. Butler, thus, quite logically and seriously asks the vital question, "Is there a '*physical*' body prior to the perceptually perceived body? An impossible question to decide."[52] Most readers may need to reread that sentence a couple of times. In short, the body is just a perception, and perceptions are formed and reformed by linguistic signs. As such, the naming of normative sex (and sexual relations) is an act of oppression and domination that must be rejected and subverted in order for humanity to be free—classic Critical Theory.

It therefore goes without saying that, in terms of this lingual nonsense machine, there is no creation order, no transcendent law, no given male and female identity, no conception of human beings made in the image of God, and no law-order for human sexual interaction in terms of marriage and family. Whatever a human being is (and they cannot tell us), language constructs reality—*words are magic!* Critical social theorists have interpreted the body as a mere biological receptacle in which the self-creating intellect is contained. The body thus awaits an identity which the individual must forge for themselves or assume from the "differences" around them. This creative intellect takes the dust of the ego's desires, the idol of an abstracted organ-less body, and breathes life into itself by a linguistic incantation. The diabolic parody of biblical creation is striking.

The task culturally and politically—for there is always a liberating societal plan of activism for the Critical Theorist—is very clear to Butler: "to overthrow the entire discourse on sex, indeed, to overthrow the very grammar that institutes 'gender'—or 'fictive sex'—as an essential attribute of humans and objects alike."[53] War must be waged against the repetition of words like man and woman, husband and wife, male and female—oppressive and rigid codes of "hierarchical binarisms." These must be displaced by

---

52. Butler, *Gender Trouble*, 155.
53. Butler, *Gender Trouble*, 154.

a new lexicon. Only then may we continue the march toward the vanishing horizon of social justice. Butler predicted thirty years ago that:

> The loss of gender norms would have the effect of proliferating gender configurations, destabilizing substantive identity, and depriving the naturalizing narratives of compulsory heterosexuality of their central protagonists: "man" and "woman."[54]

Butler realized that this could be accomplished only by greatly extending the idea of the political to include questions not traditionally regarded as political, because for Butler, and the numerous social theorists that have followed in her footsteps, the political involves the very signifying practices that establish, regulate and deregulate identity. This is why some of the most foundational theological and philosophical questions have now been made matters of politics, for political activists to campaign about and for politicians and courts to legislate and rule on. The politicization of life corresponds to the statist religion of our age. An ontology of human identity is no longer regarded as a foundation, but as a socio-*political creation*.

Roger Scruton correctly identifies this as a revolution accomplished by the literature and *language of spells*—indeed, I would argue it is a secularized form of occultism. Reality will alter itself to service human desires if the new magic words are used and repeated. He summarizes the effect of it all very astutely:

> The resulting nonsense, although it cannot be easily deciphered intellectually, can be deciphered politically. It is *directed* nonsense and it is directed at the enemy. We are to discard the old hierarchies, the binary structures, the trees of the bourgeois family and the capitalist machine and reform ourselves as... grassroots communities of underground activists....

---

54. Butler, *Gender Trouble*, 200.

The assault is aimed primarily at the language through which the enemy lays claim to the world.[55]

One can see that the real enemy in all of this is God Himself and all the laws and normative structures for social relationships revealed by Him in His Word. The order created by the living God is cast as an oppressive and even demonic power-relation—once again the Christ is accused of having a devil! Christian society has supposedly institutionalized or organised these power-relations as vehicles of blind power which must be overthrown if people are to be free to realise themselves as the centre of their own reality. To be part of or support implicitly or explicitly the society shaped by Christian commitment (most especially the one led by white, Christian, heterosexual, middle-class, able-bodied and responsible men) is to be an authoritarian personality and a collaborator with a deadly patriarchy in need of destruction. On the other hand, to come under, in any way, the "Christian patriarchy" is to be a victim of oppression. The more the convergence of ostensible victim categories and participation in marginalized groups an individual has (i.e., black, female, lesbian, pagan, disabled, poor, unemployed = intersectionality), the more "oppressed" they are and the greater the need for "liberation" by moving them, their lifestyle, practices, and ideas from the fringe to the centre of society to be celebrated and eventually mandated.

Critical Theory is clearly much more than an academic or social *tool*. It is a total world-and-life-view, a religious cult with a vision of creation (self-creation), sin (to be associated with the oppressive patriarchy in any way), justice (social justice—by making the oppressor the oppressed), and salvation (liberation from God's order). The life and death struggle against this demonic worldview infiltrating the church is one of the greatest battles of our time. The popular slogans about freedom, social justice, democracy, rights, inclusion, affirmation, and tolerance heard in both church and state today have an altered meaning and possess no reliable or lasting value. This

---

55. Scruton, *Fools, Frauds and Firebrands*, 189.

is because the true goal of the neo-Marxist is power—power from below to strike out against the One who reigns above.

## The Christian Prophetic Response

The Marxist and neo-Marxist philosophy of culture and history that we have examined has had a powerful and enduring influence around the globe in various permutations, and continues to deeply inform not only the Western academy, but also public law and policy in Western nations. There is no accounting for this influence without noticing that Marx understood biblical eschatology better than many Christians today, and sought to radically *secularize* a scriptural view of man and his historical calling to form culture. Marxism's cultural strength comes from its aping of Christian thinking, and it still represents the only serious and consistent humanistic alternative to the philosophy of meaningless cycles of recurrence in ancient paganism and eastern philosophies. Just as the myth of spontaneous generation through a form of Darwinian development gave the humanistic and secular world an alternate creation account to latch onto—in its desperate search for intellectual coherence without the God of Scripture—so too, permutations of Marxism remain the only alternative for those seeking a view of history and social order that can salvage an immanent sense of meaning from the abyss of time.

The difficulty for average Christians in responding to the neo-Marxist worldview is that they themselves do not have a robustly scriptural worldview with which to answer.[56] This is a serious problem because the encounter requires "the complete spiritual armor of the Christian religion."[57] The deficit

---

56. See Barna, *George Barna, American Worldview Inventory 2021–22: The Annual Report on the State of Worldview in the United States* (Glendale, AZ: Arizona Christian University, 2022), 6–7. Barna shows that only 6% of American adults have a biblical worldview and even amongst evangelicals and those claiming to be born again, the number lies between only 19–21%.
57. Dooyeweerd, *Roots*, 67.

is rooted in the loss of a truly Christian understanding of man's historical and cultural mission. Here, I can agree in part with Karl Löwith, who rightly argues that man needs redemption in history, from beyond history, and as such, "[t]here has never been and never will be an *immanent solution* of the problem of history, for man's historical experience is one of steady failure."[58]

Scripture makes plain that sinful man in rebellion against God is confronted with thorns, thistles, and frustration in all his historical-cultural labors. He cannot, by himself, overcome his sin-driven alienation from God, the world, other people, and his cultural calling. By his own power he cannot remake himself or the cosmos, but can only be remade in Jesus Christ, the source and root of all things (Col. 1:15–20). There is only a *transcendent* solution to the problem of history, by the incarnation, death, resurrection, ascension, and Kingdom rule of the man Jesus Christ. Only by obedience to His Word and resting repose in the providence and sovereignty of God can human beings face the future and rest secure in God's promise of the restoration and renewal for all things by the Man He has appointed.

Man's historical experience in trying to effect his own salvation is doomed to fail, but the progress of the Kingdom of God in the world, as the gospel transforms peoples and nations, is one of steady advancement. The scriptural perspective is that Jesus Christ, God the Son, is not simply saving individual souls, but is inheriting the nations and making all things new (Ps. 2:8; 111:6; Rom. 8:18–23; Heb. 1:1–2; Rev. 21:5). God clearly declares that not only Israel, but the Egyptians are His people and Assyria His handiwork (Isa. 19:24–25). The Great Commission of our Lord Jesus Himself is a directive to disciple and teach *nations and peoples* (Matt. 28:18–20). Indeed, in the course of time, the nations will bring their treasures to Him and serve Him (Ps. 72:10–11). These promises make evident the scriptural reality that "of the increase of His government and peace, there shall be no end" (Isa. 9:7); that everything is placed under Christ's feet and under His control in *this age* and the one to come (Heb. 2:8; Eph. 1:20–23). The direction of historical development is thus moving according to God's Kingdom purposes (Rom. 11:36).

---

58. Löwith, *Meaning in History*, 191; italics added.

By and large, in responding to the intimidating neo-Marxist vision of our age, Christians have tended to retreat from the civilizational conflict. Culture is often faithlessly deemed a topic best left to pious indifference, and historical development is regarded as a matter of quiet resignation because of its irrepressibility. On the restless sea of history, what *practical difference* does it make whether people in our culture believe themselves to be in the hands of a righteous God, or imagine their lives to lie trapped in the clasp of chance and fate—after all, the Kingdom of God is not of this world, and everything is going to be destroyed anyway, right?

Many Christians have also understood the drive for development, prosperity, progress, and power as inherently unchristian. It is certainly true that sin perverts the *dominion* mandate into *domination*, thereby secularizing the call to spread the gospel of the Kingdom into a humanistic agenda of creating a better world in the image of man. But the genuine and proper Christian desire to distance the faith from imperialistic political presumption or unrestrained domination has led to the collapse of a proper understanding of the historical calling of God's people as found in the biblical revelation. It has promoted a dualistic retreat into a kingdom not of this world, a world in which the Christian church is not even an historical people in the true sense, and the judgments of God to bless and curse are not active in modern history. In the face of neo-Marxism we are largely left today with a pie-in-the-sky Christianity, surrendering culture to the enemies of Christ.

Moreover, because of the influence of cultural Marxism in the church, Christians have become suspicious and afraid of *power itself*. Dooyeweerd's insight here is critical for a Christian philosophy of history and so I will quote him at length:

> Many equate power with brute force. Today many Christians, misled by this identification, consider it un-Christian to strive for the consolidation of power in organizations that aim at applying Christian principles to society. They believe that power may play no part among Christians.... Christians may speak of love and justice with an unburdened conscience, but as soon as power comes into their purview they have probably lent their ears to the devil.

Such opinions indicate that the creation motive of the Christian religion has retreated from the worldview of these Christians. As a result [they] can no longer understand humankind's fall and redemption through Jesus Christ in its full scriptural significance. The unbiblical impact of their view becomes apparent when we recall that God reveals Himself as the Creator in the original fullness of power. God is almighty. At creation God charged humankind with the cultural mandate: subdue the earth and have dominion over it....

Because of the fall, the position of power to which God called humankind in the development of culture *became directed toward apostasy*. But Christ Jesus, the Redeemer, revealed Himself as the possessor of power in the full sense of the word: "All authority in heaven and on earth has been given to me," says the risen Lord. He charged His apostles to proclaim the power of the gospel among all nations.

...[P]ower is not brute force. It is rooted in creation and contains nothing demonic.... Only sin can place power in the service of the demonic....

Insofar as power has been entrusted to human beings as creatures, it is always cultural. It implies a historical calling and task of formation for which the bearer of power is responsible and of which she must give account.[59]

There are then "moments" of truth in Marx: formation never takes place without a *struggle*. But the struggle is not between abstract oppressor and oppressed classes or identity groups. The true struggle is between true and false worship, obedience and disobedience, covenantal faithfulness or apostasy, the Kingdom of God and the kingdom of darkness. All historical formation requires *power* and as a result, it never takes place *without* a cultural struggle. Christians are, like everyone else, in the midst of a great historical struggle. We are battling the spirit of revolution which is directed against God, His creation order, and the customs and traditions which reflect that order. The revolution seeks to completely overcome the power of norms

---

59. Dooyeweerd, *Roots*, 68–69; italics added.

and tradition—the end of which would be the destruction of culture itself. However, as Dooyeweerd points out: "[H]umankind *cannot* overturn the creation order, which binds historical development to abiding norms. The creature cannot *create* in the true sense of the word. Humankind cannot create a genuine culture while completely destroying the past."[60]

In the truly Christian view, because all authority and power belong to Jesus Christ, progress is possible—and a Christian philosophy of history is possible. The facts of creation, redemption, and God's abiding law-Word for the world mean that progress can be made for God's kingdom.

Löwith describes the reality that the modern historical consciousness, especially as seen in Marxism, derives its eschatological outlook from Christianity, by opening up history to the idea of *future fulfillment*. However, Löwith errs, in my view, along with many Christians today, in not seeing that future fulfilment progressively happening within our historical existence. And this is where the Christian surrenders all his ground in culture, because Marxism *does* see a secular dominion mandate and fulfillment *in history*. This is the critical error amongst believers, for although the Kingdom of Christ is not *of* this world, in the sense that its source and power do not originate with the immanent historical action of humanity, the Kingdom of Christ is very much a reality *within the history of this world* by the Spirit, transforming this creation, and it will find its culminating fulfillment *in history* with the consummation of all things. Andrew Sandlin summarises the point incisively:

> The church, by its omission of responsible dominion work, has abetted ungodly men and Satan in their ungodly dominion. For two millennia the church has been often plagued by man-centred thought, supposedly "Christ—(or Cross, or Gospel) centred," but in actuality truncated, pietist and humanist. It is most often manifested in the idea that biblical faith is principally about man's personal salvation; it frequently is wedded to a mystical tradition, an attempt to escape the troubles of life, the wear and tear of history, and secure an eternally timeless, subjectively pious, exclusively vertical religion on earth. It fails to see that the gospel and

---

60. Dooyeweerd, *Roots*, 73

soteriology are not the end of God's plan for man; but the *means* to an end. The actual end is the subordination of all things to God through Christ by means of the earthly dominion of the godly. God's purpose is not chiefly to save man and fit him for heaven, but to restore him to covenant-keeping submission and his calling as God's dominion agent in the earth. Heaven on earth in eternity is the blissful culmination of this task faithfully prosecuted by the redeemed.[61]

A Christian philosophy of history then, undergirded by a scriptural worldview, is eschatological and truly prophetic. The bastardized eschatology of progress in our secular culture is only a *parasite* on the Christian view, because only Christianity is capable of providing true historical consciousness on the basis of biblical futurism. Which is to say, Christ is the *Alpha* and *Omega*, the beginning and the end, but also the beginning *of* the end—the final age dawns with the Kingdom of God manifest in Himself historically and His people.

The same ironic dependence is true of the possibility of radical atheism, including its expression in Marxism—it is a *parasite* in the West, living on the host of Christian belief and tradition: As Löwith points out:

> [T]he feeling that the world is thoroughly godless and godforsaken presupposes the belief in a transcendent Creator-God who cares for His creatures. To the Christian apologists, the pagans were atheists not because they did not believe in any divinity at all but because they were 'polytheistic atheists.' To the pagans the Christians were atheists because they believed in only one single God transcending the universe and the city-state, that is, everything that the ancients had consecrated.... The post-Christian world is a creation without creator, and a *saeculum* (in the ecclesiastical sense of this term) turned secular for lack of religious perspective.[62]

---

61. Andrew Sandlin, *A Postmillennial Primer: Basics of Optimistic Eschatology* (Coulterville, CA: Center for Cultural Leadership, 2023), 69–70.
62. Löwith, *Meaning in History*, 201–202.

The central theme of the Lord's Prayer, that the Kingdom would come on earth as it has in heaven, has been perverted into the secular presumption that man now remakes the world in his own image as the new god. What emerges is a realization of torment—so obvious in the perpetual struggle of Marxism—in which hope is mere illusion, a mirage on the farthest horizon, whereas Christian suffering in history always takes place in the context of indestructible hope.

The attempted synthesis by the modern West, of Christianity with the paganism of its past, productive of such dystopian secular visions of history, highlights the ambiguity and irresolute vacillation of Western culture that continues to the present moment. As Löwith correctly concludes:

> The modern mind is not single-minded: it eliminates from its progressive outlook the Christian implication of creation and consummation, while it assimilates from the ancient world view the idea of an endless and continuous movement, discarding its circular structure. The modern mind has not made up its mind whether it should be Christian or pagan. It sees with one eye of faith and one of reason. Hence its vision is necessarily dim in comparison with either Greek or biblical thinking.[63]

Truly Christian thought will thus war against the false prophecy of humanistic philosophies of history in terms of the Word of God. Not all of us are called to do philosophical and apologetic work, of course, but all Christians need a scriptural philosophy of history with which to do battle, and developing this is part of our covenantal walk with God as we prepare to pass on to the next generation what we have inherited and built upon. This is how history under God's sovereign government moves forward.

Thinking about the development, explanation, and defence of the Christian worldview and Christian philosophy of life as a form of *prophesying* reminds us of the force of the Older Testament prophetic message. As Evan Runner notes:

---

63. Lowith, *Meaning in History*, 207

> Old Testament prophecy aims to establish the supremacy of Jehovah, binding man and all creation to the Law-word of God. It views detailed events in their relation to the divine plan, which has for its purpose the absolute establishment of the supremacy and glory of Jehovah in Israel and eventually on the entire earth. This involves the Messianic prophecies: the person of the Messiah and the coming of the Kingdom of God.[64]

Clearly, the philosophical task must be carried out in the light of scriptural prophecy, "For we who wish to work at our philosophical task in the light of the witness of Jesus—we are prophets."[65] As Christians, we must not allow the false prophecy of Marx (or any other thinker or school of thought) and his heirs to go unchallenged and run the field of culture. To do so is to abandon our calling in the Kingdom of Christ. Because in a sinful and fallen world man has dislocated his thinking from God and seeks to alienate creation from Him, Christian philosophy will see that the real need in human thinking is to be *reconciled to Christ* and bound to the law-Word of God.

This need places the question of world-and-life-view and philosophical labour in its proper context, for we are not, in the first place, apologists or philosophers, academics, scholars, or anything else. As Christians, "We are prophets, and... our being engaged in philosophical work, must be understood as a moment of our lives as prophets. We may not, we cannot actually, separate our philosophical task from our prophetic calling as men, and it is the prophetic calling which works through in our philosophizing, not vice versa."[66] Our task in all our vocations, including apologetic and philosophical thinking, is to bear witness to God's grace, power and glory.

God's grace and equipping power at work in us by the Holy Spirit will bring about a passion in our being for the supremacy of the Word of God to be made manifest in our individual lives, our families, society and nation. This enlivening passion points to the true *direction* of history. For

---

64. Runner, *Walking in the Way of the Word*, 500.
65. Runner, *Walking in the Way of the Word*, 503.
66. Runner, *Walking in the Way of the Word*, 507.

we must come to see the Word of God as the "only Power to sustain us, to heal us, to renew us, to liberate us, to bring the whole of the creation to its intended fulfillment."[67]

So, what specifically is happening when, in philosophical and apologetic work, we set forth the transformative wisdom of the Word of God?

> [W]e are prophetically—thus not by our own wisdom or in our own strength, but in the power of the Holy Spirit—to bring to the light in our critical analyses the spirit of the lie, of suppression and distortion that is at work in the world, however many traces of the truth may be found therein, and at the same time to point to the gracious revelation of the Way, the Truth and the Life and the age-old community of the Truth and fellowship in the Way and the Life, the Church of Jesus Christ.... [A]s Christians engaged in our philosophical task, we are to go on the offensive to extend God's prophecy to the ends of the earth, to all the nations of the world, and, in pushing outward, always to be busy proving, that is, putting to the test, the spirits that are at work everywhere in the world, confident that He who is in us, and who by His Spirit binds us together in the bonds of love, is greater than he that is in the world, and that our Lord's intention is, as He has told us, the establishment of His supremacy over all His creation and the fulfilment of the creation design.[68]

It is in this everlasting hope, in this sense of vocation, and in this biblical vision for history that Christians today must root themselves, prophetically expounding the Christian philosophy of life and history against the lie. And we must do so in view of the note of victory that characterizes Jesus' witness to the truth and the witness of all biblical prophecy. For though the founding thinkers of the world, with their humanistic "-isms," false prophecies, and distorted eschatology, come and go, "God's plan *will* be carried out. His Kingdom *will triumph*."[69]

---

67. Runner, *Walking in the Way of the Word*, 516.
68. Runner, *Walking in the Way of the Word*, 508.
69. Runner, *Walking in the Way of the Word*, 506.

The truth about the Christ-centered character of history is summarized most aptly and memorably for us by the prophet Daniel:

> He was given authority to rule,
> and glory, and a kingdom;
> so that those of every people,
> nation, and language
> should serve Him.
> His dominion is an everlasting dominion
> that will not pass away,
> and His kingdom is one
> that will not be destroyed (Dan. 7:14, HCSB).

CHAPTER 10

# Think Christianly About Race and Racism

*From one man He has made every nationality to live over the whole earth and has determined their appointed times and the boundaries of where they live. He did this so they might seek God, and perhaps they might reach out and find Him, though He is not far from each one of us.*
— Acts 17:26-27 (HCSB)

## The Origin of Race and Racism

**I**T IS AN INTERESTING CHALLENGE to reflect on Christianity and the notion of racism because biblical faith does not recognize the modern conception of "race." As such, addressing the topic necessitates reframing the subject within biblical presuppositions. Scripture surely does speak of tribes, peoples, and nations (Gen. 10–11; Rev. 7:9), but the word "race" is not part of the lexicon of the New Testament nor is the idea of "races" part of the DNA of inspired revelation. In Scripture there is only one "race" or "blood" in Adam (Acts 17:26), and so, although now greatly extended, there is ultimately only one human family—a fact vital to our theological understanding of the unity of all mankind in both our fallenness and potential inclusion within redeemed humanity in Jesus Christ, the last Adam (1 Cor. 15:21–28), our kinsman-redeemer (Isa. 59:20). The gospel itself is at stake when we consider the root-unity of all humanity. It was this barrier-breaking message of the gospel of peace in the early church that overcame the old division, prejudice, and resentment obtaining between Jews and Gentiles (Eph. 2:11–22).

The ancient world into which the Christian church was birthed by the preaching of this gospel was in many respects remarkably cosmopolitan due to growing trade, increased mobility, and the expansion of Roman Empire. Ancient peoples no doubt had their tribal and ethnic prejudices, but they tended to think of themselves in terms of religious and political collective identities rather than in the modern sense of "races," and certainly not in the "racial" denominators of Mongoloid, Negroid, and Caucasoid—a largely arbitrary European classification for the members of the human family.[1] Instead, *religion* tied to politics was the defining factor for life and so at times, religious discrimination and prejudice were widespread. Throughout the centuries, Christian peoples have certainly had some ugly and violent episodes in this regard, but as a missionary faith, biblical Christianity has been pre-eminently concerned to win and persuade various peoples into embracing the faith, unifying them in Jesus Christ, not oppressing or forcing them into it.

The modern idea of "race relations" emerged when, after some centuries of relative isolation during the Middle Ages, explorers among European nations began discovering hitherto unknown lands and peoples from the fifteenth and sixteenth centuries onward. With the so-called Enlightenment

---

1. Preston N. Williams, "Race Relations," in *The Westminster Dictionary of Christian Ethics*, ed. James F. Childress and John Macquarrie, 523–26 (Philadelphia, PA: Westminster, 1986), 523.

and a growing exposure to foreign peoples, a *race consciousness* began to emerge in Europe, simultaneously developing a hierarchical pattern in which ethnic groups were arranged in order of superiority. This hierarchy was not confined to black, white, and yellow "races"; differences amongst Slavs, Jews, Europeans, and even Anglo-Saxons were often referred to as "racial differences" as well—so Europeans themselves were divided into Nordic, Alpine, and Mediterranean.[2] Cultural differences in civilizational advancement, technological development, and moral rectitude and refinement began to be seen not as the end result or outworking of vital *religious* differences between peoples—resulting in the "opening" or "closing" of cultures to the reality of God's law-order and kingdom—but as inherent, natural, or even God-ordained limitations within a biological type.

This way of thinking was given a massive boost in the nineteenth century with the evolutionary speculations and hypotheses of Charles Darwin, who advanced an inherently racial theory in which distinct "races" of people were thought to have evolved at different times and rates. This implied that some people were closer to and much more similar to their supposedly apelike progenitors than others. Australian Aborigines, for example, were classified by some as "missing links" between pre-hominid ancestors and modern humans. A leading Darwin historian has pointed out that

> by the time he [Darwin] writes *The Descent of Man* in 1871, it's pretty clear that he by that time shares the growing suspicion or conviction of many Europeans. The non-white races simply do not have the capacity to be elevated properly into civilized human beings, that they are mentally and morally at a more limited level. In a sense they are stuck at an early stage in the biological evolution of the human species.[3]

---

2. See Thomas Sowell, *Intellectuals and Society* (New York, NY: Basic Books, 2011), 381.
3. Peter Bowler, cited in Carl Wieland, *One Human Family: The Bible, Science, Race and Culture* (Powder Springs, GA: Creation Book Publishers, 2011), 43.

As such, noted evolutionist Stephen Jay Gould has admitted, "Biological arguments for racism may have been common before 1859, but they increased by orders of magnitude following the acceptance of evolutionary theory."[4] This Enlightenment movement from a *theological* understanding of humanity to a *"pseudo-scientific"* one is highly significant. As social critic and theologian, R. J. Rushdoony, has pointed out:

> In the modern era, as Christianity's influence receded and science began to govern together with humanism, biology came to predominate over theology. The differences between men were seen increasingly as biological and racial rather than religious....
>
> The theory of evolution fueled this developing scientific racism.... The human race was no longer the human race! It was a collection of possibly human races, a very different doctrine.[5]

So, while ethnic prejudice is as old as the Tower of Babel (Gen. 11), "racism" as a category of thought is a distinctly modern notion in the Western world. It is characterized by specific ideas of superiority and inferiority, and correlated to behavioral practices involving domination and subordination on the basis of particular *recognizable external features*. In general, what are best described as *racial ideologies* hold that human relationships should, at least in part, be ordered and structured hierarchically in terms of the outward biological and physical features of various races, whose lives and cultures are considered superior or inferior—in some measure *because* of those inherent or natural features—necessitating varying degrees of social separation or segregation. When this kind of thinking, whether arising religiously or "scientifically," becomes embedded in societal norms or institutions, so-called

---

4. Stephen Jay Gould, *Ontogeny and Phylogeny* (Cambridge, MA: Belknap-Harvard Press, 1977), 127.
5. Rushdoony, *An Informed Faith*, 21.

"racism" can be viewed as a socio-political reality and result in various forms of discrimination in human societies.

It was, for example, paler-skinned outside invaders who brought Hinduism (Brahmanism) to India. Unsurprisingly, the Brahman (priestly) upper caste in Hindu society are typically much paler-skinned, while the lowest caste "untouchables" are the darker-skinned descendants of the indigenous defeated population. The vile caste system has a religious root in the Hindu conception of the divine, and at the cultural level this system serves to keep a class of people in perpetual servitude.

Similar examples abound from across the world. In Japan, around the time of World War II, doctrines of Japanese racial superiority blended effectively with evolutionary thought and were widely propagated, leading to great cruelty—the hairy long-armed Europeans were thought closer to apes! In Shintoism, the Japanese people are considered direct descendants of the gods. Perhaps predictably, this did not include Korean or Chinese peoples. The Yamato people, in particular, were considered a superior race, and others were brutalized and discriminated against as a result.

In Europe, a notorious and murderous ideology arose in Nazi Germany around a romanticized and mythic notion of an Aryan line of racial purity to be recovered and selectively bred to facilitate the reemergence of a superior race. Blending with evolutionary ideas, this folk religion of blood and soil required the "purification" of Germanic stock and greater segregated "living space" at the expense of Slavic peoples, Jews, and all people of color.

In the United States, "Jim Crow" laws in the late nineteenth and early twentieth centuries were introduced because black Americans were considered inferior to whites. Miscegenation laws were also enacted in many Southern and Western states, forbidding "interracial" marriages—typically these laws involved prohibiting marriages between whites and blacks, Asians, or native American Indians, though nine U.S. states never enacted such laws. In a similar vein, the eugenics program in America and the work of Planned Parenthood led by race ideologues like Margaret Sanger viewed Italians and

Jews, not just blacks, as inferior undesirables to be targeted for abortion and sterilization.[6]

Tragically, some Christians, lacking a clear scriptural understanding, have all too easily been caught up in attitudes of ethnic superiority rooted in some form of race biology. Charles Kingsley, for example, was a clergyman and one of Darwin's close friends. He was an avid promoter of Darwinian ideas and wanted them synthesized with Christianity. Kingsley wrote:

> The black people of Australia, exactly the same race as the African Negro, cannot take in the Gospel... all attempts to bring them to a knowledge of the true God have as yet failed utterly...; poor brutes in human shape... they must perish off the face of the earth like brute beasts.[7]

It is clear, then, that much of this virulent prejudice, including the attitudes of domination or inherent superiority, was based not just in fear of the unknown but in rationalistic assumptions and, as we have noted, in false understandings of human origins. In the West this initially involved hierarchical Enlightenment notions of *polygenesis* held by people like Voltaire and David Hume (over against the biblical view of monogenesis), notions that later assumed evolutionary form. Despite the perennial appeal for intellectuals in East and West of an idea of *hierarchy* in nature leading to a hierarchy of peoples—whereby Aristotle held some people were slaves by nature—biblical Christianity rejects any notion of superiority and subordination of one people to another that is based in physical, biological, or so-called "racial" characteristics.

---

6. See Weikart, *From Darwin to Hitler*.
7. Charles Kingsley, cited in Wieland, *One Human Family*, 30–31.

## Ethnicity and People Groups

Despite this climate of thought and historical background, it was becoming clear to scientists after World War I that it was simply impossible to establish with any certainty the popular notion of "race" in the biological sense. In fact, our growth in understanding of human genetics has come increasingly to consign the concept of *race biology* to the historical garbage bin of ideas that really needs to be discarded at the popular level and emphatically rejected by Christians. In my view, the terms "races" and "racism" no longer serve a constructive purpose and lead only to misunderstandings and confusion. Rather, "people groups" and "ethnic prejudice" are much more accurate and useful expressions that could help move us away from both the reductionistic biological and the social constructivist conceptions of "race."

The remarkable reality is that in terms of our biological make up, human beings are all 99.9% the same.[8] According to contemporary genetics only about 0.01% of our DNA causes what people think of as "racial" differences,[9] and even these are rapidly breaking down because of interethnic mating. Richard Lewontin, a leading zoology professor at Harvard University noted in 2006:

> Over the last thirty-five years a major change has taken place in our biological understanding of the concept of human "race," largely as a consequence of an immense increase in our knowledge of human genetics. As a biological rather than

---

8. Theresa M. Duello et al., "Race and Genetics versus 'Race' in Genetics," *National Center for Biotechnology Information*, https://www.ncbi.nlm.nih.gov/pmc/articles/PMC8604262/#:~:text=The%20completion%20of%20the%20Human%20Genome%20Project%20in%202003%20confirmed,no%20genetic%20basis%20for%20race (accessed September 2023).
9. Natalie Angier, "Do Races Differ? Not Really, Genes Show," *The New York Times*, August 22, 2000, https://www.nytimes.com/2000/08/22/science/do-races-differ-not-really-genes-show.html (accessed September 2023).

a social construct, "race" has ceased to be seen as a fundamental reality characterizing the human species.[10]

None of this means there are not identifiable people groups or ethnic families with greater genetic similarity to each other emerging in the process of time, being geographically separated from one another, so that the various regions of the world are dominated by a particular genetic "deck" which codes for specific features. Nor is it illegitimate to scientifically notice generalizations "on average" of particular traits that various people groups exhibit; for example, no one would expect pygmy peoples from the tropical rainforest areas in Africa to produce basketball players challenging the Los Angeles Lakers or Olympic high jumpers to challenge the Dutch. And yet it is tiny variations in genes that control things like skin pigmentation, nose and eye shape, height and so on. These are the things that we think of as "racial features," but as Carl Wieland points out:

> generally no group has anything 'unique' not shared by any other group. For example, the Asian or almond eye differs from a typical Caucasian or round eye in having a tiny ligament that pulls the eyelid down a little. All babies are born with the ligament, but non-Asians usually lose it before 6 months of age.[11]

Because of these "genetic decks" coding for similar characteristics among given peoples (and thus coding for the same copying mistakes in the DNA called mutations), it is also noteworthy that intermarriage between ethnic groups helps reduce the risk of inherited genetic diseases in the process of human reproduction. Tribes and groups that don't marry outside of small communities are prone to above average rates of rare genetic conditions.

In a similar fashion, the notion that some form of genetic determinism is *decisive* in the relative *success* of various peoples, an idea that drives much

---

10. Lewontin, "Confusions about human race"; cited in Wieland, *One Human Family*, 74–75
11. Wieland, *One Human Family*, 94.

'racist' thinking, also fails to withstand serious scrutiny. The claim of an early president of Stanford University, that "a nation's blood determines its history," is simply nonsense. China was for centuries technologically and economically more advanced than any European country,[12] and as Thomas Sowell has pointed out:

> Progressive-era intellectuals disdained the peoples of Southern Europe, who had by all indices once been far more advanced in ancient times than the Nordics who were said to be genetically superior. The Greeks and Romans had the Parthenon and the Coliseum, not to mention literature and giants of philosophy, at a time when there was not a single building in Britain, a country inhabited at that time by illiterate tribes.[13]

What accounts for relative differences in attainment and achievement at given periods among various peoples or ethnic groups in different nations, or even within the same nation, are multiple commitments involving matters of environment, skills, behaviors, values, attitudes, as well as social and familial structures—all having a religious root. This complex of factors, not to mention God's sovereign providence in which "righteousness exalts a nation" (Prov. 14:34), means that we must avoid the mistake of thinking that what *conveys* differences in attainment in a particular context (in this case a given ethnic background) is the *cause* of those differences.

This is *not* to agree with multiculturalism that foolishly declares all *cultures* to be equal—thereby dissipating all aspiration and sealing off in their current practices, behaviors, and values those people who belong to a lagging or backward group or country. To do so is to imprison them in the very things that have left them behind. Rather it is to recognize that we cannot give simplistic and ignorant 'racial' explanations to causes that are highly complex and multidimensional. For instance, in the United States, on average, married families are much wealthier than single-parent families,

---

12. Sowell, *Intellectuals and Society*, 383, 393.
13. Sowell, *Intellectuals and Society*, 403.

and there is little difference in income between black and white *married* families. Thus, income disparity between black and white families in America is driven primarily by this fact: by a significant order of magnitude more black families are headed by single parents.[14] Interestingly, it has been socialistic welfare policies that have helped to devastate the black family, and with the collapse of biblical faith, the rate of black Christian married families has declined sharply. Whatever other socio-cultural factors may play a part in this, income disparity clearly has nothing to do with black *ethnicity*.[15]

## The Cultural and Philosophical Context of Contemporary Racial Tension

When it comes to the present social fixation with 'racism,' context is very important. The Western world is currently in a profound state of crisis. Complete societal disintegration and collapse are ominously looming. As Christian conviction and a biblical worldview have eroded, leaving a deep sense of spiritual uprootedness, a loss of cultural and national identity has quickly ensued. Our broken social order has become rudderless to the point where the populations of Western nations (especially the indigenous working classes) are no longer aware of who they are or who they were. Having been deliberately demoralized and de-Christianized through a process of indoctrination and social subversion, the ideology of multiculturalism or secularized religious pluralism has been invoked to offer a new identity and sense of belonging. The problem is that it hasn't worked. Multiculturalism and religious pluralism as ideologies under the supervision and endorsement

---

14. More than half (51.2%) of all black children lived with one parent in 2022, compared with about one in five (21.3%) white children. See "Living arrangement of children by race/ethnicity."
15. See Wieland's excellent discussion in Wieland, *One Human Family*, 358–60.

of the secular state have, not unexpectedly for the Christian, utterly failed, and instead of harmony, radical divisions are emerging everywhere.[16]

As people who are culturally very different are forced to integrate through technocratic social engineering, including near unrestricted legal or mass illegal immigration, tensions are reaching a boiling point. The migrant crisis in both America and Europe is very real, stoking both frustration and resentment.[17] Pointing out the self-destructive urge involved in such immigration practices gets one labelled a "racist." Yet "race riots" have frequently broken out across Europe and America,[18] while serious prejudice and hatred between the Black and Asian communities in Britain, as well as between Indians and Pakistanis, are commonplace; here the problems of the Indian subcontinent are simply exported to the United Kingdom.[19] This resentment is exacerbated by the political meaning of multiculturalism summed up perfectly by Sowell: "What multiculturalism boils down to is that you can praise any culture in the world except Western culture—and you cannot blame any culture in the world except Western culture."[20] This pro-

---

16. See Malise Ruthven, "How Europe lost faith in multiculturalism," *Financial Times*, https://www.ft.com/content/dd122a8c-8720-11e7-8bb1-5ba57d47eff7, accessed September 2023.
17. See Georgina Cutler, "Massachusetts Forced to Deploy National Guard to Deal with Migrant Crisis: 'This Is an Emergency!'" *GB News*, https://www.gbnews.com/news/us/massachusetts-national-guard-migrant-crisis-emergency (accessed September 2023). See also Nick Squires, "Germany Refuses to Take Any More EU Migrants as Boats Forced to Queue in Italian Docks," *The Telegraph*, September 13, 2023, https://www.telegraph.co.uk/world-news/2023/09/13/germany-refuses-more-eu-migrants-boats-queue-italian-docks/ (accessed September 2023).
18. "Thousands Defy Bans in France to Rally Against Police Violence," *Al Jazeera*, July 8, 2023, https://www.aljazeera.com/news/2023/7/8/paris-memorial-march-banned-as-fresh-protests-planned-in-france (accessed September 2023). And for the USA, see Stephanie Pagones, "Protests, Riots That Gripped America in 2020," *Fox News*, https://www.foxnews.com/us/protests-riots-nationwide-america-2020 (accessed September 2023).
19. See Colin Drury, "Leicester Riots a Warning That Violence in UK Can Be Sparked by Global Events, Experts Say," *The Independent*, https://www.independent.co.uk/news/uk/home-news/leicester-riots-hindu-muslim-violence-b2173293.html (accessed September 2023).
20. Sowell, cited in Wieland, *One Human Family*, 316.

gressive agenda is utter folly because it is directed at the evident superiority of Western *culture* that has endured at least four centuries. However, that undeniable advancement and superiority (now in rapid decline) is *grounded* not in biological facts, but in values, beliefs, and common faith—in short, in religion. Any attempt to reduce the cultural success of the Western world (i.e., European peoples) to biology is a fool's errand – and a dangerous one.

The socio-political landscape of multiculturalism provides the backdrop for this still deeper problem: the crisis of meaning pervading Western thought. When the meaning and thereby ordering of life shifts its center from Jesus Christ, the triune God, and His Word, it is inevitably sought elsewhere; and because all such meaning is an imitation, a counterfeit, it will inevitably fail. One vital aspect of the question of meaning since the beginning of philosophical inquiry has been the source and ground of *unity* in *diversity*. It is this problem, expressed at the religious and cultural level, which lies at the root of the West's social travails—including the problem of so-called "racism."

Finding unity in degrees of diversity is a necessary pursuit of every nation and culture. What can provide the unity to bind societies together—whether we are speaking of various tribes in the Congo, or Black, Hispanic, and White Americans, or something as apparently simple as the ancient United Kingdom of England, Scotland, Wales, and Northern Ireland, or the various provinces of Canada? Central to the answer is the need for shared meaning and purpose within a common understanding of cultural identity. A lingual unity facilitates the deeper language of meaning. But as a shared meaning declines, identity disintegrates and tribalist movements for devolution or separation become commonplace. As Christianity has collapsed in Scotland, the Celtic ethnic heritage and sympathies with republicanism have replaced it, stoking a powerful Scottish Nationalist movement, just as it has in Northern Ireland. In de-Christianizing Canada, French language and identity perennially feed an independence movement in the province of Quebec. The root and source of meaning for any society is inherently teleological and eschatological—that is, it involves purpose and direction or fulfillment—its movement is toward the source of ultimate meaning and cohesion which is an inescapably *religious* matter. As long as the West refuses to acknowledge and grapple with the central *religious* dimension of shared language, meaning, virtues, values, and purpose in society, it will neither understand nor be able to overcome the present problem of "racism."

The tension between peoples living in the West is further complicated today because it is now embroiled in a three-way eschatological-meaning conflict between utopian/globalist-Marxian and ethno-nationalistic views of society over against that of the gospel of the Kingdom in and through Jesus Christ. Having been variously influenced by faulty Enlightenment and Marxian conceptions of "race," ethnic origins, and hierarchy, both competing groups, falling short of the truly Christian answer, propose a false solution to the difficulties. On the Marxian side Critical Race Theorists (CRT) presently dominate the political landscape. They believe that only by permanent revolution against the *white* oppressor can we move toward the vanishing horizon of so-called "racial justice." On the growing ethno-nationalistic side, reacting to the false gospel of Marxism, advocates have their own socio-political solution to the tensions, involving a need for greater "race consciousness" (whether in the language of ethnicity or nation) and some measure of ethnic segregation along with a troubling rise in antisemitism. On this view, a careful study of nature's law by reason is said to reveal inherent distinctions between "races" or ethnicities—differences also grasped intuitively by our natural instincts regarding kith and kin to be acknowledged and applied socio-politically. This can take an Aristotelian form rooted in ancient conceptions of Natural Law, social order, and custom, or an evolutionary and Darwinian form rooted in biology and heredity.[21] Ethnocentric nationalists tend to have a *primordial* view[22] of identity in which one's "race" (blood) and

---

21. For example, see J. Philippe, *Race, Evolution and Behavior: A Life History Perspective* (Port Huron, MI: Charles Darwin Research Institute, 2000).
22. Primordialism is the idea that nations or ethnic identities are fixed, natural, and ancient. On this view, each individual possesses a single inborn ethnic identity, independent of historical processes. Ethnicity is viewed as embedded in inherited biological attributes, a long history of practicing cultural differences, or a combination of both.

"place" (socio-geographic heredity) are at the *centre* of defining who one is—the Romantic call of blood and soil—whilst Critical Theorists subscribe to a *constructionist* view of "race" as a real but culturally invented social category used to exploit and oppress people.[23] The primordial nationalists tend toward absolutizing ethnic *particularity* (diversity) for truly living well, whilst the Marxian globalists tend toward absolutizing *universality* (unity), where all distinctions must be leveled and erased. Both poles are reductionistic, holding only a *partial* truth, and are consequently erroneous.

## Marxian Inverse Racism and Christian Culture

Paradoxically, despite the very idea of "race" as human biological stocks and subgroups being scientifically debunked, and whilst appealing to a *constructionist* view of race, the Marxian Critical Race Theorists hold that the world can nonetheless be divided up into two groups—"whites" and everyone else. The "white" group (notice that this is a *biological or racial* feature, not a cultural marker) are the oppressors and to varying degrees, people of color are the oppressed. This injustice is said to be embedded in the laws, structures, and institutions of "white" society. The sociological invention of "white privilege" and "white guilt" has become an effective tool the revolutionaries use to stoke "racial" division in modern Western society. It has also meant that revisionist views of colonialism and slavery have become popular topics, serving to "prove" white guilt and the subsequent need for political penance, reparations, and so forth.

Slavery in human history and around the world has certainly played a role in *fomenting* "racism," because slaves were often despised due to their *social* rank. But just as war, conquest, and empire have been the constant story of human civilization, so slavery has been ubiquitous throughout

---

23. Race Constructionists argue that "races" are social rather than natural groups. Critical Race Theories posit on this basis that "racial justice" requires us to recognize the mechanisms of "racial formation" to subvert the present racial order and to liberate the oppressed.

human history in all civilizations and is not *caused* by "racism." Most slaves historically were enslaved by their own peoples—Asians enslaving Asians, Africans enslaving other Africans, Europeans enslaving Europeans; the European "Slavic" peoples get their name from being such frequent victims of enslavement. Though modern people are vaguely conscious of the transatlantic slave trade, notably brought to an end by faithful Christian activism in 1808, Muslim Moors enslaved Europeans for 800 years during their occupation of the Iberian Peninsula, and from the sixteenth century, Muslim states in North Africa supported piracy and the enslavement and trade of white peoples. Additionally, even in America and the Caribbean during the years of a transatlantic slave trade there were thousands of free black slave owners. Ultimately, because of the biblical teaching about human beings as made in the image and likeness of God, it was only Christian civilization in the West that finally turned against institutionalized slavery on religious principle and sought to crush it throughout the world, at great expense and in the face of much opposition. These realities have been discussed at great length by the brilliant African-American intellectual Thomas Sowell.[24]

Nonetheless, in the mythic Marxian (CRT) account of the world, only the "white" group can be "racist," so the oppressed can never be oppressors; non-white cultures generally get a free pass for their injustice, ethnic prejudice, atrocities, enslavement of others, and so forth. Where these are mentioned, it is usually blamed on colonialism or some other alleged sin of the "white" Western world. This not only means that black people (or someone in the so-called BIPOC grouping)[25] alone have a right to speak about racism, but that there can be no true collaboration of "whites" with "blacks" to resolve these issues because whites will help only when black or BIPOC interests "converge" with their own interests—thus whites cannot be allowed to speak about it. Since "white" knowledge and action will proceed

---

24. Thomas Sowell, "Facts about Slavery Never Mentioned in School," *Thomas SowellTV*, YouTube video, https://www.youtube.com/watch?v=lyPWjjWs7-w (accessed September 2023).
25. The acronym BIPOC stands for Black, Indigenous, People Of Color.

only from their *standpoint*[26] and in their interests, they can never be believed or trusted. As such, "racism" (a "sin" able to be committed only by whites) is inherently *structural* and thereby permanent, and it can never be finally overcome. Furthermore, on this view, political equality cannot be measured by opportunity under the law, but only by *outcomes*, hence the need for perpetual revolutionary action. Neither can education bring victory—there is only the endless revolutionary struggle against the "white" oppressor. This is an eschatological claim, and an important one. "Racial justice" is always only on the horizon and never fully realized, and so true peace is never possible.

This ideological perspective is self-evidently an inverse form of "racism" in which ethnically white peoples are scapegoated as the oppressive cause of the world's problems and so must be punished by becoming the oppressed. It is also significant to note that the structure and root of these ideas did *not* originate with African or Asian thinkers but with neo-Marxist European intellectuals—largely atheists from Germany, Hungary, and Italy, determined to destroy through political masochism what was left of Christendom.[27] By assigning guilt to one ethnicity, the punishment for all global ills must be *sadistically* laid upon that group as a false form of atonement to expiate the guilt of all. No amount of penance or burden-bearing on their part is ever sufficient to atone for "white" sins, real or imagined, because the structural "sin" of "whiteness" embedded in all institutions is permanent.

As the Christian mind has feebly surrendered to this diabolic critique, a *masochistic* urge has been nurtured in Western nations to *punish* themselves in an effort to atone for the crimes of which they stand accused—usually

---

26. This refers to the Critical Theorist's notion of *Standpoint Epistemology*. Standpoint theory proposes that your social location in life governs your interpretation of reality and therefore your knowledge base. In turn, authority is thought to be rooted in the individual's personal knowledge and perspectives and the power that such authority exerts.
27. This has reference to the infamous "Frankfurt School" of thought emerging from the Institute for Social Research founded in 1923 in Germany. These thinkers sought to advance Marxian Critical Theories that would subvert Western culture and realize Communism by cultural destruction of Western societal institutions as opposed to an economically focused workers revolution.

through various forms of reparations, payments, burden-bearing, false confessions and apologies, surrender of its institutions, or self-dispossession by giving up its territory as well as promoting unrestricted legal or illegal migration from developing countries, etc. In short, with the problem of guilt no longer being addressed through biblical faith at the Lord's table, an increasingly faithless Western culture seeks to alleviate the guilt of its apostasy from Christ in a kind of self-immolation.

However, the Marxian root of the self-condemning "white man" (and other ethnic groups have joined the chorus who frequently live in and off the benefits of Western civilization) is not finally about *skin color* but about the religious commitment of historic Christendom itself. Targeting a "white" or "European mentality" makes no sense at all, because such a mentality must logically be applied to *pre-Christian* white Europe as a "racial" factor, and yet pre-Christian Europe was barbarous, pagan, and engaged in all manner of Canaanitic sins. Until converted to Christ, the Vikings from the Nordic countries even practiced human sacrifice.[28] This proves that the real target is not "whiteness" as such (that is merely a useful identifier of the enemy for contemporary Marxists), but the *Christian culture* that Western peoples represented for over a thousand years. The Western mentality and culture, at least in its advances and despite its sins and failures, was unquestionably a product of biblical religion—it cannot be understood on any other terms.[29] There is no more a "White" mentality than there is an "Asiatic" soul or "African" mind. It is only a "racial" concept of man that can maintain such notions. From the scriptural standpoint the mindset of any nation is not a "racial" inheritance but a product of religion, and the culture that such religion produces. It is not "race" but sin and righteousness, obedience or disobedience to God, that is the *principal* factor in causing peoples to differ.

---

28. See "Prehistoric Period (until 1050) / The Viking Age / Religion, Magic, Death and Rituals / Human Sacrifices?" *National Museum of Denmark,* https://en.natmus.dk/historical-knowledge/denmark/prehistoric-period-until-1050-ad/the-viking-age/religion-magic-death-and-rituals/human-sacrifices/ (accessed September 2023).
29. See Mangalwadi, *The Book That Made Your World.*

## Primordial Nationalism and Romanticism

It was entirely predictable that this inverse racism of the Marxian perspective, overtly assaulting and suppressing a given ethnicity, should eventually break out in a reactionary, ethnically oriented nationalism. And it is significant to observe that certain features are shared by both the primordial nationalists—who see "racial" division and kinship rooted in inherent, unchangeable natural intuitions or biological structures and instincts—and the Critical Race Theorists who likewise, in their own way, see culturally originating "racial" division as structural and permanent. Neither provides adequate ground for unity in diversity and both have an implicit eschatology of defeat in regard to "race relations."

Primordial nationalism (i.e., ethnocentric nationalism as opposed to a patriotic and principled commitment to one's country) is actually a product of Romanticism which stressed the *uniqueness* of both the individual and their nationalities, their folklore, and origins. Steadily, in the late eighteenth and nineteenth century, nationalisms began to replace Christianity as the focal point of life in Europe. As social critic R. J. Rushdoony explains:

> Just as for the Romantic hero, the good of the individual is paramount and takes precedence over all other considerations, so for the nation, in the Romantic faith, the good or concern of the nation is the highest good and takes precedence over Christian concerns. National self-interest went hand in hand with a belief in national superiority and self-glorification.... In earlier eras, men felt loyal to a lord or a king, not to the nation as such; now allegiance was to a nation state.... [W]hile Romanticism stressed at the beginning the individual, it came in time to stress the freedom of the national state, or the worker's state, or a racial state, at the cost of personal freedom.[30]

Most modern nation-states consist of very different groups of peoples or ethnicities. In my own home country of Great Britain, we are historically

---

30. Rushdoony, *An Informed Faith*, 595–96.

an amalgamation of ancient Britons or Celts, Romans, Saxons, Franks, and Nordic peoples—not always the happiest of neighbors—and due to the British Empire and now Commonwealth, since World War II, significant numbers of people from the Caribbean Islands, the Indian subcontinent, as well as parts of Africa have settled in the United Kingdom—most of whom see themselves as British (with substantial exceptions in the Muslim communities and large numbers of contemporary migrants). What is true of Britain as a collage of peoples is true of much of Europe, and parts of Central America like Mexico, not to mention Canada and the United States, which are relatively new countries built from various European settler communities and nineteenth-century migrations. The formation of nation-states has in most cases throughout history resulted from the union of various states of differing characters—France and Germany being very good examples. Furthermore, few countries have natural boundaries separating them and historically emerging geographical boundaries have constantly changed with war, mass migrations, conflict, and political upheaval. All this makes a romanticized *primordial* or ethnocentric nationalism just as irrational as Marxian globalism.

The history of *primordial* nationalism is extremely ugly,[31] and it is no more possible to speak of this kind of nationalism as having been misapplied or misinterpreted awaiting a better application than it is to use the endless excuses of Marxists as to why Marxism is yet to work anywhere it has been tried. In part due to the long story of empire since the Pharaohs of Egypt, the identities of nations and peoples have been remarkably fluid throughout human history and there is no pure "race" or ethnicity to which anyone can point back, as any study of an individual's DNA will show. Most of us are a considerable mixture of ethnic heritage. One of my best friends in Canada, originally from the United Kingdom, discovered to his surprise that he was a descendant on his father's side of an African slave. Many of us would find similar results that we would never have anticipated.

---

31. The most notorious examples in the twentieth century are Nazi Germany and Shinto Imperial Japan.

For the sake of argument, and if the term retains any value at all, we can say it is true that our "race" or nationality is *partially* socio-culturally constructed. By this I mean that it is within the multi-faceted historical-cultural process of development that a national and ethno-geographic identity emerges amongst clans, tribes, and peoples. In many respects the emergence my own nation (a "British race") was a ninth-century development when Alfred the Great, by preventing an island-wide invasion of the Danes, formed the beginnings of an Anglo-Saxon identity and a united England in the south—to the north, it remained a Viking realm under Danelaw. The four kingdoms of England eventually came together as a united England in A.D. 927. However, it would not be until 1707 and the Acts of Union that England (including Wales) would unite with Scotland creating the Kingdom of Great Britain, with Ireland joining a century later in 1801, cementing what we today call a *British* nationality. These countries all have their own historic languages and cultural distinctives. The united English and subsequent British identity was possible only because of the cultural development of a common faith, law, and purpose—it was not the result of an ethnic or geographic unity, and not even a lingual unity. Without this common faith, tribal war would have been unremitting. Most of Europe has a similar, if not more complex, history.

At the same time, it is also true that our "race" (or national identity) *partially* involves the reality of a bloodline, a familial-ethnic inheritance. By this I mean that we all have a family history and there are certain genetic markers and dominant traits that offer a general indication of which part(s) of the globe our ancestors are from. My own immediate ancestry, just back as far as my great grandfathers and grandmothers, includes people from the countries of England, Scotland, the Netherlands, and likely even India.

Consequently, only by bringing together a variety of complex aspects can we speak of national identities. And whilst these intermingled factors all have a role in forming a sense of identity, the *defining quality* of those nations is rooted *ultimately* not in a "racial" bloodline, geographical locale, language, or social development, but in their religious commitments—a reality proved by the older concept of "Christendom."

## The Biblical View of Race and Nationhood

The Bible, and thereby Christianity, is intrinsically opposed to the modern concepts of race and racism. We noted from the outset that the unity of the "human race" in the first man Adam is one of the fundamental tenets of biblical truth, despite the fact that professing Christians with ulterior motives have at times chosen to ignore or distort this reality. In the scriptural account of human origins there is a "genetic bottleneck" at the time of the Great Flood, when humanity was reduced to Noah, his wife, their three sons, and their wives. All human beings today are descended from this family, which, having greatly expanded, was dispersed across the earth in diverse language groups at the Tower of Babel (cf. Gen. 11). I understand this to be true history and basic to the Christian view of "race."

No people group born of this family has an entirely good history in which to boast. All the peoples from around the world have had evil practices in their past and many vices in their present. This includes ancient Britons, the Saxon peoples, Scandinavians, Germanic tribes, the peoples of the Mediterranean, the numerous peoples of Asia, the Caribs of the West Indies, as well as South American civilizations, African peoples, the clans of the Pacific Islands, and native American tribes (anachronistically called "first nations"), all of whom, prior to their conversion to Christianity or coming under its widespread influence, practiced human sacrifice, cannibalism, or both. In the case of native American peoples this continued well into the eighteenth century[32] and it continues to this day in sub-Saharan Africa.[33] We have industrial-scale abortion, euthanasia, and even infanticide being widely practiced in the West today, and the world is facing the scourge of human

---

32. See Mark Nicholls, "'Thing Which Seame Incredible': Cannibalism in Early Jamestown," *Colonial Williamsburg*, https://research.colonialwilliamsburg.org/Foundation/journal/Winter07/jamestown.cfm#:~:text=Cannibalism%20was%20practiced%20in%20some,endured%20into%20the%20eighteenth%20century (accessed September 2023).
33. See Lawrence E. Y. Mbogoni, *Human Sacrifice and the Supernatural in African History* (n.p.: Mkuki na Nyota Publishers, 2013).

trafficking and sexual slavery. This universality of sin is another basic fact of Christian thought, amply demonstrated in history, and no ethnic group is exempt from just condemnation (Rom. 3:9–18).

The ideas of nation and ethnicity are related in the Bible, but certainly not identical, because what creates and makes a cohesive nation cannot be reduced to blood ties but is always grounded in a common faith. Biblical revelation gives us even deeper insight into this as we notice the specific *character* of the nation formed by God's calling and purpose—the nation of Israel. When God sovereignly determined to establish a specific nation and its boundaries he did so with a missiological purpose (Gen. 22:18), as is the case with all the nations (Acts 17:26–28). That purpose was redemptive, with the ultimate goal of uniting in Christ one new humanity gathered from all the peoples of the earth into a kingdom of priests unto God (Rev. 5:10).

There are a number of critical things to notice about the people whose national history is recounted in Scripture as both a warning and example for all (1 Cor. 10:11–13). First, Abraham was called out from amongst his pagan people by God to be the father of Israel in whom *all the nations* of the world would be blessed. There is no favoritism with God (Rom. 2:11)! There was nothing sacrosanct about Abraham's culture, homeland, or background—he was called out of it. Neither was there anything in his biological or "racial" lineage that especially fitted him to be the father of Israel or that led to God's special deliverance and dealings with his descendants—it was simply the electing love of God (Deut. 7:7–8). Second, the nature and foundation of Israel's unique national identity was covenantal (that is: religious), not ethnic. It was not by virtue of being from Abraham's loins that someone became a member of the nation—after all, Abraham had eight sons and only Isaac born through Sarah was a child of the promise through whom Jacob would come and be renamed Israel. Third, we know from the apostle Paul that the fulfillment of the promise that Abraham's seed would bless the nations was realized in Christ Jesus who is *the* "seed" of Abraham (singular: Gal. 3:16), and Christ is the final and true Priest-King, the Kinsman-Redeemer of humanity and the last Adam (1 Cor. 15:45). This sheds light on why Abraham paid a tithe to Melchizedek, the priest-King of Salem (Gen. 14:20), because the final priesthood was not to be Aaronic (from Abraham's loins ethnically), but a priesthood in the order of Melchizedek who preceded and transcended the ethnic Jew and Gentile distinction (Ps. 110:4; Heb. 7:17). Fourth, Paul is also clear that the benefit and blessing of Jewish heritage as an Israelite was not ethnic but religious: "So what advantage does the Jew have? Or what is the benefit of circumcision? Considerable in every way. First, *they were entrusted with the spoken words of God*" (Rom. 3:1–2). Likewise, the deficit position of the Gentile was not "racial" or biological but religious:

> So then, remember that at one time you were Gentiles in the flesh—called "the uncircumcised" by those called "the circumcised," which is done in the flesh by human hands. At that time you were without the Messiah, excluded from the citizenship of Israel, and foreigners to the covenants of the promise, without hope and without God in the world. But now in Christ Jesus, you who were far away have been brought near by the blood of the Messiah. For He is our peace, who made both groups one and tore down the dividing wall of hostility.... When the Messiah came, He proclaimed the good news of peace to you who were far away and peace to those who were near. For through Him we both have access by one Spirit to the Father. So then you are no longer foreigners and strangers, but fellow citizens with the saints, and members of God's household (Eph. 2:11–14; 17–19).

Fifth, the religious, not "ethnic," character of the nation is amply demonstrated in that frequently non-ethnic Hebrews became members of the covenant people of Israel, often having a significant role or impact. For example, Joseph married an Egyptian named Asenath who became the mother of two tribes of Israel, Ephraim, and Manasseh (Gen. 41:50–52); Moses married Zipporah from an ancient Arab tribe called the Midianites (though descendants of Abraham) known by tradition for their dark skin, not a Hebrew. Jethro, Moses' father-in-law, also had a significant role as an advisor in the governing of the people of Israel (Exod. 18:14–26). We are also told that when the Israelites left Egypt after the plagues, they left as a "mixed multitude" (Exod. 12:38), indicating that there were numerous non-Hebrews who left with Moses in the Exodus, having believed God, possibly even placing the sign of the covenant in blood over their thresholds, thereby joining the covenant people.[34] Rahab is perhaps the most famous non-Jew in the Older Testament—a Canaanite prostitute in Jericho who exercised faith in God and married Salmon of the tribe of Judah and so became the mother of Boaz, who married another non-Jew, Ruth. Their son Obed was the grandfather of King David, and so a Gentile prostitute was in the direct ancestry of Christ. We can presume also that many of King Solomon's wives were converted pagans.

The reality is that, despite Israel's overall failure to be the missionary people they were called to be (Exod. 19:6; Deut. 4:4–8; Isa. 49:6), there was provision for pagan Gentiles to convert and become members of the covenant nation as described in Esther 8:17; and Israel was given an explicit command concerning other ethnic peoples coming to live with and under the God of Israel: "When a foreigner lives with you in your land, you must not oppress him. You must regard the foreigner who lives with you as the native-born among you. You are to love him as yourself, for you were foreigners in the land of Egypt; I am Yahweh your God" (Lev. 19:33–34). In fact, in Ezekiel, *full inclusion* in the covenant for foreigners is clearly required when God's terms are met, *including* inheritance in the land with God's people.

> You are to divide this land among yourselves according to the tribes of Israel. You will allot it as an inheritance for yourselves and for the foreigners living among you, who have fathered children among you. You will treat them like native-born Israelites; along with you, they will be allotted an inheritance among the tribes of Israel. In whatever tribe the foreigner lives, you will assign his inheritance there. This is the declaration of the Lord God (Ezekiel 47:21–23).

These things demonstrate why Jesus was dismissive of those who claimed *ethnic privilege* as children of Abraham and part of the nation of

---

34. See Aaron Sherwood, "The Mixed Multitude in Exodus 12:38: Glorification, Creation, and Yhwh's Plunder of Israel and the Nations," *Horizons in Biblical Theology* 34, no. 2 (2012): 139–54, https://doi.org/10.1163/187122012X627821.

Israel: "I tell you that God is able to raise up children for Abraham from these stones" (Matt. 3:9).

In addition, and critically, the land they were granted to establish their nation was not an absolute *ethnic* right either—as though some ancient mystical connection with "place" or "blood and soil" was what constituted them as a people. They had been wanderers in the wilderness and slaves in Egypt and were told that if they rebelled against God, then the land of the Canaanites, which they were being given *because* of the idolatry and atrocities of the pagans, would spew them out just as it had done the peoples living there before them. Obedience to the covenant law of God was thus a *condition* of the right to keep the land:

> Do not defile yourselves by any of these practices, for the nations I am driving out before you have defiled themselves by all these things. The land has become defiled, so I am punishing it for its sin, and the land will vomit out its inhabitants. But you are to keep My statutes and ordinances. You must not commit any of these detestable things—not the native or the foreigner who lives among you. For the men who were in the land prior to you have committed all these detestable things, and the land has become defiled. If you defile the land, it will vomit you out as it has vomited out the nations that were before you. Any person who does any of these detestable practices must be cut off from his people. You must keep My instruction to not do any of the detestable customs that were practiced before you, so that you do not defile yourselves by them; I am Yahweh your God (Lev. 18:24–30).

As a result of their disobedience, they went into exile and were finally dispossessed.

Israel then was not defined as a nation "racially," but religiously. What made Abraham's descendants a nation, what provided their national *unity* amidst considerable *diversity*, was that they were a people of faith called to a purpose by the living God—a national covenant made them as a people. When they fell into idolatry, the kingdom was divided, and they became hostile to each other. Thus, while the Bible clearly supports the independence of nations (specifically, nation-states with real borders), calling them to fulfill their purpose and obligations to God and to stand against an imperial globalism of the pagan order (note that no empire was ever offered to an Israelite king or patriarch, because empire belongs to Christ alone),[35] the nation is not *defined* racially and is always relativized by the concerns of the kingdom of God. This means there is no *absolute* right of nations to continue their culture or maintain their lands. All such land grants in history are given or rescinded by God Himself under His sovereign authority—this personal activity of God in history is what explains all the historical changes down through the centuries (Dan. 2:21).

It is God's own counsel and eternal decree that causes nations and civilizations to rise, fall, and even to disappear altogether. For the nations are to God as a drop in a bucket and counted in all their pride and conceit as less than nothing and emptiness (Is. 40:17; Ps. 22:28). There can therefore be patriotism, pride, and gratitude for our nation's faith and accomplishments but no absolute nationalistic loyalty to country, land, or people. I am British by birth, live in England, and consider myself a patriot (and enjoy dual citizenship as a British-Canadian, having lived in Canada for nearly twenty years). I am genuinely proud of the venerable history of my nation (and that of my adopted nation of Canada) and the accomplishments of my people, despite our sins and failures of past and present. But we cannot stand with our nation in its evils or rebellion against God any more than we can stand with an apostate family member against Christ in the name of familial loyalty (Luke 14:26) or with a faithless and heretical church in the name of denominational loyalty (2 Cor. 6:17; Rev. 2:2–5). Scripture teaches explicitly that both familial and national loyalties are subordinate to religious loyalty—that is, loyalty to God and His Kingdom. The priority is always worshiping the living God and pursuing a culture that eschews idolatry:

> If your brother, the son of your mother, or your son or daughter, or the wife you embrace, or your closest friend secretly entices you, saying, "Let us go and worship

---

35. For a detailed discussion of the biblical idea of nationhood over against utopian globalism, see Boot, *Ruler of Kings: Toward a Christian Vision of Government.*

other gods"—which neither you nor your fathers have known, any of the gods of the peoples around you, near you or far from you, from one end of the earth to the other—you must not yield to him or listen to him. Show him no pity, and do not spare him or shield him (Deut. 13:6–8).

I gave you a land you did not labor for, and cities you did not build, though you live in them; you are eating from vineyards and olive groves you did not plant.

Therefore, fear the Lord and worship Him in sincerity and truth. Get rid of the gods your fathers worshiped beyond the Euphrates River and in Egypt, and worship Yahweh. But if it doesn't please you to worship Yahweh, choose for yourselves today the one you will worship: the gods your fathers worshiped beyond the Euphrates River or the gods of the Amorites in whose land you are living. As for me and my family, we will worship Yahweh (Josh. 24:13–15).

As a consequence of God's requirement, family, church, and state are relativized in relationship to God's kingdom. There have been and will be times when the faithful need to leave behind family, people, and even an apostate nation or order worship and serve the living God:

Naomi said, "Look, your sister-in-law has gone back to her people and to her god. Follow your sister-in-law." But Ruth replied: "Do not persuade me to leave you or go back and not follow you. For wherever you go, I will go, and wherever you live, I will live; your people will be my people, and your God will be my God. Where you die, I will die, and there I will be buried." (Ruth 1:15–17).

We can and must plead with God for our family, people, and nation, and live faithfully before the Lord amongst them for their good and blessing, for "Happy is the nation whose God is Yahweh" (Ps. 33:12). But we cannot stand with them *against* the Lord. This will mean prophetically declaring the warnings of God's law for peoples that rebel against Him. After all, the purpose of the nations is the extension of the knowledge and Kingdom of God, not some form of *racial realization*.

This is not to deny that different nations have a variety of distinctive cultural expressions that are part of a diverse tapestry of God's work in history. All the nations will ultimately bring their cultural treasures to the Lord in worship and service (Isa. 60:11; Rev. 21:24). The end goal of unity amidst the diversity of peoples is well expressed in John's Revelation: "You were slaughtered, and you redeemed people for God by your blood from every tribe and language and people and nation. You made *them a kingdom and priests* to our God, and they will reign on the earth" (Rev. 5:9–10).

The institutional church, of all places, should manifest this reality as we gather around both Word and sacrament as God's people. The most powerful witness against ethnic prejudice, hatred, or resentment should be seen amongst the multiethnic people of God (Gal. 3:28). When even the apostle Peter himself was drawn into a deeply engrained social separation between ethnic groups in the life of the church (Jew and Gentile, or the circumcised and uncircumcised), the apostle Paul withstood him to his face for behaving hypocritically and seeking to compel others to conform to a national particularity, i.e., to live as a Jew. In fact, Paul regarded his behavior as "deviating from the truth of the gospel" (Gal. 2:14), so how we handle our relationships in the church with people of ethnic backgrounds different than our own is critically important for maintaining gospel fidelity.

I had the privilege of serving as the founding pastor of a multiethnic church in Toronto, Canada, for fourteen years. Toronto is one of the most ethnically diverse cities in the world and it was an immense privilege to witness the unity in diversity of our urban church community. The distinctive characteristics of various people groups greatly enriched the church in countless ways, furthering our growth in grace and truth together as we learned from and challenged one another. There were difficulties, of course, both practical (sometimes we were doing simultaneous translation with headsets into several languages during sermons) and pastoral—there were periodic tensions within and between some of these groups. But it was amidst these joys and challenges that we grew and drew in the nations, testifying to the beauty and truth of the gospel.

As important, then, as the nations are in God's economy, to *absolutize* the nation is idolatry. They are always *relativized* in relation to the only totalizing principle Scripture allows—the Kingdom of God. A danger always lurks during culturally challenging times, even for Christians, of drifting into *primordial* forms of nationalism as well as statism in hopes of rescuing a nation from decline. Here "racial" identity or ethnicity is exaggerated in its importance, and at the same time, in reductionist fashion, ethnic heritage is made synonymous with nationhood itself, with the nation-state then seen as the central and highest institution in earthly life.

As a distinct structure ordered by the Lord, a nation functions in *multiple dimensions* of created reality, not merely the biological and social aspects. A nation can be *numerically* counted with other nations, and it exists within a given *spatial* boundary, and yet that boundary typically *moves* and changes over time. The nation has a *physical* character in terms of the territory it occupies and consists of *living* persons who have a *sense* of identity by which they *logically* distinguish themselves from other nations. Nations emerge in the context of *historical-cultural* development and will have one or more *language* groups through which the *social* life of the nation is enriched. The nation has an *economic* aspect essential to its existence and survival, and an *aesthetic* side expressed in both harmony amidst diversity and the cultural products of the people. There is an essential *juridical* function to a nation-state, for without a common law there can be no conception of nationhood, and every nation will be governed by an idea of *moral* order. This order is inescapably bound to the *faith* of the people, indicating the religious root of nationhood. The individuality structure of a nation is therefore highly complex and cannot be reduced to ethnic particularity within its biological (strictly "biotic") aspect.

## "Christian" Nationalism

Even ostensibly well-intentioned forms of ethno-nationalism rightly concerned with the *Christian* character of a people risk falling into "racial" reductionism with its ethnic particularity at the expense of unity and universality. Stephen Wolfe, for example, in *The Case for Christian Nationalism*, regards ethnicity and nationhood as basically synonymous and suggests that at the beating heart and *centre* of living well in this world is both ethnic and territorial particularity, with a community in blood, custom, and kinship—not religion—being at the *root* of nationhood.[36] For Wolfe the *volk* is "the family writ large," and blood relations bind you to people and place, creating a common *volksgeist*. Similarities in such particulars are seen as the ground of *greater love for some over others*. He quotes Thomas Aquinas' arguments from nature with approval, that "we ought to love in higher degree and more intensely those who are more like us and more closely united to us,"[37] which is a rationalistic contradiction of biblical teaching (cf. Matt 5:43–48), in which the Samaritan who is neither Jew nor Arab is my neighbor (Luke 10:29–37), and where I am required to love the non-native as myself: "You must regard the foreigner who lives with you as the native-born among you. You are to love him as yourself, for you were foreigners in the land of Egypt; I am Yahweh your God" (Lev. 19:33–34).

Wolfe sees a *right* given by *nature* itself to assert ethnic difference or particularity, and an accompanying set of customary and cultural expectations for "normality" within the group to which all must conform or face some degree of social separation; again quoting Aquinas, he suggests that regular interaction with foreigners is harmful to civil life.[38] As such he writes that "perhaps in some cases amicable *ethnic separation* along political lines is mutually desired... and each person ought to (in normal circumstances) prefer their own people over others."[39] With the atheist David Hume, Wolfe seems to prefer the notion that we form the idea of our own person by encountering our own countryman—in short, by encountering one's self,[40] not by our encounter with God and the other.

---

36. Wolfe, *The Case for Christian Nationalism*, 134–35, 140.
37. Wolfe, *The Case for Christian Nationalism*, 141.
38. Wolfe, *The Case for Christian Nationalism*, 144, 146.
39. Wolfe, *The Case for Christian Nationalism*, 149; italics added.
40. Wolfe, *The Case for Christian Nationalism*, 157.

Nor does the gospel of the Kingdom transcend Wolfe's *natural* "principle of exclusion." A given country is seen as the natural *possession* of that people in terms of their ancestors,[41] and so even a Christian nation is not regarded as a suitable home for genuine believers from other countries.[42] His primordial nationalism here appears both absolute and totalizing. This is justified theologically in terms of the radical and scholastic nature-grace doctrine of Two Kingdoms that is unsupported scripturally and is simply assumed as valid.[43] For Wolfe, the unity of Christians is only an eschatological and "spiritual" reality in terms of the heavenly kingdom, made possible by *grace*, not *nature*. This unity is therefore purely heavenly, not earthly, and is yet to be realized. This is true for both the institutional church and the state, implying the appropriateness of forms of segregation even in ethnically mixed Christian nations. Human brotherhood is good for a heavenly "spiritual kingdom," but not for our earthly reality now. Thus, for Wolfe, our unity in Christ with "foreign" believers, along with our mutual submission to His law-Word, provides no unifying basis for living well in *this world*—an incredible claim which spiritualizes into Never-Never Land the reality of the Kingdom of God and the promises of God for history (cf. Isa. 60). In Wolfe's Two Kingdoms view, one cannot base a "civic" brotherhood on the "spiritual" brotherhood of God's kingdom. Even the culturally diverse expressions of other Christian peoples would allegedly harm civil unity and prevent the

---

41. This is a bizarre argument for a scholar to make in a work seeking to justify a "Heritage America" ethno-nationalism. If the above contention were true, then the North American continent is in fact the "natural possession" of the indigenous Indian tribes (first nations) who lived there (including their present ancestors) prior to the arrival of European settlers—a claim he would strenuously deny as an American nationalist. By contrast, the religious-covenantal perspective on the character and root of nations under God's sovereignty can account for the *dispossession* of these pagan indigenous tribes by Christian European settlers as a matter of covenantal judgment within history within the providence of God.
42. Wolfe, *The Case for Christian Nationalism*, 179.
43. For a thoroughgoing critique of this false dualism, and an exploration of the biblical ideas of nationhood and the Kingdom of God, see: Boot, *The Mission of God: A Manifesto of Hope for Society*; Boot, *Gospel Culture: Living in God's Kingdom*; and Boot, *Ruler of Kings: Toward a Christian Vision of Government*.

national community (whether secular or Christian) from acting for its own good. Here even Christian diversity supposedly *destroys* unity and therefore unity must be abolished as pure sentimentality.[44] All this means that the Kingdom of God is *not* the totalizing principle for human life and existence in this world (including family, institutional church, and state); that principle is the *primordial nation*, regardless of whether it has a Christian character.

This inability to reconcile unity and diversity, insisting instead that the one destroys the other, is the Achilles heel of even Christian versions of ethno-centric nationalism, and is rooted in the absolutization of the nation-state within a Scholastic framework. This approach is entirely unnecessary in the battle to assert the importance of independent nation-states (biblical nationhood) in a context of encroaching Marxian globalism, because bonds of loyalty and national cohesion are rooted in religious worldview, and not in "racial" identity—as modern American politics amply demonstrates. The polarization of Democrats and Republicans in the United States is obviously not "whites" versus the rest, but an increasingly neo-pagan social-democratic progressive secularism versus a republicanism more strongly influenced by Christianity and biblical values. Even the non-Christian philosopher Yoram Hazony, in his proposals for a biblically rooted idea of nationhood, avoids primordialism:

> The overwhelming dominance of a single cohesive nationality, bound together by indissoluble bonds of *mutual loyalty*, is in fact the only basis for domestic peace within a free state. By this I do not mean that the entire population must be drawn from a single nationality, for *no such thing exists anywhere on earth*. Moreover, there is no evidence that such a complete homogeneity is necessary for the cohesion, stability, and success of the state. Rather, what is needed for the establishment of a stable and free state is a majority nation whose cultural dominance is plain and unquestioned, and against which resistance appears to be futile. Such a majority nation is strong enough not to fear challenges from national minorities, and so

---

44. Wolfe, *The Case for Christian Nationalism*, 199–204.

is able to grant them rights and liberties without damaging the internal integrity of the state.⁴⁵

Furthermore, by romantically regarding people and place as basically one (i.e., the people as a whole *are* the place—existing in a symbiosis), thereby strictly identifying nation and ethnicity, Wolfe, in my view, adopts an essentially primitivist and "racial" view of humanity and nationhood: "This people-place symbiosis is held together by ties of affection, based fundamentally on *natural* affection toward kin."⁴⁶ Herman Dooyeweerd shows how badly misguided and self-contradictory this perspective is:

> It is the opening-up process of human culture also which *alone can give rise to national individualities*. A nation viewed as a socio-cultural unit should be sharply distinguished from the primitive *ethnical unity* which is called a popular or tribal community. A real national cultural whole is not a natural product of blood and soil, but the result of a process of differentiation and integration in the cultural formation of human society. In a national community all ethnical differences between the various groups of a population are integrated into a new individual whole which lacks the undifferentiated totalitarian traits of a closed and primitive unit of society.
>
> It was, therefore, unmistakable proof of the reactionary character of the Nazi myth of blood and soil that it tried to undermine the national consciousness of the Germanic peoples by reviving the primitive ethnic idea of "folk" ("*volkstum*").⁴⁷

One of the most serious consequences of Wolfe's idea of natural right and affection in which ethnicity (i.e., nation) is absolutized, is that it logically eliminates the possibility of the development and improvement of backward cultures or the transformation of cultures under the Lordship of

---

45. Yoram Hazony, *The Virtue of Nationalism* (New York: Basic Books, 2018); italics added
46. Wolfe, *The Case for Christian Nationalism*, 162; italics added.
47. Dooyeweerd, *Christian Philosophy and the Meaning of History*, 62; italics added.

Christ. Wolfe is clear that the foreigner should mute his own customs, even if they are neither bad nor inferior to the customs of the nation in which he lives: "Indeed, his customs might be superior and more refined than the host country's. But the foreigner has a duty not to disrupt the host people's way of life, and the hosts have every right to hold such people to these duties, even to the point of deportation."[48]

This is an astonishing claim given the causal relation obtaining between religion and cultural customs. Wolfe seems oblivious to the fact that, had his view of making a given country the absolute cultural possession of its people—simultaneously absolutizing a "natural right" of ethnic and cultural particularity—been adopted by missionaries to the Anglo-Saxon world, none of us would be Christians today, but would still be drinking the blood of the dead! Nor would William Carey, the remarkable British missionary to India, have worked *against* his host culture to abolish the heinous custom of Sati (burning the living wife on the funeral pyre of her dead husband). In his enthusiasm to preserve the remnants of the Anglo-European Christian culture of America, Wolfe fails to grasp its religious, not ethnic, root, and cuts a re-paganizing America off from the possibility of godly transformation by incoming Christian missionaries from around the world calling the nation to repentance. As Rushdoony powerfully observed, this is a *static* and racial view of a people where priority is given to fallen man and his ethnic heritage rather than to Christ and His Word:

> Providentially, the early missionaries to Europe, coming from North Africa, Asia Minor, and the Mediterranean world generally, had no such regard for the European mind. They regarded it as unregenerate and in need of being broken and redeemed. All the plagues and evils of "the European mind" are products of the fallen man and the relics of barbarian cultures, not of Christ and His Word. All that is good in "the European Mind" is a result of Christian culture, not of race.[49]

---

48. Wolfe, *The Case for Christian Nationalism*, 168.
49. Rushdoony, *An Informed Faith*, 24.

The teaching of the apostle Paul to the church in Corinth constitutes a strong correction to those of any nation or people who wish to glory in their blood and ethnicity, "For who makes you so superior? What do you have that you didn't receive? If, in fact, you did receive it, why do you boast as if you hadn't received it?" (1 Cor. 4:8)

In summing up this chapter's argument, whilst we must insist that cultures, as the public manifestation of the religion of a people, are *not* equal, we dare not fall back into the errors of the medieval church in its synthesis with Greek culture, and argue that theologically and metaphysically *persons* are equally God's image bearers, but here on earth they possess inequalities grounded in *nature* intended by God. Rather, all tribes and nations are to be brought into subjection to Christ and His Word so that in their application of that Word to the totality of life, we worship the Lord together in the beauty of holiness, all the peoples of the earth in their diversity adding to the great chorus of Kingdom unity, glorifying God as His royal priesthood.

# CHAPTER 11

# *Think Christianly About Identity and Sexuality*

*Then God said, "Let Us make man in Our image, according to Our likeness. They will rule the fish of the sea, the birds of the sky, the livestock, all the earth, and the creatures that crawl on the earth." So God created man in his own image; He created him in the image of God; He created them male and female. God blessed them, and God said to them, "Be fruitful, multiply, fill the earth, and subdue it.*
— *Genesis 1:26–28 (HCSB)*

## The Denial of Reality

A PERSON TRULY ROOTED IN BIBLICAL religious commitments and the normative structure of the Christian family has an established identity based in God-created reality and is therefore difficult to manipulate or control. Imposing an abstract ideology designed to remake the world on such a person is nearly impossible. The individual rooted in Christ is not part of an amorphous "public" swayed this way and that by the sophisticated absurdities of elite opinion. The spiritual and moral bond of commitment to the triune God and the social tie of the family provide a stable and vital foundation that must be unequivocally shattered if people are to be seduced into a world of anchorless expressive individualism, licentious sexual gratification and self-definition. In her important work, *The Global Sexual Revolution*, Gabriele Kuby lays out the stakes and implications of our subject for human culture:

> *As sex goes, so goes the family; as the family goes, so goes society....* [I]f this model [lifelong marriage and family] is undermined through constant mass sexualization and a hollowing-out and distorting of the concept of marriage and family, then the foundation on which the culture rests is destroyed.[1]

The undermining of that foundation is now far advanced in our society, having been inculcated in media, education, law and politics. We find ourselves in a surreal world of "trans" ideologies where various people and movements uninterested in the given realities of *human* life are determined to overturn every creational distinction set out in the Word of God, and consequently, the essential fabric of Western culture is being shredded. This is occurring both in relation to real distinctions between men and women, but also with respect to the fundamental distinction between animals and human beings, persons and machines.

A telling article in the Canadian media illustrating this acute crisis recently caught my attention. A female Canadian powerlifter, April Hutchinson, is facing a two-year suspension from her sport by the Canadian Powerlifting Union for voicing concerns that men masquerading as women were dominating and ruining female powerlifting competitions.[2] This fact is

---

1. Gabriele Kuby, *The Global Sexual Revolution: Destruction of Freedom in the Name of Freedom,* trans. James Patrick Kirchner (Kettering, OH: LifeSite, 2015), 40 (italics original), 175.
2. In view here is not whether powerlifting is an appropriate sport for the female frame and the God-ordained nature of women—something which deserves analysis as a separate subject and a theological elaboration—but only the calamity taking place in female sports.

well-documented. Among many such current examples, a Canadian "transgender" athlete who is a biological male has been setting multiple records in the female division, shattering the women's world record by beating his closest female competitor by a massive 441 pounds (200 kilograms).[3] It is one thing for the man concerned to live in his psychological fantasy by seeking entrance into women's athletic divisions (maintaining any degree of self-respect is something else); it is another for professional bodies to take such athletes and records seriously. Hutchinson commented:

> I now face a 2-year ban by the CPU for speaking publicly about the unfairness of biological males being allowed to taunt female competitors and loot their winnings.... Apparently, I have failed in my gender-role duties as "supporting actress" in the horror show that is my sport right now.[4]

The absurdity of this situation would be comic if it weren't for the real lives, careers, and accomplishments being destroyed. A recent book on the Sexual Revolution by a leading young feminist, Louise Perry, who is not a Christian, offers a scathing critique of the irrational denial of inescapable differences between men and women.[5] With respect to the physiological differences, and referring copiously to various scientific studies, she writes:

---

3. Madeline Coggins, "Trans Athlete Sparks Outrage After Toppling Women's Powerlifting World Record: 'Completely Unfair,'" *Fox Business*, https://www.fox-business.com/politics/trans-athlete-sparks-outrage-toppling-womens-powerlifting-world-record-completely-unfair (accessed November 2023).
4. Clare Marie Merkowsky, "Canadian Female Powerlifter Faces Two-Year Suspension for Criticizing Men Competing Against Women," *LifeSite News*, https://www.lifesitenews.com/news/canadian-female-powerlifter-suspension-men-competing/ (accessed November 2023).
5. Feminist writers are increasingly recognizing the destruction of female sports divisions and private spaces as a real threat to women, and yet these writers invariably fail to recognise that feminism itself has fed and nurtured this "queer" dragon by undermining marriage and family and the distinct gender roles and functions taught in scripture which lie at the root of the success of Western civilization.

Adult women are approximately half as strong as adult men in the upper body and two-thirds as strong in the lower body. On average, men can bench press more mass than women can by a factor of roughly two and a half and can punch harder by a similar factor. In hand grip strength, 90 per cent of females produce less force than 95 per cent of males. In other words, almost all women are weaker than almost all men, and any feminist analysis of the power dynamic between men and women has to begin with the recognition of this fact.

And men can out-run women.... At the 2016 summer Olympics, for instance, Elaine Thompson of Jamaica won gold with a time of 10.71 seconds.... [S]he would have been easily out-run by Jamaican boys competing in the under-seventeen category, just as the United States women's national football team in 2017 were beaten by the Dallas under-fifteen boys' team.... The women's category has traditionally been protected in elite sports because, if it were not protected, there would be no women in elite sports.[6]

This conclusion is, for the vast majority of people, a predictable outcome, as equally apparent to common sense as it is to scientific analysis and as uncontroversial as it would have been to people in the Victorian Age. However, some radical feminist ideologues, quickly followed by queer Critical Theorists, have been determined to overturn these creational realities in the abstract world of academia. However, the new academic orthodoxy is now being imposed upon the real world, despite numerous actual women born with female chromosomes and organs, who work in professional sports and strongly oppose it.[7] As anti-Christian worldviews are pushed to this

---

6. Perry, *The Case Against the Sexual Revolution*, 27–28.
7. In a recent victory for sanity, the Supreme Court in the UK ruled that under British law, the terms "man" and "woman," "male" and "female," refer exclusively to *biological sex*. This was the result of years of campaigning, largely by sportswomen. See Sharron Davies, "The Fact We Needed a Court Ruling to Remove Men from Women's Sports Is Nothing Short of Shameful," *MailOnline*, published April 29, 2025, updated April 29, 2025, https://www.dailymail.co.uk/news/article-14660931/SHARRON-DAVIES-fact-needed-court-ruling-remove-men-womens-sport-short-shameful.html (accessed June 17, 2025).

self-conscious and logical extreme, the question taking centre stage is that of creational distinctions, or what we might also refer to as transcendence.

## The Maker's Instructions

The Christian scholar Hans Jurgen Baden in the last century perceived that:

> The coming religious controversy will no longer take place on the basis of the logical *pro* and *contra*, but on a basis which grips man utterly. It will change from the sphere of the word and of words into the sphere of *being and life-form*. The final legitimation of the truth lies in the possibility of its incarnation.[8]

It is hard to overstate the prophetic character of this insight. Baden saw that the central struggle of the future would be over the very nature of being human. In our generation, in the West, the bounds of acceptable speech and action have shifted from the sphere of logical argument for and against biblical faith, to an attempt to redefine reality itself and so incarnate a new word in terms of a reimagined *mode of being* and life-form. In short, we are confronting nothing less than an attempted de-creation followed by self-creation.

In the Scriptures, the foundation for a biblical world and life view is laid in the first chapter of the book of beginnings, which sets forth the crucial distinction between the absolute *Creator* and the *creature*—namely, relative created being. Genesis then addresses the unique nature of the human person, as well as the ineradicable normative distinctions built into creation—darkness and light, land and sea, and plant and animal life as distinct from man himself (Gen. 1). There is no true parallel anywhere in human thought to the creation account found in Genesis, or its Christological deepening in

---

8. Cited in Denzil G. M. Patrick, *Pascal and Kierkegaard: A Study Strategy in Evangelism*, 2 vols. (Cambridge: James Clarke and Co., 1947), 2.395; italics added.

the first chapter of John's Gospel, and without it there is no envisioning the Hebrew commonwealth or the development of Western civilization. We are told in Genesis that the most important thing to know about human beings is that they are *made in the image of God*—that is, our nature as created beings in accountable relation to another—and that we are made *male and female*. Critically, we are taught that this necessary creational structure is life-giving and life-affirming, and has in view a specific cultural task in God's plan for history (Gen. 1:28). It is only within this context that human beings, the *pinnacle* of God's creational theater of wonder, are enabled to flourish and find fulfillment.

Perhaps unsurprisingly, poets have reflected with marvel on the human lords of creation. Shakespeare's Hamlet says:

> What a piece of work is a man! how noble in reason! how infinite in faculty! in form and moving how express and admirable! in action how like an angel! in apprehension how like a god! the beauty of the world! the paragon of animals! And yet, to me, what is this quintessence of dust?

The Psalmist, under the inspiration of the Holy Spirit, likewise marvels at God's image-bearer:

> What is man that You remember him,
> the son of man that You look after him?
> You made him little less than God
> and crowned him with glory and honor.
> You made him lord over the works of Your hands;
> You put everything under His feet:
> all the sheep and oxen,
> as well as the animals in the wild,
> the birds of the sky,
> and the fish of the sea
> that pass through the currents of the seas (Ps. 8:4–8).

The glory, beauty, and dignity of humanity are therefore seen both in our *relatedness* to God and in our *role* in creation to live *coram deo* (before the face of God), performing a task for which we are each accountable. The problem, from a theological standpoint, is the fallenness and pride of man in sin and rebellion against God. Man wills to be his own god, which is a defiant lurch toward death in the attempt to alienate creation from its Maker by overturning its normative structure and vainly seeking to use creaturely freedoms to thwart creation's movement toward total restoration and renewal.

## The Trans*gender* Movement

Inevitably, how a society answers the searching question "Who is man?" determines the direction of that culture and shapes the lives of the individuals within it. The political demolition of sexual norms brought about by the Sexual Revolution was necessarily rooted in the underlying question of the nature of human beings, and the answer was given in atheistic, Freudian, and Marxian terms. With the biblical view discarded as passé, the genie was out of the bottle. As Carl Trueman explains:

> The acceptance of Freud's basic insight, that *sexual desire is constitutive of identity*, and this from infancy onward, is therefore an anthropological, philosophical, and political watershed. To concede this point means that debates about the limits of acceptable sexual expression become almost pointless because any attempt to corral sexual behavior is then rendered an oppressive move designed to make the individual inauthentic.... [A]ny attempts to set limits based on the intrinsic nature of certain sexual acts are ultimately arbitrary and politically motivated.[9]

For neo-Marxists then, sexuality and identity are essentially political matters, because any form of sexual discipline and direction, social or legal

---

9. Carl R. Trueman, *The Rise and Triumph of the Modern Self: Cultural Amnesia, Expressive Individualism and the Road to Sexual Revolution* (Wheaton, IL: Crossway, 2020), 264; italics added.

(unless legislating against the Christian position), is interpreted as *oppression*. As a result, all forms of sexual deviance and perversion demand *liberation* in the form of a psychosexual politics that emerges from various Critical Theories—that is, theories that "liberate" from the allegedly repressive structures of the Christian order.

This is not only a grand emancipation from so-called traditional mores of sexual restraint within the bond of marriage between a man and a woman, but is the far more comprehensive attempt to throw off *every form* of structural limitation on human autonomy:

> Modern and post-modern man have emancipated themselves—from God, from nature, from the family, from tradition—woman from man, children from parents and individuals from themselves as man or woman. They stand naked, restrained by nothing and defined by nothing other than their own wishes, desires and drives. They think they are free to self-actualize, and do not notice that, in their vulnerability and lack of inhibitions, they are more malleable than ever before.[10]

Evidently, this is no longer simply a matter of demanding the social toleration of timeworn promiscuity, or even a matter of making legal space for male homosexuality and lesbianism to be practiced without censure. The new expressive individualism seeks only the chimera of inner psychological well-being by stripping away *all* moral, cultural, and biologically structured norms, to facilitate the emergence of a true *noble savage*. Biology itself, with its gender binary, must be overcome and replaced by a "queer" psychologized idea of sex and gender. In the therapeutic society, sex (your biological reality) is separated from gender (your self-actualizing psychological self) so that either-or (binary) gender norms are effectively eliminated.

For radical theorists like the notorious Judith Butler, who influenced a generation of intellectuals to think this way, your gender is simply *performative*—the way you act like a man or woman—it has no ontological status in creation. There is no created male or female "being" behind the

---

10. Kuby, *The Global Sexual Revolution*, 174.

performative doing, no essential gender *identity* before gender *expressions*.[11] You are not born a man or woman but become such, or neither. The cultural concepts of man and woman, male and female, husband and wife (along with the traditional roles associated with them) are socially fabricated, the fictive creations of language repetition. Marriage is a social construct, a political power play promoted in the interests of white, male, heterosexual capitalists. Changing the "language game" by destroying its normative meaning is therefore the essence of the politics that aims to remake social reality.

The fact is that the concrete reality of being a woman, of menstruation, childbearing, and all that this presupposes in terms of real biological essence is ignored by Butler as a lesbian, who believes that in the abstract private world of her personal psychology, she transcends the categories of male or female. Thus, as Trueman correctly notes, "transgenderism is merely the latest iteration of self-creation that becomes necessary in the wake of decreation."[12]

## The Trans*humanist* Movement

An important connection largely unexplored in this context is the clear relationship between *transgenderism* and *transhumanism*—both of which, as recent developments within Western thinking on selfhood, hold that people can transition and transcend, by their own psychological and technological power, the bounds of our given human nature. For example, the acronym LGBTQQIP2SA refers to people who are Lesbian, Gay, Bisexual, Transgender, Queer, Questioning, Intersex, Pansexual, Two-Spirited, and Asexual. This ever-evolving acronym reflects a farcical refusal to conform to created reality. In my view, transgenderism is actually a form of transhumanism, sharing its basic assumptions. Transgenderism has a degree of cultural acceptability and plausibility today only because of its popular and cultish

---

11. Butler, *Gender Trouble*, 25–26.
12. Trueman, *The Rise and Triumph*, 363.

*de-creation narrative*, in conjunction with the advance of human technique, being facilitated by the *technological ability* to artificially manipulate and impersonate biological realities.

Transhumanism is at root a religious worldview in which man self-consciously seeks to become a god, remaking himself in a new image, placing faith in his own technological capacity as ultimate. Rooted in atheistic materialism, the movement "projects a new phase in evolutionary history on the basis of the use of technology."[13] In a promotional video for a transhumanist Global Future Congress in New York, this new era for humanity is set forth:

> Yet what we need is not just a new technological revolution but a new civilization or paradigm; we need a new philosophy and ideology, new ethics, new culture, new psychology and even a new metaphysics. We must reset our limits and go beyond ourselves, beyond the earth and beyond the solar system.... Thus a new reality and future man will arise.[14]

This is an unmistakable statement of faith or religion with a new divinity concept. As the theologian Paul Tillich noted:

> What in the idea of God constitutes divinity? The answer is: It is the element of the unconditional and of ultimacy. This carries the quality of divinity. If this is seen, one can understand why almost everything "in heaven and on earth" has received ultimacy in the history of human religion.[15]

Leading transhumanist thinker Natasha Vita-More drafted a transhumanist manifesto in 1994 in which she asserts that as our *ideas* and *tools* continue to evolve, so shall we—both in terms of our bodies and values. The goal moves well beyond the *enhancement* of the body and its senses.

---

13. Geertsema, *Homo Respondens*, 319.
14. "2045: A New Era for Humanity" (May 2013), cited in David Herbert, *Becoming God: Transhumanism and the Quest for Cybernetic Immortality* (Ontario: Joshua Press, 2014), 139–40.
15. Paul Tillich, *Dynamics of Faith* (New York: Harper Colophon Books, 1957), 10.

These ideologues seek a world of "diversity and multiplicity" with transhuman rights of "morphological freedom."[16] This is the "freedom" to alter and change the body, in the hope of manipulating the essential nature of human beings.

Transhumanism aims finally at the creation of a *cyborg*—a cybernetically controlled organism where the person no longer merely utilizes, but actually *merges* with, human technology. In science fiction there have been both positive and negative representations of this ideal. In *Star Trek the Motion Picture* (the first Star Trek film in 1979), the story revolves around the discovery of a self-conscious machine that is searching for its creator. It turns out the machine is the twentieth-century earth satellite Voyager which, having gathered knowledge for centuries in terms of its original programing, became self-aware and now wants to find the creator to fulfill its purpose of uploading all that it has learned. The movie ends with one of the main characters literally *merging* with the machine and the birth of a new immortal species.

Although the film is indirectly raising interesting questions about the human search for God—picked up again in Star Trek V, *The Final Frontier*—the vital point of the story is that *man* is the creator, and merging with his own technology man becomes a godlike being, shattering and rising above all established human limitations. The film offers an idealistic picture of a glorious future for humanity, merging with its own creation. Similarly, more recent films like the 2014 movie *Transcendence,* offer an explicitly positive and essentially eschatological transhumanist message, with man's technology portrayed as offering divine transcendence. The lead character, an artificial intelligence scientist, passes away, but his wife uploads his consciousness into a quantum computer and connects it to the Internet.

By contrast, in the later Star Trek film *First Contact* (1996), a subsequent generation with a new Enterprise ship and crew encounters the quintessential embodiment of the cyborg represented by an alien race known as the Borg (the name obviously riffing off cyborg). The Borg are a hive mind with a queen, and there are no true individuals, but the Borg collective

---

16. Natasha Vita-More, cited in Herbert, *Becoming God*, 122.

consciousness is manifested in separate humanoid drones, supposedly superior entities seamlessly combining the organic with the synthetic and connected via carrier waves. Interestingly, given the battle over pronouns and individual identity in our culture, when a distinct humanoid drone unit introduces itself, the pronoun used is the plural "we" rather than "I"—so, "we are Borg." The transcending of the biological norm has actually eliminated the essential individuality of the human being. They forcibly assimilate organic species into their collective, incorporating their biological and technological distinctives with their own in the pursuit of perfection and immortality. Here, although human beings (and other alien humanoid beings) are merged with technology transcending their biological limitations, existence as a cyborg is depicted in nightmarish and dystopian terms where all that is truly human—personal identity, self-determination, creative thought, freedom, and indeed human imperfection—is abolished. This film offers a negative appraisal of transhumanist aspirations.

Today, with rapid and highly publicized developments in artificial intelligence, as well as the notable hysteria surrounding it, metaphysical questions regarding the distinction between the human and the machine are being raised—some even suggesting this vital demarcation is breaking down. However, as Henk Geertsema has pointed out, the machine, no matter how sophisticated, remains a *physical device* designed by humans to perform certain functions. The notion that sophistication, "learning" capacity and processing power eviscerate the boundary between man and his creation, or overcomes the irreducibility of the sensitive, psychical and ethical aspects of reality to the purely physical, is rightly dismissed by Geertsema: "Technological developments in relation to human and machine do not warrant the use of *cyborg* as a symbol for a boundary evasion between them."[17]

The reductionistic *physicalism* involved in the transhumanist view inevitably tries to reduce self-awareness, human choice, emotion, as well as ethical and legal accountability to purely *physical* phenomena—potentially downloadable into another substrate (i.e., a computer of some kind), because

---

17. Geertsema, *Homo Respondens*, 325.

the human organism and machine are considered merely materialistically as information processing devices. The outcome is that the very idea of truly *mental* causation (that cannot be reduced to physics) is destroyed, along with notions of individual personhood and human freedom.

Just as the origin myth of transgenderism must reject the biblical account of male and female creation in God's image as distinct and essential identities, so the cyborg story of transhumanism must not only deny the unique creation of human beings, whose life is more than physics due to animation by the very breath of God (Gen. 2:7), but it must also dispense with any notion of the fall of human beings into sin and ruin and their need to be redeemed and restored. Instead, the new cyborg ontology has its own soteriology and eschatology. Denis Alexander, Director of the Faraday Institute for Science and Religion at Cambridge University, articulates the religious hope of transhumanism:

> The messianic hope in this case is placed in technology that will shape the enhanced, better human, perhaps a new species altogether, the posthuman. And then in the far future lies the hope of immortality when the posthuman will become substrate-independent, delivered from the constraints of flesh and blood *to live on in a digital heaven*.[18]

Combining an allegedly *objective* naturalistic scientific method (destroying freedom) with the *subjective* projection of the inner self (destroying law-order), in both transgenderism and transhumanism we encounter the individual's pretended radical autonomy from God, expressed in its socialistic form, "freedom over against oppression, inclusivity over against exclusion. Cyborg becomes the icon of protest against fixed oppositions."[19] In short, away with the distinction between the divine and human, male and female, man and machine—all such oppositions are oppression!

---

18. Denis Alexander, cited in Herbert, *Becoming God*, 138; italics original.
19. Geertsema, *Homo Respondens*, 351.

Without an original unity and integrity to a given creation-order that has fallen and been disrupted by sin, requiring restoration and redemption, the cyborg concept of remaking human nature by technique becomes a totalizing political myth that seeks to replace the biblical worldview. Human organization, planning, technique, and technology will bring humanity to new birth, manipulate reality to fulfil our desires, and save us from despair, finally delivering us into a digital heaven. The political myth thus becomes a pseudo-messianic cult.

## The Garden of God

Responding faithfully to the *trans* religious mythos requires that we not only analyze its philosophical presuppositions and religious content, but also that we notice with compassionate understanding the inherent desperate struggle to find the self, pointing its captives toward the only true fulfillment of the struggle for identity in Christ Jesus alone. Geertsema has insightfully pointed out: "Our sense of personal identity does not start to develop out of an inner subjectivity, even less out of scientific knowledge; it begins as a *response* to somebody who relates to me as a person."[20]

In the garden of God, Adam and Eve were placed in the immediacy of personal relationship to God and to each other. In the context of this relationship, they were given responsibility to *freely form* creation as the cultural task for which the entire human family is accountable (Gen. 1:26–28; 2:15–17, 21–25). This responsibility and accountability to a personal God who made us for fellowship with Himself is the *essence of life's meaning* and basis of human identity from the Christian standpoint. In the biblical world and life view, the first humans used this freedom to distance themselves from God by seeking to become their own god (Gen 3:5). And so, the Lord God came looking for a *response* from the couple He had created and animated in spiritual relation to Himself, calling out to Adam: "Where art thou?" (Gen. 3:9).

---

20. Geertsema, *Homo Respondens*, 354.

Critically, then, in this fall from right relation to his Creator, man lost, not only the living God, but *himself*. It is noteworthy that, in the grip of shame, this finds initial expression with our first parents trying to cover their *sexual identities*. By human *technique*, in the sewing of fig leaves to cover themselves, they hid from God and from each other (Gen. 3:7–10). From this time on, human beings have wrestled with an identity crisis.

It is clear from Genesis and the rest of Scripture that human sin, alienation, and the subsequent loss of the self, are not simply a predicament of the intellect, but also of the heart and of the will (Prov. 4:23)—it is the problem of *defiance* (Gen. 3:1–6; Matt. 15:18–20; Rom. 8:6–8). The reality of this spiritual apostasy comes to stark and disturbing expression in a poem of the young Karl Marx:

> In a prayer of despair, I will build myself a throne.
> Cold and huge will be its summit,
> Its bulwark will be superhuman horror,
> And its marshal will be gloomy agony.[21]

Because God created human beings as a "relation," the only true and stable *ground* of the self is the Triune God, who, as the infinite personal, is in eternal relation to Himself. To try to find or define the self apart from this relation to God is a form of *despair*. It seeks to transfer to man the freedom and prerogatives of God, and its outcome is only agony and horror. The subjective freedom and independence of the human person that people experience is only a creaturely and relative freedom—which is to say: it is a created freedom, temporal, embodied, and historical. Man never can and never will be God, remaking reality after his own image. Unlike the living God, we are not self-established or self-defining, nor can we create ourselves out of nothing. We are "selves" established by another. It is God alone who declares "I AM WHO I AM" (Exod. 3:14). The only human being who has or

---

21. Karl Marx, "Invocation of One in Despair," *All Poetry*, https://allpoetry.com/Invocation-Of-One-In-Despair (accessed November 2023).

can authentically make this claim is the Lord Jesus Christ who declared, "I assure you: Before Abraham was, I am" (John 8:58).

## Reflecting on Ourselves

To properly understand the basic motive of the trans movements it is important to notice that, as self-conscious beings, we are able to step back from ourselves and reflect on who we are—in this sense, we *relate to ourselves*. As we do, we encounter the self we *are* and have *become*, as well as the self we hope to be and strive to become, the one we *project*. Because as creatures we inescapably relate to ourselves through relation to something other and higher (outside the self), there are ultimately only *two paths* for understanding ourselves: either we accept that we have an identity established by our Creator and so choose to truly be our created selves by living accountably *coram deo*, or we choose to pretend to a radical autonomy and imagine we can establish ourselves by relating to a different criterion. This alternate criterion might be sought in socio-political life, an ideal of the same or opposite sex, a given sexual desire, an abstract principle or human technique; in fact, any number of things may offer an alternate basis for establishing the self. However, because God alone is the true criterion of human identity, the *choice* of an idol, being a false measure of the self, leads only to confusion, despair, and agony.

The existentialist philosopher Jean-Paul Sartre realized that human beings "are a choice, and for us, to be is to choose ourselves."[22] But rather than choosing ourselves as created and intended by our maker, Sartre alleged that human consciousness is an attempt to *become God*—to be totally original and create *de novo*. Admitting this was impossible, he despaired, saying, "Man is a useless passion."[23] Whenever human beings fail to become themselves in

---

22. Jean-Paul Sartre, *The Wisdom of Sartre: A Selection* (New York: Philosophical Library, 1956), 55.
23. Jean-Paul Sartre, *Being and Nothingness*, trans, Hazel E. Barnes (New York: Washington Square, 1992), 754.

relation to the living God, by trying to ground and construct their identity in God-substitutes, ruin is the inevitable result. Scripture identifies the futile attempt to define ourselves and our lives in this way as sin.

## The Nature of Despair

We hear a great deal in our present culture about "authenticity" and "being yourself" or expressing yourself as an individual, and in one sense the Christian can agree that we *must* be ourselves. Indeed, God calls us to become our *unique selves* in terms of His purposes. Even though each person belongs to the human family, the individual is not exhausted by the abstract unity called *humanity*, as though we are each simply one example of a species, like an earthworm or ant. On the contrary, our uniqueness is ordained—as God says to the prophet Jeremiah:

> The word of the Lord came to me:
>
> I chose you before I formed you in the womb;
> I set you apart before you were born.
> I appointed you a prophet to the nations (Jer. 1:4–5).

In a similar fashion the psalmist writes:

> For it was You who created my inward parts;
> You knit me together in my mother's womb.
> I will praise You
> because I have been remarkably and wonderfully made.
> Your works are wonderful,
> and I know this very well....
>
> Your eyes saw me when I was formless;
> all my days were written in Your book and planned
> before a single one of them began (Ps. 139:13, 14, 16).

The Scriptures are crystal clear that each human being is made with a distinctive purpose and plan in mind. The apostle Paul tells us that God the Father is the source "from whom every family in heaven and on earth is named" (Eph. 3:15). We might say that each of us has a *divine* name; God has created and defined our being. This is the *givenness* of the self, the aspect of necessity in all our lives. It is one of the reasons God sometimes *renames* His servants in the Bible in terms of their specific character and calling. Abram becomes Abraham; Sarai becomes Sarah; Jacob becomes Israel; Solomon becomes Jedediah; Simon becomes Peter. It is a reminder that each of us is intended, called forth, wanted, loved, with a specific mission to become and do that for which we were made. Yet, both the prophet Jeremiah and King David, though destined by God from the womb for a purpose, had to *choose* to become themselves—they did not arrive in the world fully actualized as prophet or king. They grew and developed, choosing their course amidst a host of possibilities, and they both sinned and grappled with despair.

Recognizing that sin inevitably leads to despair is important for understanding our culture, and for sharing the truth of the gospel with those in the grip of *trans* ideologies. A helpful guide in this regard is Søren Kierkegaard, who wrote long before *trans* movements ever emerged. He argued that despair is not simply an emotion, but a sinful *condition* a person lives in by refusing to choose to be the person God created them to be—and it manifests itself in a variety of different ways. Each of us has at times lived in despair, because it is the *misrelation* of ourselves to God, to our own being, and to others. In fact, all sin has the character of a misrelation. Human creatures are spiritual beings oriented to our maker, with eternity in our hearts (Eccl. 3:11), and each of us is placed in a particular time, family, and context to fulfil an historical calling. As we have seen, the self is partly a *given*, but is not perfectly or fully *actualized*. We must grow and develop, accountable in the context of God's order, as we confront the daily reality of possibility and choice. It is here in the historical realm of both necessity and possibility that we can flounder.

In his remarkable book, *The Sickness unto Death*, Kierkegaard helps us to understand the specific nature of despair. In particular, what he calls the *despair of defiance*, is helpful for understanding and responding to *trans* ideologies. In this despairing state, a person correctly recognizing that the self is a *task* or calling, wills to be a self, but not the true self they were created to be. Instead, they demand to decide for themselves what and who they are, and who they are to become. This defiance can be the result of being overwhelmed by a sense of *infinite possibility* (a dizziness of freedom), whilst seeking to throw off the real constraints of *finite necessity*. However, as Kierkegaard puts it, "actuality is a *unity* of possibility and necessity."[24] That is, human flourishing requires both possibility and necessity, and where either is denied, we live in the sinful condition of despair. The person in the grip of *necessity* without God-given possibility, for example, becomes fatalistic, deterministic, and so narrow that they lack the will or courage to break out of conformity to the spirit of the world—they never discover who they were made and called to be.

However, of particular relevance to the *trans* movements is the despair of *possibility*. When we lose sight of our created finitude, and the *givenness* of our personhood, our God-given imagination becomes an end in itself, and life starts to be lived through a kind of inner fantasy, leading us away from ourselves. In other words, where we lack a proper sense of created divine necessity, the reality of possibility runs wild and unrestrained. The philosopher Stephen Evans points to the illustration of oxygen in understanding the concept of possibility: "A human person cannot breathe, and thus cannot live, without oxygen, but it is also impossible to breathe pure oxygen. Similarly, the self cannot breathe as spirit without possibility, though it is impossible to live on possibility alone."[25]

Persons claiming to be *transgendered*, in desperately seeking to find the self in an ideal of the opposite sex, or the abstract fiction of gender fluidity, are trying to breathe pure oxygen (i.e., pure possibility), and have become tragically lost in the imagination. Whilst believing they are becoming *more*

---

24. Søren Kierkegaard, *The Sickness unto Death*, in *Kierkegaard's Writings*, vol. 19, ed. and trans. Howard V. Hong and Edna H. Hong (Princeton, NJ: Princeton University Press, 1980), 36; italics added.
25. C. Stephen Evans, *Kierkegaard and Spirituality: Accountability as the Meaning of Human Existence* (Grand Rapids: Eerdmans, 2019, 26.

*real*, by choosing themselves in relation to an idol, they lose contact with the necessary structure of their created self, and so the self actually becomes increasingly *unreal*. The same can be said for the *transhumanist* who, gripped in the imagination by the myth of self-creation, reaches for infinitude and immortality through pure possibility, dreaming of defying all necessity by an apostate use of the gift of free formation—in this case, technology. Both refuse to obey or submit to their created limitations and the necessary conditions of life.[26]

## Becoming Yourself

The situation is one of tragic *parody*. In one sense, unlike many less thoughtful people, those involved in the *trans* movements are sufficiently self-conscious and spiritually aware to understand that human beings have a freedom and responsibility to be and choose themselves. But they do so in open defiance of their Maker, enslaved to a sinful imagination. Kierkegaard prophetically saw that such a person refuses to begin "*at* the beginning," but parodies a godlike absoluteness by seeking to start "*in* the beginning": "the self in despair wants to be master of itself or to create itself, to make his self into the self he wants to be, to determine what he will have or not have in his concrete self."[27]

The tragedy, however, is that all such ephemeral choices are wholly arbitrary because, lacking contact with the God-given self, they have no stability, and can always come apart or be undone, only for the person to try and reinvent themselves all over again. For those whose change of mind is the result of *God's claim* on their true self, like those who wish to de-transition after horrific surgeries conducted in a hopeless attempt to match their bodies with their imagination, they still have to live with the physical damage that has been done. As such, those who promote and propagate *trans*

---

26. Kierkegaard, *The Sickness unto Death*, 36.
27. Kierkegaard, *The Sickness unto Death*, 68.

ideologies occupy a shadowland without borders, without unity, and without law. Total insurrection and rebellion are legitimate at any moment. Thus, the illusion of absolute freedom finally makes for an empty self and empty life.[28] Disillusionment and despair dog the steps of those in this land of illusions.

I called the *trans idea* a tragic parody, a hopeless striving, because we have seen that it entails a creation myth, as well as a narrative that counterfeits the new birth, either by emergence into a new sexual identity, or new species—by a pseudo-spiritual merging with technology. It is a form of spirituality involving "coming out" testimonials of conversion or confessions of faith in the divinity of man. But it is a *demonic* form of religious life because of its self-conscious rebellion.

However, when God, by His Spirit, reveals Himself to the individual in the absolute Person, Jesus Christ, the despair of defiance is exposed for the dreadful sin it is, and the only possible *resolution* to our radical brokenness is brought to light in a genuine *recreation*. This is possible only through repentance and faith in the atoning death and resurrection life of the eternal Son, who made us for relationship with Himself. It requires the surrender of our illusions, the throwing down of our arms, and trading defiance for devotion. The Lord Jesus grants new creation, new life, and new birth, to those who come to Him, abolishing death, and bringing life and immortality to light, satisfying all our infinite longings (2 Tim. 1:10). He alone offers true rest for the self, by bringing to an end the wearisome struggle for our identity. The Savior's gentle yoke of *necessity* makes sense of our human *possibility*: "Come to Me, all of you who are weary and burdened, and I will give you *rest*. All of you, take up My yoke and learn from Me, because I am gentle and humble in heart, and you will find rest for *yourselves*. For My yoke is easy and My burden is light" (Matt. 11:28–30).

It is in the Son of God, the Son of man, our creator *and* brother, that we discover who we truly are, and through whom we are finally liberated to be

---

28. See Evans, *Kierkegaard*, 38.

and to choose ourselves. In the words of C. S. Lewis, "It will never be lawful simply to 'be ourselves' until 'ourselves' have become sons of God."[29]

---

29. C. S. Lewis, *God in the Dock: Essays on Theology and Ethics,* ed. Walter Hooper (Grand Rapids, MI: Eerdmans, 1972), 286.

CHAPTER 12

# Think Christianly About Life

*Before I formed you in the womb I knew you,
and before you were born I consecrated you.*
— *Jeremiah 1:5 (NRSV)*

## Life and Revolution

WHILE THE WORLDVIEW THAT PROMOTES abortion is an ancient one, the flashpoint of the modern Western abortion movement is the Sexual Revolution of the 1960s. This ideological revolution set out to change *culture* in toto, rather than just political life, and deemed the Christian sexual ethic that had formed and shaped Western society as "retrogressive and stifling and the enemy of The

Good Life."[1] Its goal was to undermine the norm of sexual union and pleasure within the sanctity of the marriage relationship, and to reduce sex to a libidinous form of individual recreation—that is, an end in itself—wholly disconnected from God, commitment, family, and childrearing. Pharmaceutical birth control was seen as key to advancing this agenda and so-called "abortion rights" were thought to provide the ultimate fail-safe. As a result, almost every form of adult consensual sex was gradually normalized and legalized, from fornication to adultery and sodomy.[2]

The so-called "pro-choice" position, brought into the mainstream of culture by this lascivious revolution, has had terrible, dehumanizing effects on women, children, fathers, and families, not to mention a devastating impact on Western demography. It has led what we once called Christendom into the pornification of culture and a regard for women, in particular, as essentially sexual objects, rather than as persons whose sexual being is fulfilled in a monogamous, complementary relationship to their gender-opposite—a covenant relationship of duties and responsibilities, which include those toward the unborn child.[3]

As a result of the Sexual Revolution and the changing social attitude to sexuality and family, our age is facing a fertility crisis because we are producing fewer and fewer children—an ideal promoted on every side, since children are increasingly seen as a drag on individual mobility, freedom, prosperity and independence. The murder of unborn children has contributed significantly to these declining birth rates. As an aspect of the deep hostility amongst cultural elites toward the Christian view of the family, a culture of death has been growing up around us. Aside from some important

---

1. P. Andrew Sandlin, "Are Christian Sexual Ethics Outdated?" *Ezra Institute*, last modified July 3, 2013, https://www.ezrainstitute.com/are-christian-sexual-ethics-outdated/.
2. P. Andrew Sandlin, *The Christian Sexual Worldview: God's Order in an Age of Sexual Chaos* (Coulterville, CA: Center for Cultural Leadership, 2015), 20.
3. It is telling that the Playboy Foundation was from the very beginning an advocate of abortion rights. Cf. Carrie Pitzulo, "The Battle in Every Man's Bed: Playboy and the Fiery Feminists," *Journal of the History of Sexuality* 17, no. 2 (2008): 259–89, available at https://doi.org/10.1353/sex.0.0004, 259–89.

exceptions in the United States, most Western politicians still steadfastly refuse even to open up debate around the moral issue of abortion, while our courts continue to imprison people engaging in peaceful Christian prayer and witness near the many abortion clinics.

Ominously, many elites think the revolution hasn't gone far enough. Leading medical intellectuals and "experts" writing in the *Journal of Medical Ethics* are calling for the legitimization of "afterbirth abortion" (i.e., infanticide), for the same reasons someone would have an abortion now, declaring that the newborn infant is only a "potential person," without a moral right to life.[4] The British Medical Association has advised doctors that there may be grounds for abortion solely on the basis of the sex of the baby. A recent investigative journalistic operation found that sex-selective abortion (i.e., the abortion of baby girls) was prevalent, even though it remains against the law. Subsequent inspections of clinics in the UK found that the illegal pre-signing of abortion forms by doctors, without any contact with the woman seeking to acquire an abortion, as well as the photocopying of doctors' signatures to pre-approve abortions, was widespread.4 In Canada, there is no law restricting abortion at all. Abortion is available on demand up to term, with infanticide being tacitly practiced already, as late-term aborted babies are left to die and thrown in the garbage like soiled garments.

Despite the incalculable deleterious effects of destroying unborn children in any society, this bizarre death-wish is propagated in one cultural message after another. In media, film, and educational materials, we are perpetually told that human beings are infesting the planet, destroying "Mother Nature," and using up her resources. The result has been proposals and policies promoting zero population growth, zero industrial growth, net zero, and personal carbon footprint reduction through any and all means, including abortion, as practical political orthodoxy. Alongside this, the children in government schools are taught that sex is primarily for the purpose of recreation with anyone, not procreation with one's married spouse; the

---

4. Stephen Adams, "Killing Babies No Different from Abortion, Experts Say," *Daily Telegraph*, http://www.telegraph.co.uk/health/healthnews/9113394/Killing-babies-no-different-from-abortion, accessed April 29, 2013.

killing of unborn babies is a mother's right; euthanizing the very sick and the elderly is compassionate; and governmental social engineering, not God, governs our lives.

## Precious Thoughts

Into this contemporary chaos and hatred of life speaks the Lord and author of life in the sublime Psalm 139, through David's marvelous prayer:

> Lord, You have searched me and known me.
> You know when I sit down and when I stand up;
> You understand my thoughts from far away.
> You observe my travels and my rest;
> You are aware of all my ways.
> Before a word is on my tongue,
> You know all about it, Lord.
> You have encircled me;
> You have placed Your hand on me.
> This extraordinary knowledge is beyond me.
> It is lofty; I am unable to reach it.
>
> Where can I go to escape Your Spirit?
> Where can I flee from Your presence?
> If I go up to heaven, You are there;
> if I make my bed in Sheol, You are there.
> If I live at the eastern horizon
> or settle at the western limits,
> even there Your hand will lead me;
> Your right hand will hold on to me.
> If I say, "Surely the darkness will hide me,
> and the light around me will be night" —
> even the darkness is not dark to You.

The night shines like the day;
darkness and light are alike to You.

For it was You who created my inward parts;
You knit me together in my mother's womb.
I will praise You
because I have been remarkably and wonderfully made.
Your works are wonderful,
and I know this very well.
My bones were not hidden from You
when I was made in secret,
when I was formed in the depths of the earth.
Your eyes saw me when I was formless;
all my days were written in Your book and planned
before a single one of them began.

God, how difficult Your thoughts are
for me to comprehend; how vast their sum is!
If I counted them, they
would outnumber the grains of sand;
when I wake up, I am still with You.

God, if only You would kill the wicked—
you bloodthirsty men, stay away from me —
who invoke You deceitfully.
Your enemies swear by You falsely.
Lord, don't I hate those who hate You,
and detest those who rebel against You?
I hate them with extreme hatred;
I consider them my enemies.

Search me, God, and know my heart;
test me and know my concerns.

See if there is any offensive way in me;
lead me in the everlasting way.

This well-known psalm is a personal petition to know and to be led by the infinite and yet personal God, though surrounded by the wickedness of ungodly people. The psalm celebrates God's intimate omniscience, His omnipotence, His omni-competence in all human affairs (otherwise known as providence), and His mercy and wonderful judgments. This is the triune God of Scripture who knows all men, their aims, purposes, and desires, a God from whom nothing is hidden, and yet who enters into covenant relationship with His people using His personal name, I AM. This almighty Lord of hosts tests and searches the heart as creator-God and King, and in particular confronts humanity with His absolute sovereignty, providence, and predestinating grace from womb to tomb.

## The Intimate Providence of God

The first verse of Psalm 139 reads literally, "I AM, you searched me and you know me." The covenant God searches the depths of our being. He knows a man better than he knows himself. We see in verses 2–4 the comprehensive extent and exhaustive character of that knowledge. This kind of intimate, all-encompassing knowledge is beyond our human ability to fully grasp; it is high and impregnable to our limited understanding, a wonder and mystery which humbles us, and calls us to bow before it (v. 6).

David reminds the reader that there is nowhere we can flee from the all-seeing omniscience of God—it hems us in (v. 5). There is no hiding place from the presence of the divine gaze, neither in the heavens nor in the tomb can we escape His intimate knowledge and sovereignty (vv. 7–9). To the believer, this is a great comfort and joy, but to the enemies of God, it is an intolerable terror and an insult to their self-professed autonomy. Man's inability to escape the living God at any point or in any place is dramatically set forth in verse 8, which literally reads, "If I spread out my bed in the grave, behold, you are there!" As John Calvin wrote about verse 5, we "cannot move a hair's breadth without his knowledge."⁵ King David is not frightened by this thought, and neither are all those who love the Lord. Søren Kierkegaard's prayer is apropos: "Father in Heaven! When the thought of Thee wakes in our hearts, let it not awaken like a frightened bird that flies about in dismay, but like a child waking from its sleep with a heavenly smile."⁶

The reality of God's Fatherly presence and motherly proximity is wondrous and important, but there is yet more to marvel at in this psalm. It is not simply that God *knows all things*; He is *involved*. He lays His hand upon His covenant people—each one individually (v. 5). This is a hand of care and protection, as well as of discipline and correction. For God to lay a hand upon someone represents His full and total authority over them in a profoundly personal way. As a parent, when I laid my hand upon my children as they were growing up, I did so sometimes to protect or carry them, sometimes to restrain or discipline them, but always to demonstrate my authority as their father. This is why grabbing or restraining someone whom we have no right to control can be construed as assault; it is an illegitimate exercise of authority.

Sometimes the biblical writers, like Job, call upon God to *remove* His hand of discipline or judgment in the midst of His mysterious working, and yet how grateful believers ought to be for the sovereign hand of God, even when it seems heavy upon them (cf. Job 6:9, 13:21). Were it not for the forceful hand of God whose authority and jurisdiction are total, Abraham's nephew Lot would have remained in Sodom on the eve of its destruction. Yet, by grace, when Lot lingered, the angels grabbed him by the hand and led him out to safety (Gen. 19:1–38). If it were up to man in his ruined condition, he would cradle and nurse his sins, looking back longingly to the rebel city and so persist with a stony and defiant heart in insurrection against God. But through Christ, God calls all peoples out of darkness into His marvelous

---

5. John Calvin, *Commentary on Psalms*, trans. James Anderson, vol. 5 (Grand Rapids, MI: Christian Classics Ethereal Library, 1849), 191, http://www.ccel.org/ccel/calvin/calcom12.pdf, accessed October 7, 2013, ad loc.
6. Søren Kierkegaard, *The Prayers of Kierkegaard*, ed. Perry D. Lefevre (Chicago: University of Chicago Press, 1956), 48.

light, raising those who come to him from spiritual death to life and transposing them from the kingdom of darkness to the kingdom of light.

Sometimes, God's hand is also upon us as He cares for and comforts us. It is an immeasurable mercy to know the consoling and reassuring hand of God in all things. This ever-present, all-knowing, and all-pervasive reality is the personal *presence* of the Holy Spirit. This reality is so overwhelming to contemplate, that sometimes even Christians are tempted to run away and hide in the shadows from their ever-present God. But King David declares that "even the darkness is not dark to you; the night is bright as the day, for darkness is as light with you" (v. 12).

## God's Studio

Nowhere is this mysterious, all-conditioning providence more dramatically illustrated than in the marvel that is human conception and gestation. At the center of this great prayer of Psalm 139 is one of the most beautiful and important declarations in the Psalms, emphatically revealing the total sanctity of life as God's precious gift (vv. 13–16).

So remarkable are these things that David declares, "God, how difficult Your thoughts are for me to comprehend; how vast their sum is!" God's total providence and sovereignty are not seen simply in His pervasive presence and exhaustive knowledge of our activities; they are manifest in His artisanship, His personal creativity and foreordination within our lives, from conception to our last breath. Here therefore, creation and predestination (that is, God's calling) are seen to be entirely and intimately involved with each other.

The womb itself is God's *studio*, poetically described as "the depths of the earth," a place totally hidden (v. 15). From conception through gestation, "it was You who created my inward parts; You knit me together in my mother's womb. I will praise You because I have been remarkably and wonderfully made." (Ps. 139:13–14). The psalm thus reveals that each person was or is personally crafted, ordained, shaped by God's benevolent will and design, called into being for the purposes of God; all of which manifests the inscrutable kindness, goodness and love of God.

In verse 16 we have a critical statement in relation to our subject of the sanctity of human life. The Hebrew text literally reads, "My embryo [Heb. *golmi*] your eyes saw." This unique phrase refers to an incomplete vessel; the life is young and undeveloped. The rest of the verse goes on to strikingly relate the active creation of the human embryo in terms of God's wholly personal predestination, expressed in the totality of the life of His beloved creatures. The sovereign Lord has established and appointed our days and our steps: "in your book were written every one of them, the days formed for me, *when as yet there was none of them*" (v. 16). As if to reinforce this mysterious truth, the word "formed" carries the sense of the development of a plan prior to its enactment. God is not just counting a person's days in His secret work, He is *forming* the person's future before their heart begins to beat, giving meaning to every moment in terms of His eternal decree. Every person is therefore fashioned in terms of God's wonderful and excellent purposes. Both the Old and New Testaments provide specific examples of this prodigious wonder. Consider Jeremiah 1:5: "Before I formed you in the womb I knew you, and before you were born I consecrated you"; and St. Paul in Galatians 1:15–16: "He who had set me apart before I was born, and who called me by His grace, was pleased to reveal His son to me."

## God's Judgment on the Wicked

Following these powerful statements about the all-conditioning providence and loving care of God from conception to the grave, King David calls on God to *judge* the wicked. David hands his life over to God as one formed for the purpose of doing battle against wickedness. The wicked men of blood come under the censure of God and David for their lawlessness. These lawless deeds include murder (v. 19), a violation of the Sixth Commandment, and blasphemy (v. 20), a violation of the Third Commandment. Verse twenty makes clear that there is premeditation and forethought involved in their scheming against God. Remarkably, some of these murderers use the name of God as though He were supportive of their evil deeds and plans. This demonstrates and reminds us that apostate churchmen are involved in blasphemy whenever they endorse or support what God condemns.

In verses frequently passed over in both the reading and consideration of this psalm, David declares *his* hatred of those who, in their murderous lawlessness, hate *God* (v. 21). This reflects God's own detesting of the wicked seen in Psalm 5:4–6: "For you are not a God who delights in wickedness; evil may not dwell with you. The boastful shall not stand before your eyes; you hate all evildoers. You destroy those who speak lies; the Lord abhors the bloodthirsty and deceitful man."

Linguistically, the term "hate" here means the strongest possible aversion to lawless works and an abhorrence of the people who delight in them. David thus declares that he loathes those who in this way rebel, oppose, and rise up against God. John Calvin correctly noted in his comment on verse 21: "Our attachment to godliness must be inwardly defective if it does not generate an abhorrence of sin."[7]

We should not read into this text a childish, vindictive, self-centered motive, or a merely emotional understanding of David's divinely inspired words. He is highlighting a real spiritual battle between truth and falsehood, God and Satan, light and darkness, in which good and evil, life and death are very literally at stake—in this conflict there is no middle ground, no irenic third way. We are for or against the Lord. And King David's words are not unloving. According to the Scriptures, love is the fulfillment of the law (Rom. 13:8–10). Jesus' commandment to love our enemies should not be read as an impossible task of stirring up warm emotional feelings and connections to those people who oppose the Lord, but rather requires that we obey God's law concerning them (Matt. 5:44). We do not steal from them or bear false witness against them, for example. Moreover, we obey the Lord's command to make known to them the gospel of Jesus Christ which calls them to repentance (Matt. 28:18–20). As law-abiding people, lawlessness must be a horror to us, or we cannot be a people of love. In this sense, then, to abhor the *wicked*

---

7. Calvin, *Commentary on the Psalms*, ad loc.

(not just lawlessness in the abstract) is an aspect of love toward God, because love fears God and obeys His law.

Scripture requires the Christian to maintain an abhorrence of evil and the strongest possible censure of those who hate and blaspheme God in their murderous ways. To approve of such people and their works is to participate in their evil. In Luke 14:26, Jesus said that if a person does not "hate his own father and mother and wife and children, brothers and sisters and yes, even his own life, he cannot be my disciple." Obviously, by this, He did not mean a person should cultivate an *emotion* of hatred toward one's own family. Rather, Jesus taught that anything that comes before God in our lives, even familial relationships, is a form of idolatry. To fail to have the strongest possible aversion to the evil man in terms of God's law is to put sentimentality before what God requires, which is likewise a form of idolatry.

## Despoiling the Masterpiece—Killing the Future

Given that the womb is the master craftsman's studio for sculpting the future, now that we have considered this *mercy* of God (the womb), and His providential care in the creation of the human embryo, we can begin to fully appreciate the evil of abortion. One of the tragic ironies of abortion is that it constitutes murder *in the life of the family*, so that the first cradle of life is turned into a chamber of death. Considering the Bible's clear teaching, the wickedness of abortion should be obvious to all true Christians—but surveys show that many who claim to be Christians (though evangelicals are holding up relatively well here) are confused or downright unscriptural on abortion.[8] The influence of secularism and pagan religions is creating syncretistic people in the West whose moral compass is broken. In America

---

8. See, for example, "America's Abortion Quandary," *Pew Research Center*, May 6, 2022, https://www.pewresearch.org/religion/2022/05/06/americas-abortion-quandary/#:~:text=Among%20religious%20groups%20analyzed%20in%20the%20survey%2C,should%20be%20illegal%20in%20most%20cases%20(53%), accessed June 11, 2025.

today, only four out of every ten adults (39%) share the biblical view that life is sacred. And sadly, despite some visible and effective pro-life activists amongst the millennial generation, studies show that not only are they the generation *least likely* to believe life is sacred, they are the age group *most likely* to claim the Bible is ambiguous about abortion and that human life has no inherent value. They are also the generation least likely, since polling began, to have an interest in having children.[9] The silence on this issue in the church is too often deafening (unless it is a voice *for* abortion, as a recent survey of *United Church Observer* readers found), because to address the subject is seen as "political," and politics, people are often told, should not mix with the pulpit—though leftist progressive politics has found a comfortable platform precisely there for decades.[10] Nevertheless, the true church has long viewed the destruction of the human embryo as murder according to biblical standards. The grounds for this are seen clearly in the Sixth Commandment ("you shall not murder") and in Exodus 21:22–25:

> When men get in a fight and hit a pregnant woman so that her children are born prematurely but there is no injury, the one who hit her must be fined as the woman's husband demands from him, and he must pay according to judicial assessment. If there is an injury, then you must give life for life, eye for eye, tooth for tooth, hand for hand, foot for foot, burn for burn, bruise for bruise, wound for wound.

This case law sets out, by a minimal illustration, certain applications and implications of the Sixth Commandment. First, the specific case here involves an *accidental* abortion. If the penalty for causing an abortion, not by premeditated violence but by criminal negligence, is so severe, it is obvious

---

9. See George Barna, *American Worldview Inventory 2021–22: The Annual Report on the State of Worldview in the United States* (Glendale, AZ: Arizona Christian University, 2022), 102–103.
10. Cf. Patrick Craine, "Poll: United Church Members Significantly More Liberal than Canadian Public on Abortion, Euthanasia," *LifeSite News*, http://www.lifesitenews.com/news/pollunited-church-members-more-liberal-than-canadian-public-onabortion-eu, accessed July 12, 2012.

that an abortion deliberately induced is strongly forbidden. We see from this text that abortion carried with it the maximum sentence of death and is therefore considered in God's law to be *murder*. Even if mother and child were not injured in the incident mentioned in Exodus 21, the negligent man must still be fined. In other words, God's law sets a hedge of protection, second to none, around a pregnant woman and her embryo. In Scripture, even a mother bird with eggs or already-hatched young is protected by God's law, to prevent the exploitation of God's creation (Deut. 22:6); if birds are to be protected, how much more expectant mothers with their unborn child!

The challenge we face today—since the late 1960s—in applying God's law to the matter of abortion is not new. The early church had to confront the widespread reality of abortion in the Greco-Roman world. The Greek philosophers often advocated both abortion and infanticide whenever these were perceived to be in the interests of the pagan state. Plato's *Republic* argues that the state is the ultimate order and functional god and can order abortion, infanticide, and incest as it sees fit.[11] Aristotle's ideal society required abortions when state-permitted births were exceeded.[12] Furthermore, in Roman law, abortion and infanticide were not essentially distinguished. Infants did not actually have legal status until the head of the family, the "*pater familias*," accepted the child into the family. Until that acceptance was extended, an infant could be destroyed.[13]

In contradistinction to so much of the modern church infected with radical feminism—an ideology that sees biblical norms for men and women as oppression, being a wife and mother as a form of servitude, and the destruction of children in the womb simply a matter of "rights" over one's own body—the early church quickly and unequivocally condemned abortion. Tertullian wrote: "To hinder a birth is merely a speedier man-killing; nor

---

11. Plato, *Republic*, trans. Allan Bloom (New York, NY: Basic Books, 1968), Book VIII, 546a–547a.
12. Michael J. Gorman, *Abortion and the Early Church: Christian, Jewish and Pagan Attitudes in the Greco-Roman World* (Downers Grove, IL: InterVarsity Press, 1982), 20–25.
13. Allen Mason Ward, Fritz M. Heichelheim, and Cedric A. Yeo, *A History of the Roman People* (Englewood Cliffs, NJ: Prentice Hall, 1983), 35–38.

does it matter whether you take away a life that is born, or destroy one that is coming to birth. That is a man which is going to be one; you have the fruit already in its seed."[14] The early Apostolic Constitutions likewise call for vengeance upon those who destroy the unborn child. So serious was this to the church that, because the Roman Empire did not see abortion as a crime in the way the Bible does, many church communities pronounced their own ecclesiastical sentence of "penance for life," to indicate the capital nature of the offense. The Council of Ancyra in AD 314 noted this earlier practice and limited the restitution period to ten years.[15] Among the pagans, by contrast, Tacitus, the Roman historian and senator, found it repugnant that the Jews *would not* kill babies.

In many countries today, abortion is not only legal but seen as a basic human right, being demanded in the name of spurious euphemisms like "reproductive healthcare." As biblical faith has declined in the West, abortions have correspondingly increased. In the United Kingdom, although the procurement of an abortion remains, in a technical sense, a criminal offense (Offenses Against the Person Act of 1861), ever since abortion was made available under certain conditions in 1967 by the Abortion Act, we have taken the lives of ten million people in the womb. This has usually been carried out, prior to 24 weeks gestation, under the lying pretense that having the baby risks injury to the physical or mental health of the pregnant woman. It has effectively meant a blank check for abortion on demand, since this is the reason cited in 98% of cases.[16] In Canada today, abortion is sponsored and funded by the so-called "Ministry of Health" (Orwellian speak for what is increasingly a ministry of death to young and old), and as already noted,

---

14. Tertullian, *Apologia* 9.6, available at http://www.ccel.org/ccel/schaff/anf03.iv.iii.ix.html, accessed October 7, 2013.
15. Council of Ancyra, Canon 21, in *Nicene and Post-Nicene Fathers*, 2nd series, vol. 14, ed. Philip Schaff and Henry Wace, trans. Henry Percival, rev. Kevin Knight (Buffalo, NY: Christian Literature Publishing Co., 1900), http://www.newadvent.org/fathers/3802.htm.
16. "Abortion in the United Kingdom," *Wikipedia*, https://en.wikipedia.org/wiki/Abortion_in_the_United_Kingdom#:~:text=Although%20a%20number%20of%20abortions,abortions%20in%20the%20United%20Kingdom, accessed June 2024.

is permissible all the way to full-term.[17] American research shows that the reasons most often cited for an abortion are people claiming they are "not ready for the responsibility," or have "inadequate finances." Only 1% involve rape.[18] Other common motivations for having an abortion found in various studies include the preservation of beauty; the continued enjoyment of freedom and irresponsibility; a hatred of life; a hatred of men; and the alleged imperfection of a fetus. Concerning the ostensible imperfection of a fetus argument, two American doctors, writing back in the 1960s, rightly noted:

> No human being is perfect. Would the world, moreover, really be a better place after the destruction of the millions of defective individuals? Has the world gained or lost from the services of the epileptic Michelangelo, of the deaf Edison, of the hunchback Steinmetz, of the Roosevelts—both the asthmatic Theodore and the polio-paralyzed Franklin? It must be recognized that liberalized abortion laws would logically be followed by pressures for legalized euthanasia. The attack on life is essentially the same.[19]

This juridical assault on life began with the abolition of laws against abortion, and the fight is escalating and expanding. Some years ago, in the UK's *Daily Mail Online*, an article was published about the National Health Service (the UK's socialized system of healthcare), regarding the case of a doctor who had blown the whistle on the NHS allegedly euthanizing 130,000 elderly patients every year because "they are difficult to manage or to free up beds."[20] There is now mounting pressure on the UK parliament to fully

---

17. In 2015 (the most recent statistic available). there were 100,104 registered abortions that our taxes paid for. "Statistics: Abortion in Canada," *Abortion Rights Coalition of Canada*, http://www.arcc-cdac.ca/backrounders/statistics-abortion-in-canada.pdf, accessed April 5, 2017.
18. "Abortion Statistics," *Orlando Women's Center*, http://www.womenscenter.com/abortion_stats.html, accessed November 5, 2013.
19. A. C. Mietus and Norbert J. Mietus, "Criminal Abortion: 'A Failure of Law' or a Challenge to Society?" *American Bar Association Journal* 51, no. 10 (October 1965): 924–28, 926.
20. Steve Doughty, "Top Doctor's Chilling Claim: The NHS Kills Off 130,000 Elderly Patients Every Year," *Daily Mail Online*, June 19, 2012, http://www.dailymail.co.uk/

decriminalize abortion (the activists want this available up to term) *and* to decriminalize euthanasia. Euthanasia (euphemistically called MAID: Medical Assistance in Dying) has been legal in Canada since 2016. The number of people killed by the state in the name of MAID has skyrocketed in an alarming and unprecedented manner in Canada since it was first introduced.[21] Canada has gone from legalizing abortion to a legalization and mass-expansion of euthanasia in fewer than fifty years. From a worldview standpoint, the logical and juridical link between abortion and euthanasia establishes the reality that the generation which kills its children will be killed by its children.

These overt attacks on life, as well as being motivated by rampant self-centered individualism, are a modern form of eugenics—the attempt to direct a supposed evolutionary process by controlling who reproduces and who is born. Hitler's sterilization laws and eugenics programs were actually first modeled in the United States by the work and legislative preparation of American evolutionary biologist Dr. Harry Laughlin. The founder of the modern pro-abortion, birth control movement, (and Planned Parenthood) was the racist eugenicist, Margaret Sanger (1879–1966). She was a white supremacist, and even addressed a meeting of the *Ku Klux Klan*. She argued that "the brains of Australian Aborigines were only one step more evolved than chimpanzees and just under blacks, Jews, and Italians."[22] Her early clinics were initially strategically located to control the births of Slavs, Latins, and Jews. She later targeted African American communities.[23] Planned Parenthood itself reported that of the 132,314 abortions it performed in 1991

---

news/article-2161869/Top-doctors-chilling-claim-The-NHS-kills-130-000-elderly-patients-year.html.

21. Leyland Cecco, "Canada's Assisted Dying Laws in Spotlight as Expansion Paused Again," *The Guardian*, February 25, 2024, https://www.theguardian.com/world/2024/feb/25/canada-assisted-dying-laws-in-spotlight-as-expansion-paused-again, accessed June 2024.
22. Wieland, *One Human Family*, 65.
23. H. A. Washington, *Medical Apartheid: The Dark History of Medical Experimentation on Black Americans from Colonial Times to the Present* (New York: Doubleday, 2006), 196.

in the USA, 42.7% involved African Americans and other minorities, even though they constitute only 19.7% of the population.[24]

## Choose Life

It should be clear to every Christian that great spiritual evil is at work in the destruction of the life of the most helpless and innocent of all human beings. There is something profoundly malevolent in this wanton killing, a love of death fundamental to sinful man's spiritual condition. This orientation toward death, the Bible tells us, marks men and cultures that are in rebellion against God—which is to say, by their hostility to God they become suicidal in their inclinations (Prov. 8:36). Scripture tells us there is a dreadful linkage between sin and death. Spiritual separation from the source of life in Jesus Christ means a growing tendency toward death in every respect, because Christ alone is the resurrection and the life and the light that leads to life (John 8:12; 11:25). His atonement, resurrection, and total Lordship alone break the chains that bind, by separating us from the power of sin and death, consecrating us to life and righteousness—for in Christ the power of death is broken (1 Cor. 15).

In the pagan Greco-Roman world, into which this gospel was first declared, the great entertainment for the masses was death, paraded as games. Whether gladiators were fighting to the death or Christians were being tossed to lions to be torn apart before a gleeful mob, death was a spectator sport. As the gladiators entered the arena they cried, "Hail Caesar. We who are about to die salute you." The Christian faith in the Lord of life eventually brought an end to the blood-letting and human sacrifices of the arena.

Not unlike the claims of the Caesars of the ancient Roman world, or the pagan ideals of the Greek philosophers, life and law today are being redefined in terms of whatever a statist elite says they are; life has value and is worth living only when the humanistic state says so. The state has again

---

24. Wieland, *One Human Family*, 65.

sought to make itself the ultimate order. As a consequence, abortion is seen as simply a matter of politics, either unrelated to or above the law of God. The promotion and practice of abortion is thus, at root, a return to paganism and to a fundamental denial of the truth of the Word of God and teaching of Psalm 139. The psalmist asserts the total authority of the plans and purposes of God; in a retrogressive contrast to this in our day, the control of life by human agencies is the alternate plan of predestination *of man, by man*.

If in our thinking we deny sovereign and predestinating power to God, we simply transfer that power to man and to the state (which is simply man on a larger scale). Whenever belief in God's predestination declines, faith in the planning or predestination of the state over life and death rapidly takes its place. Abortion expresses this extraordinary usurpation. It is a fatuous attempt to play God par-excellence—to govern, to grant, and to take life on man's own terms without reference to the living God or His Word. It is supremely ironic that the modern pagan State is against capital punishment for lawless murderers (actual evildoers) where God requires it, but will exercise capital punishment against innocent unborn children whom God's law protects. If man can play God and write his own ad hoc law to suit his desires, questions of life and death become open questions to be decided by the so-called "democratic will," embodied by State planners and legislatures.

Under God, the ministry of the doctor is meant to be a ministry of life and healing; under humanistic man-gods, doctors are increasingly required to become murderers of babies and the elderly. Womb and tomb are claimed by the all-powerful State. And yet all this is done along with the blasphemous claim that the modern secular State reverences and affirms life and liberty. The reality, however, is that human worth, dignity, and life are no longer affirmed or protected on the grounds that all human beings bear God's image; rather, the weak are murdered by the strong in the name of another person's right to choose. The psalmist makes abundantly clear that judgment looms over such an age and culture dominated by "men of blood" (v. 19), where God's name is mocked and blasphemed.

## Abstracting Evil

The reason even many Christians find passages of Scripture like Psalm 139 difficult in our day is because numerous believers have unwittingly adopted the Aristotelian and humanistic notion of a clear division between intention and action, thereby depersonalizing sin by abstracting a man's *actions* from his true moral *nature*. Because the life of man, and the human history that emerges due to man's actions, undeniably manifest real evil, only by resorting to pagan dualistic assumptions, erecting an artificial division between intent (spirit) and act (matter), can humanistic thinking retain the notion of a natural goodness or moral neutrality within man, over against the biblical doctrine of a fallen and sinful nature in all human beings, revealed by their deeds. This means that, as we see in Gnosticism, the spirit or mind can supposedly remain pure, while the material and historical environment is thought to be impure, by nature inferior because of its dependence on the physical world. This being the case, many pagans thought that what a person does in the body does not define their true moral character. People may say of a criminal, "Yes, he is a murderer (or rapist, or pornographer, or paedophile), but in his heart he's a good chap with good intentions." This sharp and artificial separation of moral nature from moral action seeks to preserve an anti-biblical view of man. It results in a denial of real responsibility whereby intent (or character) and act are divorced from one another, rather than being seen as involved in each other. Works of evil can then be seen, not as an expression of man's sinful and lawless heart, but as a form of strange social sickness produced by the person's environment, upbringing, or defective education.

Scripture makes clear, however, that sin does not have abstract, objective existence; rather, sin is lawlessness and therefore both sin and righteousness are essential moral qualities *of a man* (1 John 3:4), affecting all aspects of his life. Sin is something *a person thinks and does*. Murder and adultery have no existence apart from the person who commits them. Crimes do not happen without a criminal—there is no sin without a sinner. Sin is not an abstract *idea* but an expression of a sinful and immoral *nature*. Murder is evil and so murderers are evil, since men do not murder out of the goodness of their hearts. Jesus made clear that a good tree does not bring forth bad fruit and *vice versa* (Matt. 7:18). Sin can and does manifest itself in thoughts, words, and deeds, in historical events and their results, but it does not thereby gain independent metaphysical being—this would require the view that evil has a metaphysical ultimacy alongside God. This is why it is not sin-in-the-abstract (merely as a category or idea) that the psalmist says we are to hate; we are also to have an established moral aversion of the strongest kind to evil men.

## The Cosmology of Killing: Moloch Worship Repackaged

Given the inescapable reality of evildoers masquerading as righteous, it should come as no surprise that Christian morality in our time is largely rejected and sneered at as judgmental, divisive, intolerant, or even an expression of hatred. To be faithful and wise witnesses in such a context, we need to relearn to understand our faith and make our case as the early Christian apologists did amongst the pagans—not simply pragmatically, but also cosmologically. Cosmology concerns the origin and ordering of created reality. The Christ who ordered the world, who called it into existence, who by His incarnation condescended to hallow the womb, holds all things together by His powerful Word (Col. 1:17). The implications flowing from this fact are profound.

Two things become clear in Scripture in light of the appearing of Christ's Kingdom. First, ultimately, there really are *only two religions* and all people, necessarily, participate in one or the other—the worship and service of the *Creator* or of the *creation*. And second, as a consequence, we are in a cosmic spiritual conflict between the kingdom of Satan and the Kingdom of God that manifests itself in the ideas and practices of every social order. Social and cultural norms and practices are not neutral, coincidental, or peripheral to fundamental beliefs; rather these manifest our deepest religious commitments.

The origins of this struggle go much further back than Greece and Rome, of course. We see it even amongst the Hebrews as they copied the pagans around them. As Jeremiah 32:33-35 makes plain, the Hebrews were drawn into the cult of creature worship and offered their children to Moloch. *Melek* is the common Hebrew word for king and is related to Moloch and Milcom, the god of the Ammonites, as explained in 1 Kings 11:7. A culture that exchanges the truth about God for *the lie* (Rom. 1:21-27) that man can be as god (Gen. 3:5) is a culture that worships and serves creation, not the Creator, and in the personification of nature with various gods (of which man is part), he in fact worships himself and his own will and idea, usually in the form of the State, a king, or an emperor. Moloch worship was in reality State worship—it was man worship. The brass statue of the god had a human form with outstretched hands and had a bull's head. A fire was stoked to incredible heat in the statue's belly, and parents were required to offer up their babies to this terrifying embrace without any sign of protest, and then watch the horror unfold.

God's Word warns against this practice, making it clear that this was an aspect of religious paganism and occultism, in Deuteronomy 18:10-11: "No one among you is to make his son or daughter pass through the fire, practice divination, tell fortunes, interpret omens, practice sorcery, cast spells, consult a medium or a familiar spirit, or inquire of the dead."

It is unsurprising that these occult practices are widely and actively pursued by many in our culture today, concurrent with abortion on demand. The cosmology of killing is thus pagan and occultic to its core, and originates in the first temptation, that man could play God, determining good and evil for himself—to be beyond good and evil. The contemporary justification of the killing of the unborn, then, on the sole basis of personal "choice" (the woman's right to choose), is the essence of Moloch worship. We moderns might not place our children in the fire, but the meaning, and the result, are the same. We satisfy self-will and the will of the State (which is man writ large) by offering up our children on the altar of our own godhood—our convenience, desires, lusts, and selfishness—worshiping and serving the creature.

Our society, in abandoning the life-giving and life-affirming reality of the incarnate living Word, has adopted a cosmology of death and killing, in which we reveal "Choice" to be our god. We deny the truth of any value higher than our choices and recognize no end greater than our will—all of which leaves us with nothing but the existential self and therefore reduces us to nothing. As with the worship of Moloch, it is the "free and voluntary" aspect of our killing that is the all-important basis of action in our contemporary pagan culture. And as we play the fool, sterile and clinical abortuaries that seek to sanitize our sacrifices on the altar of self (with the State's strict limit on public protest around the killing centers), provide the deafening silence that shields mothers and cowardly men from comprehending the consequences of their evil actions.

## Choosing Life

To illustrate the fundamental cosmology of the pro-life position, let's briefly consider a cosmological critique of two common arguments for abortion: abortion as a matter of health, and a human right. The two are related. By identifying abortion as a human right, and thus as an absolute value, one of the more pernicious aspects of the contemporary practice of baby killing in the West has developed: abortion has been identified as a matter of women's *health* and personal well-being. In the United States, the publications of the National Organization for Women (NOW) repeatedly refer to abortion as "the most fundamental right of women," *ahead* of the right to vote and the right to free speech. The protection of abortion rights is its top priority.[25] The Christian faith is seen as enemy number one in this struggle for "health" and "rights." I once saw a shocking and blasphemous placard displayed at a pro-choice march which demonstrated the antipathy

---

25. In a 1999 speech celebrating the 30th anniversary of the passage of Trudeau's omnibus bill C-150, Senator Lucie Pépin similarly argued that its abortion legislation provided a new freedom which "proved to be a stepping stone for many other freedoms and options that have altered women's place in [Canadian] society—self-esteem, education, jobs, a voice and empowerment." See Lucie Pépin, *Debates of the Senate*, 2nd Sess., 36th Parl., vol. 138, no. 7, available at http://www.parl.gc.ca/Content/Sen/Chamber/362/Debates/pdf/007db_1999-11-16-e.pdf.

of the cosmology of killing to Jesus Christ as the Lord of life. It read, "If Mary had had an abortion, we wouldn't be in this mess."

The Christian cosmology, by contrast, is one of life and compassion. We are *pro-life* because God is life and the author of life. It is particularly revealing to notice that the triune God's very being and nature is defined by *begetting*. The Incarnation reminds us that the Son, though born into the world at a certain point in history, is the *eternally begotten* of the Father. The wonder here is that the unity of the Trinity is manifest as a self-giving familial community of love. In the incarnation, where "veiled in flesh the godhead see," we discover the divine community.

As male and female creatures made in God's image, His familial nature is reflected in the human family where, out of the union of man and woman, *begetting* takes place and *generation* occurs, bringing life. To *abort begetting* is thus contrary to the very nature of God, who has revealed Himself in the familial categories of Father and Son, where the Son is begotten not made. In the antithetical view, the cosmology of killing, there is no eternal begetting. Ultimate reality is not the triune God, an infinite-personal divine community, but only an impersonal, empty, and lifeless unity of being or non-being. Hence death and annihilation are the goal of existence in pagan thought, which means abortion becomes entirely *logical* in an anti-Christian worldview. We can see from this that when opposing abortion, we are not simply moralizing; we are applying a scriptural worldview and cosmology by describing the true God as He reveals Himself, and the nature of the world He has made.

A final dimension must be added to this with regard to the nature of the gospel itself, an aspect that the incarnation of Christ so clearly sets forth. Christ is *born* into the world as a human being, as the last Adam and head of a new humanity. God's people would be "born again" by the Spirit of God and become representatives of the new creation. So, the process of our salvation is likewise one of birth and generation. Human birth, in Scripture, becomes a type of the new birth—we must be born again (John 3:1–21). The believer is re-*generated* through the work of the Holy Spirit, by the imperishable *seed* of the Word of God. By this, we are given life and brought into the *family* of God (1 Pet. 1:23). Thus, to abort birth is to reject its ultimate end in the new birth, just as to deny creation is to reject the new creation, and to deny the fruition of family is to reject the family of God. Abortion is thus a logical extension of the cosmology of death, whilst God's very being and nature, as well as the plan of salvation itself, militate against abortion and contradict the practice.

In the cosmology of compassion, God is at work in all history by His providential and salvific work to bring about His life-giving purposes. Jesus said, "I have come that you might have life, and life in all its fullness" (John 10:10). John's prologue tells us, "In him was life and the life was the light of men." Jesus Christ is life, not death. This reminds us that the creation of life is God's work, not man's, and as such it is entirely in His hands, so that life is always on His terms. God's terms are set out in His Word. By prohibiting murder, the Sixth Commandment includes the positive duty to *promote life* and protect the innocent—in so doing, we are fulfilling the law and working with God's purposes for creation. The cosmology of compassion calls on us to reveal to others the love and mercy of the triune God. This love is manifest not only in His eternal begetting and the incarnation of the Son of God, but also by the good gift of life in every womb.

## The Everlasting Way

All human beings are sinners. The apostle Paul counted himself foremost amongst them (1 Tim. 1:15). And yet mercifully, our sin *can be forgiven* by and through the atoning death of Jesus Christ, when we come to him in true repentance and faith; this includes the sin of abortion. Scripture is clear that because of our sinful nature, all have sinned and come short of God's glorious righteous standard (Rom. 3:23). We are lawless and rebellious by nature due to sin. Some of God's greatest servants were guilty of murder and adultery, including King David, the author of Psalm 139, and yet they found mercy, grace, new life, and renewal. Thus, David does not condemn evil in Psalm 139 out of a sense of self-righteous superiority. In verses 23–24 he prays, "Search me, God, and know my heart." This is to be our starting point. We must ask God to try us and know our thoughts in His intimate omniscience. And, like David, in such a case we should be quickly aware that our own integrity, such as it is, is not enough; we can stand only in Christ's righteousness. We must all be tried and searched by God, and we all need him to lay His hand of covenant faithfulness upon us to guard, guide, discipline, and preserve us. This is why David prays in verse 24, "See if there is any offensive way in me," and then: "lead me in the everlasting way."

What is that way? It is the way in which we pray that God's right hand will hold us fast. It is the way of Christ, the way of obedience to His law, the way of righteousness and justice, the way of the kingdom of God. It is the only way in which we can walk by the power of the Holy Spirit—it is the path that leads to life!

# Bibliography

"Abortion in the United Kingdom." *Wikipedia*. https://en.wikipedia.org/wiki/Abortion_in_the_United_Kingdom#:~:text=Although%20a%20number%20of%20abortions,abortions%20in%20the%20United%20Kingdom. Accessed, June 2024.

"Abortion Statistics." *Orlando Women's Center*. Available at http://www.womenscenter.com/ abortion_stats.html. Accessed November 5, 2013.

"America's Abortion Quandary." *Pew Research Center*. https://www.pewresearch.org/religion/2022/05/06/americas-abortion-quandary/#:~:text=Among%20religious%20groups%20analyzed%20in%20the%20survey%2C,should%20be%20illegal%20in%20most%20cases%20(53%). Accessed June 11, 2025.

"Living arrangements of children by race/ethnicity." *Office of Juvenile Justice and Delinquency Prevention*. Available at https://ojjdp.ojp.gov/statistical-briefing-book/population/ faqs/qa01202. Accessed September 2023.

"Prehistoric Period (until 1050) / The Viking Age / Religion, magic, death and rituals / Human sacrifices?" Available at https://en.natmus.dk/historical-knowledge/denmark/prehistoric-period-until-1050-ad/the-viking-age/religion-magic-death-and-rituals/human-sacrifices/. Accessed September, 2023.

"Statistics - Abortion in Canada." *Abortion Rights Coalition of Canada*. Available at http://www.arcc-cdac.ca/backrounders/statistics-abortion-in-canada.pdf. Accessed April 5, 2017.

"Thousands defy bans in France to rally against police violence." Available at https://www.aljazeera.com/news/2023/7/8/paris-memorial-march-banned-as-fresh-protests-planned-in-france. Accessed September 2023.

Adams, Stephen. "Killing Babies no different from abortion, experts say." *Daily Telegraph*. Available at www.telegraph.co.uk/health/healthnews/9113394/Killing-babies-no-different-from-abortion. Accessed April 29, 2013.

Adamson, Peter. *Classical Philosophy: A History of Philosophy Without Any Gaps*. Croydon: Oxford University Press, 2014.

———. *Classical Philosophy: A History of Philosophy Without Any Gaps*. Vol. 1. Croydon, UK: Oxford University Press, 2014.

Adler, David. "Darwin's Illness." *Israel Journal of Medical Sciences*. 25.4 (April 1989): 218–21.

Angier, Natalie. "Do Races Differ? Not Really, Genes Show." Available at https://www.nytimes.com/2000/08/22/science/do-races-differ-not-really-genes-show.html. Accessed September, 2023.

Aquinas, Thomas. *Summa Theologica*. Translated by the Fathers of the English Dominican Province. Revised by Daniel J. Sullivan. 2 vols. Great Books of the Western World 19–20. Chicago: Encyclopedia Britannica, 1952.

Aristotle. *The Basic Works of Aristotle, Metaphysics: Book 12, 1072b*. Edited by Richard McKeon. New York: Random House, 1941.

Averbeck, Richard E. "The Law and the Gospels." In *The Oxford Handbook of Biblical Law*. Edited by Pamela Barmash. 409–23. New York: Oxford University Press, 2019.

Bahnsen, Greg L. *Presuppositional Apologetics: Stated and Defended*. Edited by Joel McDurmon. Powder Springs, GA: The American Vision, 2008.

———. *Theonomy in Christian Ethics*. Texas: Covenant Media, 2002.

Barcellos, Richard C. *In Defense of the Decalogue: A Critique of New Covenant Theology*. Enumclaw, WA: WinePress Publishing, 2001.

Barna, George. *American Worldview Inventory 2021–22: The Annual Report on the State of Worldview in the United States*. Glendale, AZ: Arizona Christian University, 2022.

Bergman, Jerry. *The Dark Side of Charles Darwin: A Critical Analysis of an Icon of Science*. Green Forest, AR: Master Books, 2011.

Berman, Harold J. *Law and Revolution*. Vol. 1: *The Formation of the Western Legal Tradition*. London: Harvard University Press, 1983.

———. *Law and Revolution*. Vol. 2: *The Impact of the Protestant Reformations on the Western Legal Tradition* (London: Harvard University Press, 2003

Berthoud, Jean-Marc. *In Defense of God's Law*. Translated by Molly Anderson Orr. Tallahassee, FL: Zurich Publishing, 2022

Blamires, Harry. *The Christian Mind: How Should A Christian Think?* London: SPCK, 1963.

# BIBLIOGRAPHY

Boettner, Loraine. *The Millennium*. Phillipsburg, NJ: Presbyterian and Reformed Publishing, 1957; rev. 1984.

Bonhoeffer, Dietrich. "On Stupidity." In *Dietrich Bonhoeffer Works*. Vol. 8: *Letters and Papers from Prison*. Edited by Christian Gremmels, et al. English Edition edited by John W. de Gruchy. 43–44. "After Ten Years" translated by Barbara and Martin Rumscheidt. Minneapolis, MN: Fortress, 2009.

Boot, Joseph. *Gospel Culture: Living in God's Kingdom*. London: Wilberforce Publications, 2017.

———. *Ruler of Kings: Toward a Christian Vision of Government*. London: Wilberforce Publications, 2022.

———. *The Mission of God: A Manifesto of Hope for Society*. Toronto: Ezra, 2016.

———. *Why I Still Believe: A Journey into Christian Apologetics*. n.p. Toronto: Ezra, 2021.

Brooke, George J. "Christ and the Law in John 7–10." In *Law and Religion: Essays on the Place of the Law in Israel and Early Christianity*. Edited by Barnabas Lindars. 102–112. Worcester: James Clarke & Co., 1988.

Burnside, Jonathan. "Old Testament: Torah and Constitutionalism." In *Christianity and Constitutionalism*. Edited by Nicholas Aroney and Ian Leigh. 33–57. Oxford University Press, 2022.

———. *God, Justice, and Society: Aspects of Law and Legality in the Bible*. New York: Oxford University Press, 2011.

Butler, Judith. *Gender Trouble: Feminism and the Subversion of Identity*. New York, NY: Routledge, 1990.

Butt, Riazat. "Half of Britons do not believe in evolution, survey finds." *The Guardian*. Available at https://www.theguardian.com/science/2009/feb/01/evolution-darwin-survey-creationism#:~:text=The%20poll%20found%20that%2025,theory%20or%20confused%20about%20it. Accessed July, 2024.

Calvin, John. *Commentary on Psalms*. Translated by James Anderson. Vol. 5. Grand Rapids: Christian Classics Ethereal Library, 1849), 191. Available at http://www.ccel.org/ccel/ calvin/calcom12.pdf. Accessed October 7, 2013.

Cayley, David. *George Grant in Conversation*. Concord, ON: House of Anansi Press, 1995.

Cecco, Leyland. "Canada's Assisted Dying Laws in Spotlight as Expansion Paused Again." *The Guardian*. Available at https://www.theguardian.com/world/2024/feb/25/canada-assisted-dying-laws-in-spotlight-as-expansion-paused-again. Accessed, June, 2024.

Cheng-Morris. "Striking Image Shows Police Forming Ring Around Churchill Statue to Stop Clash Between Rival Protesters." *Yahoo! News*. https://uk.news.yahoo.com/police-guard-winston-churchill-statue-171822582.html. Accessed June 2023.

Clauson, Marc A. "The Mosaic Judicial Law in the Early Church." Unpublished paper. Liberty University, 1990.

———. "Theonomy in the Middle Ages: The Case of Thomas Aquinas." Lecture delivered at the 2005 American Political Science Association Annual Meeting in Washington DC. 2005. Available at http://www.theonomyresources.com/pdfs/Theonomy-in-the-Middle-Ages-Aquinas.pdf. Accessed May, 2023.

Clouser, Roy. "Is there a Christian View of Everything from Soup to Nuts?" *Pro Rege*. 31.4: 1–10, 2003.

———. *Knowing with the Heart: Religious Experience and Belief in God*. Downers Grove, IL: InterVarsity, 1999.

Coggins, Madeline. "Trans Athlete Sparks Outrage After Toppling Women's Powerlifting World Record: 'Completely Unfair.'" *Fox Business*. Available at https://www.foxbusiness.com/ politics/trans-athlete-sparks-outrage-toppling-womens-powerlifting-world-record-completely-unfair. Accessed November, 2023.

"Council of Ancyra, Canon 21," in *Nicene and Post-Nicene Fathers, Second Series*. Vol. 14. Edited by Philip Schaff and Henry Wace. Translated by Henry Percival. Revised and edited for New Advent by Kevin Knight. Buffalo, NY: Christian Literature Publishing Co., 1900. Available at http://www.newadvent.org/fathers/3802.htm.

Craine, Patrick. "Poll: United Church Members Significantly More Liberal than Canadian Public on Abortion, Euthanasia." *Lifesite News*. Available at http://www.lifesitenews.com/news/ pollunited-church-members-more-liberal-than-canadian-public-onabortion-eu. Accessed July 12, 2012.

Cutler, Georgina. "Massachusetts forced to deploy National Guard to deal with migrant crisis: 'This is an emergency!'" Available at Available at https://www.gbnews.com/news/us/ massachusetts-national-guard-migrant-crisis-emergency. Accessed September, 2023.

Dalai Lama. *Beyond Religion: Ethics for a Whole World* . New York: Mariner Books, 2012.

Darwin, Charles. *The Autobiography of Charles Darwin 1809–1882*. Edited by Nora Barlow. London: Collins, 1958.

Davies, Sharron. "The fact we needed a court ruling to remove men from women's sports is nothing short of shameful. *MailOnline*. Published 29 April 2025. Updated

29 April 2025. https://www.dailymail.co.uk/news/article-14660931/SHARRON-DAVIES-fact-needed-court-ruling-remove-men-womens-sport-short-shameful.html. Accessed June 17, 2025.

Dodds, E. R. *Pagan and Christian in an Age of Anxiety*. Cambridge: Cambridge University Press, 1965.

Dooyeweerd, Herman. *Christian Philosophy and the Meaning of History*. In *The Collected Works*, vol. 21. Edited by D. F. M. Strauss. Jordan Station, ON: Paideia Press, 2023.

———. *A New Critique of Theoretical Thought*. In *The Collected Works*. Series A, vol. 1: *The Necessary Presuppositions of Philosophy*. Translated by David H. Freeman and William S. Young. Jordan Station, ON: Paideia Press, 1984.

———. *A New Critique of Theoretical Thought*. In *The Collected Works*. Series A, vol. 2: *The General Theory of the Modal Spheres*. Translated by David H. Freeman and H. de Jongste. Jordan Station, ON: Paideia Press, 1984.

———. *Reformation and Scholasticism in Philosophy*. In *The Collected Works*. Series A, vols. 5/1 and 5/2. Translated by M. Verbrugge. Jordan Station, ON: Paideia Press, 2013.

———. *Roots of Western Culture: Pagan, Secular and Christian Options*. In *The Collected Works*. Series B, vol. 15. Edited by D. F. M. Strauss. Translated by John Kraay. Jordan Station, ON: Paideia Press, 2012.

———. *Time, Law and History: Selected Essays*. In *The Collected Works of Herman Dooyeweerd*. Series B, vol. 14. Edited by D. F. M. Strauss. Jordan Station, ON: Paideia Press, 2017.

Doughty, Steve. "Top Doctor's Chilling Claim: The NHS Kills Off 130,000 Elderly Patients Every Year." *Daily Mail Online*. Available at http://www.dailymail.co.uk/news/article-2161869/Top-doctors-chilling-claim-The-NHS-kills-130-000-elderly-patients-year.html. Accessed June 19, 2012.

Douma, J. *The Ten Commandments: Manual for the Christian Life*. Translated by Nelson D. Kloosterman. Phillipsburg, NJ: Presbyterian and Reformed, 1996.

Downie, Rex. "Natural Law and God's Law: An Antithesis." *The Journal of Christian Reconstruction: Symposium on Politics*. Vol. 5. Vallecito CA, Chalcedon Foundation, 1978.

Drury, Colin. "Leicester riots a warning that violence in UK can be sparked by global events, experts say." Available at https://www.independent.co.uk/news/uk/home-news/leicester-riots-hindu-muslim-violence-b2173293.html. Accessed September, 2023.

Duello, Theresa M., et al., "Race and genetics versus 'race' in genetics." Available at https://www.ncbi.nlm.nih.gov/pmc/articles/PMC8604262/#:~:text=The%20

completion%20of%20the%20Human%20Genome%20Project%20in%202003%20 confirmed,no%20genetic%20basis%20for%20race. Accessed September, 2023.

Einstein, Albert. *Ideas and Opinions*. Translated by Sonja Bargmann. Souvenir, 1973.

Einwechter, William O. *Walking in the Law of the Lord: An Introduction to the Biblical Ethics of Theonomy*. Pennsylvania: Darash, 2010.

Elazar, Daniel J. and Stuart A Cohen. *The Jewish Polity*. Bloomington, IN: Indiana University, 1985.

Eliot, T. S. "The Love Song of J. Alfred Prufrock." In *T. S. Eliot: Selected Poems and A Critical Reading of the Selected Poems of T. S. Eliot*. Croydon, UK: Faber and Faber, 1954.

Ellul, Jacques. *The Theological Foundation of Law*. Translated by Marguerite Wieser. Garden City, New York: Doubleday and Company, 1960.

Engels, Friedrich. *Fourth Thesis on Feuerbach*. "Das Buch der Offenbarung." In *Marx-Engels Werke*. Berlin, 1959. III.

Evans, C. Stephen. *Kierkegaard and Spirituality: Accountability as the Meaning of Human Existence*. Grand Rapids: Eerdmans, 2019.

Evans, James Allan. *The Empress Theodora: Partner of Justinian*. Austin: University of Texas, 2002.

Flew, Antony. *There is a God: How the World's Most Notorious Atheist Changed his Mind*. New York: HarperCollins, 2007.

Forbes, Hugh Donald. *George Grant: A Guide to His Thought*. Toronto: University of Toronto Press, 2007.

Frame, John. *A History of Western Philosophy and Theology*. Phillipsburg, NJ: Presbyterian and Reformed, 2015.

Franke, John R. *Barth for Armchair Theologians*. Louisville: Westminster John Knox, 2006.

Geertsema, Hendrik G. *Homo Respondens: Essays in Christian Philosophy*. Edited by Govert J. Buijs and Perry Huesmann. Jordan Station, ON: Paideia Press, 2021.

Gentry, Kenneth. *Postmillennialism Made Easy*. n.p.: Victorious Hope Publishing, 2020.

González, Justo L. *The Story of Christianity: The Early Church to the Present Day*. Peabody, MA: Prince, 1984.

Gorman, Michael J. *Abortion and the Early Church: Christian, Jewish and Pagan Attitudes in the Greco-Roman World*. Downers Grove, IL: InterVarsity, 1982.

Gould, S. J. *Ontogeny and Phylogeny*. Cambridge, MA: Belknap-Harvard Press, 1977.

Grandjonc, Jacques and Karl Marx. *Editionsrichtlinien der Marx-Engels-Gesamtausgabe (MEGA)*. I. Abt. II. Berlin: Dietz, 1993.

Grant, George P. *Lament for a Nation: The Defeat of Canadian Nationalism.* Toronto: McClelland and Stewart, 1965.

———. *Philosophy in the Mass Age.* Toronto: Copp Clark Publishing, 1959.

Green, Vivian. *A New History of Christianity.* Bridgend: Blitz Editions, 1998.

Griffith, Sidney H. *The Church in the Shadow of the Mosque: Christians and Muslims in the World of Islam.* Princeton, NJ: Princeton University Press, 2008.

Harris, Sam. *The End of Faith: Religious Terror and the Future of Reason.* USA: W. W. Norton, 2004.

———.*The Moral Landscape: How Science Can Determine Human Values.* New York: Free Press, 2010.

Harrisond, Peter. *The Fall of Man and the Foundations of Science.* Cambridge: Cambridge University Press, 2007.

Hazony, Yoram. *The Virtue of Nationalism.* New York: Basic Books, 2018.

Herbert, David. *Becoming God: Transhumanism and the Quest for Cybernetic Immortality.* Ontario: Joshua Press, 2014.

Horkheimer, Max. *Critical Theory: Selected Essays.* Translated by Matthew J. O'Connell et al. New York, NY: Continuum, 2002.

——— and Theodor W. Adorno. *Dialectic of Enlightenment: Philosophical Fragments.* Edited by Gunzelin Schmid Noerr. Translated by Edmund Jephcott. Stanford, CA: Stanford University Press, 2002.

Hunter, Cornelius G. *Darwin's God: Evolution and the Problem of Evil.* Grand Rapids: Brazos Press, 2001.

Jammer, Max. *Einstein and Religion.* Princeton: Princeton University Press, 1999.

Jones, Peter. *The Other Worldview: Exposing Christianity's Greatest Threat.* Bellingham, WA: Kirkdale, 2015.

Kierkegaard, Søren. "From the Papers of One Still Living." In *Early Polemical Writings*, edited and translated by Julia Watkin. Princeton, NJ: Princeton University Press, 1990.

———. *Kierkegaard's Writings.* Vol. 14: *Two Ages: The Age of Revolution and the Present Age. A Literary Review.* Edited and translated by Howard V. Hong and Edna H. Hong. Princeton, NJ: Princeton University Press, 2009.

———. *On Authority and Revelation. The book on Adler, or A Cycle of ethico-religious essays.* Princeton, NJ: Princeton University Press, 1955.

———. *The Essential Kierkegaard*. Edited by Howard V. Hong and Edna H. Hong. Princeton, NJ: Princeton University Press, 2000.

———. *The Humor of Kierkegaard: An Anthology*. Edited by Thomas C. Oden. Princeton, NJ: Princeton University Press, 2004.

———. *The Prayers of Kierkegaard*. Edited by Perry D. Lefevre. Chicago, IL: University of Chicago Press, 1956.

———. *The Sickness unto Death*. Kierkegaard's Writings 19. Edited and translated by Howard V. Hong and Edna H. Hong. Princeton, NJ: Princeton University Press, 1980.

———. *Training in Christianity*. Translated by Walter Lowrie. New York: Vintage Books, 2004.

Kirschner, Marc. "Missing Links." In *The Boston Globe*. Oct 23, 2005, 77.

Knapton, Sarah, "Big Bang theory is wrong, claim scientists. *The Telegraph*. June 10, 2025. Available at https://www.telegraph.co.uk/news/2025/06/10/big-bang-theory-is-wrong-claim-scientists/.

Knudsen, Robert D. *Roots and Branches: The Quest for Meaning and Truth in Modern Thought*. Jordan Station, ON: Paideia Press, 2009.

Krauss, Laurence. "Something from Nothing." Dialogue with Richard Dawkins, Arizona State University. Feb 4, 2012. Available at https://dangerousintersection.org/2012/04/22/richard-dawkins-and-lawrence-krauss-discuss-something-from-nothing/.

Kuby, Gabriele. *The Global Sexual Revolution: Destruction of Freedom in the Name of Freedom*. Translated by James Patrick Kirchner. Kettering, OH: LifeSite, 2015.

Kuyper, Abraham. *Lectures on Calvinism*. Grand Rapids: Eerdmans, 1978.

———. *Principles of Sacred Theology*. New York: Charles Scribner's Sons, 1898.

Kymlicka, Will. *Contemporary Political Philosophy: An Introduction*. Guildford: Clarendon Press/Oxford University Press, 1990.

Lane, Tony. *The Lion Concise Book of Christian Thought*. Oxford: Lion Publishing, 1984.

Lecler, J. *Toleration and Reformation*. 2 vols. Translated by T. L. Westow. London: Longmans, 1960.

Leeman, Jonathan and Mark Dever. "On the Mission of the Church." Available at https://www.9marks.org/interview/episode-25–on-the-mission-of-the-church/. Accessed November 16, 2017.

Legutko, Ryszard. *The Demon in Democracy: Totalitarian Temptations in Free Societies*. New York: Encounter Books, 2016.

# BIBLIOGRAPHY

Leithart, Peter J. *Defending Constantine: The Twilight of an Empire and the Dawn of Christendom*. Downers Grove, IL: InterVarsity Academic, 2010.

Lewis, C. S. "The Humanitarian Theory of Punishment." *Issues in Religion and Psychotherapy*. 13.1, Article 11: 147–53. Available at: https://scholarsarchive.byu.edu/irp/vol13/iss1/11. Accessed February, 2025.

———. *God in the Dock: Essays on Theology and* Ethics. Edited by Walter Hooper. Grand Rapids: Eerdmans, 1972.

Lewontin, Richard. "Confusions about human race." Available at https://raceandgenomics.ssrc.org/Lewontin/. 7 June 2006. Accessed September, 2023.

Löwith, Karl. *Meaning in History*. Chicago, IL: University of Chicago Press, 1949.

Löwy, Michael. *Georg Lukács: From Romanticism to Bolshevism*. Translated by Patirck Camiller. London: NLB, 1979.

MacCulloch, Diarmaid: *Christianity: The First Three Thousand Years* (New York: Penguin Books, 2009.

Malantschuk, Gregor. *The Controversial Kierkegaard*. Translated by Howard V. Hong and Edna H. Hong. Waterloo, ON: Wilfred Laurier University, 1980.

Mangalwadi, Vishal. *The Book That Made Your World: How the Bible Created the Soul of Western Civilisation*. Nashville: Thomas Nelson, 2011.

Maraniss, David. *When Pride Still Mattered: A Life Of Vince Lombardi*. New York: Simon and Schuster, 1999.

Marcuse, Herbert. *Eros and Civilization: A Philosophical Inquiry Into Freud*. Boston: Beacon Press, 1974.

Marx, Karl. "Invocation of One in Despair." *All Poetry*. Available at https://allpoetry.com/Invocation-Of-One-In-Despair. Accessed November, 2023.

———. *Theses on Feuerbach: A New English Translation Based on the New Marx-Engels-Gesamtausgabe*. Translated by Carlos Bendaña-Pedroza. By permission of the International Marx-Engels-Foundation. Second revised edition. Bonn: 2022.

Mayr, Ernst. *One Long Argument: Charles Darwin and the Genesis of Modern Evolutionary Thought*. Cambridge: Harvard University Press, 1991.

Mbogoni, Lawrence E. Y. *Human Sacrifice and the Supernatural in African History*. n.p.: Mkuki na Nyota Publishers, 2013.

McGuckin, John A. *The Ascent of Christian Law: Patristic and Byzantine Formulations of a New Civilization*. New York: St Vladimir's Seminary, 2012.

McManners, John, ed. *The Oxford Illustrated History of Christianity*. Oxford: Oxford University Press, 1990.

Merkowsky, Clare Marie. "Canadian Female Powerlifted Faces two-year Suspension for Criticizing Men Competing Against Women." *LifeSite News*. Available at https://www.lifesitenews.com/news/canadian-female-powerlifter-suspension-men-competing/. Accessed November, 2023.

Meyer, Stephen. *Darwin's Doubt: The Explosive Origin of Animal Life and the Case for Intelligent Design*. New York: HarperCollins, 2013.

Mietus, A. C. and Norbert J. Mietus. "Criminal Abortion: 'A Failure of Law' or a Challenge to Society?" *American Bar Association Journal*. 51.10 (October 1965): 924–28.

Molnar, Thomas. *Utopia: The Perennial Heresy*. New York: University Press of America, 1990.

Nagel, Thomas. *Mind and Cosmos: Why the Materialist Neo-Darwinian Conception of Nature Is Almost Certainly False*. Oxford: Oxford University Press, 2012.

Nicholls, Mark. "'Thing which seame incredible': Cannibalism in Early Jamestown." *Colonial Williamsburg*. Available at https://research.colonialwilliamsburg.org/Foundation/journal/Winter07/jamestown.cfm#:~:text=Cannibalism%20was%20practiced%20in%20some,endured%20into%20the%20eighteenth%20century. Accessed September, 2023.

North, Gary. *The Judeo-Christian Tradition*. Tyler, TX: Institute for Christian Economics, 1990.

O'Connor, D. J. *Aquinas and Natural Law*. New Studies in Ethics. London: Macmillan, 1967.

Ouweneel, Willem. *The Eternal Word: God Speaking to Us*. An Evangelical Introduction to Reformational Theology. Vol. 1, Part 1: Scripture: The Revealed Source for Theology. Jordan Station, ON: Paideia Press, 2021.

Ouweneel, Willem. *The World is Christ's: A Critique of Two Kingdoms Theology*. Toronto: Ezra, 2017.

Pagones, Stephanie. "Protests, riots that gripped America in 2020." Available at https://www.foxnews.com/us/protests-riots-nationwide-america-2020. Accessed September, 2023.

Patrick, Denzil G. M. *Pascal and Kierkegaard: A Study Strategy in Evangelism*. 2 vols. Cambridge: James Clarke and Co, 1947.

Pearcey, Nancy. *Finding Truth: 5 Principles for Unmasking Atheism, Secularism, and Other God Substitutes*. Colorado Springs, CO: David C. Cook, 2015.

Pelikan, Jaroslav. *The Christian Tradition: A History of the Development of Doctrine*. Vol. 1: *The Emergence of the Catholic Tradition 100-600*. Chicago, IL: University of Chicago, 1971.

Pépin, Lucie. *Debates of the Senate*. 2nd Session, 36th Parliament. Vol. 138, no. 7. Available at: http://www.parl.gc.ca/Content/Sen/Chamber/362/Debates/pdf/007db_1999-11-16-e.pdf.

Perkins, Liz. "St Paul's Cathedral branded Winston Churchill a 'white supremacist' and 'unashamed imperialist'." *The Telegraph*. 24 June 2023. Accessed June, 2023.

Perks, Stephen C. *The Politics of God and the Politics of Man: Essays on Politics, Religion and Social Order*. Taunton, England: Kuyper Foundation, 2016.

Perry, Louise. *The Case Against the Sexual Revolution: A New Guide to Sex in the 21st Century*. Padstow, Cornwall: Polity, 2022.

Peterson, Jordan. "Why I love Great Britain." *The Telegraph*. Dec. 14, 2021. Available at https://www.telegraph.co.uk/news/2021/12/14/love-great-britain/.

Philippe, J. *Race, Evolution and Behavior: A Life History Perspective*. Port Huron, MI: Charles Darwin Research Institute, 2000.

Pitzulo, Carrie, "The Battle in Every Man's Bed: Playboy and the Fiery Feminists." *Journal of the History of Sexuality*. 17.2 (2008): 259–89. Available at https://doi.org/10.1353/sex.0.0004.

Plato, *Republic*. Translated by Allan Bloom. New York, NY: Basic Books, 1968.

Popper, Karl. *Philosophy after Darwin*. Princeton, NJ: Princeton University Press, 2010.

Poythress, Vern S. *The Shadow of Christ in the Law of Moses*. Brentwood, TN: Wolgemuth and Hyatt, 1991.

Rae, Murray A. *Kierkegaard's Vision of the Incarnation: By Faith Transformed*. Chippenham: Clarendon, Oxford, 1997.

Raehn, Raymond V. "The Historical Roots of Political Correctness." In *Political Correctness: A Deceptive and Dangerous Worldview. Its Pedigree, History and Practices*. Edited by William S. Lind and Richard W. Hawkins. 16–29. United States: Nehemiah Institute, 2020.

Reich, Wilhelm. *The Sexual Revolution*. Translated by Therese Pol. New York: Farrar, Straus and Giroux, 1986.

Ridderbos, Herman. *The Coming of the Kingdom*. Edited by Raymond O. Zorn. Translated by H. de Jongste. St. Catharines, ON: Paidea, 1978.

Runner, H. Evan. *Walking in the Way of the Word*. In *The Collected Writings of H. Evan Runner*. Vol. 1. Jordan Station, ON: Paideia Press, 2016.

Ruse, Michael. ed. *Philosophy After Darwin*. Princeton: Princeton University Press, 2010.

Rushdoony, R. J. *An Informed Faith: The Position Papers of R. J. Rushdoony*. Vol. 2: *Ecclesiology, Doctrine and Biblical Law*. Vallecito, CA: Ross House Books, 2017.

———. *Faith and Action*. Vol. 1: *Authority, Humanism and Morality*. Vallecito, CA: Ross House Books, 2019.

———. *Foundations of Social Order: Studies in the Creeds and Councils of the Early Church*. Vallecito, CA: Ross House Books, 1968.

———. *The One and the Many: Studies in the Philosophy of Order and Ultimacy*. Vallecito, CA: Ross House Books, 2007.

Ruthven, Malise. "How Europe lost faith in multiculturalism." Available at https://www.ft.com/ content/dd122a8c-8720-11e7-8bb1-5ba57d47eff7. Accessed September, 2023.

Ryan, Alan. *On Politics: A History of Political Thought From Herodotus to the Present*. London: Allen Lane, 2012.

Sandlin, P. Andrew. "Introducing Cultural Theology." Center for Cultural Leadership. Last modified July 12, 2017. https://docsandlin.com/2017/07/12/introducing-cultural-theology/.

———. *The Christian Sexual Worldview: God's Order in an Age of Sexual Chaos*. Coulterville, CA: Center for Cultural Leadership, 2015.

———. "Are Christian Sexual Ethics Outdated?" *Ezra Institute*. Last modified July 3, 2013. Available at https://www.ezrainstitute.com/are-christian-sexual-ethics-outdated/.

———. *A Postmillennial Primer: Basics of Optimistic Eschatology*. Coulterville, CA: Center for Cultural Leadership, 2023.

Sartre, Jean-Paul. *Being and Nothingness*. Translated by Hazel E. Barnes. New York: Washington Square, 1992.

———. *The Wisdom of Sartre: A Selection*. New York: Philosophical Library, 1956.

Schaff, Philip. *The Creeds of Christendom*. Vol. 2: *The Greek and Latin Creeds, with Translations*. New York: Harper and Brothers, 1890.

———. *History of the Christian Church*. Revised edition. Vol. 3: *Nicene and Post-Nicene Christianity. From Constantine the Great to Gregory the Great, A.D. 311–600*. New York: Scribner's, 1884.

Schrödinger, Erwin. *My View of the World*. Cambridge: Cambridge University Press, 1964.

———. *Nature and the Greeks and Science and Humanism*. Cambridge: Cambridge University Press, 2014.

Schuurman, Egbert. *Technology and the Future: A Philosophical Challenge*. Translated by H. Donald Morton. Jordan Station, ON: Paideia Press, 2009.

*Science Can Determine Human Values*. New York, NY: Free Press, 2010.

Scruton, Roger. *Fools, Frauds and Firebrands: Thinkers of the New Left*. Croydon: Bloomsbury Publishing, 2015.

Searle, John. *Mind, Language and Society: Philosophy in the Real World*. New York, NY: Basic Books, 1998).

Seerveld, Calvin. *A Christian Critique of Art and Literature*. Revised edition. Sioux Center, IA: Dordt College, 1995.

Sherwood, Aaron. "The Mixed Multitude in Exodus 12:38: Glorification, Creation, and Yhwh's Plunder of Israel and the Nations." *Horizons in Biblical Theology* 34.2 (2012): 139–54. Doi: https://doi.org/10.1163/187122012X627821.

Sixsmith, Ben. "Peckham, protests and 'parasitic merchants'." Available at https://thecritic.co.uk/ peckham-protests-and-parasitic-merchants/. Accessed September, 2023.

Sowell, Thomas. "Facts about Slavery Never Mentioned in School." Thomas SowellTV. Available at https://www.youtube.com/watch?v=lyPWjjWs7-w. Accessed September, 2023.

———. *Intellectuals and Society*. New York, NY: Basic Books, 2011.

Spier, J. M. *An Introduction to Christian Philosophy*. Translated by D. H. Freeman. Philadelphia, PA: Presbyterian and Reformed, 1966.

Spykman, Gordon J. *Reformational Theology: A New Paradigm for Doing Dogmatics*. Grand Rapids: Eerdmans, 1995.

Squires, Nick. "Germany refuses to take any more EU migrants as boats forced to queue in Italian docks." Available at https://www.telegraph.co.uk/world-news/2023/09/13/germany-refuses-more-eu-migrants-boats-queue-italian-docks/. Accessed September, 2023.

Stark, Rodney. *Discovering God: The Origins of the Great Religions and the Evolution of Belief.* New York: HarperOne, 2007.

———. *How the West Won: The Neglected Story of the Triumph of Modernity.* Wilmington, DE: ISI Books, 2015.

Stauffer, Ethelbert. *Christ and the Caesars.* Translated by K. and R. Gregor Smith. Eugene, OR: Wipf and Stock, 2008.

Stevenson, J., ed. *A New Eusebius: Documents Illustrating the History of the Church to AD 337.* Revised by W. H. C. Frend. Cambridge: SPCK, 1987.

Strauss, D. F. M. "Scholasticism and Reformed Scholasticism at Odds with Genuine Reformational-Christian Thinking." *Nederduitse Gereformeerde Teologiese Tydskrif.* 5.2 (March 1969): 97–114.

———. *Philosophy: Discipline of the Disciplines.* Jordan Station, ON: Paideia Press, 2009.

———. *Soul and Body.* Jordan Station, ON: Paideia Press, 2020.

———. *The Philosophy of Herman Dooyeweerd.* Jordan Station, ON: Paideia Press, 2024.

———. "What Happened to Evolution?" In *Discovering Dooyeweerd.* Edited by D. F. M. Strauss. 273–82. Jordan Station, ON: Paideia Press, 2023.

Taylor, E. L. Hebden. *The Christian Philosophy of Law, Politics and the State.* Nutley, NJ: Craig, 1966.

———. *The New Legality.* Philadelphia, PA: Craig, 1967.

Tertullian, *Apologia* 9.6. Available at http://www.ccel.org/ccel/schaff/anf03.iv.iii.ix.html. Accessed October 7, 2013.

*The Holy Bible: A Translation from the Latin Vulgate in the Light of the Hebrew and Greek Originals.* Translated by Ronald Knox. Baronius, 2012.

Thomas, Jeremy A. *The Nation's Gospel: Spreading the Christian Faith in Britain Since the Reformation, Vol 1 (1516-1791) Reformation to Revolution.* Exeter: Wilberforce Publications, 2017.

Tillich, Paul. *Dynamics of Faith.* New York: Harper Colophon Books, 1957.

———. *Systematic Theology.* 3 vols. Chicago, IL: University of Chicago, 1951.

Troost, Andree. *What is Reformational Philosophy: An Introduction to the Cosmonomic Philosophy of Herman Dooyeweerd.* Translated by Anthony Runia. Jordan Station, ON: Paideia Press, 2012.

Trueman, Carl R. *The Rise and Triumph of the Modern Self: Cultural Amnesia, Expressive Individualism and the Road to Sexual Revolution.* Wheaton, IL: Crossway, 2020.

University of Michigan. "Evolution now accepted by majority of Americans." *Science-Daily*. 20 August 2021. www.sciencedaily.com/releases/2021/08/210820111042.htm. Accessed July, 2024.

Van Der Walt, Bernie. *Thomas Aquinas and the Neo-Thomist Tradition: A Christian Philosophical Assessment*. Jordan Station, ON: Paideia Press, 2021.

Van Riessen, Hendrik. *The Society of the Future*. Translated by David Hugh Freeman. Philadelphia, PA: Presbyterian and Reformed Publishing, 1957.

Van Til, Cornelius. "My Credo." In *Jerusalem and Athens*. Edited by E. R Geeham. Phillipsburg, NJ: Presbyterian and Reformed, 1971.

———. *The Defense of the Faith*. Phillipsburg, NJ: Presbyterian and Reformed, 1967.

———. *The Ten Commandments*. Jordan Station, ON: Cantaro Publications, 2023.

———. *The New Modernism: An Appraisal of the Theology of Barth and Brunner*. Philadelphia: Presbyterian & Reformed, 1946.

Voegelin, Eric. "Saint Thomas Aquinas on History, Politics, and Law." Available at https://voegelinview.com/saint-thomas-aquinas-history-politics-law-part-1/. Accessed January 13, 2025.

Vollenhoven, Dirk H. *Introduction to Philosophy*. Translated by John H. Kok. Sioux Center, IA: Dordt College, 2005.

Ward, Allen Mason, Fritz M. Heichelheim, and Cedric A. Yeo. *A History of the Roman People*. Englewood Cliffs, NJ: Prentice Hall, 1983.

Washington, H. A. *Medical Apartheid: The Dark History of Medical Experimentation on Black Americans from Colonial Times to the Present*. New York: Doubleday, 2006.

Weikart, Richard. *From Darwin to Hitler: Evolutionary Ethics, Eugenics, and Racism in Germany*. New York, NY: Palgrave Macmillan, 2004.

Weinberg, Steven. "Without God." *The New York Review of Books*. 55.14 (September 25, 2008): 1–3.

Wells, H. G. *A Modern Utopia*. Lincoln, NE: University of Nebraska, 1967.

Whale, John Seldon. *The Protestant Tradition*. Cambridge: Cambridge University Press, 1962.

Wieland, Carl. *One Human Family: The Bible, Science, Race and Culture*. Powder Springs, GA: Creation Book Publishers, 2011.

Williams, Preston N. "Race Relations." In *The Westminster Dictionary of Christian Ethics*. Edited by James F. Childress and John Macquarrie. 523–26. Philadelphia, PA: Westminster, 1986.

Wolfe, Stephen. *The Case for Christian Nationalism*. Moscow, ID: Canon, 2022.

Wolters, Albert. *Creation Regained: Biblical Basics for a Reformational Worldview*. 2nd edition. Grand Rapids, MI: Eerdmans, 2005.

Zuidema, S. U. *Communication and Confrontation: A Philosopohical Appraisal and Critique of Modern Society and Contemporary Thought*. Assen/Kampen: Royal VanGorcum and J. H. Kok, 1972.

# *About the Author*

**Rev. Dr. Joseph Boot (MA, PhD)** is a Christian thinker, writer, and cultural apologist-theologian. He is the Founder and President of the Ezra Institute for Contemporary Christianity and the Ezra Centre for Christian Thought (U.K.), and serves as an adjunct instructor in culture and apologetics at Bryan College, Tennessee.

A dual citizen of the U.K. and Canada, Dr. Boot was the founding pastor of Westminster Chapel in Toronto, where he ministered for fourteen years. Now residing once again in Great Britain, he has worked in Christian apologetics, worldview education, and church leadership for more than thirty years on both sides of the Atlantic. He has spoken and lectured globally at universities, seminaries, churches, colleges, and conferences, regularly addressing pastors and Christian leaders as well as professionals in academic, medical, business, legal, and political fields. He has also publicly debated leading atheistic thinkers and philosophers in Canada, the United Kingdom, and the United States.

Dr. Boot completed his undergraduate studies in Theology at Birmingham Christian College (U.K.), earned an MA in Mission Theology with a dissertation on Christian cultural philosophy and apologetics at the University of Manchester (U.K.), and holds a PhD in Christian Intellectual Thought from Whitefield Theological Seminary (Florida, USA).

His published works include *Searching for Truth* (Crossway), *Why I Still Believe* (Baker Books), *How Then Shall We Answer* (New Wine), *The Mission of God* (Ezra Press), *Ruler of Kings: Toward a Christian Vision of Government*

(Wilberforce Publications), and his latest work, *Think Christianly: Developing an Undivided Mind* (Ezra Press). Other recent volumes developing a cultural apologetic include *Gospel Culture* and *Gospel Witness* (Ezra Press/Wilberforce Publications), which serve as introductions to a scriptural worldview and a Christian philosophy of culture. His most noted contributions to Christian thought are systematic works of cultural apologetics and philosophy elucidating the biblical worldview as it relates to the Christian's calling in the world.

Dr. Boot is widely recognized as a Reformed evangelical cultural theologian and leading Christian apologist. He serves as Senior Fellow of Cultural Philosophy and Apologetics at several think tanks and training organizations, including TruthXchange and the Center for Cultural Leadership in California, as well as The Wilberforce Academy (Christian Concern) in London, England. In 2011, he was honoured by Toronto's Centre for Mentorship and Theological Reflection, founded by Dr. Dennis Ngien, as "Best Preacher Apologist" for his contribution to apologetic and expository preaching. He is also the founding chancellor of Westminster Classical Christian Academy in Toronto, one of Canada's first Classical Christian elementary schools.

Joe is married to Jenny, and they have three adult children.

# About Ezra Press

**Ezra Press** is the publishing ministry of the Ezra Institute for Contemporary Christianity, dedicated to advancing a reformational worldview rooted in the Lordship of Jesus Christ over every area of life. We publish books, articles, and resources that equip Christians to think faithfully, live courageously, and engage culture with biblical truth.

Ezra Press titles include works of theology, cultural apologetics, worldview formation, and applied Christian philosophy, written to serve the church, train leaders, and bear faithful witness in the world.

## Recent Ezra Press Titles

— *The Mission of God: A Manifesto of Hope for Society (10th Anniversary Edition)* — Dr. Joseph Boot

— *Keep Faith in Medicine* — Dr. Ted Fenske

— *A Time to Search: Discovering the Meaning and Purpose of Life* — Dr. Joseph Boot

— *Why I Still Believe: A Journey into Christian Apologetics* — Dr. Joseph Boot

— *Sacred Streaming?: Pastoral Warnings Against Digitizing Church* — Nick Thompson

— *Covenant Sexuality: Essays on Religion, Sexuality, and Identity* — Various Authors

*Find more books and resources at*
**EZRAPRESS.COM**

www.ingramcontent.com/pod-product-compliance
Lightning Source LLC
Chambersburg PA
CBHW020730130526
44580CB00019B/110/J